W9-CTP-153

ANNUAL EDITIONS

Computers in Society 10/11
Sixteenth Edition

EDITOR

Paul De Palma
Gonzaga University

Paul De Palma is Professor and Department Chair of Computer Science at Gonzaga University. When he discovered computers, he was working on a doctorate in English (at Berkeley). He retrained and spent a decade in the computer industry. After further training (at Temple), he joined the computer science faculty at Gonzaga. He is currently studying computational linguistics (at the University of New Mexico). His research interests include the social impact of computing and speech processing.

The McGraw·Hill Companies

Connect
Learn
Succeed™

ANNUAL EDITIONS: COMPUTERS IN SOCIETY, SIXTEENTH EDITION

Published by McGraw-Hill, a business unit of The McGraw-Hill Companies, Inc., 1221 Avenue
of the Americas, New York, NY 10020. Copyright © 2011 by The McGraw-Hill Companies, Inc.
All rights reserved. Previous edition(s) 2005, 2007, 2008. No part of this publication may be reproduced or distributed in any form or by any means, or stored in a database or retrieval system,
without the prior written consent of The McGraw-Hill Companies, Inc., including, but not limited
to, in any network or other electronic storage or transmission, or broadcast for distance learning.

Some ancillaries, including electronic and print components, may not be available to customers
outside the United States.

Annual Editions® is a registered trademark of The McGraw-Hill Companies, Inc.

Annual Editions is published by the **Contemporary Learning Series** group within the
McGraw-Hill Higher Education division.

1 2 3 4 5 6 7 8 9 0 WDQ/WDQ 1 0 9 8 7 6 5 4 3 2 1 0

ISBN 978–0–07–352858–8
MHID 0–07–352858–7
ISSN 1094–2629

Managing Editor: *Larry Loeppke*
Developmental Editor: *Dave Welsh*
Editorial Coordinator: *Mary Foust*
Editorial Assistant: *Cindy Hedley*
Production Service Assistant: *Rita Hingtgen*
Permissions Coordinator: *Lenny J. Behnke*
Senior Marketing Manager: *Julie Keck*
Senior Marketing Communications Specialist: *Mary Klein*
Marketing Coordinator: *Alice Link*
Director Specialized Production: *Faye Schilling*
Senior Project Manager: *Joyce Watters*
Design Specialist: *Margarite Reynolds*
Production Supervisor: *Sue Culbertson*
Cover Graphics: *Kristine Jubeck*

Compositor: Laserwords Private Limited
Cover Image: RF/CORBIS (inset); © Don Bishop/Getty Images (background)

Library in Congress Cataloging-in-Publication Data
Main entry under title: Annual Editions: Computers in Society. 2010/2011.
1. Computers in Society—Periodicals. De Palma, Paul, *comp.* II. Title: Computers in Society.
658'.05

www.mhhe.com

Editors/Academic Advisory Board

Members of the Academic Advisory Board are instrumental in the final selection of articles for each edition of ANNUAL EDITIONS. Their review of articles for content, level, and appropriateness provides critical direction to the editors and staff. We think that you will find their careful consideration well reflected in this volume.

ANNUAL EDITIONS: Computers in Society 10/11
16th Edition

EDITOR

Paul De Palma
Gonzaga University

ACADEMIC ADVISORY BOARD MEMBERS

Charles Bauer
Illinois Institute of Technology

Paula Bell
Lock Haven University of Pennsylvania

Maria I. Bryant
College of Southern Maryland

Peter A. Danielson
University of British Columbia

Michael J. Day
Northern Ilinois University

J. Kevin Eckert
University of Maryland—Baltimore County

Kenneth Fidel
DePaul University

Laura Finnerty Paul
Skidmore College

David C. Gibbs
University of Wisconsin—Stevens Point

Kenton Graviss
Indiana University—Southeast

Patricia A. Joseph
Slippery Rock University

Donna Kastner
California State University—Fullerton

Eugene J. Kozminski
Aquinas College

Lyn Lazar
Western Carolina University

Richard A. Lejk
University of North Carolina—Charlotte

Michael Martel
Ohio University

Daniel Mittleman
DePaul University

Ottis L. Murray
University of North Carolina, Pembroke

Gail Niklason
Weber State College

Therese D. O'Neil
Indiana University of Pennsylvania

Morris Pondfield
Towson University

Robert B. Sloger
Amarillo College

John C. Stoob
Humboldt State University

Lawrence E. Turner
Southwestern Adventist University

Lih-Ching Chen Wang
Cleveland State University

Haibo Wang
Texas A & M International University

Fred Westfall
Troy University

Rene Weston-Eborn
Weber State College

Nathan White
McKendree University

Preface

In publishing ANNUAL EDITIONS we recognize the enormous role played by the magazines, newspapers, and journals of the public press in providing current, first-rate educational information in a broad spectrum of interest areas. Many of these articles are appropriate for students, researchers, and professionals seeking accurate, current material to help bridge the gap between principles and theories, and the real world. These articles, however, become more useful for study when those of lasting value are carefully collected, organized, indexed, and reproduced in a low-cost format, which provides easy and permanent access when the material is needed. That is the role played by ANNUAL EDITIONS.

In a well-remembered scene from the 1968 movie, *The Graduate,* the hapless Ben is pulled aside at his graduation party by his father's business partner. He asks Ben about his plans, now that the young man has graduated. As Ben fumbles, the older man whispers the single word, "plastics," in his ear. Today, Ben is eligible for the senior discount at movie theatres. What advice would he offer a new graduate? Surely not *plastics,* even though petrochemicals have transformed the way we live over the past four decades. Odds are that computers have replaced plastics in the imaginations of today's graduates, this despite the tech bubble that burst in 2000. To test this hypothesis, I did a Google search on the words "plastics," and "plastic." This produced about 226,000,000 hits, an indication that Ben was given good advice. I followed this with a search on "computers," and "computer," to which Google replied with an astonishing 1,120,000,000 hits. The point is that computers are a phenomenon to be reckoned with.

In netting articles for the 16th edition of *Computers in Society* from the sea of contenders, I have tried to continue in the tradition of the previous editors. The writers are journalists, computer scientists, lawyers, economists, and academics, the kinds of professions you would expect to find represented in a collection on the social implications of computing. They write for newspapers, business and general circulation magazines, academic journals, and professional publications. Their writing is free from both the unintelligible jargon and the breathless enthusiasm that prevents people from forming clear ideas about computing. This is by design, of course. I have long contended that it is possible to write clearly about any subject, even one as technically complex and clouded by marketing as information technology. I hope that after reading the selections, you will agree.

Annual Editions: Computers in Society is organized around important dimensions of society rather than of computing. The introduction begins the conversation with an article by the late Neil Postman who says "that every technology has a philosophy which is given expression in how the technology makes people use their minds." Sherry Turkle, one of the earliest and most eloquent commentators on the psychological changes wrought by computing, begins the final unit with a similar thought: "computational objects do not simply do things *for* us, they do things *to* us as people, to our ways of being [in] the world, to our ways of seeing ourselves and others." In between, with

the help of many other writers, a crucial question recurs like a leitmotif in a complex piece of music: To what extent is technology of any kind without a bias of its own and to what extent does it embody the world view, intentionally or not, of its creators? If the answer were simply that the good and the ill of computing depend upon how computers are used, those of us interested in the interaction of computers and society would be hard-pressed to claim your attention. We could simply exhort you to do no evil, as Google tells its employees. Good advice, certainly. But information technology demands a more nuanced stance.

Sometimes, computing systems have consequences not intended by their developers. Threats to privacy in an era of social networking is one (Articles 11, 12, 25, 26, 29). A growing inability to concentrate is another (Articles 13, 14). And at all times, "embedded in every technology there is a powerful idea" (Article 1). An essential task for students of technology is to learn to tease out these ideas, so that the consequences might be understood *before* the technology is adopted.

The book's major themes are the economy, community, politics considered broadly, and the balance of risk and reward. In a field as fluid as computing, the intersection of computers with each of these dimensions changes from year to year. Many articles in the 10th edition examined the growing importance of e-commerce. By the time of the 13th edition, e-commerce had nearly disappeared. This is not because e-commerce had become unimportant. Rather, in just a few years, it had moved into the mainstream. The 14th edition replaced over half of the articles from the 13th. The 15th edition eliminated a third from the 14th. The 16th edition removes 40 percent of the articles from the 15th edition, replacing them with eighteen new ones. Computing is a rapidly moving target. We race to keep up.

In 1965, Gordon Moore, who would go on to found Intel, published a paper in which he observed that the number of transistors that could be squeezed onto a silicon chip had doubled each year since the invention of integrated circuits. In a slightly modified form this has come to be called Moore's Law. Scholars have been predicting its demise ever since, usually pointing out that integrated circuits, like everything else in the universe, must conform to the laws of physics, and nothing, not even the ingenuity of Silicon Valley engineers, is without limits. Nevertheless, despite the inevitable day of reckoning, Paul Ceruzzi

(Article 2) points out that Moore's Law has been operating for almost a half century.

To see why the articles in this volume describe a world not conceivable even a decade ago, perform this thought experiment. Imagine you have a chessboard and a supply of pennies. Put one penny on the upper left-most square. Put two pennies on the next square and so on, doubling each stack of pennies for each subsequent square. At the end of the first row, you will have a stack 256 pennies high. Lots, but still manageable. By the end of the second row, the stack will have grown to 65,536 pennies, a big stack and worth a lot of money, but still within the budget of a college student. By end of the third row—twenty-four years of the nearly fifty that Moore's Law has been operating—you will have a stack of 17 million pennies, over sixteen miles high and worth in the neighborhood of $200,000. This pile of pennies tells you everything you need to know about how it is that bloggers and assorted online sources are putting newspapers out of business (Articles 4, 19, 24), how Google has publishers and libraries worried (Article 22), how Twitterers in Iran held the world's attention last spring (Article 33), and, above all, why the term "computer," refers to so much more than the device on your desk (or even in your backpack). Computing has expanded beyond the constraints of the computer—to your running shoes (Article 18), to robot soldiers (Article 21), to Google's cloud (Articles 39, 40)—for the same reason that the stack of pennies grew incomprehensibly large. Any good thing that doubles in size with regularity is going to change its world in unimaginable ways.

More than other technologies, computers force us to think about limits. What does it mean to be human? Are there kinds of knowledge that should not be pursued? One of our contributors, Sherry Turkle, asks, apropos of any complex technology, "Are you really you if you have a baboon's heart inside, had your face resculpted by Brazil's finest plastic surgeons, and are taking Zoloft to give you a competitive edge at work?" (Turkle, 2003, p. 6). Are we developing "increasingly intimate relationships with machines," as Turkle claims (Article 37), and, do we really need to build computers that are self-aware (Article 41)?

A word of caution. Each article has been selected because it is topical, interesting, and nicely written. To say that an article is interesting or well-written, however, does not mean that it is right. This is as true of the facts presented in each article as it is of the point of view. When reading startling claims, whether in this volume or anywhere else, it is wise to remember that writers gather facts from other sources who gathered them from still other sources, who may, ultimately, rely upon a selective method of fact-gathering. There may be no good solution to the problem of unsupported assertions, beyond rigorous peer review. But, then, most of us don't curl up each night with scientific journals, and even these can be flawed. The real antidote to poorly supported arguments is to become critical readers, no less of experts. With the demise of newspapers and at least the semblance of professional accountability, blogs and opinion pieces have moved into the vacuum. We have to be more vigilant then ever. Having said that, I hope you will approach these articles as you might approach a good discussion among friends. You may not agree with all opinions, but you will come away nudged in one direction or another by reasoned arguments, holding a richer, more informed, view of important issues.

This book includes several features that I hope will be helpful to students and professionals. Each article listed in the table of contents is preceded by a short abstract with key concepts in bold italic type. The social implications of computing, of course, are not limited to the eight broad areas represented by the unit titles. A topic guide lists each article by name and number along still other dimensions of computers in society.

We want *Annual Editions: Computers in Society* to help you participate more fully in some of the most important discussions of the time, those about the promises and risks of computing. Your suggestions and comments are very important to us. If you complete and return the postage-paid article rating form in the back of the book, we can try to incorporate them into the next edition.

Reference

Turkle, S. (2003). Technology and Human Vulnerability. *Harvard Business Review*, 81(9): 43–50.

Paul De Palma
Editor

Contents

UNIT 1
Introduction

UNIT 2
The Economy

The concepts in bold italics are developed in the article. For further expansion, please refer to the Topic Guide.

UNIT 3
Work and the Workplace

UNIT 4
Computers, People, and Social Participation

The concepts in bold italics are developed in the article. For further expansion, please refer to the Topic Guide.

UNIT 5
Societal Institutions: Law, Politics, Education, and the Military

The concepts in bold italics are developed in the article. For further expansion, please refer to the Topic Guide.

UNIT 6
Risk and Avoiding Risk

The concepts in bold italics are developed in the article. For further expansion, please refer to the Topic Guide.

UNIT 7
International Perspectives and Issues

UNIT 8
The Frontier of Computing

The concepts in bold italics are developed in the article. For further expansion, please refer to the Topic Guide.

The concepts in bold italics are developed in the article. For further expansion, please refer to the Topic Guide.

Correlation Guide

The *Annual Editions* series provides students with convenient, inexpensive access to current, carefully selected articles from the public press. **Annual Editions: Computers in Society 10/11** is an easy-to-use reader that presents articles on important topics such as *the economy, the workplace, social participation, risk,* and many more. For more information on *Annual Editions* and other *McGraw-Hill Contemporary Learning Series* titles, visit www.mhhe.com/cls

This convenient guide matches the units in **Annual Editions: Computers in Society 10/11** with the corresponding chapters in three of our best-selling McGraw-Hill Computer Science textbooks by O'Brien/Marakis, Haig/Cummings, and Baltzan/Phillips.

Annual Editions: Computers in Society 10/11	Introduction to Information Systems, 15/e by O'Brien/Marakas	Management Information Systems for the Information Age, 8/e by Haag/Cummings	Business Driven Technology, 4/e by Baltzan/Phillips
Unit 1: Introduction	**Chapter 1:** Foundations of Information Systems in Business	**Chapter 1:** The Information Age in Which You Live: Changing the Face of Business	
Unit 2: The Economy	**Chapter 2:** Competing with Information Technology **Chapter 7:** Electronic Business Systems **Chapter 8:** Electronic Commerce Systems	**Chapter 1:** The Information Age in Which You Live: Changing the Face of Business **Chapter 2:** Major Business Initiatives: Gaining Competitive Advantage with IT **Chapter 5:** Electronic Commerce: Strategies for the New Economy	**Chapter 1:** Business-Driven Technology **Chapter 2:** Identifying Competitive Advantages **Chapter 3:** Strategic Initiatives for Implementing Competitive Advantages **Chapter 4:** Measuring the Success of Strategic Initiatives
Unit 3: Work and the Workplace	**Chapter 7:** Electronic Business Systems **Chapter 8:** Electronic Commerce Systems **Chapter 10:** Developing Business/IT Solutions	**Chapter 2:** Major Business Initiatives: Gaining Competitive Advantage with IT **Chapter 4:** Decision Support and Artificial Intelligence: Brainpower for Your Business	**Chapter 16:** Integrating Wireless Technology in Business **Chapter 17:** Building Software to Support an Agile Organization
Unit 4: Computers, People, and Social Participation		**Chapter 9:** Emerging Trends and Technologies: Business, People, and Technology Tomorrow	
Unit 5: Societal Institutions: Law, Politics, Education, and the Military			
Unit 6: Risk	**Chapter 11:** Security and Ethical Challenges	**Chapter 8:** Protecting People and Information: Threats and Safeguards	
Unit 7: International Perspectives and Issues	**Chapter 12:** Enterprise and Global Management of Information Technology		
Unit 8: The Frontier of Computing		**Chapter 9:** Emerging Trends and Technologies: Business, People, and Technology Tomorrow	**Chapter 19:** Outsourcing in the 21st Century **Chapter 21:** Developing a 21st Century Organization

Topic Guide

This topic guide suggests how the selections in this book relate to the subjects covered in your course. You may want to use the topics listed on these pages to search the Web more easily.

On the following pages a number of websites have been gathered specifically for this book. They are arranged to reflect the units of this Annual Editions reader. You can link to these sites by going to *http://www.mhhe.com/cls*.

All the articles that relate to each topic are listed below the bold-faced term.

Internet References

The following Internet sites have been selected to support the articles found in this reader. These sites were available at the time of publication. However, because websites often change their structure and content, the information listed may no longer be available. We invite you to visit http://www.mhhe.com/cls for easy access to these sites.

Annual Editions: Computers in Society 10/11

General Source

Livelink Intranet Guided Tour
http://www.opentext.com

Livelink Intranet helps companies to manage and control documents, business processes, and projects more effectively. Take this tour to see how.

UNIT 1: Introduction

Internet and American Life
http://www.pewinternet.org

Provides "reports exploring the impact of the Internet on families, communities, work and home, daily life, education, health care, and civic and political life."

Beyond the Information Revolution
http://www.theatlantic.com/issues/99oct/9910drucker.htm

Peter Drucker has written a three-part article, available at this site, that uses history to gauge the significance of e-commerce— "a totally unexpected development" —to throw light on the future of, in his words, "the knowledge worker."

Short History of the Internet
http://ei.cs.vt.edu/~wwwbtb/book/chap1/index.html

Shahrooz Feizabadi presents the history of the World Wide Web as well as the history of several ideas and underlying technologies from which the World Wide Web emerged.

UNIT 2: The Economy

CAUCE: Coalition against Unsolicited Commercial Email
http://www.cauce.org

This all-volunteer organization was created to advocate for a legislative solution to the problem of UCE, better known as spam. Read about the fight and how you can help at this Web page.

E-Commerce Times
http://www.ecommercetimes.com

E-Commerce Times is a gateway to a wealth of current information and resources concerning e-commerce.

Fight Spam on the Internet
http://spam.abuse.net

This is an anti-spam site that has been in operation since 1996. Its purpose is to promote responsible net commerce, in part, by fighting spam. Up-to-date news about spam can be found on the home page.

The Linux Home Page
http://www.linux.org

This website explains that Linux is a free Unix-type operating system, originally created by Linus Torvalds, that is causing a revolution in the world of computers. The site features the latest news about Linux, and everything else you would need to know to switch to the service.

AllAdvantage—The Rise of the Informediary
http://en.wikipedia.org/wiki/AllAdvantage

This Wikipedia article describes AllAdvantage's pathfinding role as, arguably, the first Internet infomediary.

Smart Cards: A Primer
http://www.smartcardbasics.com/overview.html

This site describes the smart card, its applications, and its value in e-commerce.

Smart Card Group
http://www.smartcard.co.uk

This website bills itself as "the definitive website for Smart Card Technology." At this site you can download Dr. David B. Everett's definitive "Introduction to Smart Cards."

UNIT 3: Work and the Workplace

American Telecommuting Association
http://www.knowledgetree.com/ata-adv.html

What is good about telecommuting is examined at this site that also offers information regarding concepts, experiences, and the future of telecommuting.

Computers in the Workplace
http://cpsr.org/prevsite/program/workplace/workplace-home.html

"Computers in the Workplace (initiated by the CPSR/Palo Alto chapter) became a national level project in 1988. The Participatory Design conferences have explored workplace issues since the conference's inception in 1992."

InfoWeb: Techno-rage
http://www.cciw.com/content/technorage.html

Techno-rage is becoming more and more common. This site provides information and resources regarding techno-rage and techno-stress.

STEP ON IT! Pedals: Repetitive Strain Injury
http://www.bilbo.com/rsi2.html

Data on carpal tunnel syndrome are presented here with links to alternative approaches to the computer keyboard and links to related information.

What About Computers in the Workplace
http://law.freeadvice.com/intellectual_property/computer_law/computers_workplace.htm

This site, which is the leading legal site for consumers and small businesses, provides general legal information to help people understand their legal rights in 100 legal topics—including the answer to the question, "Can my boss watch what I'm doing?"

UNIT 4: Computers, People, and Social Participation

Alliance for Childhood: Computers and Children
http://drupal6.allianceforchildhood.org/computer_position_statement

How are computers affecting the intellectual growth of children? Here is one opinion provided by the Alliance for Childhood.

Internet References

The Core Rules of Netiquette
http://www.albion.com/netiquette/corerules.html

Excerpted from Virginia Shea's book *Netiquette,* this is a classic work in the field of online communication.

SocioSite: Networks, Groups, and Social Interaction
http://www.sociosite.net

This site provides sociological and psychological resources and research regarding the effect of computers on social interaction.

UNIT 5: Societal Institutions: Law, Politics, Education, and the Military

ACLU: American Civil Liberties Union
http://www.aclu.org

Click on the Supreme Court's Internet decision, plus details of the case *Reno v. ACLU,* and the ACLU's campaign to restore information privacy, "Take Back Your Data"; and cyber-liberties and free speech for opinions on First Amendment rights as they apply to cyberspace.

Information Warfare and U.S. Critical Infrastructure
http://www.twurl.com/twurled_world/ullman/cover.htm

The "twURLed World" contains a pie chart of URLs involved in IW (information warfare) as well as report main pages that list Internet domains, keywords in contexts and by individual terms, and listing of all URLs and links to details.

Living in the Electronic Village
http://www.rileyis.com/report

This site addresses the impact of information in technology on government. Shown is the executive summary, but seven other sections are equally pertinent.

United States Patent and Trademark Office
http://www.uspto.gov

This is the official homepage of the U.S. Patent and Trademark Office. Use this site to search patents and trademarks, apply for patents, and more.

World Intellectual Property Organization
http://www.wipo.org

Visit the World Intellectual Property Organization website to find information and issues pertaining to virtual and intellectual property.

UNIT 6: Risk and Avoiding Risk

AntiOnline: Hacking and Hackers
http://www.antionline.com/index.php

This site is designed to help the average person learn how to protect against hackers.

Copyright & Trademark Information for the IEEE Computer Society
http://computer.org/copyright.htm

Here is an example of how a publication on the Web is legally protected. The section on Intellectual Property Rights Information contains further information about reuse permission and copyright policies.

Electronic Privacy Information Center (EPIC)
http://epic.org

EPIC is a private research organization that was established to focus public attention on emerging civil liberties issues and to protect privacy, the First Amendment, and constitutional values. This site contains news, resources, policy archives, and a search mechanism.

Internet Privacy Coalition
http://www.epic.org/crypto

The mission of the Internet Privacy Coalition is to promote privacy and security on the Internet through widespread public availability of strong encryption and the relaxation of export controls on cryptography.

Center for Democracy and Technology
http://www.cdt.org/crypto

These pages are maintained for discussion and information about data privacy and security, encryption, and the need for policy reform. The site discusses pending legislation, Department of Commerce Export Regulations, and other initiatives.

Survive Spyware
http://reviews.cnet.com/4520-3688_7-6456087-1.html

Internet spying is a huge problem. Advertisers, Web designers, and even the government are using the Net to spy on you. CNET.com provides information about spyware and detecting spying eyes that will help you eliminate the threat.

UNIT 7: International Perspectives and Issues

The Internet and State Control in Authoritarian Regimes
http://www.carnegieendowment.org/files/21KalathilBoas.pdf

The authors describe how the Internet can be a countering force against government control of information delivery.

UNIT 8: The Frontier of Computing

Introduction to Artificial Intelligence (AI)
http://www-formal.stanford.edu/jmc/aiintro/aiintro.html

This statement describes A.I. Click on John McCarthy's home page for a list of additional papers.

Kasparov vs. Deep Blue: The Rematch
http://www.research.ibm.com/deepblue/home/html/b.html

Video clips and a discussion of the historic chess rematch between Garry Kasparov and Deep Blue are available on this site.

PHP-Nuke Powered Site: International Society for Artificial Life
http://www.alife.org/

Start here to find links to many alife (artificial life) websites, including demonstrations, research centers and groups, and other resources.

UNIT 1

Introduction

Unit Selections

1. **Five Things We Need to Know about Technological Change,** Neil Postman
2. **Moore's Law and Technological Determinism: Reflections on the History of Technology,** Paul E. Ceruzzi

Key Points to Consider

- All U.S. school children learn that the first message Samuel F.B. Morse transmitted over his newly invented telegraph were the words, "What hath God wrought." What they probably do not learn is that Morse was quoting from the poem of Balaam in the Book of Numbers, chapter 23. Read the text of this poem. The overview to this unit presents two ways to understand technical and scientific discoveries. In which camp is Morse?

- Early on in *Walden,* Thoreau famously remarks that "Our inventions are wont to be pretty toys, which distract our attention from serious things. They are but an improved means to an unimproved end, an end that it was already but too easy to arrive at. . . . We are in great haste to construct a magnetic telegraph from Maine to Texas; but Maine and Texas, it may be, have nothing important to communicate." Substitute "Internet" for "magnetic telegraph." Do you agree or disagree with Thoreau? How do you think Paul Ceruzzi ("Moore's Law and Technological Determinism") might respond?

- Richard Lewontin, a Harvard geneticist, says ("The Politics of Science," *The New York Review of Books,* May 9, 2002) that "The state of American science and its relation to the American state are the product of war." What does he mean? Is Lewontin overstating his case? Use the Internet to find out more about Richard Lewontin.

- The two poles of thought that Paul Ceruzzi ("Moore's Law and Technological Determinism") discusses are usually referred to as *social constructionism* and *technological determinism.* Use the Internet to explore both. Ceruzzi says that "public acceptance of technological determinism is evident among the many visitors where I work, at the National Air and Space Museum." Why?

- Referring to the last question, do you think Postman ("Five Things We Need to Know about Technological Change"), is a social constructivist or a technological determinist (or something else, altogether)?

Student Website
www.mhhe.com/cls

Internet References

Internet and American Life
http://www.pewinternet.org

Beyond the Information Revolution
http://www.theatlantic.com/issues/99oct/9910drucker.htm

Short History of the Internet
http://ei.cs.vt.edu/~wwwbtb/book/chap1/index.html

This book, *Annual Editions: Computers in Society,* is part of a larger series of books published by Dushkin/McGraw-Hill. The series contains over seventy titles, among them *American History, Sociology, and World Politics.* It is instructive to note that not one of them carries the final prepositional phrase, "in Society." Why is that? Here is a first approximation. History, sociology, world politics, indeed, most of the other titles in the *Annual Editions* series are not in society, they *are* society. Suppose we produced an edited volume entitled, "History in Society." If such a volume contained reflections on the social implications of the academic study of history, it would have a tiny and specialized readership. But you know that when we speak of "computers in society," we are not talking about the social implications of the academic study of computing. Here is one difference between this volume and the others in the series: It is possible to study computers without studying their social dimension.

But is it? Until not long ago, most people interested in the philosophy and sociology of science considered it value-neutral. That is, a given technology carried no values of its own. The ethics of this or that technology depended on what was done with it. A vestige of this thinking is still with us. When people say, "Guns don't kill people. People kill people," they are asserting that technology somehow stands outside of society, waiting to be put to use for good or ill. The concern about intoxicated drivers is similar. All of us would live happier, safer lives if campaigns to remove drunken drivers from their cars were successful. But this still would not get to the heart of highway carnage that has to do with federal encouragement for far-flung suburbs, local patterns of land use, and a neglect of public transportation. Drunk driving would not be the issue it is if driving were not so vital to American life, and driving would not be so vital to American life if a cascade of social and political decisions had not come together in the middle of the twentieth century to favor the automobile.

The first article, "Five Things We Need to Know About Technological Change," makes this point eloquently: "Embedded in every technology there is a powerful idea. . . ." The observation is an important one and is shared by most of the more reflective contemporary commentators on technology. The idea that technology can be studied apart from its social consequences owes some of its strength to the way many people imagine that scientific discoveries are made—since technology is just science applied. It is commonly imagined that scientists are disinterested observers of the natural world. In this view, science unfolds, and technology unfolds shortly after, according to the laws of nature and the passion of scientists. But, of course, scientists study those things that are socially valued. The particular expression of social value in the United States is the National Science Foundation and National Institute of Health funding. We should not be surprised that the medical and computing sciences are funded generously, or, indeed, that our research physicians and computer scientists are paid better than English professors.

Perhaps a more accurate view of the relationship between technology and computing to society is that social values affect technical discovery that, in turn, affect social values. It is this

© Photodisc/Getty Images

intricate dance between computers and society—now one leading, now the other—that the writers in this volume struggle to understand, though most of them do it implicitly. But, before we try to understand the dance, it seems reasonable to understand what is meant by the word "computer." You will find in this volume a decided bias toward networked computers. A networked computer is one that can communicate with many millions of others through the global Internet. This is a new definition. As recently as 1996, less than 1 in 5 Americans had used the Internet (Blendon et al., 2001). Just as we mean networked computers when we use the word "computer" today, in the late 1980s someone using the word would have meant a stand-alone PC, running, maybe a word processor, a spreadsheet, and some primitive games. A decade before that, the word would have referred to a large, probably IBM, machine kept in an air-conditioned room and tended by an army of technicians. Prior to 1950, the word would have meant someone particularly adept in arithmetic calculations. The point here is that as the meaning of a single word has shifted, our understanding of the dance has to shift with it.

That this shift in meaning has occurred in just a few decades helps us understand why so many commentators use the word "revolution" to describe what computing has wrought. Just as technologies come with hidden meanings, so do words, themselves. The word "revolution" when it is applied to political upheaval is used to describe something thought bad, or at least chaotic—the single counter example is the American Revolution. Not so when the word is applied to computing. Computing is thought to change quickly, but more, it is thought to bring many benefits. A survey conducted not long ago by the Brookings Institution (Blendon et al., 2001) indicated that 90 percent of

Americans believe that science and technology will make their lives easier and more comfortable. The real question to ask is more basic: not whether Americans believe it, but is it true? First, does the spread of computing constitute a revolution, or just, in Thoreau's words, "an improved means to an unimproved end"? Second, revolutionary or not, have we grown smarter, healthier, happier with the coming of the computer? This is still an open question—but, as the Internet morphs from a novelty to an appliance, to a shrinking number of commentators.

Nevertheless, as I warned in the preface to this volume, read each of the articles critically, including this one. Paul Ceruzzi, a distinguished historian of computing, offers in his piece, "Moore's Law and Technological Determinism," disagrees with me. Despite his natural affinity for the social constructionist perspective, he tells us that "computing power must increase because it can." This is raw technological determinism. Read the essay and see if you're convinced.

Reference

Blendon, R., Benson, J., Brodie, M., Altgman, D., Rosenbaum, M., Flournoy, R., Kim, M. (2001). Whom to Protect and How? *Brookings Review,* 9(1): 44–48.

Five Things We Need to Know about Technological Change

Neil Postman

Good morning your Eminences and Excellencies, ladies, and gentlemen.

The theme of this conference, "The New Technologies and the Human Person: Communicating the Faith in the New Millennium," suggests, of course, that you are concerned about what might happen to faith in the new millennium, as well you should be. In addition to our computers, which are close to having a nervous breakdown in anticipation of the year 2000, there is a great deal of frantic talk about the 21st century and how it will pose for us unique problems of which we know very little but for which, nonetheless, we are supposed to carefully prepare. Everyone seems to worry about this—business people, politicians, educators, as well as theologians.

The human dilemma is as it has always been, and it is a delusion to believe that the technological changes of our era have rendered irrelevant the wisdom of the ages and the sages.

At the risk of sounding patronizing, may I try to put everyone's mind at ease? I doubt that the 21st century will pose for us problems that are more stunning, disorienting or complex than those we faced in this century, or the 19th, 18th, 17th, or for that matter, many of the centuries before that. But for those who are excessively nervous about the new millennium, I can provide, right at the start, some good advice about how to confront it. The advice comes from people whom we can trust, and whose thoughtfulness, it's safe to say, exceeds that of President Clinton, Newt Gingrich, or even Bill Gates. Here is what Henry David Thoreau told us: "All our inventions are but improved means to an unimproved end." Here is what Goethe told us: "One should, each day, try to hear a little song, read a good poem, see a fine picture, and, if possible, speak a few reasonable words." Socrates told us: "The unexamined life is not worth living." Rabbi Hillel told us: "What is hateful to thee, do not do to another." And here is the prophet Micah: "What does the Lord require of thee but to do justly, to love mercy and to walk hum-

bly with thy God." And I could say, if we had the time, (although you know it well enough) what Jesus, Isaiah, Mohammad, Spinoza, and Shakespeare told us. It is all the same: There is no escaping from ourselves. The human dilemma is as it has always been, and it is a delusion to believe that the technological changes of our era have rendered irrelevant the wisdom of the ages and the sages.

. . . all technological change is a trade-off. . . . a Faustian bargain.

Nonetheless, having said this, I know perfectly well that because we do live in a technological age, we have some special problems that Jesus, Hillel, Socrates, and Micah did not and could not speak of. I do not have the wisdom to say what we ought to do about such problems, and so my contribution must confine itself to some things we need to know in order to address the problems. I call my talk *Five Things We Need to Know About Technological Change*. I base these ideas on my thirty years of studying the history of technological change but I do not think these are academic or esoteric ideas. They are the sort of things everyone who is concerned with cultural stability and balance should know and I offer them to you in the hope that you will find them useful in thinking about the effects of technology on religious faith.

First Idea

The first idea is that all technological change is a trade-off. I like to call it a Faustian bargain. Technology giveth and technology taketh away. This means that for every advantage a new technology offers, there is always a corresponding disadvantage. The disadvantage may exceed in importance the advantage, or the advantage may well be worth the cost. Now, this may seem to be a rather obvious idea, but you would be surprised at how many people believe that new technologies are unmixed blessings. You need only think of the enthusiasms with which most people approach their understanding of computers. Ask anyone who knows something about computers to talk about them, and you will find that they will, unabashedly and relentlessly, extol the wonders of computers. You will also find that in most cases they will completely neglect to mention any of the liabilities of computers. This is a dangerous imbalance, since the greater the wonders of a technology, the greater will be its negative consequences.

Think of the automobile, which for all of its obvious advantages, has poisoned our air, choked our cities, and degraded the beauty of our natural landscape. Or you might reflect on the paradox of medical technology which brings wondrous cures but is, at the same time, a demonstrable cause of certain diseases and disabilities, and has played a significant role in reducing the diagnostic skills of physicians. It is also well to recall that for all of the intellectual and social benefits provided by the printing press, its costs were equally monumental. The printing press gave the Western world prose, but it made poetry into an exotic and elitist form of communication. It gave us inductive science, but it reduced religious sensibility to a form of fanciful superstition. Printing gave us the modern conception of nation-wide, but in so doing turned patriotism into a sordid if not lethal emotion. We might even say that the printing of the Bible in vernacular languages introduced the impression that God was an Englishman or a German or a Frenchman—that is to say, printing reduced God to the dimensions of a local potentate.

Perhaps the best way I can express this idea is to say that the question, "What will a new technology do?" is no more important than the question, "What will a new technology undo?" Indeed, the latter question is more important, precisely because it is asked so infrequently. One might say, then, that a sophisticated perspective on technological change includes one's being skeptical of Utopian and Messianic visions drawn by those who have no sense of history or of the precarious balances on which culture depends. In fact, if it were up to me, I would forbid anyone from talking about the new information technologies unless the person can demonstrate that he or she knows something about the social and psychic effects of the alphabet, the mechanical clock, the printing press, and telegraphy. In other words, knows something about the costs of great technologies.

Idea Number One, then, is that culture always pays a price for technology.

Second Idea

This leads to the second idea, which is that the advantages and disadvantages of new technologies are never distributed evenly among the population. This means that every new technology benefits some and harms others. There are even some who are not affected at all. Consider again the case of the printing press in the 16th century, of which Martin Luther said it was "God's highest and extremest act of grace, whereby the business of the gospel is driven forward." By placing the word of God on every Christian's kitchen table, the mass-produced book undermined the authority of the church hierarchy, and hastened the breakup of the Holy Roman See. The Protestants of that time cheered this development. The Catholics were enraged and distraught. Since I am a Jew, had I lived at that time, I probably wouldn't have given a damn one way or another, since it would make no

difference whether a pogrom was inspired by Martin Luther or Pope Leo X. Some gain, some lose, a few remain as they were.

Let us take as another example, television, although here I should add at once that in the case of television there are very few indeed who are not affected in one way or another. In America, where television has taken hold more deeply than anywhere else, there are many people who find it a blessing, not least those who have achieved high-paying, gratifying careers in television as executives, technicians, directors, newscasters and entertainers. On the other hand, and in the long run, television may bring an end to the careers of school teachers since school was an invention of the printing press and must stand or fall on the issue of how much importance the printed word will have in the future. There is no chance, of course, that television will go away but school teachers who are enthusiastic about its presence always call to my mind an image of some turn-of-the-century blacksmith who not only is singing the praises of the automobile but who also believes that his business will be enhanced by it. We know now that his business was not enhanced by it; it was rendered obsolete by it, as perhaps an intelligent blacksmith would have known.

The questions, then, that are never far from the mind of a person who is knowledgeable about technological change are these: Who specifically benefits from the development of a new technology? Which groups, what type of person, what kind of industry will be favored? And, of course, which groups of people will thereby be harmed?

. . . there are always winners and losers in technological change.

These questions should certainly be on our minds when we think about computer technology. There is no doubt that the computer has been and will continue to be advantageous to large-scale organizations like the military or airline companies or banks or tax collecting institutions. And it is equally clear that the computer is now indispensable to high-level researchers in physics and other natural sciences. But to what extent has computer technology been an advantage to the masses of people? To steel workers, vegetable store owners, automobile mechanics, musicians, bakers, bricklayers, dentists, yes, theologians, and most of the rest into whose lives the computer now intrudes? These people have had their private matters made more accessible to powerful institutions. They are more easily tracked and controlled; they are subjected to more examinations, and are increasingly mystified by the decisions made about them. They are more than ever reduced to mere numerical objects. They are being buried by junk mail. They are easy targets for advertising agencies and political institutions.

In a word, these people are losers in the great computer revolution. The winners, which include among others computer companies, multi-national corporations and the nation state, will, of course, encourage the losers to be enthusiastic about computer technology. That is the way of winners, and so in the beginning they told the losers that with personal computers the average person can balance a checkbook more neatly, keep better track of recipes, and make more logical shopping lists. Then they told them that computers will make it possible to vote at home, shop at home, get all the entertainment they wish at home, and thus make community life unnecessary. And now, of course, the winners speak constantly of the Age of Information, always implying that the more information we have, the better we will be in solving significant problems—not only personal ones but large-scale social problems, as well. But how true is this? If there are children starving in the world—and there are—it is not because of insufficient information. We have known for a long time how to produce enough food to feed every child on the planet. How is it that we let so many of them starve? If there is violence on our streets, it is not because we have insufficient information. If women are abused, if divorce and pornography and mental illness are increasing, none of it has anything to do with insufficient information. I dare say it is because something else is missing, and I don't think I have to tell this audience what it is. Who knows? This age of information may turn out to be a curse if we are blinded by it so that we cannot see truly where our problems lie. That is why it is always necessary for us to ask of those who speak enthusiastically of computer technology, why do you do this? What interests do you represent? To whom are you hoping to give power? From whom will you be withholding power?

I do not mean to attribute unsavory, let alone sinister motives to anyone. I say only that since technology favors some people and harms others, these are questions that must always be asked. And so, that there are always winners and losers in technological change is the second idea.

Third Idea

Here is the third. Embedded in every technology there is a powerful idea, sometimes two or three powerful ideas. These ideas are often hidden from our view because they are of a somewhat abstract nature. But this should not be taken to mean that they do not have practical consequences.

The third idea is the sum and substance of what Marshall McLuhan meant when he coined the famous sentence, "The medium is the message."

Perhaps you are familiar with the old adage that says: To a man with a hammer, everything looks like a nail. We may extend that truism: To a person with a pencil, everything looks like a sentence. To a person with a TV camera, everything looks like an image. To a person with a computer, everything looks like data. I do not think we need to take these aphorisms literally. But what they call to our attention is that every technology has a prejudice. Like language itself, it predisposes us to favor and value certain perspectives and accomplishments. In a culture without writing, human memory is of the greatest importance, as are the proverbs, sayings and songs which contain the accumulated oral wisdom of centuries. That is why Solomon was thought to be the wisest of men. In Kings I we are told he knew 3,000 proverbs. But in a culture with writing, such feats of memory are considered a waste of time, and proverbs are merely irrelevant fancies. The writing person favors logical organization and systematic analysis, not proverbs. The telegraphic person values speed, not introspection. The television person values immediacy, not history. And computer people, what shall we say of them? Perhaps we can say that the computer person values information, not knowledge, certainly not wisdom. Indeed, in the computer age, the concept of wisdom may vanish altogether.

The consequences of technological change are always vast, often unpredictable and largely irreversible.

The third idea, then, is that every technology has a philosophy which is given expression in how the technology makes people use their minds, in what it makes us do with our bodies, in how it codifies the world, in which of our senses it amplifies, in which of our emotional and intellectual tendencies it disregards. This idea is the sum and substance of what the great Catholic prophet, Marshall McLuhan meant when he coined the famous sentence, "The medium is the message."

Fourth Idea

Here is the fourth idea: Technological change is not additive; it is ecological. I can explain this best by an analogy. What happens if we place a drop of red dye into a beaker of clear water? Do we have clear water plus a spot of red dye? Obviously not. We have a new coloration to every molecule of water. That is what I mean by ecological change. A new medium does not add something; it changes everything. In the year 1500, after the printing press was invented, you did not have old Europe plus the printing press. You had a different Europe. After television, America was not America plus television. Television gave a new coloration to every political campaign, to every home, to every school, to every church, to every industry, and so on.

That is why we must be cautious about technological innovation. The consequences of technological change are always vast, often unpredictable and largely irreversible. That is also why we must be suspicious of capitalists. Capitalists are by definition not only personal risk takers but, more to the point, cultural risk takers. The most creative and daring of them hope to exploit new technologies to the fullest, and do not much care what traditions are overthrown in the process or whether or not a culture is prepared to function without such traditions. Capitalists are, in a word, radicals. In America, our most significant radicals have always been capitalists—men like Bell, Edison, Ford, Carnegie, Sarnoff, Goldwyn. These men obliterated the 19th century, and created the 20th, which is why it is a mystery to me that capitalists are thought to be conservative. Perhaps it is because they are inclined to wear dark suits and grey ties.

I trust you understand that in saying all this, I am making no argument for socialism. I say only that capitalists need to be carefully watched and disciplined. To be sure, they talk of family, marriage, piety, and honor but if allowed to exploit new technology to its fullest economic potential, they may undo the institutions that make such ideas possible. And here I might just give two examples of this point, taken from the American encounter with technology. The first concerns education. Who, we may ask, has had the greatest impact on American education in this century? If you are thinking of John Dewey or any other education philosopher, I must say you are quite wrong. The greatest impact has been made by quiet men in grey suits in a suburb of New York City called Princeton, New Jersey. There, they developed and promoted the technology known as the standardized test, such as IQ tests, the SATs and the GREs. Their tests redefined what we mean by learning, and have resulted in our reorganizing the curriculum to accommodate the tests.

A second example concerns our politics. It is clear by now that the people who have had the most radical effect on American politics in our time are not political ideologues or student protesters with long hair and copies of Karl Marx under their arms. The radicals who have changed the nature of politics in America are entrepreneurs in dark suits and grey ties who manage the large television industry in America. They did not mean to turn political discourse into a form of entertainment. They did not mean to make it impossible for an overweight person to run for high political office. They did not mean to reduce political campaigning to a 30-second TV commercial. All they were trying to do is to make television into a vast and unsleeping money machine. That they destroyed substantive political discourse in the process does not concern them.

Fifth Idea

I come now to the fifth and final idea, which is that media tend to become mythic. I use this word in the sense in which it was used by the French literary critic, Roland Barthes. He used the word "myth" to refer to a common tendency to think of our technological creations as if they were God-given, as if they were a part of the natural order of things. I have on occasion asked my students if they know when the alphabet was invented. The question astonishes them. It is as if I asked them when clouds and trees were invented. The alphabet, they believe, was not something that was invented. It just is. It is this way with many products of human culture but with none more consistently than technology. Cars, planes, TV, movies, newspapers—they have achieved mythic status because they are perceived as gifts of nature, not as artifacts produced in a specific political and historical context.

When a technology become mythic, it is always dangerous because it is then accepted as it is, and is therefore not easily susceptible to modification or control. If you should propose to the average American that television broadcasting should not begin until 5 P.M. and should cease at 11 P.M., or propose that there should be no television commercials, he will think the idea ridiculous. But not because he disagrees with your cultural agenda. He will think it ridiculous because he assumes you are proposing that something in nature be changed; as if you are suggesting that the sun should rise at 10 A.M. instead of at 6.

The best way to view technology is as a strange intruder.

Whenever I think about the capacity of technology to become mythic, I call to mind the remark made by Pope John Paul II. He said, "Science can purify religion from error and superstition. Religion can purify science from idolatry and false absolutes."

What I am saying is that our enthusiasm for technology can turn into a form of idolatry and our belief in its beneficence can be a false absolute. The best way to view technology is as a strange intruder, to remember that technology is not part of God's plan but a product of human creativity and hubris, and that its capacity for good or evil rests entirely on human awareness of what it does for us and to us.

Conclusion

And so, these are my five ideas about technological change. First, that we always pay a price for technology; the greater the technology, the greater the price. Second, that there are always winners and losers, and that the winners always try to persuade the losers that they are really winners. Third, that there is embedded in every great technology an epistemological, political or social prejudice. Sometimes that bias is greatly to our advantage. Sometimes it is not. The printing press annihilated the oral tradition; telegraphy annihilated space; television has humiliated the word; the computer, perhaps, will degrade community life. And so on. Fourth, technological change is not additive; it is ecological, which means, it changes everything and is, therefore too important to be left entirely in the hands of Bill Gates. And fifth, technology tends to become mythic; that is, perceived as part of the natural order of things, and therefore tends to control more of our lives than is good for us.

If we had more time, I could supply some additional important things about technological change but I will stand by these for the moment, and will close with this thought. In the past, we experienced technological change in the manner of sleepwalkers. Our unspoken slogan has been "technology über alles," and we have been willing to shape our lives to fit the requirements of technology, not the requirements of culture. This is a form of stupidity, especially in an age of vast technological change. We need to proceed with our eyes wide open so that we may use technology rather than be used by it.

"Five Things We Need to Know About Technological Change," Address to *New Tech 98* Conference, Denver, Colorado, March 27, 1998. Copyright © 1998 by Neil Postman. Reprinted by permission of the author.

Moore's Law and Technological Determinism

Reflections on the History of Technology

PAUL E. CERUZZI

Just over a year ago, the arrival in my mailbox of a book I had agreed to review triggered some thoughts about technology I had been meaning to articulate. The book was Ross Bassett's *To the Digital Age: Research Labs, Start-up Companies, and the Rise of MOS Technology* (Baltimore, 2002).[1] In it, Bassett describes the development of metal-oxide semiconductor (MOS) technology, which enabled semiconductor firms to place more and more transistors on a single silicon chip.[2] This became the basis for what is now known as Moore's law, after Gordon E. Moore. In April 1965, Moore, then the director of research and development at the semiconductor division of Fairchild Camera and Instrument Corporation, published a paper in which he observed that the number of transistors that could be placed on an integrated circuit had doubled every year since integrated circuits had been invented and predicted that that trend would continue.[3] Shortly afterward, Moore left Fairchild to cofound Intel—a company, Bassett notes, that staked its future on MOS technology.

It is important to note at the outset that Moore's law was an empirical observation; it is not analogous to, say, Ohm's law, which relates resistance to current. Moore simply looked at the circuits being produced, plotted their density on a piece of semi-log graph paper, and found a straight line. Furthermore, he made this observation in 1965, when the integrated circuit was only six years old and had barely found its way out of the laboratory. The name "Silicon Valley" did not even exist; it would be coined at the end of that decade. Nonetheless, Moore's prediction that the number of transistors that could be placed on an integrated circuit would continue to double at short, regular intervals has held true ever since, although the interval soon stretched from twelve to eighteen months.[4]

Moore's law has been intensively studied, mainly by those wondering when, if ever, fundamental physical constraints (such as the diameter of a hydrogen atom) will interrupt the straight line that Moore observed. These studies note the lengthening of the interval mentioned already: chip densities now double about every eighteen to twenty months, although no one is sure why.[5] Analysts have been predicting the failure of Moore's

law for years. Interestingly, the moment of its demise seems always to be about ten years from whenever the prediction is made; that is, those writing in 1994 anticipated that it would fail in 2004, while some today put the likely date at about 2015. Obviously one of these predictions will pan out someday, but for now Moore's law is very much in force, as it has been for over forty-five years—a fact from which the lengthening of the doubling interval should not distract us. Over the same period, computer-disk memory capacity and fiber-optic cable bandwidth have also increased at exponential rates. Thus, in 2005 we see memory chips approaching a billion (10^9) bits of storage, Apple iPods with forty-gigabyte (3×10^{11} bits) disks, and local networks capable of transmitting a full-length Hollywood feature film in seconds.

But while industry analysts, engineers, and marketing people have studied Moore's law intensively, historians of science and technology have shown less interest. That is surprising, since it cuts to the heart of an issue that they have debated over the years: technological determinism.

Mel Kranzberg and his colleagues organized the Society for the History of Technology in part to foster a view of technology running counter to the notion that technology is an impersonal force with its own internal logic and a trajectory that human beings must follow. The society's founders spoke of a "contextual" approach to technology, in which the linear narrative of events from invention to application was accompanied by an understanding of the context in which those events occurred.[6] They named the society's journal *Technology and Culture* to emphasize the importance of all three words. Of course, the founding of SHOT and the establishment of *T&C* did not settle the framework for studying technology once and for all, and periodically the concept of determinism is revisited.[7] Nor did the contextual approach remain static. Led by a second generation of scholars including Thomas Parke Hughes, Wiebe Bijker, and Donald MacKenzie, it evolved into the notion (borrowed from elsewhere) of the "social construction" of technology.[8] At the risk of telescoping a complex and rich story, recall that part of the context of the founding of the Society for the History of Technology in 1957 was the Soviets' launch of *Sputnik* and its effect on the perception of U.S. and British technology.[9] The idea of free peoples choosing their destiny freely was very much on the minds of Americans and Britons, then engaged in a cold war with a nation whose citizens lacked such freedom.

I agree with and support this approach to the history of technology. But it must confront a serious challenge: the steady and unstoppable march of semiconductor density, which has led to the rapid introduction of an enormous number of new products, services, and ways of working and living. Think of all the cultural, political, and social events that have occurred in the West since 1965. Think of our understanding of the history of science and technology today compared to then. Now consider that throughout all of these years, the exponential growth of chip density has hardly deviated from its slope. Can anything other than the limit implied by Planck's constant have an effect on Moore's law?

That Moore's law plays a significant role in determining the current place of technology in society is not in dispute. Is it a determinant of our society? The public and our political leaders believe so. In the popular press, the term "technology" itself is today synonymous with "computers." Historians of technology find that conflation exasperating, as it excludes a vast array of technology-driven processes, such as textiles or food production.

The public acceptance of technological determinism is evident among the many visitors where I work, at the National Air and Space Museum, and a recent essay in this journal indicates that determinism is again very much on the minds of historians of technology as well. In "All that Is Solid Melts into Air: Historians of Technology in the Information Revolution," Rosalind Williams recounts her experiences as dean of students at the Massachusetts Institute of Technology during that institution's transition from a set of internally generated, ad hoc administrative computing systems to one supplied by a commercial vendor, SAP.[10] Williams noted that MIT faculty and administrators felt powerless to shape, much less resist, the administrative model embodied in the new software. Such feelings of powerlessness might be understandable elsewhere, but MIT faculty are supposed to be the masters of new technology—they are the ones who create the science and engineering that underpin SAP's products. How could *they* be powerless?

A close reading of Williams's essay reveals that MIT faculty and staff were not exactly passive consumers of SAP R/3. They may have conformed to the software's rigid structure, but not without a fight. The final implementation of this "reengineering," as it was called, was much more than a simple top-down process. Is that not a refutation of the notion that increases in semiconductor density drive society? If one looked instead at a liberal arts college, less technologically savvy than MIT, would the deterministic nature of computing assert itself more strongly?

Williams used her own institution and her own role as a dean as data points (although she did exclaim "There must be an easier way to do research").[11] I propose that we do the same: look not at other people and institutions but rather at ourselves, historians of

technology who live and work in a digital environment and who assert the right to criticize the blind acceptance of the products of the information age. How do we, as individuals, handle the consequences of Moore's law?

I begin with the ground on which we stand—or, more accurately, the chairs in which we sit. We spend our days in offices, staring into computer screens, using software provided by corporations such as Microsoft, Adobe, AOL, Novell, Lotus. We do not design or build the hardware or write the software, nor do we have more than a rudimentary notion of how to repair either when something breaks. "Wizards" install new applications for us; we insert a disk and press "Enter." The computer recognizes when a new device is attached, a process called "plug and play." How far removed this is from the days when many of us used jacks, wrenches, screwdrivers, and other tools to replace broken or worn parts on our cars, reinstalled everything, tested it, and then drove off![12]

We are trying to have it both ways. We pass critical and moral judgment on Harry Truman for his decision to use atomic bombs against Japan, we criticize a museum for showing, out of context, the aircraft that carried the first bomb, yet we ignore our inability to exert more than a smidgen of control over technologies that affect—determine—our daily lives.[13] In her recent book *User Error,* Ellen Rose, a professor of education and multimedia at the University of New Brunswick, writes that when it comes to software people uncritically accept technology without regard to its context or social dimension.[14] This time the villains are not Harry Truman, the Air Force Association, or senior management at the Smithsonian. We are responsible. Historians of technology find determinism distasteful. Yet we validate it every day.

Consider the tools that I and my colleagues used when I began my career as a historian of technology and a teacher:

16 mm movies
Triplicate 3″ × 5″ library cards (author, title, subject)
5″ × 8″ note cards, some with edge notches sorted by a
    knitting needle
35 mm film camera, producing color slides or 8″ × 10″
    black-and-white prints
Blackboard and chalk
Cassette tape recorder
Drafting table, for producing hand-drawn maps and charts
Hewlett-Packard pocket calculator
Microfilm
Mimeograph machine
Overhead transparencies, hand drawn on the fly during
    a lecture
Photocopier
Preprints or offprints of published papers
Telephone, rotary dial, leased from AT&T
Typed letters, sent through U.S. mail
Typewriter, manual

Now consider the tool set we use today in our daily work of teaching, researching, and writing. This list is based on an informal look around my own office and at nearby universities

Hardware	Software
Blackberry or PDA	JPEG image files
Compact disks	PDF files (plus Adobe Reader)
Cell phone	Electronic mail
Digital camera	Instant messaging or chat
DSL or cable modem	Groupware (Lotus Notes or
DVD player	Microsoft Outlook)
GPS receiver	Adobe Photoshop
MP3 player	Microsoft Excel
Laptop computer	Microsoft PowerPoint
Desktop personal computer	Microsoft Word
Scanner with digitizing software	Worldwide Web browser
Sony MiniDisc recorder	Amazon.com
VoIP telephone	Blackboard.com
Wireless ethernet (Wi-Fi)	Blogs
networking device	Google
	HTML documents
	JSTOR
	Listservs, Usenet or similar
	discussion groups
	ProQuest on-line newspaper
	retrieval
	QuickTime Virtual Reality
	Turnitin.com

in Maryland and Virginia where I have taught or lectured. For convenience I divide it into software and hardware. Strictly speaking only hardware obeys Moore's law, but in practice the advances in semiconductor technology allow for more and more complex software products, so both lists are appropriate.

I have probably left some out. Few readers will be enthusiastic users of every device or program or service listed above (though some will be). But I have made my point: Moore's law is at work.

Every three years, as chip capacity quadruples, a new generation of electronic products appears, along with new versions of existing software or new software products. Six years from now probably half the devices in my list of current hardware will be superseded. We see Moore's law at work in the progression of personal computer system software from CP/M to MS-DOS to Windows in its numerous versions, each integrating more and more functions (and triggering antitrust actions, to little avail). We see it, too, in the progression of personal computers, laptops, cell phones, digital cameras, MP3 players, and other devices far more powerful than the computer that accompanied Neil Armstrong, Michael Collins, and Buzz Aldrin to the Moon in 1969.[15]

It is this progression that drives the current relationship between culture and technology. Right now, many of us are abandoning film for digital photography. For those of us who took pleasure in working in a darkroom, this transition is painful. Do we have a choice? I vividly remember getting a pocket calculator and putting away my beloved slide rule.[16] It was a conscious decision that I made with an appreciation of its cultural

implications. But who thinks about the wholesale transition to digital technology? Ellen Rose argues that we adopt these things en masse, without questioning them. And if we do not question them, we are at the mercy of those who produce and sell them to us. How can we espouse theories of the social shaping of technology when our daily interaction with technology is driven to such a great extent by the push of engineering?

This phenomenon seems, furthermore, without regard for the themes of gender, race, and class to which historians of technology have devoted so much attention. This journal, for example, has published an excellent study of women's involvement with programming early computers.[17] The popular press carries almost daily reports on, for example, how technologies such as the cell phone are used in less-developed countries lacking extensive wired phone infrastructure, how such technologies are differently adopted in various developed countries, how such devices are manufactured in Asia, or the outsourcing of software production to countries like India.

These are second-order examples of social construction. Silicon Valley firms frequently introduce products that fail in the marketplace, and the consumer plays a role in that process. Race, class, and gender factor into consumers' decisions. But transistor density and memory capacity never stop growing. The MIT faculty may balk at implementing a particular database product, but not at the doubling of chip capacity every eighteen months. It is a prerequisite for employment at MIT, Microsoft, or in Silicon Valley that one buy into the perpetuation of Moore's law. People who do not believe it must find work elsewhere.

Is this belief, then, an indication of the social construction of computing? I think not. Rather, it is an indication of the reality of technological determinism. Computing power must increase because it can.

PowerPoint

In an earlier version of this essay I examined the debate over Microsoft PowerPoint as a possible refutation of the thesis of determinism. Many scholars have criticized this program. Edward Tufte, the well-known author of books on the visual presentation of information, is especially harsh, arguing that PowerPoint "elevates format over content, betraying an attitude of commercialism that turns everything into a sales pitch."[18] Vint Cerf, coinventor of the Internet protocols, prefers old-fashioned overhead transparencies and typically begins his public talks with the admonition, "Power corrupts; PowerPoint corrupts absolutely." For Cerf it is more of an apology; at most conferences he is the only speaker who does not use the program.[19] Originally I intended to add my own critique, but in the interval between early draft and later revision the debate was flattened by the steamroller of Moore's law. Neither Tufte nor Cerf has made the slightest dent in the adoption of PowerPoint. And if they could not, who can? Two years ago it was still possible to warn scholars not to use PowerPoint. Now that sounds like a crusty old newspaper reporter waxing nostalgic about his old Underwood (and the bottle of bourbon in the top desk drawer).

Comparing PowerPoint to Stalin, as Tufte does, does not advance the debate over technological determinism. Nor will it do to deny determinism because one uses only a fraction of the electronic devices listed above—or even none of them. In a famous and now fairly old essay titled "Why I Am Not Going to Buy a Computer," Wendell Berry raised many of the objections found in more recent critiques, albeit with a succinct eloquence that few can match.[20] One objection not found in many later commentaries that Berry nonetheless advanced was that his wife did the typing for him. That brought him a lot of criticism, of course, but no argument he could have raised would have made a difference. As Ellen Rose points out, even if one writes an essay in longhand, someone else will have to scan or key it into a computer before it can be published.[21] Who is kidding whom? All of these critiques wither before Moore's law. When I was preparing these remarks I found Berry's famous essay not by going to the library and looking for a print copy but by typing the title into Google. The full text came up in seconds. Whether Berry knows or cares that his writings can be found that way, I cannot say. Nor do I know if whoever put the essay onto the Worldwide Web did so with a sense of irony. It does not matter. That is how one retrieves information nowadays.

A common method by which scholars communicate today is via Microsoft Word files attached to e-mail messages. Most publishers and publications (including this journal) ask that manuscripts be submitted as e-mail attachments. Microsoft Word has its flaws; most of us who use it, for example, have encountered instances where the font suddenly changes, randomly, for no apparent reason.[22] Word is also a voracious consumer of memory, but thanks to Moore's law that does not matter. Attaching Word files to e-mail is simple and it works, and so the practice is ubiquitous. I compare it to the $4'8\frac{1}{2}''$ railroad gauge, which experts say is slightly narrower than the optimum, in terms of engineering efficiency. That drawback is overshadowed by the virtue of being a standard.[23] But remember that the encoding of text in Word is controlled by Microsoft, and Microsoft has the right to change the code according to its needs—not ours. Indeed, Microsoft has done so in the past, and we may assume that it will do so again.[24] The same holds true of another "standard" now taking hold, Adobe's Portable Document Format (PDF). PDF files also take up a lot of memory, but that is not the problem. The coding of these files is owned by Adobe, not by the person who wrote the words or created the document. Before reading such a file, we have to look at a page of dense legalese that states that we "accept" whatever terms of use Adobe wants us to accept (I have never read it).

One response to these concerns is to adopt "open source" programs that do what Word and Acrobat do but run under some other operating system, such as Linux, and adhere to the GNU general public license. Such programs are available and their numbers are increasing. By definition, their source code is available publicly, without charge, and cannot ever come under the control of a private entity.[25] Users are encouraged to modify the software to fit their needs. The historian who learns how to write open-source code would be the present-day counterpart to one who could repair and modify his own automobile in the dim past.

But can open-source software refute the thesis that historians have no ability to control the pace of digital technology? Thus far, the number of historians of technology who use these programs is miniscule. Perhaps open source will prevail, but the movement is mature and yet has not had much effect on us.

An Internal Logic at Work

Historians need to be cautious when predicting the future—or, for that matter, assessing the present. Using ourselves as data points, as I (like Rosalind Williams) have done, is also dangerous. Yet the data are there, and it would be foolish to ignore our own actions. Readers interested in critiques of the pace of digital technology besides the ones cited here can find a range of studies.[26] I have not dwelled more on them because, like everything else, they have had no effect on Moore's law. For the same reason, I do not offer this essay as yet another critique of digitization. My goal is more modest: to ask that we step back from a social constructionist view of technology and consider that, in at least one instance, raw technological determinism is at work. Only then can we begin to make intelligent observations about the details of this process. Ross Bassett's *To the Digital Age* is one such study. There ought to be many more, and they ought to address the question of why the exponential advance of computer power is so impervious to social, economic, or political contexts.

I do not deny that the digital world we inhabit is socially constructed. I am reminded of it every time I observe the celebrity status afforded to Steve Jobs—who, by the way, is not an engineer. Biographies of individuals like Jobs tell how they willed the future into being through the strength of their personalities. One must read these biographies with care, but their arguments are valid. Studying the history of computing in the context of social, political, and economic forces makes sense. It identifies us as like-minded thinkers who do not embrace every new gadget. But if we assert the right to look at technology that way, we must also recognize that in at least one case, Moore's law, an internal logic is at work, and that it is based on old-fashioned hardware engineering that an earlier generation of historians once celebrated.

Notes

1. My review appeared in the October 2004 issue of this journal, *Technology and Culture* 45 (2004): 892–93.

2. A variant, in which PNP-type transistors alternate with NPN types, is called "complementary MOS," or CMOS, and has the advantage of requiring very little power.

3. Gordon E. Moore, "Cramming More Components onto Integrated Circuits," *Electronics,* 19 April 1965, 114–17.

4. The mathematical relationship described by Moore is $n = 2^{((y - 1959) \div d)}$, where n is the number of circuits on a chip, y is the current year, and d is the doubling time, in years. For a doubling time of eighteen months, or $d = 1.5$, this equation predicts chip densities of about one billion in 2005. Chips with that density are not yet available commercially as far as I know, but are being developed in laboratories.

5. For early discussions on this topic among the principals, see Gordon E. Moore, "Progress in Digital Integrated Electronics" (paper presented at the International Electronic Devices Meeting, Washington, D.C., 1–3 December 1975, technical digest 11–13); Robert N. Noyce, "Microelectronics," *Scientific American* 237 (September 1977): 65.

6. See, for example, Stephen H. Cutcliffe and Robert C. Post, eds., *In Context: History and the History of Technology—Essays in Honor of Melvin Kranzberg* (Bethlehem, Pa., 1989).

7. See, for example, Merritt Roe Smith and Leo Marx, eds., *Does Technology Drive History? The Dilemma of Technological Determinism* (Cambridge, Mass., 1994).

8. For example, Donald MacKenzie and Judy Wajcman, eds., *The Social Shaping of Technology,* 2nd ed. (Buckingham, 1999); Wiebe Bijker, Thomas P. Hughes, and Trevor Pinch, eds., *The Social Construction of Technological Systems* (Cambridge, Mass., 1987).

9. Mel Kranzberg, "The Newest History: Science and Technology," *Science,* 11 May 1962, 463–68.

10. Rosalind Williams, "All that Is Solid Melts into Air: Historians of Technology in the Information Revolution," *Technology and Culture* 41 (2000): 641–68. See also her more recent book, *Retooling: A Historian Confronts Technological Change* (Cambridge, Mass., 2002).

11. Williams, "All that Is Solid," 641.

12. I can no longer make such repairs, as the engine and basic components of the car I now drive are inaccessible. Its ignition, fuel, brake, and other systems are all heavily computerized.

13. Robert C. Post, "A Narrative for Our Time: The *Enola Gay* 'and after that, period,'" *Technology and Culture* 45 (2004): 373–95. But see also his "No Mere Technicalities: How Things Work and Why It Matters," *Technology and Culture* 40 (1999): 607–22, which expresses Post's concerns about the way historians of technology react to claims that "life without technology isn't an option."

14. Ellen Rose, *User Error: Resisting Computer Culture* (Toronto, 2003).

15. The Apollo Guidance Computer had a read-write memory capacity of two thousand sixteen-bit words, or four thousand bytes. See the History of Recent Science and Technology project web pages for the Apollo Guidance Computer, http://hrst.mit.edu/ hrs/apollo/public/, accessed July 2005.

16. The calculator was a Hewlett-Packard HP-25C. The letter "C" meant that it used CMOS chips, novel at that time.

17. Jennifer S. Light, "When Computers Were Women," *Technology and Culture* 40 (1999): 455–83.

18. Edward Tufte, "Power Corrupts: PowerPoint Corrupts Absolutely," *Wired,* September 2003, 118–19; also Ian Parker, "Absolute PowerPoint," *New Yorker,* 28 May 2001, 86–87.

19. This is the title of Tufte's article cited above, of course, but I heard Cerf use the phrase on the two occasions when we were on the same program as speakers; we were the only two who did not use PowerPoint.

20. The essay was published in print in various places, but I found it on the Worldwide Web at http://www.tipiglen.dircon.co.uk/berrynot.html (accessed July 2005).

21. Rose (n. 14 above), 175. She is referring to Neil Postman, who proudly claimed that he wrote all his work by hand.

22. This happened to me as I was preparing this essay.

23. George W. Hilton, *American Narrow Gauge Railroads* (Stanford, Calif., 1990).

24. And this does not address the question whether one can still read the disk on which a document was stored.

25. Paul Ceruzzi, "A War on Two Fronts: The U.S. Justice Department, Open Source, and Microsoft, 1995–2000," *Iterations,* an on-line journal, http://www.cbi.umn.edu/iterations/ceruzzi.html (accessed July 2005). Among colleagues in SHOT, I note that Bryan Pfaffenberger, of the University of Virginia, uses open source software. At home I use several open-source programs, but my employer in general does not allow them at work. GNU, a recursive acronym for "GNU's Not UNIX," is, among other things, an open-source operating system.

26. The best are written by computer-industry insiders. See, for example, Clifford Stoll, *Silicon Snake Oil: Second Thoughts on the Information Superhighway* (New York, 1996); Ben Shneiderman, *Leonardo's Laptop: Human Needs and the New Computing Technologies* (Cambridge, Mass., 2003); Steve Talbott, *The Future Does Not Compute* (Sebastopol, Calif., 1995); Thomas K. Landauer, *The Trouble with Computers: Usefulness, Usability, and Productivity* (Cambridge, Mass., 1995); Donald A. Norman, *The Invisible Computer: Why Good Products Fail, the Personal Computer Is so Complex, and Information Appliances Are the Solution* (Cambridge, Mass., 1998).

PAUL CERUZZI is curator of aerospace electronics and computing at the Smithsonian's National Air and Space Museum. A second edition of his book *A History of Modern Computing* appeared in 2004.

From *Technology and Culture,* July 2005, pp. 584–593. Copyright © 2005 by Society for the History of Technology. Reprinted by permission.

UNIT 2
The Economy

Unit Selections

Key Points to Consider

- Paul Farhi's article ("Online Salvation") was published in late 2007. Use the Internet to see if you can answer the question posed in the table of contents: "Will the Internet save the beleaguered newspaper business?"

- What is very new for the United States in terms of health care is old hat elsewhere. Use the Internet to learn about the French *carte vitale.* How do online health records figure into current proposals for health care reform in the United States? Has the *carte vitale* solved some of the problems associated with insurance billing and coordination of health care?

- For a follow-up on Grow and Elgin's piece ("Click Fraud . . ."), see an article by Jason Pontin MIT's *Technology Review* ("But Who's Counting?," March/April, 2009).

Student Website
www.mhhe.com/cls

Internet References

CAUCE: Coalition against Unsolicited Commercial Email
   http://www.cauce.org
E-Commerce Times
   http://www.ecommercetimes.com
Fight Spam on the Internet
   http://spam.abuse.net
The Linux Home Page
   http://www.linux.org
AllAdvantage—The Rise of the Informediary
   http://en.wikipedia.org/wiki/AllAdvantage
Smart Cards: A Primer
   http://www.smartcardbasics.com/overview.html
Smart Card Group
   http://www.smartcard.co.uk

Living in the United States in the beginning of the 21st century, it is hard to imagine that the accumulation of wealth once bordered on the disreputable, at least among a certain class. Listen to William Wordsworth, writing two hundred years ago:

> The world is too much with us; late and soon,
> Getting and spending, we lay waste our powers:
> Little we see in nature that is ours;
> We have given our hearts away, a sordid boon!

© Creatas/PunchStock

These are words that would quicken the pulse of any young protester of globalization. And no wonder. Wordsworth was writing a generation after James Watt perfected the steam engine. England was in the grips of the Industrial Revolution. Just as the developed world now appears to be heading away from an industrial and toward a service economy, so Wordsworth's world was moving from an agrarian to an industrial economy. And just as the steam engine has become the emblem of that transformation, the computer has become the symbol of this one.

People, of course, did not stop farming after the Industrial Revolution, nor have they stopped producing steel and automobiles after the Information Revolution, though many commentators write as if this is exactly what has happened. It is true that we in the United States have largely given up factory work. In the last three decades, the number of Americans employed has increased by over 50 million. During this same period, the number of manufacturing jobs declined by several hundred thousand. A large handful of these new workers are software and computer engineers, website developers, manipulators of digital images—the glamor jobs of the information age. A much larger portion provide janitorial, health, food, and child care services, leading to the charge that the American economy works because we take in one another's laundry.

A service that Americans provide in abundance is advertising. One model in use on the Web is for businesses to pay their Internet hosts only when a potential buyer actually clicks on their site. Sounds good? Read about Martin Fleichmann ("Click Fraud"), who calculates that invalid clicks have cost his company $100,000. Web advertising is increasingly important for some traditional companies, betting on the wild world of Internet advertising to save them. Read Paul Farhi's piece, "Online Salvation," for a look at just how complex the newspaper business has become.

Now what of the decline in manufacturing? It is a rare week when the papers do not include coverage of a plant closure, the weakness of trade unions, or the drop in living wage manufacturing jobs. A large part of this is due to plant relocations to countries with lower labor costs. To be convinced, take a look at where almost anything you purchase is made. Lay the blame on computing. It is impossible to imagine how a global manufacturing network could be coordinated without computers. Products manufactured abroad—with or without the productivity benefits of computers—pass through a bewildering array of shippers and distributors until they arrive on the shelves of a big box retailer in a Phoenix suburb, or just-in-time to be bolted to the frame of an automobile being assembled outside St. Louis. Or, imagine how Federal Express could track its parcels as they make their way from an office in a San Jose suburb to one in Manhattan. "Technology giveth and technology taketh away."

Only in the world of computing could a multibillion dollar company founded by a twenty-something challenge another multibillion dollar company founded by pair of twenty-somethings. Read Fred Vogelstein's fascinating report ("Great Wall of Facebook: The Social Network's Plan to Dominate the Internet—and Keep Google Out") to learn about Facebook's challenge to Google. Stephen Baker and Heather Green ("Beyond Blogs") is another of those "only in computing" pieces. When authors refer to a 2005 article on blogs as an "outdated relic," you know we're in the land of computer technology.

We end this unit with a topic that is very much in the news as of this writing (August 2009), namely healthcare reform. Robert Steinbrook reports on proposals for online, and personally controlled, health care records.

Click Fraud

The Dark Side of Online Advertising

BRIAN GROW AND BEN ELGIN

Martin Fleischmann put his faith in online advertising. He used it to build his Atlanta company, MostChoice .com, which offers consumers rate quotes and other information on insurance and mortgages. Last year he paid Yahoo! Inc. and Google Inc. a total of $2 million in advertising fees. The 40-year-old entrepreneur believed the celebrated promise of Internet marketing: You pay only when prospective customers click on your ads.

Now, Fleischmann's faith has been shaken. Over the past three years, he has noticed a growing number of puzzling clicks coming from such places as Botswana, Mongolia, and Syria. This seemed strange, since MostChoice steers customers to insurance and mortgage brokers only in the U.S. Fleischmann, who has an economics degree from Yale University and an MBA from Wharton, has used specially designed software to discover that the MostChoice ads being clicked from distant shores had appeared not on pages of Google or Yahoo but on curious websites with names like insurance1472.com and insurance060 .com. He smelled a swindle, and he calculates it has cost his business more than $100,000 since 2003.

Fleischmann is a victim of click fraud: a dizzying collection of scams and deceptions that inflate advertising bills for thousands of companies of all sizes. The spreading scourge poses the single biggest threat to the Internet's advertising gold mine and is the most nettlesome question facing Google and Yahoo, whose digital empires depend on all that gold.

The growing ranks of businesspeople worried about click fraud typically have no complaint about versions of their ads that appear on actual Google or Yahoo Web pages, often next to search results. The trouble arises when the Internet giants boost their profits by recycling ads to millions of other sites, ranging from the familiar, such as cnn.com, to dummy Web addresses like insurance1472.com, which display lists of ads and little if anything else. When somebody clicks on these recycled ads, marketers such as MostChoice get billed, sometimes even if the clicks appear to come from Mongolia. Google or Yahoo then share the revenue with a daisy chain of website hosts and operators. A penny or so even trickles down to the lowly clickers. That means Google and Yahoo at times passively profit from click fraud and, in theory, have an incentive to tolerate it. So do

smaller search engines and marketing networks that similarly recycle ads.

Slipping Confidence

Google and Yahoo say they filter out most questionable clicks and either don't charge for them or reimburse advertisers that have been wrongly billed. Determined to prevent a backlash, the Internet ad titans say the extent of click chicanery has been exaggerated, and they stress that they combat the problem

---

Rogues Glossary

The murky world of Web advertising has its own jargon

Click Fraud

Clicking on Internet advertising solely to generate illegitimate revenue for the website carrying the ads; those doing the clicking typically also get paid.

Parked website

A site typically with little or no content except for lists of Internet ads, often supplied by Google or Yahoo; many of them are the source of false clicks.

Paid-to-Read

A PTR site pays members to look at other websites and offers from marketers; often used to generate fake clicks on parked websites.

Clickbot

Software that can be used to produce automatic clicks on ads; some versions employed in click fraud can mask the origin and timing of clicks.

Botnet

A collection of computers infected with software that allows them to be operated remotely; networks of thousands of machines can be used in click fraud.

vigorously. "We think click fraud is a serious but manageable issue," says John Slade, Yahoo's senior director for global product management. "Google strives to detect every invalid click that passes through its system," says Shuman Ghosemajumder, the search engine's manager for trust and safety. "It's absolutely in our best interest for advertisers to have confidence in this industry."

That confidence may be slipping. A *BusinessWeek* investigation has revealed a thriving click-fraud underground populated by swarms of small-time players, making detection difficult. "Paid to read" rings with hundreds or thousands of members each, all of them pressing PC mice over and over in living rooms and dens around the world. In some cases, "clickbot" software generates page hits automatically and anonymously. Participants from Kentucky to China speak of making from $25 to several thousand dollars a month apiece, cash they wouldn't receive if Google and Yahoo were as successful at blocking fraud as they claim.

"It's not that much different from someone coming up and taking money out of your wallet," says David Struck. He and his wife, Renee, both 35, say they dabbled in click fraud last year, making more than $5,000 in four months. Employing a common scheme, the McGregor (Minn.) couple set up dummy websites filled with nothing but recycled Google and Yahoo advertisements. Then they paid others small amounts to visit the sites, where it was understood they would click away on the ads, says David Struck. It was "way too easy," he adds. Gradually, he says, he and his wife began to realize they were cheating unwitting advertisers, so they stopped. "Whatever Google and Yahoo are doing [to stop fraud], it's not having much of an effect," he says.

Spending on Internet ads is growing faster than any other sector of the advertising industry and is expected to surge from $12.5 billion last year to $29 billion in 2010 in the U.S. alone, according to researcher eMarketer Inc. About half of these dollars are going into deals requiring advertisers to pay by the click. Most other Internet ads are priced according to "impressions," or how many people view them. Yahoo executives warned on Sept. 19 that weak ad spending by auto and financial-services companies would hurt its third-quarter revenue. Share prices of Yahoo and Google tumbled on the news.

Google and Yahoo are grabbing billions of dollars once collected by traditional print and broadcast outlets, based partly on the assumption that clicks are a reliable, quantifiable measure of consumer interest that the older media simply can't match. But the huge influx of cash for online ads has attracted armies of con artists whose activities are eroding that crucial assumption and could eat into the optimistic expectations for online advertising. (Advertisers generally don't grumble about fraudulent clicks coming from the websites of traditional media outlets. But there are growing concerns about these media sites exaggerating how many visitors they have—the online version of inflating circulation.)

The success of Google and Yahoo is based partly on the idea that clicks are reliable.

Most academics and consultants who study online advertising estimate that 10% to 15% of ad clicks are fake, representing roughly $1 billion in annual billings. Usually the search engines divide these proceeds with several players: First, there are intermediaries known as "domain parking" companies, to which the search engines redistribute their ads. Domain parkers host "parked" websites, many of which are those dummy sites containing only ads. Cheats who own parked sites obtain search-engine ads from the domain parkers and arrange for the ads to be clicked on, triggering bills to advertisers. In all, $300 million to $500 million a year could be flowing to the click-fraud industry.

Law enforcement has only lately started focusing on the threat. A cybercrime unit led by the FBI and U.S. Postal Inspection Service just last month assigned two analysts to examine whether federal laws are being violated. The FBI acted after noticing suspected cybercriminals discussing click fraud in chat rooms. The staff of the Senate Judiciary Committee has launched its own informal probe.

Many advertisers, meanwhile, are starting to get antsy. Google and Yahoo have each settled a class action filed by marketers. In late September a coalition of such major brands as InterActive Corp.'s Expedia.com travel site and mortgage broker Lending-Tree is planning to go public with its mounting unease over click fraud, *BusinessWeek* has learned. The companies intend to form a group to share information and pressure Google and Yahoo to be more forthcoming. "You can't blame the advertisers for being suspicious," says Robert Pettee, search marketing manager for LendingTree, based in Charlotte, N.C. "If it's your money that's going out the door, you need to be asking questions." He says that up to 15% of the clicks on his company's ads are bogus.

In June, researcher Outsell Inc. released a blind survey of 407 advertisers, 37% of which said they had reduced or were planning to reduce their pay-per-click budgets because of fraud concerns. "The click fraud and bad sites are driving people away," says Fleischmann. He's trimming his online ad budget by 15% this year.

Google and Yahoo insist there's no reason to fret. They say they use sophisticated algorithms and intelligence from advertisers to identify the vast majority of fake clicks. But the big search engines won't disclose the specifics of their methods, saying illicit clickers would exploit the information.

Some people who have worked in the industry say that as long as Google and Yahoo distribute ads to nearly anyone with a rudimentary website, fraud will continue. "Advertisers should be concerned," says a former Yahoo manager who requested anonymity. "A well-executed click-fraud attack is nearly impossible, if not impossible, to detect."

Although 5 feet 6 and 135 pounds, Marty Fleischmann is no one to push around. He barked orders at much bigger oarsmen while serving as coxswain on the varsity crew team at Yale in the mid-1980s. His shyness deficit surfaced again when he later played the role of Jerry Seinfeld in the student follies at Wharton. Married and the father of three children, he tends to pepper his conversation with jargon about incentives and efficiencies.

Follow the Money

Click fraud schemes vary and often involve a complicated chain of relationships. Here's one way the process can work:

1. XYZ Widgets signs up with Google or Yahoo to advertise on the Internet, agreeing to pay the search engine every time somebody clicks on an XYZ ad.
2. Google or Yahoo displays the ad on its own site but also recycles it to millions of affiliates, including "domain parking" companies.
3. Domain-parking outfits feed the Google or Yahoo ad to thousands of "parked" websites, some of which are nothing more than lists of ads.
4. A fraud artist who owns a parked site circulates it to "paid to read" (PTR) groups, whose members receive small payments to visit sites and click on ads.
5. When a PTR member clicks on the XYZ ad, the company is billed. Yahoo or Google shares the proceeds with the domain parker, the fraudster, and the clickers.

Before he and partner Michael Levy co-founded their financial-information company in 1999, Fleischmann worked in Atlanta at the management consulting firm A.T. Kearney Inc., advising major corporations in the shipping and pharmaceutical industries. One lesson he says he learned is that big companies are loath to cut off any steady source of revenue. Google and Yahoo are no different, he argues.

That cynicism several years ago contributed to MostChoice's assigning an in-house programmer to design a system for analyzing every click on a company ad: the Web page where the ad appeared, the clicker's country, the length of the clicker's visit to MostChoice's site, and whether the visitor became a customer. Few companies go to such lengths, let alone companies with only 30 employees and revenue last year of just $6.4 million.

To Fleischmann, the validity of his clicks, for which he pays up to $8 apiece, has become an obsession. Every day he pores over fresh spreadsheets of click analysis. "I told Yahoo years ago," he says, "'If this was costing you money instead of making you money, you would have stopped this.'"

Google, he says, does a better job than Yahoo of screening for fraud. But neither adequately protects marketers, he argues. Until March, 2005, Google, based in Mountain View, Calif., charged advertisers twice for "double clicks," meaning those occasions when a user unnecessarily clicks twice in quick succession on an ad. Confirming this, Google's Ghosemajumder says that before the company made the change, it felt it had to focus "on issues of malicious behavior," though now it identifies double clicks and bills for only one.

Korean Clones

Fleischmann's daily immersion in click statistics fuels his indignation. How, he wants to know, did he receive traffic this summer from PCs in South Korea which are clicking on insurance1472 .com and insurance060.com? The only content on these identical sites—and five other clones with similar names—are lists of Yahoo ads, which occasionally have included MostChoice promotions. Fleischmann's spreadsheets revealed, not surprisingly, that all of the suspected Korean clickers left his site in a matter of seconds, and none became customers. The two individuals registered as owning the mysterious insurance sites are based in South Korea. They didn't respond to requests for comment, and most of the sites disappeared in late summer, after MostChoice challenged Yahoo about them.

"If this was costing [Yahoo] money instead of making it," they would have stopped it.

Fleischmann, like most other advertisers, has agreed to let Google and Yahoo recycle his ads on affiliated sites. The search engines describe these affiliates in glowing terms. A Google "help" page entitled "Where will my ads appear?" mentions such brand names as AOL.com and the website of *The New York Times*. Left unmentioned are the parked websites filled exclusively with ads and sometimes associated with click-fraud rings.

Google and Yahoo defend their practice of recycling advertising to domain-parking firms and then on to parked sites, saying that the lists of ads on the sites help point Internet surfers toward relevant information. Google notes that it allows advertisers to identify sites on which they don't want their ads to run.

But this Google feature doesn't apply to many parked sites, and Yahoo doesn't offer the option at all. In any event, excluding individual sites is difficult for marketers that don't do the sort of time-consuming research MostChoice does. Whether they know it or not, many other companies are afflicted in similar ways. At *BusinessWeek's* request, Click Forensics Inc., an online auditing firm in San Antonio, analyzed the records of its 170 financial-services clients and found that from March through July of this year, 13 companies had received clicks from websites identified as dubious by MostChoice.

Yahoo declined to comment on insurance1472, -060, and other suspect sites in its ad network. The Sunnyvale (Calif.) search giant stressed that in many cases it doesn't deal directly with parked sites; instead, it distributes its ads by means of domain-parking firms.

BusinessWeek's independent analysis of the MostChoice records turned up additional indications of click fraud. Over the past six months, the company received 139 visitors through an advertisement on the parked site healthinsurancebids.com, which offers only ads supplied by Yahoo. Most of these visitors were located in Bulgaria, the Czech Republic, Egypt, and

Taking the Search Engines to Court

Under pressure from advertisers, Google Inc. and Yahoo! Inc. are adjusting the way they deal with click fraud. Several lawsuits filed on behalf of hundreds of advertisers have helped fuel the modest changes.

In June, Yahoo agreed to settle a class action filed in federal court in Los Angeles on behalf of advertisers alleging they had been billed for fake clicks. Without admitting wrongdoing, Yahoo said it would grant refunds for bad clicks since January, 2004, that advertisers bring to its attention. The potential cost to Yahoo isn't clear. The company also agreed to appoint an in-house advocate to represent advertisers. The search engine said it would periodically invite marketers to inspect its now-secret fraud-detection systems. Separate from the settlement, Yahoo says that next year it will give marketers more control over where their ads appear.

Google reached its own settlement with unhappy advertisers in July in state court in Texarkana, Ark., where a judge approved a pact valued at $90 million. The agreement provides $30 million in cash for lawyers but only advertising credits for class members. Dissatisfied, a group of advertisers is seeking to challenge the settlement in appellate court. "The rot is so pervasive," says Clarence E. Briggs, III, a leader of the breakaway group. Briggs, a former Army ranger, says his company, Advanced Internet Technologies in Fayetteville, N.C., has detected $90,000 of bad clicks on its Google ads.

Google, which denied any liability, has since announced it will pull back its cloak of secrecy and show individual advertisers the proportion of their clicks it has deemed invalid and for which they weren't billed.

—Ben Elgin and Brian Grow

Evolution of a Scam

The purpose of click fraud has changed in recent years.

Version 1.0

Companies clicked on a rival's Internet advertisements, running up its ad bills and squeezing the competition. The ads in question typically appeared on Google, Yahoo and other search engine sites.

Version 2.0

Today click fraud is much more likely to occur on small websites that carry ads recycled from Yahoo and Google. Fraudsters arrange for fake clicks on the ads and split the resulting revenue with the search engines.

Ukraine. Their average stay on MostChoice.com was only six seconds, and none of them became a customer.

Healthinsurancebids.com offers a revealing entry point into the click-fraud realm. It is one of several parked sites registered to Roland Kiss of Budapest. Kiss also owns BestPTRsite .com. "PTR" refers to "paid to read." In theory, paid-to-read sites recruit members who agree to read marketing e-mails and websites tailored to their interests. PTR site operators pay members for each e-mail and website they read, usually a penny or less.

In reality, many PTR sites are click-fraud rings, some with hundreds or thousands of participants paid to click on ads. BestPTRsite says it has 977 members. On Aug. 23 its administrator sent an e-mail to members containing a list of parked sites filled with ads. One of these sites, mortgagebg.com, which is also registered to Kiss, has been a source of apparently bogus clicks on MostChoice. The e-mail instructed members to click on different links every day, a common means to avoid detection. Members were also told to cut and paste text from the Web pages they click as proof of their activity. "If you send us back always the same link you will get banned and not paid! So take care and visit everyday a new link," the e-mail said.

Reached by telephone, Kiss says that his registration name is false and declines to reveal the real one. He says he's the 23-year-old son of computer technicians and has studied finance. He owns about 20 paid-to-read sites, he says, as well as 200 parked sites stuffed with Google and Yahoo advertisements. But he says he will take down healthinsurancebids.com to avoid discovery. He claims to take in $70,000 in ad revenue a month, but says that only 10% of that comes from PTRs. The rest, he says, reflects legitimate clicks by real Web surfers. He refrains from more PTR activity, he claims, because "it's no good for advertisers, no good for Google, no good for Yahoo." It's not unusual for people who are involved in PTR activity to profess that they restrict their behavior in some way for the good of advertisers and the big search engines.

After joining several PTR groups, *BusinessWeek* reporters received a torrent of e-mail showcasing hundreds of parked sites filled with Google and Yahoo ads. The groups urged participants to click aggressively on ads. "People don't click because they're interested in the subject," says Pam Parrish, a medical editor in Indianapolis who has participated in PTR sites. "They're clicking on ads to get paid."

Parrish, 52, says that when she started three years ago, PTR sites drew clickers like herself: potential customers looking to pick up a few spare dollars. At one point, she says she belonged to as many as 50 such sites but earned only about $200 all told. More recently, she says, most PTR sites have dropped the pretense of caring whether members are interested in the sites they visit. Parrish and others active on PTR sites say click fraud became more blatant as Google and Yahoo made their ads more widely available to parked sites.

Google and Yahoo say they filter out most PTR activity. "We manage that very well," says Google's Ghosemajumder. "It hasn't been an issue across our network, but it's something we take very seriously." Yahoo adds that PTR sites carrying its ads are in "very serious violation" of its standard distribution

Advertisers in China Are Getting Burned, Too

China has a reputation in the U.S. as a haven for click-fraud artists. Now, Chinese advertisers say they, too, have fallen victim to the proliferating racket.

In August, Chinese advertisers carrying placards even staged a small demonstration in front of the Beijing office of Baidu.com. China's top search engine. Leading the protest was Dr. Liu Wenhua, director of the Beijing Zhongbei Cancer Medical Research Center. Liu claims that his center, which advertises its services online, has suffered from fraudulent clicks on its ads on a Baidu-affiliated music and entertainment site. Baidu has offered a refund, Liu says, but he turned it down, preferring to take Baidu to court. "I'm not satisfied," the doctor says.

Zhang Xinwei, a partner with the Beijing Hetong Law Office, represents Liu and four other advertisers that also have sued Baidu, alleging fraud. "The problem is very serious," says Zhang. Another plaintiff, Land of Maples Tourism & Culture Exchange, a Beijing travel agency specializing in trips to Canada, has hired a different lawyer. Steven Donne, who runs the agency, says he became suspicious of a batch of 600 clicks this summer because they all came from one source. But Donne feared he wouldn't be able to prove click fraud, so his suit focuses on a claim that Baidu manipulates search results to punish certain advertisers. The legal cases are all in a preliminary stage.

Baidu officials declined to comment but provided a statement denying any impropriety. "Baidu places the highest priority on preventing fraudulent clicks," it said. "We have set up numerous measures both through automated technology and manual efforts to prevent fraudulent clicks and the effectiveness of which [has] been verified by [an] independent third party. . . . We are, however, continuing to invest aggressively in safeguarding measures which will help ensure that our customers and users continue to have the best possible experience."

Despite such assurances, advertisers say concern is spreading. Executives at Analysys International, an info tech researcher in Beijing, noted earlier this year that clicks on its ads on Baidu soared without any uptick in business. In April alone, Analysys burned through one-third of its modest yearly online marketing budget of $3,800. "It was like crazy," says CEO Edward Yu.

This spring, Analysys conducted a survey of 2,000 online advertiser in China and found that one-third believe they have been click-fraud victims. Yu continues to patronize Google's Chinese affiliate, but he has stopped buying advertising from Baidu and Yahoo China, which is owned by Alibaba.com. Porter Erisman, a spokesman for Alibaba, said in an e-mail that "click fraud is a serious but manageable issue," adding that less than 0.01% of his company's customers have complained.

—Bruce Einhom

agreement. Yahoo says it scans its network for PTR activity, but declines to describe its methods.

PTR impresarios often don't fit the profile of an illicit kingpin. Michele Ballard runs a 2,200-member network called the-Owl-Post.com from her home in the small town of Hartford, Ky. On disability since a 1996 car accident, Ballard, 36, lives with her ailing mother and her cat, Sassy. She says she works day and night running Owl-Post, a five-year-old group named after the postal system in the Harry Potter novels. Sometimes, Ballard says she takes a break at lunchtime to tend her vegetable garden or help her elderly neighbors with theirs.

She sends her members a daily e-mail containing links to parked webpages, many of them filled with Google ads. Her e-mails, decorated with smiley faces, suggest to members: "If you could just give a click on something on each page." She owns some of the parked pages, so she gets a share of the revenue when ads on them are clicked. She claims her take amounts to only about $60 a month, noting that if she made more than $85, the government would reduce her $601 monthly disability check.

In August, Google cut off a domain parking firm that hosted some of Ballard's sites. Showing her resilience, she moved the sites to other domain parkers, although none of those currently distributes Google ads. "Google would prefer you not to send out ads on paid e-mails, because they get too much crappy traf-fic," she says in a phone interview. She realizes that advertisers would get angry "if they knew we were just sitting here, clicking and not interested" in their wares. But, she adds, "They haven't figured that out yet."

Despite these views, Ballard says she doesn't think she's doing anything improper, let alone illegal. While investigations of some Internet criminals have revealed evidence of click fraud, the activity itself hasn't been the subject of prosecution. Ballard says Owl-Post is "like a huge family" whose members sometimes help out colleagues in financial distress. She says the network includes people who have low incomes and are desperate to earn cash to pay their bills. "A lot of people would be hurt if [the PTR business] crashed," she says.

Google's Ghosemajumder says any operation inviting people to click on ads is encouraging fraud, but he expresses skepticism about the overall scale of PTR activity: "People have a great tendency to exaggerate when they say they can attack Google's service."

Networks of human clickers aren't the only source of fake Web traffic. Scores of automated clicking programs, known as clickbots, are available to be downloaded from the Internet and claim to provide protection against detection. "The primary use is to cheat advertising companies," says Anatoly Smelkov, creator of Clicking Agent, a clickbot he says he has sold to some 5,000 customers worldwide.

The brazen 32-year-old Russian software developer lives in the city of Novosibirsk in western Siberia and says he received a physics degree from the state university there. A fan of the British physicist and author Stephen W. Hawking, Smelkov says Clicking Agent is a sideline that generates about $10,000 a year for him; he also writes software for video sharing and other purposes.

"A lot of people would be hurt [if the paid-to-read business] crashed," says one organizer.

Clickbots are popular among online cheats because they disguise a PC's unique numerical identification, or IP address, and can space clicks minutes apart to make them less conspicuous. Smelkov shrugs off his role in facilitating deception. He points out that the first four letters of the name of his company, Lote-Soft Co., stand for "living on the edge." Teasing, he asks: "You aren't going to send the FBI to me, are you?"

Past Media Scandals

Allegations that some publishers and TV companies deceive advertisers go back many decades. Now the problem has moved online:

Newspapers and Magazines

Outrage over circulation fraud, employed to boost ad rates, led to the 1914 creation of the Audit Bureau of Circulations. But that didn't stop some publishers from faking the numbers. In 2004 a scandal tainted Tribune's *Newsday* and its Spanish-language *Hoy*, Belo's *Dallas Morning News*, and Sun-Times Media's *Chicago Sun-Times*.

Television

Broadcasters set ad rates using surveys of how many people are tuned in during four "sweeps" periods a year. Advertisers complain that some networks and local stations use contests and other stunts to attract extra attention during sweeps. The American Association of Advertising Agencies says this practice "has been going on for decades."

Internet

Click fraud, generating bogus mouse clicks on an online ad, isn't the only way advertisers can get ripped off on the Internet. Some ads are priced according to "impressions," the number of Web surfers who see it, regardless of whether they click. Now there is concern that some media companies commit impression fraud by overstating the number of visitors to their sites.

Google and Yahoo say they can identify automated click fraud and discount advertisers' bills accordingly. Jianhui Shi, a Smelkov customer who goes by the name Johnny, says that for this very reason he steers away from Google and Yahoo ads. An unemployed resident of the booming southern Chinese city of Shenzhen, Jianhui says he has used Clicking Agent to click all sorts of ads on sites he controls, making about $20,000 a year from this activity. While he doesn't click on Google and Yahoo ads, he says that more skilled Chinese programmers modify Clicking Agent to outwit the American search engines. "Many in China use this tool to make money," he wrote in an e-mail to *BusinessWeek.*

Back at the bare-bones MostChoice offices in north Atlanta, Marty Fleischmann continues to demand recompense. He says he has received refunds from Google and Yahoo totaling only about $35,000 out of the $100,000 he feels he is owed. In one exchange, MostChoice e-mailed Google to point out 316 clicks it received in June from ZapMeta.com, a little-known search site. MostChoice paid an average of $4.56 a click, or roughly $1,500 for the batch. Only one converted into a customer. Google initially responded that "after a thorough manual review" some bad clicks were filtered out before MostChoice was charged. Refund request: denied.

But as clicks from ZapMeta kept arriving, Fleischmann demanded in an Aug. 7 e-mail to Google: "You should be trusting us and doing something about [ZapMeta] as a partner, instead of finding more ways to refute our data or requests." (*BusinessWeek's* e-mail to ZapMeta's site and its registered owner, Kevin H. Nguyen, elicited no response.)

Finally, on Aug. 8, Google admitted that clicks from ZapMeta "seem to be coming through sophisticated means." A Google employee who identified himself only as "Jason" added in an e-mail: "We are working with our engineers to prevent these clicks from continuing." MostChoice received a $2,527.93 refund that included reimbursement for suspect clicks from an additional site as well.

Google says it has refunded MostChoice for all invalid clicks and won't charge for any additional ZapMeta clicks until the situation is resolved. But Google also says it doesn't believe ZapMeta has done anything improper. As of late September, ZapMeta continued to carry ads that had been recycled from Google, although not MostChoice ads.

Randall S. Hansen, a professor of marketing at Stetson University in Deland, Fla., sees a larger lesson in tales of this sort. "We are just beginning to see more and more mainstream advertisers make the Internet a bigger part of their ad budget, and move dollars from print and TV," says Hansen, who has held marketing jobs at *The New Yorker* and *People* magazines. "But if we can't fix this click-fraud problem, then it is going to scare away the further development of the Internet as an advertising medium. If there is an undercurrent of fraud, then why should a large advertiser be losing $1 million, or maybe not know how much it is losing?"

With Moira Herbst.

From *BusinessWeek*, October 2, 2006, pp. 46, 48–52, 54–57. Copyright © 2006 by BusinessWeek. Reprinted by permission of the McGraw-Hill Companies.

Online Salvation?

The embattled newspaper business is betting heavily on Web advertising revenue to secure its survival. But that wager is hardly a sure thing.

PAUL FARHI

Even the most committed newspaper industry pessimist might begin to see a little sunshine after talking to Randy Bennett. Yes, the print business is "stagnant," acknowledges the Newspaper Association of America's new-media guru. And yes, he says, newsrooms are under pressure. But—and here comes the sun—newspapers have staked out a solid position on the Internet, he says. Internet revenue is growing smartly: In 2003, Bennett points out, newspapers collected a mere $1.2 billion from their online operations; last year the figure was nearly $2.7 billion. "We're growing at a double-digit rate," he says.

This is the kind of news that soothes beleaguered publishers and journalists. As print circulation and advertising swoon, the newspaper industry, and news providers generally, have looked for a lifeboat online. Newspapers were the first of the mainstream media to extend their traditional news franchises into the world of pixels, giving them an important "first mover" advantage. Websites run by local newspapers typically remain the most popular sources of news and the largest sources of online advertising in their local communities.

Predictions about where the Internet is headed are, of course, hazardous. A dozen or so years after it began to become a fixture in American life, the Internet is still in a formative stage, subject to periodic earthquakes and lightning strikes. Google didn't exist a decade ago. Five years ago, no one had heard of MySpace. Facebook is just four years old, and YouTube is not quite three. Washington Post Executive Editor Leonard Downie Jr. compares the current state of the Internet to television in the age of "Howdy Doody."

Even so, a few dark clouds are starting to form in the sunny vista. Consider a few distant rumbles of thunder:

- After years of robust increases, the online newspaper audience seems to have all but stopped growing. The number of unique visitors to newspaper websites was almost flat—up just 2.3 percent—between August 2006 and August 2007, according to Nielsen/NetRatings. The total number of pages viewed by this audience has plateaued, growing just 1.8 percent last year.
- Newspaper websites are attracting lots of visitors, but aren't keeping them around for long. The typical visitor

to nytimes.com, which attracts more than 10 percent of the entire newspaper industry's traffic online, spent an average of just 34 minutes and 53 seconds browsing its richly detailed offerings in October. That's 34 minutes and 53 seconds per month, or about 68 seconds per day online. Slim as that is, it's actually about three times longer than the average of the next nine largest newspaper sites. And it's less than half as long as visitors spent on the Web's leading sites, such as those run by Google, Yahoo! and Microsoft.

Many news visitors—call them the "hard-core"—linger longer online, but they're a minority. Greg Harmon, director of Belden Interactive, a San Francisco-based newspaper research firm, estimates that as many as 60 percent of online newspaper visitors are "fly-bys," people who use the site briefly and irregularly. "Everyone has the same problem," says Jim Brady, editor of washingtonpost.com. The news industry's continuing challenge, Brady says, is to turn "visitors into residents."

- As competition for visitors grows, news sites are rapidly segmenting into winners and losers. In a yearlong study of 160 news-based websites (everything from usatoday.com to technorati.com), Thomas E. Patterson of Harvard University found a kind of two-tier news system developing: Traffic is still increasing at sites of well-known national brands (the New York Times, CNN, the Washington Post, etc.), but it is falling, sometimes sharply, at mid-size and smaller newspaper sites.

"The internet is redistributing the news audience in ways that [are] threatening some traditional news organizations," concluded Patterson in his study, produced for the Joan Shorenstein Center on the Press, Politics and Public Policy. "Local newspapers have been the outlets that are most at risk, and they are likely to remain so."

Patterson suggests that some of the declines at newspaper sites may be due to increased competition from local broadcast stations, particularly TV. Although they got a late start on the Internet, local TV stations are beginning to catch up, thanks to copious video news clips and strong promotional capabilities.

"A lot of papers are close to maxing out their local audiences," Patterson said in an interview. "It's hard to know where more readers will come from. . . . They have to figure out how to deal with a pretty difficult future."

In other words, for many, that first-mover advantage has vanished.

Most ominous of all is that online ad growth is beginning to slow. Remember those confidence-building double-digit increases in online advertising revenue? They're fading, fast. In the first quarter of this year, the newspaper industry saw a 22 percent gain in online revenue. Not exactly shabby, but still the smallest uptick (in percentage terms) since the NAA started keeping records in 2003. In the second quarter, the industry rate slipped again, to 19 percent. The third quarter promises even less, considering what various companies have been reporting lately. E.W. Scripps Co. saw a 19 percent increase. The Washington Post Co. said its online revenue was up 11 percent in the period, the same as Gannett's. Tribune Co. saw a gain of 9 percent. McClatchy was almost in negative territory, with a weak 1.4 percent increase for the quarter and the year to date.

All of which begins to hint at one of the deeper economic challenges facing online news providers. Even as advertisers move from traditional media to new media, a big question lingers: Can online ad revenue grow fast enough to replace the dollars that are now being lost by the "old" media? And what happens if they don't?

At the moment, the Internet has a long way to go. Newspapers collected $46.6 billion from print advertisers last year; they took in another $11 billion in circulation revenue in 2004, the last time the NAA compiled the total. Even with the double-digit increases online, that's more than 20 times what they're generating from the Internet. Among the industry's most cutting-edge publishers, the Internet still accounts for only a fraction of the overall pie. The leading online newspaper company, the New York Times Co., derives only about 11 percent of its revenue from the Web. This fall, MediaNews Group, which publishes 57 daily newspapers, including the Denver Post and the San Jose Mercury News, touted plans to increase its share of Internet revenue to 20 percent—by 2012.

Philip Meyer, author of "The Vanishing Newspaper" and a former journalist and University of North Carolina journalism professor, believes that it's "in the interest of both newspapers and advertisers to shift content to the Internet." Advertisers get narrower target audiences for their products, he notes, and greater accountability, since they can monitor consumers' behavior. "Newspapers can at last grow their businesses without being held back by the variable costs of newsprint, ink and transportation," he said in an e-mail interview. "In the recent past, newspaper owners have preferred to cut fixed costs, like editorial staff, which gives a quick boost to the bottom line but weakens their hold on the audience. Using technology to cut the variable costs is a better strategy even though the payoff takes longer."

Shedding the big overhead costs of the old media is certainly an attraction of the new one. The problem is, an Internet visitor isn't yet as valuable as a print or broadcast consumer. The cost of reaching a thousand online readers—a metric known in advertising as CPM, or cost per thousand—remains a fraction of the print CPM. The price differential can be as much as 10-to-1, even though many newspaper websites now have online audiences that rival or exceed the number of print readers.

Some of this disparity is a result of the witheringly competitive nature of the Web. Unlike the print business, in which newspaper publishers generally enjoy near-monopoly status, the online news world is littered with entrants—from giants like MSNBC .com and AOL.com, to news aggregators like drudgereport.com, to blogs by the millions. This makes it tough for any online ad seller to do what newspaper publishers have done for years—keep raising their ad rates. "Ultimately, it comes down to supply and demand," observes Leon Levitt, vice president of digital media for Cox Newspapers. "And there's an awful lot of supply out there."

Harvard's Patterson offers a more intriguing, and perhaps more unsettling, theory about why it's hard to squeeze more money out of online advertisers: Web ads may not be as effective as the traditional kind. "I'm not sure [advertisers] are convinced yet about how terrific a sales tool [a Web display ad] is," he says. "The evidence isn't strong yet that it can drive people into a store the way a full-page newspaper ad can. They're less confident about what they're getting online." Moreover, unlike their here-and-gone counterparts on the Internet, print subscribers still stay around long enough to see an ad. Some 80 percent of print readers say they spent 16 or more minutes per day with their newspaper, according to Scarborough Research.

These dynamics could change, perhaps as stronger news sources emerge on the Web and weaker ones disappear. But even if the newspaper industry continued to lose about 8 percent of its print ad revenue a year and online revenue continued to grow at 20 percent a year—the pace of the first half of 2007—it would take more than a decade for online revenue to catch up to print.

Journalists, or indeed anyone with an interest in journalism, had better pray that doesn't happen. Because online revenue is still relatively small and will remain so even at its current pace, this scenario implies years of financial decline for the newspaper industry. Even a 5 percent decline in print revenue year after year might look something like Armageddon. Newspapers were already cutting their staffs before this year's advertising downturns. A sustained frost of similar intensity would likely lead to even more devastating slashing. The cuts could take on their own vicious momentum, with each one prompting a few more readers to drop their subscriptions, which would prompt still more cuts. Some daily papers would undoubtedly fold.

Some remain confident that these dire scenarios won't come to pass. "I don't foresee [print dying] in my lifetime," says Denise F. Warren, chief advertising officer for the New York Times Co. and its websites. "I'm still bullish on print. It's still an effective way to engage with the audience." On the other hand, she adds, "The business model will keep evolving."

Yes, says Phil Meyer, but it may evolve in ways that render many daily newspapers unrecognizable to today's subscribers: "You want a prediction?" he says. "There will be enough ads for ink on paper to survive, but mainly in niche products for specialized situations."

Adding It Up

Here is how much print and online ad revenue newspapers have attracted in recent years:

Year	Print Total		Online Total		Print and Online Total	
	$Mill	%change	$Mill	%change	$Mill	%change
2000	$48,670	5.10%				
2001	$44,305	−9.00%				
2002	$44,102	−0.50%				
2003	$44,939	1.90%	$1,216		$46,156	
2004	$46,703	3.90%	$1,541	26.70%	$48,244	4.50%
2005	$47,408	1.51%	$2,027	31.48%	$49,435	2.47%
2006	$46,611	−1.68%	$2,664	31.46%	$49,275	−0.32%
2007						
Quarter						
First	$9,840.16	−6.40%	$750.04	22.30%	$10,590.20	−4.80%
Second	$10,515.23	−10.20%	$795.68	19.30%	$11,310.90	−8.60%

Source: Newspaper Association of America.

Question: Do you see a smart online business model for traditional media that will permit newspapers and other publications to continue to do deep reporting and attract talented journalists?

Craig Newmark: Not yet. While there are people working on it . . . no one's figured it out yet.

—From an online Q&A with Craigslist founder Newmark, posted on nytimes.com on October 10.

To restore the industry's momentum online, executives like Denise Warren suggest the key may simply be more. More new editorial features that will attract new visitors and keep the old ones engaged on the site for longer.

The Times, for instance, expanded three "vertical" news and feature sections last year (real estate, entertainment and travel) and this year is fleshing out similar sections on business, health and technology. In early December, the paper will launch a Web version of its fashion and luxury goods magazine, called T. The paper has also stopped charging for its op-ed columns, after having determined that it could attract more readers—and hence more advertising dollars—by removing the "pay wall" that blocked unlimited access. (The Wall Street Journal is also considering doing away with online subscriptions and moving to a free, ad-supported model, the Journal's new owner, Rupert Murdoch, said in mid-November.)

Washingtonpost.com has added more blogs, more video and special features, like a religion and ethics discussion called On Faith. In June, it started a hyper-local site-within-the-site called LoudounExtra.com that focuses on exurban Loudoun County in Virginia. Coming next summer: a complete redesign of the site. With so much movement, Brady isn't concerned about traffic slowing down. "I'm not worried that people's interest in the Internet has peaked," he says. "There's a whole generation coming up that uses the Internet a lot more."

Cox Newspapers is focusing on its papers' local markets with freestanding niche offerings that target specific demographic groups underserved by the main newspaper, such as young mothers and pet owners and local sports fans, says Leon Levitt. The idea is to assemble a larger, geographically concentrated online readership bit by bit, with as many as seven to nine specialized publications, he says.

Harvard's Patterson has a simpler idea: Just play the news better online. His study of news sites found "substantial variation" in how local sites display news, with some pushing blogs, ads and "activity lists" over breaking news. "If local news is downplayed, local papers are conceding a comparative advantage in their competition with other community sites for residents' loyalties," the study concluded. "If national and international news is downplayed, local papers may increase the likelihood that local residents will gravitate to national brand-name outlets."

The news may be the primary product, but the way the news is served online needs to be updated, too, says Mark Potts, a Web-news entrepreneur and consultant. He says newspaper-run sites are falling behind the rest of the industry in their use of technology. "For the most part, once you get past the bigger papers, newspapers are not up to date" online, he says. "They've got some video, a podcast, some blogs, yes, but mostly . . . they're just pasting the newspaper up on the screen. That was barely OK five years ago." Potts ticks off the tools that news sites usually lack: social networking applications, database-search functions, mapping, simplified mobile-device delivery technology, services that let readers interact with one another, etc. His one-word description for the state of newspapers online: "Stodgy."

On the ad side, traditional news organizations are starting to join, rather than trying to fight, some of the Internet's giants. In recent months, major newspaper companies have struck alliances with Yahoo! and Google in an attempt to pair newspapers' strength in selling local advertising with the search engines' superior technology and national reach.

In the first phase of a multipart alliance, some 19 newspaper companies that own 264 daily papers have linked their online help-wanted advertising to Yahoo!'s HotJobs recruitment site. When an advertiser seeking to hire, say, a nurse, in St. Louis buys an ad through the St. Louis Post-Dispatch, the newspaper places the ad on its site, which is co-branded with HotJobs and automatically linked to HotJobs' national listings. As a result, the advertiser gets his message in front of both local job candidates and others across the country. HotJobs, in turn, gets a local sales agent—the Post-Dispatch—to sell more listings. Although the partners have revealed few financial details about the arrangement, revenue from such ads is split between the newspaper and Yahoo!, with the newspapers taking a majority of each dollar generated.

In a second phase of the alliance that is now being tested, publishers such as McClatchy, Lee Enterprises, Media General, Cox and others will attempt to do something similar with display ads. Using Yahoo!'s search capabilities and technology, the companies hope to marry national and local display ads to their visitors' interests. People interested in, say, pickup trucks (as identified by tracking software and registration questionnaires), would likely see national ads for Ford, and perhaps for local Ford dealers, when they logged on to a newspaper's site. Such highly targeted advertising would command much higher CPMs than plain old banner ads, says Cox's Levitt.

While it's still too early to declare victory, the general scheme of the partnership has drawn praise from Wall Street. Deutsche Bank analyst Paul Ginocchio has estimated that some members of the consortium could see online ad growth rates of 40 percent for the next two years, thanks in large part to revenue generated by the Yahoo! tie-in.

However, other publishers have declined to join the Yahoo! consortium, in part out of concern that newspapers may be giving away too much to Yahoo! and leaving readers little reason to visit the newspapers' own sites. For example, Gannett and Tribune Co. are developing a display advertising network of their own.

Another group of publishers, including Hearst, E.W. Scripps and the New York Times Co., have turned to Google. Under an experimental program that was expanded this summer, Google is running auctions that enable thousands of smaller advertisers to bid on ad space—size, section and date of their choosing—on some 225 newspaper websites. The newspapers are free to accept the offer, reject it or make a counteroffer (Google says more than half the bids have been accepted). The process is streamlined by Google's technology, which automates billing and payments.

A little less cooperation might help, too. Some argue that news providers made a huge strategic mistake when they decided to make their content available to others online. "Free riders" like Yahoo.com, MSN.com, Google and AOL.com have built massive franchises—far larger than any traditional mainstream news site—in part by posting news stories created and paid for by others. These days, of course, anyone can assemble a series of links and headlines to become a "news" site. The Shorenstein Center put it bluntly in its recent study of news on the Internet: "The largest threat posed by the Internet to traditional news organizations . . . is

the ease with which imaginative or well positioned players from outside the news system can use news to attract an audience."

"It's a terribly unfair deal," says Randy Siegel, the publisher of Parade, the weekly newspaper magazine. "Newspapers need to negotiate a more equitable share with search engines that are making billions of dollars by selling ads around newspaper content without the costs of creating that content. . . . The book industry and the movie industry don't give their content away."

Arkansas Publisher Walter Hussman Jr. knows he sounds like a man from another century when he says it, but he thinks newspapers shouldn't be free, online or off. He rues the day that the Associated Press, which is owned by the newspaper industry, agreed to sell stories to the Yahoo!s and AOLs of the world. Free or bargain-priced news, Hussman says, cheapens everyone's news. Free, he says, "is a bad business model."

Hussman has an idea that's so old and abandoned it seems almost new: Make people pay for the news they want, even in the Internet age. Hussman obviously is swimming upstream with this notion. Not long after the New York Times stopped charging for its op-ed columns under the now-jettisoned Times-Select initiative, the Sacramento Bee dropped subscription fees for Capitol Alert, the paper's website for political news.

The newspaper Hussman publishes, the Arkansas Democrat-Gazette in Little Rock, is one of the few that charge a fee ($4.95 a month) for full access to its site. The site has a modest base of 3,000 subscribers, but Hussman says walling it off protects a more lucrative franchise: the newspaper. He believes it's no coincidence that the Democrat-Gazette's print circulation is growing—about 2,000 daily in the latest six-month period that ended in September—at a time when so many others are sliding.

But what about the ad revenue that the newspaper is giving up with such a restricted website? Hussman says ad rates are so low online that they often don't cover the cost of producing original journalism. Example: An online gallery of photos from a local high school football game might generate 4,000 page views. If an advertiser paid $25 for each thousand views—a premium figure, by the way—the photo feature might generate $100, barely enough to pay the photographer for his work.

"I know what I'm saying is going to sound too simplistic to some people, but it seems to be working," he says. "The reason I advocate this is not some ideological or esoteric reason or because of pride of authorship. I'm basing this on experience."

Hussman sees an industry that generates nearly $60 billion a year in print ad sales and subscription fees, and that supports the expenditure of roughly $7 billion a year on newsgathering operations, and worries about it all slipping away in an era in which news is so abundant—and so free. "It would be wonderful if someone could figure out a way" to do all that online, he says before concluding, "but I just don't see it now."

PAUL FARHI (farhip@washpost.com) is a Washington Post reporter who writes frequently about the media for the *Post* and *AJR*. He has written about the *San Francisco area's news blues, hyperlocal news websites* and the *business magazine Portfolio* in recent issues of *AJR*.

From *American Journalism Review*, December 2007/January 2008, pp. 18–23. Copyright © 2008 by the Philip Merrill College of Journalism at the University of Maryland, College Park, MD 20742–7111. Reprinted with permission.

Great Wall of Facebook: The Social Network's Plan to Dominate the Internet—and Keep Google Out

Instead of working together to reach the promised land of online brand advertising, Facebook and Google are racing to see who can get there first.

FRED VOGELSTEIN

Larry Page should have been in a good mood. It was the fall of 2007, and Google's cofounder was in the middle of a five-day tour of his company's European operations in Zurich, London, Oxford, and Dublin. The trip had been fun, a chance to get a ground-floor look at Google's ever-expanding empire. But this week had been particularly exciting, for reasons that had nothing to do with Europe; Google was planning a major investment in Facebook, the hottest new company in Silicon Valley.

Originally Google had considered acquiring Facebook—a prospect that held no interest for Facebook's executives—but an investment was another enticing option, aligning the Internet's two most important companies. Facebook was more than a fast-growing social network. It was, potentially, an enormous source of personal data. Internet users behaved differently on Facebook than anywhere else online: They used their real names, connected with their real friends, linked to their real email addresses, and shared their real thoughts, tastes, and news. Google, on the other hand, knew relatively little about most of its users other than their search histories and some browsing activity.

But now, as Page took his seat on the Google jet for the two-hour flight from Zurich to London, something appeared to be wrong. He looked annoyed, one of his fellow passengers recalls. It turned out that he had just received word that the deal was off. Microsoft, Google's sworn enemy, would be making the investment instead—$240 million for a 1.6 percent stake in the company, meaning that Redmond valued Facebook at an astonishing $15 billion.

As the 767 took off, Page tersely but calmly shared the news with the others on the plane and answered their questions for about 15 minutes. "Larry was clearly, clearly unhappy about it," the passenger says.

Page soon got over it, but Facebook's rejection was still a blow to Google; it had never lost a deal this big and this publicly.

But according to Facebookers involved in the transaction, Mountain View never had much of a chance—all things being equal, Microsoft was always the favored partner. Google's bid was used primarily as a stalking horse, a tool to amp up the bidding. Facebook executives weren't leaping at the chance to join with Google; they preferred to conquer it. "We never liked those guys," says one former Facebook engineer. "We all had that audacity, 'Anything Google does, we can do better.' No one talked about MySpace or the other social networks. We just talked about Google."

Today, the Google-Facebook rivalry isn't just going strong, it has evolved into a full-blown battle over the future of the Internet—its structure, design, and utility. For the last decade or so, the Web has been defined by Google's algorithms—rigorous and efficient equations that parse practically every byte of online activity to build a dispassionate atlas of the online world. Facebook CEO Mark Zuckerberg envisions a more personalized, humanized Web, where our network of friends, colleagues, peers, and family is our primary source of information, just as it is offline. In Zuckerberg's vision, users will query this "social graph" to find a doctor, the best camera, or someone to hire—rather than tapping the cold mathematics of a Google search. It is a complete rethinking of how we navigate the online world, one that places Facebook right at the center. In other words, right where Google is now.

All this brave talk might seem easy to dismiss as the swagger of an arrogant upstart. After all, being Google is a little like being heavyweight champion of the world—everyone wants a shot at your title. But over the past year, Facebook has gone from glass-jawed flyweight to legitimate contender. It has become one of the most popular online destinations. More than 200 million people—about one-fifth of all Internet users—have Facebook accounts. They spend an average of 20 minutes on the site every day. Facebook has stolen several well-known Google employees, from COO Sheryl Sandburg to chef Josef Desimone; at least 9 percent of its staff used to work for the search giant. And since last December, Facebook has launched a series of ambitious initiatives, designed to make the social graph an even more integral part of a user's online experience. Even some Googlers concede that Facebook represents a growing threat. "Eventually, we are going to collide," one executive says.

It is remarkable that the most powerful company on the Web would feel threatened by one that has yet to turn a profit. (Last year, one insider estimates, Facebook burned through $75 million plus the $275 million in revenue it brought in; Google made $4.2 billion on an astounding $15.8 billion in net revenue.) And even Facebook executives concede that Google has secured an insurmountable lead in search advertising—those little text ads that pop up next to search results—which accounts for about 90 percent of Google's net revenue. But they say they are going after an even bigger market: the expensive branding campaigns that so far have barely ventured online. Once, Google hoped an alliance with Facebook would help attract those huge ad budgets. Now, instead of working together to reach the promised land of online brand advertising, Facebook and Google are racing to see who can get there first.

Like typical trash-talking youngsters, Facebook sources argue that their competition is old and out of touch. "Google is not representative of the future of technology in any way," one Facebook veteran says. "Facebook is an advanced communications network enabling myriad communication forms. It almost doesn't make sense to compare them."

To understand Facebook's challenge to Google, consider my friend and neighbor Wayne, a PhD in computer science from UC Berkeley and a veteran of many big-time programming jobs. I know a lot about him because we are friends. I know even more because we are Facebook friends. On his online profile, I not only find the standard personal-blog-type information—his birthday, address, résumé, and pictures of his wife, son, and step-kids. I also discover that he likes to make beer, that he had dinner at one of my favorite restaurants last week, and that he likes to watch cartoons. Indeed, he has posted something about his life almost every day for the past two months—wondering whether his son's Little League game will get rained out, asking his friends what the impeller in his central heating unit does.

But if I type Wayne's name into Google, I learn very little. I am directed to an old personal website, with links that have almost all expired, and a collection of computer-science papers he has written over the years. That's about it.

Hardly any of Wayne's Facebook information turns up on a Google search, because all of it, along with similar details about the other 200 million Facebook users, exists on the social network's roughly 40,000 servers. Together, this data comprises a mammoth amount of activity, almost a second Internet. By Facebook's estimates, every month users share 4 billion pieces

Facebook's 4-Step Plan for Online Domination

Mark Zuckerberg has never thought of his company as a mere social network. He and his team are in the middle of a multiyear campaign to change how the Web is organized—with Facebook at the center. Here's how they hope to pull it off.

1. Build Critical Mass

In the eight months ending in April, Facebook has doubled in size to 200 million members, who contribute 4 billion pieces of info, 850 million photos, and 8 million videos every month. The result: a second Internet, one that includes users' most personal data and resides entirely on Facebook's servers.

2. Redefine Search

Facebook thinks its members will turn to their friends—rather than Google's algorithms—to navigate the Web. It already drives an eyebrow-raising amount of traffic to outside sites, and that will only increase once Facebook Search allows users to easily explore one another's feeds.

3. Colonize the Web

Thanks to a pair of new initiatives—dubbed Facebook Connect and Open Stream—users don't have to log in to Facebook to communicate with their friends. Now they can access their network from any of 10,000 partner sites or apps, contributing even more valuable data to Facebook's servers every time they do it.

4. Sell Targeted Ads, Everywhere

Facebook hopes to one day sell advertising across all of its partner sites and apps, not just on its own site. The company will be able to draw on the immense volume of personal data it owns to create extremely targeted messages. The challenge: not freaking out its users in the process.

of information—news stories, status updates, birthday wishes, and so on. They also upload 850 million photos and 8 million videos. But anyone wanting to access that stuff must go through Facebook; the social network treats it all as proprietary data, largely shielding it from Google's crawlers. Except for the mostly cursory information that users choose to make public, what happens on Facebook's servers stays on Facebook's servers. That represents a massive and fast-growing blind spot for Google, whose long-stated goal is to "organize the world's information."

Facebook isn't just kneecapping Google's search engine; it is also competing with it. Facebook encourages its 200 million members to use Microsoft's search engine, which it installed on its homepage late last year as part of the deal struck between the two companies. At press time, it was also planning to launch Facebook Search, allowing users to scour one another's feeds.

Want to see what some anonymous schmuck thought about the *Battlestar Galactica* finale? Check out Google. Want to see what your friends had to say? Try Facebook Search. And it will not only be for searching within Facebook. Because Facebook friends post links to outside sites, you will be able to use it as a gateway to the Web—making it a direct threat to Google. Why settle for articles about the Chrysler bankruptcy that the Google News algorithm recommends when you can read what your friends suggest? Already, Facebook is starting to horn in on Google's role as the predominant driver of Web traffic. According to Hitwise, Facebook in recent months has sent more traffic than Google to Evite, video site Tagged.com, and gossip mills Perez Hilton.com and Dlisted. That trend should only grow with the advent of Facebook Search.

These are just the latest moves in an ambitious campaign to make the social graph an integral, ubiquitous element of life online. In December, Facebook launched Connect, a network of more than 10,000 independent sites that lets users access their Facebook relationships without logging in to Facebook.com. Go to Digg, for instance, and see which stories friends recommended. Head to Citysearch and see which restaurants they have reviewed. Visit TechCrunch, Gawker, or the Huffington Post and read comments they have left. On Inauguration Day, millions of users logged in to CNN.com with their Facebook ID and discussed the proceedings with their friends in real time.

In April, Facebook announced its Open Stream API, allowing developers to create mashups using Facebook's constantly updated stream of user activity. Previously, users who wanted to read their friends' News Feeds had to go to the Facebook site. Now developers can export that information to any site—or to freestanding applications, much as Twitter desktop clients do for Tweets.

Connect and Open Stream don't just allow users to access their Facebook networks from anywhere online. They also help realize Facebook's longtime vision of giving users a unique, Web-wide online profile. By linking Web activity to Facebook accounts, they begin to replace the largely anonymous "no one knows you're a dog" version of online identity with one in which every action is tied to who users really are.

To hear Facebook executives tell it, this will make online interactions more meaningful and more personal. Imagine, for example, if online comments were written by people using their real names rather than by anonymous trolls. "Up until now all the advancements in technology have said information and data are the most important thing," says Dave Morin, Facebook's senior platform manager. "The most important thing to us is that there is a person sitting behind that keyboard. We think the Internet is about people."

But you don't build a competitor to Google with people alone. You need data. And Connect and Open Stream are intended to make Facebook a much more powerful force for collecting user information. Any time someone logs in to a site that uses Connect or Open Stream, they give Facebook the right to keep track of any activity that happens there—potentially contributing tons more personal data to Facebook's servers. Facebook Connect and Open Stream are also designed to make each user's friend network, which belongs to Facebook, even more valuable and crucial to the Web experience. Together, they aim to put Facebook users' social networks at the center of all they do online.

Mark Zuckerberg is notoriously cocky, even by the standards of Silicon Valley. Two years ago, he walked away from a reported nearly $1 billion offer from Yahoo for his company. He could have sold to Google or Microsoft for a lot more. His business cards once famously read: i'm ceo . . . bitch. And he has described Facebook as a once-in-a-century communications revolution, implying that he is right up there with Gutenberg and Marconi.

Still, you'd think he might play it a little cool when discussing Google, not wanting to antagonize the most powerful company on the Internet. But Zuckerberg doesn't pull any punches, describing Google as "a top-down way" of organizing the Web that results in an impersonal experience that stifles online activity. "You have a bunch of machines and algorithms going out and crawling the Web and bringing information back," he says. "That only gets stuff that is publicly available to everyone. And it doesn't give people the control that they need to be really comfortable." Instead, he says, Internet users will share more data when they are allowed to decide which information they make public and which they keep private. "No one wants to live in a surveillance society," Zuckerberg adds, "which, if you take that to its extreme, could be where Google is going."

It's ironic to hear Zuckerberg paint Google as Big Brother. After all, many observers worry that Facebook itself has grown too controlling. Unlike Google, Facebook makes it difficult for users to export their contacts, mail, photos, and videos—a practice Web 2.0 evangelists say is a sign that the company values its proprietary data more than its users' experience. In November 2007, Facebook launched Beacon, a ham-fisted attempt to inject advertising into News Feeds. Users felt violated; after a month of protest, Zuckerberg publicly apologized and effectively shut Beacon down. Then, in February 2009, Facebook quietly changed its terms of service, appearing to give itself perpetual ownership of anything posted on the site, even after members closed their accounts. Users complained so vociferously—millions joined Facebook groups and signed online petitions protesting the change—that the company was forced to backtrack. The event left many people fearful of the amount of personal information they were ceding to a private, profit-hungry enterprise. "Do You Own Facebook?" a *New York* magazine cover story asked warily in April. "Or Does Facebook Own You?" (Facebook executives say that the company was merely updating the terms of service to match those of other sites and that there was no nefarious intent. They reinstated a version of the amendment after subjecting it to a vote of Facebook members.)

The drumbeat of controversy surrounding Facebook illustrates the catch-22 the social network faces: It has a massive storehouse of user data, but every time it tries to capitalize on that information, its members freak out. This isn't an academic problem; the company's future depends on its ability to master the art of behavioral targeting—selling customized advertising based on user profiles. In theory, this should be an irresistible opportunity for marketers; Facebook's performance advertising program allows them to design and distribute an ad to as narrow an audience as they would like. (It has also developed a program to create ads that are designed to be spread virally.) But as the Beacon debacle showed, there is a fine line between "targeted and useful" and "creepy and stalkerish"—and so far, not enough advertisers have been willing to walk that line.

In a way, Facebook's dilemma extends from its success. Users see the site as sanctified space, a place to engage in intimate conversations with friends—not to be laser-beamed by weirdly personal advertising. But with initiatives like Connect and Open Stream, Facebook can sell ads beyond its own site. Just as Google's AdSense program sells ads on any participating website, Connect and Open Stream will eventually push Facebook-brokered advertising to any member site or app. But unlike with AdSense, Facebook's ads could be exquisitely tailored to their targets. "No one out there has the data that we have," says COO Sandberg.

That's where the big-budget brand advertisers come in. Google has courted them for four years, to no avail. That's because, while search ads are great at delivering advertising to users who are seeking specific products, they are less effective at creating demand for stuff users don't yet know they want. Google has tried everything to lure brand advertisers—from buying and selling radio ads to purchasing YouTube. And it is easy to see why it keeps trying. Today, global online brand advertising accounts for just $50 billion a year. Offline brand advertising, meanwhile, accounts for an estimated $500 billion.

Google's desire to crack the brand-advertising conundrum is so intense, some company executives have even considered swallowing their pride and pursuing another deal with Facebook. But whether or not it ultimately friends the social network, Google has clearly been influenced by it. On December 4, the same day that Facebook Connect launched, Google unveiled its own version, Friend Connect, which allows websites to link to accounts on any of the major social networks—including MySpace, LinkedIn, Ning, Hi5, and Bebo. In March, four months after Facebook reportedly offered $500 million in a failed bid for Twitter, reports surfaced that Google was holding similar talks. (A Google insider confirms the discussions.) It is easy to see the appeal: Twitter is growing even faster than Facebook—doubling its membership in March—and would give Google access to the kind of personal information that fills Facebook News Feeds. And Google recently announced Wave, a Web communications platform that encourages Facebook-like sharing and conversations. The company even seems to have conceded Zuckerberg's point about its impersonal search results. In April, Google announced a plan to allow individuals to create detailed profiles that would show up whenever anyone searches for their name. If they opt for this service—a big if—users gain greater control over how they are portrayed online, which will give them the incentive to share with Google the kind of personal information they had previously shared only with Facebook.

Google has even shown a willingness to join Facebook in gingerly tapping the third rail of Internet marketing—behavioral targeting. The search giant has long assured its users that it would never use their personal information to deliver targeted advertising, relying instead on aggregate data or search activity that preserves anonymity. ("There is a line with users that you don't want to cross," Google CEO Eric Schmidt said in the wake of the Beacon controversy.) But in March, Google started its own behavioral targeting campaign—tracking users' browsing to deliver more-customized ads. Users have the option to either edit their profiles or opt out entirely.

In September 2007, Gideon Yu was hired as Facebook's CFO. Before that, the 38-year-old had been CFO at YouTube, where he negotiated its acquisition by Google. He'd also put in four years as Yahoo's treasurer and was one of its top dealmakers. Facebook announced the hire with much fanfare. "I consider it kind of a coup that we were able to recruit him here," Zuckerberg told the *Wall Street Journal*. "He's just excellent."

Nineteen months later, Yu was gone. It was a short tenure—not unprecedented for a private-company CFO. But Zuckerberg turned Yu's departure into a kerfuffle by publicly trashing him, saying that the job had simply outgrown him and that Facebook now needed a CFO with "substantial public company experience." To many, the performance was a stark reminder that the Facebook CEO, while undeniably ambitious and brilliant, was still just 24 years old. (He's 25 now.)

Zuckerberg's youth has given Googlers some confidence. After all, even under the most sage and steady leadership, Facebook would be confronted with a difficult challenge: turning a massive user base into a sustainable business. (Just ask Friendster, MySpace, YouTube, and Twitter.) Through Google's own experience with YouTube, they have seen how expensive it can be to keep up with exploding user growth. They inked a disastrous $900 million partnership with MySpace in 2006, a failure that taught them how hard it is to make money from social networking. And privately, they don't think Facebook's staff has the brainpower to succeed where they have failed. "If they found a way to monetize all of a sudden, sure, that would be a problem," says one highly placed Google executive. "But they're not going to."

Facebook's naysayers have a point. But before they get too complacent, they might remember another upstart that figured out a new way to organize the Internet. For five years, it worked on building its user base and perfecting its product, resisting pleas from venture capitalists to figure out how to make money. It was only after it had made itself an essential part of everyone's online life that its business path became clear—and it quickly grew to become one of the world's most powerful and wealthy companies. The name of that company, of course, was Google.

Contributing editor **Fred Vogelstein** (fred_vogelstein@wired.com) wrote about Google in issue 17.02.

From *Wired*, July 2009. Copyright © 2009 by Wired. Reprinted by permission.

Beyond Blogs

Three years ago our cover story showcased the phenomenon. A lot has changed since then.

STEPHEN BAKER AND HEATHER GREEN

In the frantic news biz, where stories go stale overnight, one of our old articles is behaving very strangely. Year after year it continues to draw swarms of online readers, more than holding its own against up-to-date fare. Oddy, while technology races ahead, our story remains frozen in time. It describes a world in which YouTube has yet to emerge from the garage and Twittering, today's micro-blogging rage, is left to the birds.

The year was 2005, and the story was "Blogs Will Change Your Business." It marked our plunge into the world of bottom-up media, of news as a "conversation." Many people at the time—including a good number at this magazine and throughout the business world—considered blogs to be a publishing tool for trivia, banality, venom, and baseless attacks. This was all true, the article conceded.

But in the helter-skelter of the blogosphere, we wrote, something important was taking place: In the 10 minutes it took to set up a blogging account, anyone with an Internet connection could become a global publisher. Some could become stars and gain power. That was already happening. In this new world, any business that hoped to "control" information—and that included just about everybody—was in for a wild ride. This promised a seismic shock in our own media world. No mystery there. But it also posed challenges for businesses in practically every realm. Every e-mail or memo could be blogged. Every employee, no matter what rank, could become a voice for the company, either publicly or cloaked, some gaining more power than the entire public relations department. "Your customers and rivals are figuring blogs out," we warned, adding: "Catch up . . . or catch you later."

Following our own advice, we ended the story by linking to our new blog, Blogspotting.net. The conversation continued on the blog, as it does to this day. Who cared that the magazine piece grew a bit musty? Canaries don't read the yellowing articles lining their cages.

Serious Google Juice

Turned out it wasn't quite that simple. The magazine article, archived on our website, kept attracting readers and blog links. A few professors worked it into their curricula, sending class after class of students to the story. With all this activity, the piece gained high-octane Google juice. Type in "blogs business" on the search engine, and our story comes up first among the results, as of this writing. Hundreds of thousands of people are still searching "blogs business" because they're eager to learn the latest news about an industry that's changing at warp speed. Their attention maintains our outdated relic at the top of the list. It's self-perpetuating: They want new, we give them old.

What to do? Update the old beast, naturally. Early this year, we put out questions on Blogspotting. What needed fixing? Responses streamed in. We called the old sources and contacted some new ones. We annotated the original article, bolstering the online version with dozens of notes and clarifications. That approach works for the Net, with its pop-up windows and limitless space. But for the more cramped confines of the paper magazine, we have to cut to the chase.

So here goes. Three years ago, we wrote a big story—but missed a bigger one. We focused on blogs as a new form of printing press, one that turned Gutenberg's economics on its head, making everyone a potential publisher. This captured our attention, not least because this publishing revolution was already starting to rattle the skyscrapers in our media-heavy, Manhattan neighborhood. But despite the importance of blogs, only a minority of us participates. Chances are, you don't. According to a recent study from Forrester Research, only a quarter of the U.S. adult online population even bothers to read a blog once a month.

But blogs, it turns out, are just one of the do-it-yourself tools to emerge on the Internet. Vast social networks such as Facebook and MySpace offer people new ways to meet and exchange information. Sites like LinkedIn help millions forge important work relationships and alliances. New applications pop up every week. While only a small slice of the population wants to blog, a far larger swath of humanity is eager to make friends and contacts, to exchange pictures and music, to share activities and ideas.

These social connectors are changing the dynamics of companies around the world. Millions of us are now hanging out on the Internet with customers, befriending rivals, clicking through pictures of our boss at a barbecue, or seeing what she read at the beach. It's as if the walls around our companies are vanishing and old org charts are lying on their sides.

This can be disturbing for top management, who are losing control, at least in the traditional sense. Workers can fritter away hours on YouTube. They can use social networks to pillory a colleague or leak secrets. That's the downside, and companies that don't adapt are sure to get lots of it.

But there's an upside to the loss of control. Ambitious workers use these tools to land new deals and to assemble global teams for collaborative projects. The potential for both better and worse is huge, and it's growing—and since 2005 the technologies involved extend far beyond blogs. So our first fix is to lose "blogs" from our headline. The revised title: "Social Media Will Change Your Business."

Even when researching a story like this, it's easy to fall into old patterns. Let's see, we thought as we started out: Which top executives are embracing social media? Sun Microsystems chief executive officer Jonathan I. Schwartz is a blogger. What's he up to? IBM set up its own social network for employees, Beehive. It has 30,000 employees on it. We should definitely give them a call.

But hold on. If we're writing about new networks that extend beyond companies and break down their walls, and if these technologies are often beyond the control of executives, what are we doing calling the bosses? Like many others in business, we have developed top-down reflexes that are nearly Pavlovian. We have to deprogram ourselves.

So. How to get in touch with the grass roots? We try Twitter, the microblogging sensation. People use it to send tiny haiku-like messages (140 characters maximum) to everyone who chooses to receive their feeds. The two of us each has a few hundred people following our posts, either on the Twitter page, sites like Facebook, or (for a few fanatics) the cell phone. Who are these people? Well, they're just that, people. They're not organized by industry or rank. They're screen names, just like us (stevebaker and heatherlgreen). An estimated 1 million folks are on the Twitter service now. It's a small number, but it includes lots of influential voices, especially in tech. Some follow friends to learn what they had for breakfast or what they saw at the Vatican Museum. But they also may see what technologies their competitors

---

WE DIDN'T SEE 'EM COMING
Here are some of the important sites and services we missed

YouTube It took the service, which now has 66 million U.S. visitors, only three years to jump-start online video, unleash millions of amateur filmmakers, and undercut TV giants.

Twitter What can you say in 140 characters? The popularity of the two-year-old microblogging service shows that short can indeed be sweet—or boring, sometimes brilliant. Will it still be big in three years?

Wikipedia The grassroots encyclopedia didn't make the cut for our blogging story, but it's a social media phenom. It exploded during the last three years, becoming the seventh-most-popular site online and attracting 59 million American users, up from 5 million.

Spam Blogs Mass-produced to attract Google ads, these so-called splogs infested the blogosphere in 2005 and 2006. They now account for more than 90% of all blog postings, but filters catch most of them.

Facebook and **MySpace.** The best-known social network when we wrote our story was Friendster. That's how fast social media is changing.

iTunes Yes, we knew about Apple's music service. But we didn't guess that it would become the leading destination for podcast downloads. Countrary to our expectations, podcasts have evolved into a feature of traditional radio, not a rival to it.

From paper to cyber and back: A problem in blogistics
When we decided to update our 2005 cover story on blogs, we first did it on our website. That was a piece of cake, at least on the technical side. We just sprinkled additions and corrections through the text. Online readers could click on them and the new footnotes would pop up. But how to pull off such a trick on paper? We decided to write an entirely new story and create all sorts of tables and charts to explain the changes in social media that have occurred over the past three years. Here's a look at what we got right, what we missed, and what has changed.

---

are putting into alpha tests and get the buzz on new rounds of financing. Work and leisure, colleague and rival; they all blend on these networks.

The 140-Character Resume

We send out a few posts on Twitter (they're called "tweets") asking people how social media are changing their work. Scores of responses pour in. People learn what colleagues are up to, inside and outside the company. They see trends. They make contacts. They learn. Some even sell. A Dell employee who goes by the Twitter name of Ggroovin tells us that Dell's service on Twitter has brought in half a million dollars of new orders in the past year. Some on

We said, "Mainstream media will start to look like blogs."

Got that one right. Blogs are proliferating on mainstream sites. *BusinessWeek* alone now has 20. Big names such as Andrew Sullivan, original Wonkette Ana Marie Cox, and *Freakonomics* authors Stephen Dubner and Steven Levitt now blog for mainstream publications.

MATCH THE MEDIA OUTLETS WITH THEIR ASSOCIATED BLOGS

1 *The New York Times*	a) Andrew Sullivan's blog: Views of a political contrarian
2 *Atlantic Monthly*	
3 *Discovery Channel*	b) *Freakonomics* blog: Unorthodox economics, following best-seller
4 *Time*	c) Swampland: Political notes and (occasional) caustic asides
5 *Time Warner*	
	d) TreeHugger: Ins and outs of going green for guilt-ridden consumers
Answers: 1b, 2a, 3d, 4c, 5e	e) TMZ: Gossip, embarrassing pix, and red-carpet extravaganzas

BLOGS. UP AND UP (AND LOTS OF ZOMBIES)

In the spring of 2005, search engine Technorati reported indexing 9 million blogs. Today's figure? 74 million. It sounds impressive, but only a fraction of all bloggers has posted within the last two months. Eliminate the sleepers, and the blog universe shrivels to 5.2 million. Kevin Burton, CEO of FeedBlog, argues that there are even fewer active blogs, about 2 million to 4 million. In either case, more than enough to read. In fact, only one in four adult Americans online, according to Forrester Research, reads a blog every month.

We said, "Dooced: An expression used when someone loses a job because of blogging."

Three years later, we're not hearing that word much. Tim Bray, director of Web technologies at Sun Microsystems, thinks we exaggerated the risk. "I think there's a news story in the absence of carnage," he says, adding that 4,000 employees at Sun blog. "Nobody's been fired. Nobody has taken career damage over a blog."

Twitter sniff around for the next job. "The new résumé is 140 characters," tweets 23-year-old Amanda Mooney, who just landed a job in PR.

Still, we have to talk with a few corporate honchos. How are they dealing with this outbreak of communication tools? J.P. Rangaswami is a good person to start with. He runs technology at BT, the British telecom giant, and is famous for an approach that blends inside and outside networks. We leave a message with the press department. A day passes. We wonder if we should try another number before it strikes us how silly we've been. We can go straight to the person! That's what social media lets you do. We leave a comment on Rangaswami's blog, Confused of Calcutta, and promptly get a reply. He's flying to San Francisco, but he leaves his Facebook and Twitter contacts, along with a cell phone number.

Hours later, Rangaswami describes the changes since the 2005 article. Then, he says, there were either traditional communications or weird stuff with funny names, like blogs and wikis. People at BT now embrace a full range of online tools, and they use them more and more, especially as young workers join the company. "The new people come infected with the new world," he says.

More than 16,000 BT employees work together on wikis, using the same technology as Wikipedia, the online encyclopedia that lets anyone post or edit entries. But instead of teaming up to edit an online encyclopedia, employees gather on them to write software, map cellphone base stations, launch branding campaigns. Nearly every new project hatches a wiki. This is especially valuable in a global economy, where engineers in Asia can pick up a project as Europeans go to bed. The new groups that evolve on these wikis raze traditional hierarchies: An intern can amend the work of a senior engineer. Meanwhile, some 10,500 employees at BT (that Rangaswami knows of) are already on Facebook. BT is also offering an internal social network. But just like Facebook and Twitter, it won't work unless it attracts a crowd. Rangaswami can't force anyone to use it. It would be fruitless to try. To hear Rangaswami describe it, all his team can do is provide tools and watch.

There's a lot to look at. "We've spent years talking about the value of the water-cooler conversations," he says. "Now we have the ability to actually understand what these relationships are, how information and decision-making migrate. We see how people really work." Why does this matter? The company can spot teams that form organically, and then can place them on targeted projects. It can pinpoint the people who transmit ideas. These folks are golden. "A new class of supercommunicators has emerged," he says.

WHERE ARE THEY TODAY?

Some of the key characters in our 2005 cover

Bob Lutz The GM vice-chairman was the darling of the blogging set when he launched the company's FastLane blog in 2005. His posts are now fewer and read more like PR.

Dave Sifry Our prediction? Sifry's Technorati blog search engine would be snapped up. Not quite. Instead, it struggled with scale and was surpassed by Google. Sifry stepped down last year as Technorati's CEO, though he's still chairman.

Dan Gillmor The advocate of citizen journalism couldn't turn his passion into a business. Bayosphere, his community news startup in California, never got off the ground.

We said, "Any chance that a blog bubble could pop? The answer is really easy: No."

Strictly speaking, it's still true. Blogs alone account for minimal investment. But they aren't alone. They're part of social media, tied to YouTube and Facebook, and to sky-high projections of new ad revenue. That frothy market could tumble. Still, it wouldn't affect most blogs.

We said, "A prediction: Mainstream media will . . . take over vast commercial stretches of the blogosphere."

Whoops. In fact, in politics, tech, gossip, and media, blogs are flexing their muscles. With lower costs and bigger buzz, many are matching or topping mainstream sites in traffic and influence. Examples:

Engadget The most popular group-edited blog brings in 2.5 million readers for updates on the newest and shiniest gadgets in tech.

Huffington Post Spearheaded by Arianna Huffington, this pile-on of around 1,500 bloggers attracts more than 4 million visitors per month. Political commentary is its bread and butter.

TechCrunch Michael Arrington, a lawyer, turned this site about tech startups into a Silicon Valley powerhouse with more than half a million rabid readers.

Community-Driven Blogs Notes about secret affairs, cutesy pictures, and updates about international happenings that don't get much play in traditional media fuel a host of obsessively popular sites like PostSecret, Icanhascheezburger, and Global Voices.

Good networkers have always had their ways to work around the direct reports and dotted lines diagrammed on company charts. They've created informal networks. Now, with social media, they have a fast-expanding set of tools to extend these relationships, and even to change their companies. Charlene Li and Josh Bernoff of Forrester Research detail an example from Best Buy in their new book about social media, *Groundswell*. In 2006 two marketing managers at the company worked weekends to create an in-house social network, Blue Shirt Nation. Now it has grown to more than 20,000 participants, 85% of them sales associates. In a company with a 60% annual turnover rate, this group churns at only 8.5%, blogs Gary Koelling, one of the founders. And Blue Shirt Nation gets results. A promotional drive on the site helped persuade 40,000 employees to sign up for 401(k) retirement accounts. This bottom-up approach moves a whole lot faster than initiatives that wind through a corporate approval process. Drawbacks? The new order favors those who network, create buzz, and promote their brand. Managers have to make sure that quieter employees don't lose out.

The change is even more dramatic in media. In the world we envisioned in 2005, the old dogs of mainstream media (like us) learning the new tricks of blogging and using them to extend our reach and clout. We figured we'd be surrounded by constellations of standalone bloggers, each with his or her own niche.

Competition from the Megablogs

Steve Rubel was our example. The opening spread of our 2005 story featured a full-page photo of Rubel, PR executive and leading blog evangelist. He was stripping off a sweatshirt, Superman-style, in the vastness of Grand Central Terminal. Rubel's job was to help companies communicate in this new world. He extended his brand by blogging. It wasn't a bad gig. He remains a power in blogging, and his stature won him a job directing digital media at PR firm Edelman & Associates from an office with big windows overlooking Times Square.

Sitting there one recent morning, facing a widescreen Mac laptop, Rubel drops a bomb. He doesn't blog much anymore. He lets his popular Micropersuasion site sit fallow for days on end. That would have been sacrilege when we wrote our article. Back then he was posting a dozen times a day—even from bed.

What changed? Two big things, he says: technology and media. In 2005, a smart and hyperactive PR guy with

THE QUIET BLOGGING STAR IN OUR MIDST

Most of us didn't even know that our colleague Kerry Miller had a blog on the side. But her Passive Aggressive Notes, a compilation of hilarious scrawlings sent in by readers, turned into a far bigger sensation than our in-house efforts. Proving that one good idea can fly high under its own power, she generates 1.3 million page views per month and thousands of reader comments. In March, Miller quit our magazine to turn her blog into a book and to pursue another idea.

PODCASTING, FINALLY

We explained the importance of this grassroots form of radio. But it's only in this year that it has taken off. Still, rather than a revolutionary media propelled by indies, it's dominated by pros like NPR.

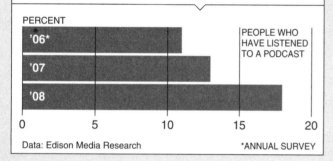

PERCENT

'06*

'07

'08

0   5   10   15   20

PEOPLE WHO HAVE LISTENED TO A PODCAST

Data: Edison Media Research   *ANNUAL SURVEY

HOW HAVE SOCIAL MEDIA AFFECTED YOUR WORLD?

We put out the question on Twitter and the Blogspotting blog and got back scores of responses—in 140 characters or less. A sampling:

mikemookie It is forcing brands to think about the person, not the target (that isn't to say that brands are actually doing it . . . yet)

jonathanfields Blogs are the big show, IM/social-hubs are backstage pass, Twitter/micro-blogging is afterparty. It's about layers of access.

AmandaMooney Just commented on ur Blogspotting post. As a graduating senior it's made a HUGE impact. The new résumé is 140 characters or less.

ekivemark The market is a flow of conversation. The best conversation happens at the water cooler. Twitter is our virtual water cooler.

ThomasEriksen Microblogging is something that 90% of us still have not figured out the purpose of. It's almost like life itself.

jspepper what's wrong is that there are a lot of snake-oil sales going on right now.

unfluff SM is instant, always-on, uber-connected communication. Great for news, chaotic in crisis, sometimes @ risk of info overload.

---

a blog could actually be a leader in tech coverage. Rubel came up with scoops. Since then, megablogs with paid staffs, such as Michael Arrington's TechCrunch and Om Malik's GigaOm, have become titans. And sites like Techmeme and Digg aggregate the hottest news—much of it from the megablogs. These are New Media champions, and they come from outside Old Media ranks. Some of them, it could be argued, wield more power than large metro dailies, or even magazines. Go to the Technorati search engine and see how many blogs link to TechCrunch, the leading source for dealmaking in Silicon Valley. Links are only one measure of influence, but a vital one in the blogosphere. The number is 170,908. That's more than (gulp) BusinessWeek.com.

Fine. TechCrunch and the others get plenty of attention. But what's it worth? Valuation is a hot question in social media. Andrew Baron, the co-founder of Rocketboom, an early video blog, had some fun with it. A few weeks ago, he announced that he was auctioning his Twitter account, which had some 1,300 followers, on eBay. Anyone who wanted an instant crowd with some influential followers could bid. (Of course, these followers might not stick around under a new regime. That was part of the risk calculation.) The bidding quickly rose above $500. As the auctioning

continued, more people (including us) signed up to follow Baron's account so they could witness this drama in action. That increase in his crowd theoretically raised the value of his Twitter property. In the end, he called it off. As we write, his following has climbed to 2,309.

While we're talking money, let's revisit one of the boldest assertions in the old article. Could a blogging bubble burst? "That's easy," we wrote, answering our own question. "No." The logic was that blogging, a free form of publishing, was anything but a highly capitalized industry. Even blog technology companies such as Six Apart and Technorati were small fry, backed by just a sliver of the venture capital in Silicon Valley. How could an industry built largely on free labor and free software develop a bubble, much less burst? It can't.

But social media sure can. Since our story, major investors and corporations have focused on the profit potential of social sites. Like Baron's Twitter crowd writ large, they promise relationships, millions of them. Such media could be worth a fortune. Strike that: They'd better be. Over the past three years, tech and media companies have been opening up their checkbooks for these properties. Google gobbled up YouTube for $1.65 billion; NewsCorp bought MySpace for $588 million; and Microsoft bought a pricey

Links

Two blogging giants, Jeff Jarvis and Arianna Huffington, give their takes on how Old Media is adjusting to the current state of the blogosphere

Jeff Jarvis, BuzzMachine

Three years ago, blogs were still a curiosity to a business audience—new enough to warrant a cover story, strange enough to require explaining. Now blogs and social media are not only better understood and accepted, but they are coming to be seen as a necessity in media and, more and more, in business.

Next, I think, *BusinessWeek*'s readers will see that social media are changing their fundamental relationship with customers to be less about serving and more about collaborating. No, I don't mean that every product will be the product of a committee. But customers who want to talk will, and smart companies will not just listen but will engage them in decisions. This will have an impact not just on PR and image but on product design, marketing, sales, customer service—the whole company.

Three years from now, I predict *BusinessWeek*'s cover won't be about blogs or tools but about companies as communities.

Arianna Huffington, Huffington Post

The growth of New Media journalism will be a hybrid combining the best aspects of traditional print newspapers with the best of what the Web brings to the table. We're getting a glimpse into this with the many changes afoot at Old Media places like the *The New York Times,* and from New Media players like, well, like the Huffington Post.

The online vs. print debate is totally obsolete. It's as musty as the old barroom argument about Ginger vs. Mary Ann. It's 2008, why not have a three-way? Traditional media have ADD: They are far too quick to drop a story. Online journalists, meanwhile, tend to have OCD—we chomp down on a story, refusing to move on until we've gotten down to the marrow.

The shifting dynamic between the forces of print and online reminds me of Sarah Connor and the T-101 in *The Terminator.* At first, the visitor from the future (digital) seemed intent on killing Sarah (print). But as the relationship progressed, the Terminator became Sarah and her son's one hope for salvation. Today, you can almost hear digital media (which for some reason has a thick Austrian accent) saying to print: "Come with me if you want to live!"

---

slice of Facebook that put a $15 billion valuation on the company. Venture firms, meanwhile, have been racing to fund scores of social media startups.

For many of them, the business plan remains blurry. Even giants like MySpace are struggling to figure out the financials. And there's no guarantee that Web masses will stay loyal for the long haul. If investors lose faith in these new ventures built on relationships, all hell could break loose.

This could convulse Wall Street, deepen the recession, sink pension funds—you name it. But you know what? The next day, we'll be back on the blogs and social networks, checking up on each other, uploading our analyses, and sussing out opportunities in the storm.

Even if the bubble bursts—and we predict it will—the power of social media to transform our businesses and society will only grow.

From *BusinessWeek,* June 2, 2008, pp. 45–50. Copyright © 2008 by BusinessWeek. Reprinted by permission of the McGraw-Hill Companies.

Personally Controlled Online Health Data—The Next Big Thing in Medical Care?

Robert Steinbrook, MD

Most physicians in the United States have paper medical records—the sort that doctors have kept for generations. A minority have electronic records that provide, at a minimum, tools for writing progress notes and prescriptions, ordering laboratory and imaging tests, and viewing test results (see line graph).[1] Yet electronic health data are poised for an online transformation that is being catalyzed by Dossia (a nonprofit consortium of major employers), Google Health, Microsoft HealthVault, and other Web services that are seeking expanded roles in the $2.1 trillion U.S. health care system.

Online repositories will allow patients to store, retrieve, manage, and share their health data—such as lists of medical problems, medical history, medications, allergies, immunizations, test results, insurance information, and doctor's visits—over the Internet. It remains uncertain, however, whether people will wish to assume these responsibilities, whether physicians and health care institutions will facilitate the process, and whether the long-term result will be improved health care and decreased costs—or simply the creation of new business opportunities.

Online repositories typically promise consumers, in the words of Google Health, "complete control over your data," meaning that personal information won't be sold or shared without the consumer's explicit permission. Repositories may have comprehensive privacy policies, and people can always delete their data or cancel their accounts. Unfortunately, promises about data privacy and security may lack legal force. Policies about advertising on repository sites vary from complete prohibitions to allowances for targeting ads and searches to users with specified personal characteristics. Data storage is usually free; there may be a fee for additional services provided by other companies or organizations.

Physicians may have little awareness of the changes that are afoot. Nonetheless, they may soon need to figure out how to work with the new services. Physicians with electronic records will have to decide whether to allow their patients to receive this information in standardized electronic formats online and use it as they wish—for example, to share it with a competing

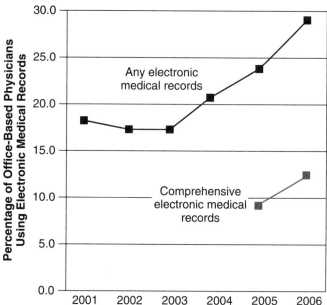

Percentage of office-based physicians in the United States using electronic medical records, 2001–2006.

Data are from Hing et al.[1] Comprehensive electronic medical records systems include, at a minimum, computerized orders for prescriptions and tests, test results (laboratory or imaging), and clinical notes.

medical group or a doctor in another part of the country. In turn, physicians will be able to receive electronic data from patients seeking care or a second opinion.

Since the 1990s, a few academic researchers have sought to develop personally controlled health records. In 2003, a working group sponsored by the Markle Foundation defined such records as "an electronic application through which individuals can access, manage and share their health information, and that of others for whom they are authorized, in a private, secure and confidential environment."

In an online survey conducted in November 2007, 91% of respondents agreed that "patients should have access to their

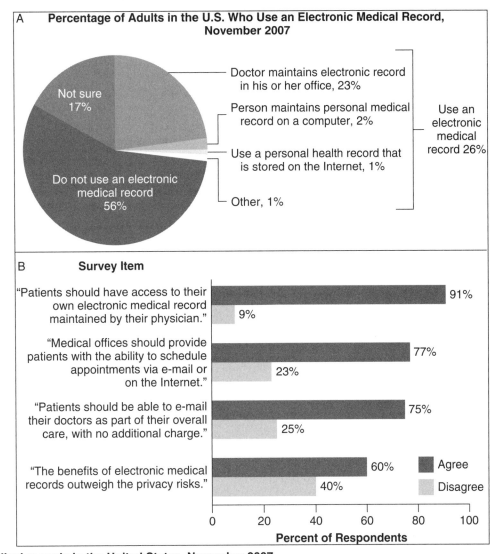

A Percentage of Adults in the U.S. Who Use an Electronic Medical Record, November 2007

Not sure 17%

Doctor maintains electronic record in his or her office, 23%

Person maintains personal medical record on a computer, 2%

Use a personal health record that is stored on the Internet, 1%

Use an electronic medical record 26%

Do not use an electronic medical record 56%

Other, 1%

B Survey Item

"Patients should have access to their own electronic medical record maintained by their physician." — 91% / 9%

"Medical offices should provide patients with the ability to schedule appointments via e-mail or on the Internet." — 77% / 23%

"Patients should be able to e-mail their doctors as part of their overall care, with no additional charge." — 75% / 25%

"The benefits of electronic medical records outweigh the privacy risks." — 60% / 40%

Agree

Disagree

Percent of Respondents

Use of electronic medical records in the United States, November 2007.

Data are from a Wall Street Journal Online/Harris Interactive Survey of 2153 adults, conducted online in the United States, November 12–14, 2007.[2] Percentages in Panel A do not sum to the total because of rounding.

own electronic medical record," and 60% agreed that "the benefits of electronic medical records outweigh the privacy risks" (see bar graph).[2] At present, however, few people have personal health records, and even fewer have personally controlled electronic health data; only 1% of respondents use a personal health record that is accessible through the Internet. Nonetheless, many patients use the Internet to e-mail their physicians, receive test results, request referrals, schedule appointments, or refill prescriptions.

If personally controlled records take off—and despite the enthusiasm of proponents, there is no assurance that they will—the electronic records maintained by physicians and hospitals will be only one component of a larger Web-based information system with national interoperability standards, in which patients increasingly control their own health data. Patients will be able to download their data from medical records, laboratories, pharmacies, and insurance-claims databases, and add data, such as measurements of weight or blood pressure. Without

carrying paper records, they will be able to share data with multiple doctors, an emergency department, or family members as necessary; renew prescriptions; manage their fitness, diet, or a chronic disease such as diabetes or congestive heart failure; communicate with people with similar health problems; or find clinical trials to participate in.

Dossia (www.dossia.org), founded by AT&T, Intel, Wal-Mart, and five other large U.S. employers, plans to offer a voluntary means of storing personally controlled health data to about 2 million employees and 5 million dependents and retirees, as well as making other services available. The platform uses an open-source technology, Indivo, developed at Children's Hospital Boston. Dossia's long-term goal is a portable and secure lifelong record that will be available regardless of a person's employer, insurance plan, or physician; employees who leave a participating organization will still be able to use the system, possibly for a fee. Pilot testing is ongoing.

Microsoft HealthVault (www.healthvault.com) allows patients to "collect, store and share health information with family members and participating healthcare providers." HealthVault, currently available only in the United States, includes a search feature, services (such as an emergency health record) to which information can be sent, and a connection center permitting the direct upload of data from compatible devices, such as those that measure heart rate, blood pressure, blood glucose, or peak airway flow. New York Presbyterian Hospital is working with Microsoft HealthVault on data exchange; however, the feature is not yet available and the exact data types are still under discussion. Microsoft indicates that it does not "use your health information for commercial purposes unless we ask and you clearly tell us we may."

Google Health is not yet publicly available. In February, the Cleveland Clinic and Google announced a pilot program that will enroll 1500 to 10,000 patients to test the platform's ability to exchange data with an electronic medical records system. Such exchanges could eventually allow patients to store all their medical records in one place and to communicate with providers, pharmacies, and online health applications.

In theory, personally controlled online health data could help to improve health, doctor–patient communications, and the coordination and quality of care and to avert medical errors—and thereby reduce the cost of care—though of course this all remains to be seen. The users who may benefit the most may be patients with complicated chronic conditions and those with episodic needs for extensive care or treatment.[3]

Because patients generally won't have to pay for storage or other costs of maintaining online health data, funding plans are largely based on anticipated revenues—revenues for hospitals and health plans from the recruitment and retention of patients who want such records, and revenues for the likes of Google and Microsoft from lucrative advertising on health-related searches. There are also anticipated savings—for insurers in the form of reductions in claims as a result of coordinating care and enrolling patients in disease-management programs, and for employers in the form of increased worker productivity and decreased health care costs for employees who become more aware of their health care needs, use wellness programs more fully, and have better-coordinated care. Of course, it is too soon to say what revenues and savings will actually materialize.

Personally controlled electronic health data may also raise new problems. The data may be incomplete, inaccurate, or difficult to verify, resulting in liability concerns for physicians who rely on them. Online data stored outside the health care system are not subject to the federal Health Insurance Portability and Accountability Act (HIPAA), which established minimum privacy and security standards for individually identifiable health information controlled by a "covered entity"—a health care provider, a health plan, or a health care clearinghouse. Because online data repositories such as Dossia, Google Health, and Microsoft HealthVault and some of their business partners are not covered entities, the data they store may not be as private as consumers assume, and a person's "control" could turn out to be limited.

Under HIPAA, every person "has a right of access to inspect and obtain a copy of protected health information," with certain exceptions (for example, psychotherapy notes). Providers, health plans, and clearinghouses must provide the information "in the form or format requested . . . if it is readily producible in such form or format," although electronic medical records are typically printed out and given to patients in paper form.

Perhaps the most widely used personal health records are hospitals' or medical groups' electronic medical records reached through a secure Web connection, or "patient portal." The portal is part of the provider's information system, and as long as patients' health data remain there, they are covered by HIPAA. Depending on state laws and organizations' policies, patients may have access to lists of their problems, medications, allergies, and test results. Progress notes are usually not available because of the level of explanation required and physicians' concerns about sharing their personal thoughts, although the patient has the right to examine the entire chart.[4] Examples of portals are PatientSite, developed at Beth Israel Deaconess Medical Center in Boston, which has about 37,000 active users, and MyChart, outpatient medical records developed by Epic Systems. Versions of MyChart are used by an estimated 2.4 million patients,[4] including about 120,000 at the Cleveland Clinic and 103,000 at the Palo Alto Medical Foundation, nearly half of all adult primary care patients. Portals can allow for secure messaging, including prescription, referral, and appointment requests, but they typically do not support data input from the patient or outside pharmacies, laboratories, physicians, or hospitals, nor do they communicate with portals at other institutions or work at all sites of care.[4]

Other personal health records, including some being established by Aetna and Well-Point, are based on insurance claims. After portability standards are implemented, patients who change coverage should be able to transfer their data between companies. Although insurers can provide data from administrative claims and can sometimes supplement them from other sources, such records lack detailed clinical information.

Dossia was announced in December 2006, Microsoft HealthVault in October 2007, and Google Health in February 2008, so their collective impact is not yet measurable. Although some physicians and patients will embrace increased use of the Internet for health care, others may prefer to watch from the sidelines as the bugs are worked out. Moreover, because legal protections have not kept pace with technological advances, Congress may wish to amend HIPAA or enact new legislation[5] to safeguard personally controlled electronic health data. If concerns about privacy, security, and commercial exploitation can be allayed, this nascent enterprise should have a smoother birth.

Notes

1. Hing ES, Burt CW, Woodwell DA. Electronic medical record use by office-based physicians and their practices: United States, 2006. Advance data from vital and health statistics. No. 393. Hyattsville, MD: National Center for Health Statistics, 2007.

2. Bright B. Benefits of electronic health records seen as outweighing privacy risks. Wall Street Journal. November 29, 2007.

3. Pagliari C, Detmer D, Singleton P. Potential of electronic personal health records. BMJ 2007;335:330-3.

4. Halamka JD, Mandl KD, Tang PC. Early experiences with personal health records. J Am Med Inform Assoc 2008;15:1–7.

5. Technologies for Restoring Users' Security and Trust in Health Information Act, HR 5442, 110th Cong. 2nd Sess (2008).

DR. STEINBROOK (rsteinbrook@attglobal.net) is a national correspondent for the *Journal*.

From *The New England Journal of Medicine,* April 17, 2008, pp. 1653–1656. Copyright © 2008 by Massachusetts Medical Society. All rights reserved. Reprinted by permission.

UNIT 3

Work and the Workplace

Unit Selections

8. **National ID: Biometrics Pinned to Social Security Cards,** Ryan Singel
9. **Dilberts of the World, Unite!,** David Sirota
10. **Computer Software Engineers,** *Occupational Outlook Handbook*
11. **How Deep Can You Probe?,** Rita Zeidner
12. **Privacy, Legislation, and Surveillance Software,** G. Daryl Nord, Tipton F. McCubbins, and Jeretta Horn Nord

Key Points to Consider

- Some European democracies require their citizens to carry government-issued identification. This has been problematic in the United States. Why do you think this is so?

- Were you surprised to learn that there is no constitutional right to privacy at work?

- Find out how workplace privacy issues are handled in other Western democracies.

- How do you feel about prospective employers searching the Internet for information about you?

- David Sirota presents the resistance of tech workers to union organization as misguided. What are two of the reasons for their resistance? Do you think that anti-union sentiment in the tech sector is misguided?

Student Website
www.mhhe.com/cls

Internet References

American Telecommuting Association
http://www.knowledgetree.com/ata-adv.html

Computers in the Workplace
http://cpsr.org/prevsite/program/workplace/workplace-home.html

InfoWeb: Techno-rage
http://www.cciw.com/content/technorage.html

STEP ON IT! Pedals: Repetitive Strain Injury
http://www.bilbo.com/rsi2.html

What About Computers in the Workplace
http://law.freeadvice.com/intellectual_property/computer_law/ computers_workplace.htm

W ork is at the center of our lives. The kind of work we do plays a part in our standard of living, our social status, and our sense of worth. This was not always the case. Read some of the great Victorian novels, and you will find a society where paid employment, at least among the upper classes, does not exist. Even those men from the nineteenth century and before, whose discoveries and writings we study and admire, approached their work as an avocation. It is hard to imagine William Wordsworth kissing his wife goodbye each morning and heading off to the English Department where he will direct a seminar in creative writing before he gets to work on a sticky line in "Ode Composed at Tintern Abbey." Or, think of Charles Darwin donning a lab coat and supervising an army of graduate students before he touches up his latest National Science Foundation proposal. In the nineteenth century, there were a handful of professionals— doctors, lawyers, professors, clergy, military officers—and a larger handful of craftsmen—joiners, millers, coopers, black-smiths, an army of agricultural workers and an increasing number of displaced peasants toiling in factories, what William Blake called England's "dark Satanic mills."

The U.S. Census records tell us that there were only 323 different occupations in 1850, the butcher, the baker, and the candle-stick maker that all children read about. The butcher is still with us, as well as the baker, but both of them work for national supermarket chains, using digitally controlled tools and managing their 401ks online. The candlestick maker has morphed into a refinery worker, watching digital displays in petrochemical plants that light up the Louisiana sky. The Canadian National Occupational Classification lists more than 25,000 occupational titles. It was once feared that, first, machines in the early twentieth century and, then, computers in the later would render work obsolete, transforming us into country gentlemen, like Charles Darwin in the utopian view or nomadic mobs of starving proletarians in the distopian.

It appears instead that fabulously productive farms and factories—as well as a third world willing to make our shoes, cloth-ing, and electronics for pennies an hour—have opened up opportunities that did not exist in Darwin's time. We are now sales clerks, health care workers, state license examiners, light truck drivers, equal opportunity compliance officers, and, yes, also software engi-neers, database analysts, website designers, and entrepreneurs.

Many of the lowest paid jobs in the new economy are held by the foreign-born, some illegally, prompting the current immigration debate. That debate, in turn, has prompted some to propose a mechanism to determine who may and may not work in the United States. One proposal is a tamper-proof Social Security card, complete with biometric data. See Ryan Singel's article, "National ID," for the details.

We have grown used to hearing stories in the news about the blush coming off the rose of software development. The computer industry is happy to reduce labor costs by outsourcing skilled work and importing cheap labor. David Sirota's piece, "Dilberts of the World, Unite!" offers a twist. Instead of just reporting on declining conditions in the computer industry, he tells us that some engi-neers in Washington State have begun to organize.

As a corrective to gloomy talk about the tech sector, take a look at the piece from the Bureau of Labor Statistics, "Computer

© The McGraw-Hill Companies Inc./John Flournoy, photographer

Software Engineers." There you will find that, news of outsourcing notwithstanding, software engineering is "expected to be among the fastest-growing occupations through the year 2016."

Another topic, much in the news, is the predictable response to employers who have learned that their applicants maintain MySpace pages. They scan them looking for information—an interest in violent films, pictures from a party that got out of hand—that didn't come up when interviewees were on their best behavior. Rita Zeidner's piece from HR Magazine, ought to please job applicants with wild oats still to sow: "Many states limit the extent to which employers can consider off duty con-duct in making a hiring decision. . . ."

We end this section with a clear advice for both employees and employers. For employees, don't expect constitutional pro-tections against unreasonable search and seizure to prevent your boss from reading your e-mail. These protections usually apply only to government action. See G. Daryl Nord and his col-leagues for a persuasive account ("Privacy, Legislation, and Surveillance Software").

National ID
Biometrics Pinned to Social Security Cards

RYAN SINGEL

The Social Security card faces its first major upgrade in 70 years under two immigration-reform proposals slated for debate this week that would add biometric information to the card and finally complete its slow metamorphosis into a national ID.

The leading immigration proposal with traction in Congress would force employers to accept only a very limited range of approved documents as proof of work eligibility, including a driver's license that meets new federal Real ID standards, a high-tech temporary work visa or a U.S. passport with an RFID chip. A fourth option is the notional tamper-proof biometric Social Security card, which would replace the text-only design that's been issued to Americans almost without change for more than 70 years.

A second proposal under consideration would add high-tech features to the Social Security card allowing employers to scan it with specially equipped laptop computers. Under that proposal, called the "Bonner Plan," the revamped Social Security card would be the only legal form of identification for employment purposes.

Neither bill specifies what the biometric would be, but it could range from a simple digital photo to a fingerprint or even an iris scan. The proposals would seem to require major changes to how Social Security cards are issued: Currently, new and replacement cards are sent in the mail. And parents typically apply for their children before they're old enough to give a decent fingerprint.

There are also logistical problems to overcome before forcing all of the nation's employers to verify a biometric card—given the nation has millions of employers, many of whom may not have computer equipment at all.

"This is an exact example of why IDs are so ludicrous as a form of security," American Civil Liberties Union legislative counsel Tim Sparapani said. "Do we really think the migrant workers are going to show up at the pickle farm and the farmer is going to demand ID and have a laptop in the field to check their ID?"

That's one of the problems that Rep. Zoe Lofgren (D-California), who heads a key House immigration subcommittee, says she's thinking about.

"There seems to be a fairly strong sentiment that there needs to be an easy way to reliably enforce whatever rules we adopt and the biometric is something being discussed in all the House bills," Lofgren told Wired News. "Obviously every small business isn't going to have a biometric card reader, but perhaps the post office might have a reader since every community in America has a post office."

The proposed biometric feature would apply to newly issued or replaced Social Security cards—you won't be asked to hand in your old one. Nevertheless, the plan doesn't sit well with privacy and civil liberties advocates like Sparapani. And immigrant-rights groups foresee rampant database errors, and an inevitable mission drift, with biometric cards—whether the Social Security card or one of the other cards pushed in the proposals—being used for purposes other than employment.

Currently, U.S. employers can accept a range of documents, including expired U.S. passports, tribal documents, refugee documents, birth certificates, driver's licenses and even school report cards, to establish an employee's eligibility for work.

Michele Waslin, the policy research director at the National Council of La Raza, a Latino civil rights group, supports immigration reform but emphasizes that employment-eligibility verification must be effective and have safeguards.

"This is one provision that would impact every single person that gets a job in the United States," Waslin said. "Given the inaccuracy of government databases, it is likely that some Americans will show documents and the answer will come back as a 'non-confirmation' and (they) could be denied employment based on a government mistake."

Waslin also fears that the existence of a document that proves immigration status will lead to widespread document checks, even from shop clerks.

"You can imagine arriving at a polling place and some people are being asked for a Real ID, while people who look 'American' aren't asked for a Real ID," Waslin said.

The controversy is likely to heat up this week. Senate Majority Leader Harry Reid is set to schedule two weeks of immigration-reform debate Tuesday, setting a deadline for a bipartisan panel of lawmakers to craft legislation that combines tighter border enforcement, avenues for current undocumented workers to earn legal status, and stringent employee-verification requirements for employers.

If they succeed, the bill will probably have roughly the same contours as the leading House bill, known as the *Strive Act*, co-authored by Reps. John Flake (R-Arizona) and Luis Gutierrez (D-Illinois).

The Strive Act would require employers to verify a new employee's credentials—by telephone or the internet—against databases maintained by the Social Security Administration and the Department of Homeland Security. If the answer comes back as a "non-confirmation," the new hire would have the opportunity to update any incorrect records.

The Strive Act's verification system is based on the Basic Pilot Program, a currently voluntary program that lets busi- nesses verify new employees' work eligibility over the web. But that program relies on databases prone to inaccuracy, according to Tyler Moran, the employment policy director at the National Immigration Law Center.

"The Basic Pilot program has given more power to employers to oppress workers," Moran said. "It's the worker's burden to prove they are work-authorized, and employers are taking adverse action when there is a problem, such as demoting or fir- ing workers before they have a chance to correct the database."

A recent report by the Social Security Administration's inspector general backs up Moran's criticism with findings that 17.8 million records in the government's employment databases contained inaccuracies that could initially and erroneously flag individuals as ineligible for employment.

From *Wired.com,* May 15, 2007, pp. online. Copyright © 2007 by Conde Nast Publications, Inc. Reprinted by permission.

Dilberts of the World, Unite!

Can a populist uprising flourish in a sector traditionally hostile to collective action?

DAVID SIROTA

In the 1990s, dot-com celebrations were happening everywhere. From Silicon Valley to Boston, from Austin to Seattle, the geeky Lambda Lambda Lambda frat brothers from *Revenge of the Nerds* were suddenly big men on campus, starting computer companies, swimming in cash—partying, as Prince might say, like it was 1999 (it actually *was* 1999). As the kegger raged upstairs, though, a group of Microsoft employees at its headquarters in Redmond, Washington, called the Washington Alliance of Technology Workers—WashTech for short—was shrieking from the basement about an impending economic massacre. Sadly, very few were listening. Now the party's over—and a white-collar uprising is on.

If you haven't heard much about this, don't blame yourself. We live in a media environment that trumpets the price of the Apple iPhone as big financial news and adultery as major political news. But the fight WashTech is contributing to is hugely important for two reasons—one is obvious, but the other is rarely discussed.

First, the obvious: the white-collar sector is growing fast. Between 1977 and 2004 the number of professional and high-skilled US workers more than doubled. The government predicts that roughly one-third of all employment growth between now and 2012 will be in the white-collar sector. In contemporary America, though, sheer size is no longer the primary determinant of change. The better gauge is demographics, which brings us to the second reason this white-collar uprising is so significant: if politics and culture still react to the mass public at all, they react almost exclusively to the upper middle professional class. That's pretty awful, but it's absolutely true. Business misbehavior, for example, was rarely a Congressional focus when CEOs were cutting blue-collar wages. But when Enron's collapse hit the stock market and undermined the retirement savings of the upper middle class, lawmakers raced to pass corporate accountability legislation. Housing affordability and predatory lending received little attention in Washington when only the working poor couldn't meet their mortgage payments. But now that defaults are convulsing Wall Street, the problem is deemed a crisis. So this white-collar uprising is not just about professional office workers and their fight. It is also about whether an uprising can flourish in the very demographic the Establishment most responds to—a demographic that also happens to be skeptical of collective action.

How did WashTech begin, and what is its role in the larger uprising roiling America? Not too long ago, on a typically gray Seattle winter day, the group's president, Marcus Courtney, sat down with me at a Starbucks in the University District to tell the story. In 1993 Courtney was one of many starry-eyed college grads who migrated to Seattle just as the tech boom was moving to warp speed. He found one of those Great Jobs at Microsoft in technical support—only his job turned out to be not so great. He was one of roughly 6,000 employees known as "permatemps," a classification that allows a company to pay a temp-agency middleman for full-time, indefinite labor. The designation, which covers roughly a quarter of Microsoft workers in the Seattle area, means employers don't have to pay regular benefits.

"Around the middle of 1997," Courtney tells me, "me and my office mate were talking about how we weren't getting real raises or cost-of-living increases, and I was like, this permatemp stuff is kinda bullshit. The contract agencies are ripping us off. I was like, God, I wonder if there's an organization to help us." So he started phoning state agencies and labor councils. "Everyone was totally fucking clueless," he says. "All anyone knew about the new economy was that people make millions. No one had any idea that here in Seattle a huge percentage of the employment is contracted out." So Courtney and two others began building an e-mail list of permatemps and other high-tech workers who were interested in getting more politically active.

In December 1997 their efforts were bolstered when the *Seattle Times* published a front-page story about how Microsoft used its connections in state government to secure a regulatory change exempting high-tech companies from having to pay temps time-and-a-half for overtime. It was a screwing of bipartisan proportions: the rule change was approved by Democratic Governor Gary Locke, and it was designed to bring the state's labor regulations into conformity with federal law, which was changed by the then-Republican Congress. The *Times* also noted that the local labor movement had hung the permatemps out to dry: two unions supported the rule change after it was revised to make sure their own members were protected.

For the uprising, the episode was like a match being dropped into a pool of gasoline. Sold out by both political parties and ignored by organized labor, "we decided to get serious," Courtney tells me. From the flames of outrage, WashTech was born. The organization's mission is straightforward: to get high-tech workers to vote to form unions so they can collectively bargain for improved wages, benefits and job security.

Microsoft countered the organizing drive by claiming that the status of the workers as permatemps meant the company had no statutory obligation to listen to the union, even though roughly two-thirds of all permatemps had been working full-time for more than a year. "Issues of collective bargaining are issues between employees and their employer," said a company spokesman at the time. "In this case, the employers are the staffing companies." The *Times* reported that when the workers and WashTech began the byzantine process of trying to bargain with four separate temp agencies, the agencies claimed that because the workers were temps, they were not "an appropriate bargaining unit under the federal labor laws." Courtney and his colleagues were caught in no man's land—call it Dilbert's Purgatory. "Permatemps were getting the worst of all worlds," Courtney says, taking a sip of coffee.

When it came to wages, they were considered high-level computer professionals, thus not entitled to overtime pay, thanks to the state ruling and change in federal law. When it came to benefits, they were treated as temps unworthy of healthcare coverage and stock options. And when it came to basic union rights, they were treated as "a second class of subordinate workers," as the former chair of the National Labor Relations Board said at the time. They had none of the organizing privileges that other company employees enjoyed.

After two failed organizing attempts, one at Microsoft and one at Amazon.com, Courtney and his allies enlisted the aid of the Communications Workers of America to build WashTech's "at large" membership—workers who are not covered by any union contract but who are sympathetic to the cause and pay $11 a month in dues. Courtney remained visible in the local media as an increasingly effective advocate for tech workers.

WashTech finally got a break in 2005. That year 900 call-center workers at Cingular in suburban Seattle voted to form a union and affiliate with WashTech. As of mid-2007 WashTech had roughly 1,500 dues-paying members—1,100 at Cingular (now AT&T) and 400 at large. It also had an e-mail list of 17,000 subscribers. Whether WashTech's work can expand the white-collar uprising beyond that, however, is very much an open question.

Certainly the conditions seem ripe. Between 2000 and 2004, 221,000 US tech jobs were eliminated as offshore outsourcing accelerated. In 2005 the Institute of Electrical and Electronics Engineers reported the first drop in median income for tech workers in the thirty-one years it had been producing annual wage and salary analyses. And WashTech's survey of IT workers found that the majority said their healthcare premiums had increased and their wages had either remained flat or dropped. As these trends have intensified, WashTech's membership has grown. Nonetheless, there are reasons that only 2 to 5.5 percent of high-tech workers are unionized—reasons that have little to do with concrete economic factors.

"Many people in these industries say, 'I hate unions' just on principle," Courtney tells me as we walk out of Starbucks. "But these same people will then go to the Mini-Microsoft website and voice their complaints because they know the company is reading the site." This constituency is a key component of today's white-collar uprising. They are swing voters, but they aren't the socially liberal, economically conservative suburbanites pundits always say are the key swing demographic in presidential elections. They are folks whose libertarianism has led them to vote Republican and dislike unions but whose economic self-interest is now pulling them in a populist direction.

According to a national poll commissioned by WashTech in late 2003, 73 percent of IT workers describe themselves as either Independents (32 percent) or Republicans (41 percent)—a demographic that is typically hostile to the ideology of the labor movement and the concept of collective action. However, an overwhelming majority of this same group told pollsters they support strongly progressive legislation to expand unemployment benefits and to prohibit government contracts from going to companies that outsource jobs. And despite decades of antiunion propaganda from industry and its allied consultants, think tanks and politicians, a majority of Americans still tell pollsters that, if given the chance, they would vote to join a union.

This sentiment persists even in the white-collar world. Groups like WashTech, however, haven't been able to expand persistent positive feelings about unions into a more mature movement because they face the Fantastic Four: a quartet of pernicious and dishonest story lines that play to tech workers' unique self-image and that discourage full participation in the uprising.

The first and most powerful of these myths is the Marlboro Man Fable. Doug, a Microsoft employee and WashTech at-large member, who asks me to use a pseudonym to protect him from blacklisting, tells me that while tech workers certainly have complaints about wages and benefits, they do not see unions as being congruent with their deeply held beliefs in "rugged individualism"—the Marlboro Man spirit that says everyone is a lone cowboy who can tough it out on his or her own. "One of the successful things the high-tech industry has done is to have sold people on the idea that if you just struggle all by yourself, you can be Bill Gates, too," he says over lunch at Microsoft's cafeteria in Redmond. "That's kind of what we sell in our whole country as the self-made man. There's no such thing, really, but that's what lots of folks believe."

The gulf between the Marlboro Man Fable and reality is one of the most combustible ingredients in today's uprising. People's economic experiences—stagnant wages, rising healthcare costs, decreasing retirement benefits—indict the fable in a far deeper way than even the best uprising leader could. However, as Doug says, the awakening has been slow in a white-collar world that matured during the go-go 1990s. The Marlboro Man Fable poses the toughest challenge to WashTech because it drills directly into white-collar workers' psychology—specifically, their belief "that interests of employers and employees are the same," as sociologist Seymour Martin Lipset found in his groundbreaking research on the subject.

Antiunionism is being sustained not solely by the Marlboro Man Fable but also by the Legend of Job Security—the second of the Fantastic Four. Shrewd corporate PR and workers' career ambitions predispose white-collar employees to view the boss and the company as inherently benevolent. Many workers believe they don't need a union because they think such benevolence will protect them from the outsourcing buzz saw. WashTech's 2005 poll showed that about half of all tech workers do not believe outsourcing will affect their jobs—even though simultaneous polls of high-tech executives show that most are planning to radically accelerate outsourcing.

Whereas surmounting the Marlboro Man Fable requires changing deep psychologies and self-images, breaking through the Legend of Job Security is a much easier task, thanks to harsh realities. Princeton economist Alan Blinder reports that up to 42 million jobs could be outsourced in the coming years, especially impersonal services like software programming. Many high-tech workers are starting to get a handle on this. "A lot of full-timers who have been at Microsoft a long time are finally believing that sometime in the next few years, five years maximum, some whole division is going to show up one Monday morning and their card keys aren't going to work," one WashTech activist tells me. "Their work will have been sent to India." WashTech has deftly played its role as information conduit to expose outsourcing practices in provocative ways. For example, the group has leaked internal Microsoft documents revealing that company managers are encouraging those under them to hire foreign workers.

The frustrations of another WashTech member, a permatemp named Rennie, illustrate the third great myth of the Fantastic Four. Like most veteran permatemps, Rennie has been trying to switch to full-time work. "I've interviewed for jobs, and they always say they are going to hire me, but before they get an offer on the table, the job gets outsourced or an H-1B gets brought in," he says in disgust. H-1B is a bland, IRS-tax-form kind of term, but it is at the heart of the Great Labor Shortage Lie.

For the better part of two decades, tech companies have complained about a dearth of high-skilled US computer programmers and engineers. This narrative is dutifully echoed by the media. A 2007 *BusinessWeek* headline is typical: Where Are All the Workers? the magazine asked, stating that "companies worldwide are suddenly scrambling to manage a labor crunch."

"They say they can't find a qualified American, but what they really mean is they can't find a *cheap* American."

—Microsoft temp worker

There's just one snag: there is no labor shortage. In 2007 a comprehensive Duke University study found "no indication of a shortage of engineers in the United States." As *BusinessWeek* admits in that same story about a supposed "global labor crunch," many "so-called shortages could quickly be solved if employers were to offer more money." But that's not happening. In fact, the magazine grudgingly acknowledged, "the strongest evidence that there's no general shortage today is that overall worker pay has barely outpaced inflation." So why is the lie still being spread? To drive down wages. To "fix" the alleged shortage, Congress in 1990 created the H-1B program, which allows employers like Microsoft to bring in temporary foreign workers for high-skill jobs. "They say they need H-1Bs because they can't find a qualified American, but what they really mean is they can't find a *cheap* American," Rennie tells me during a coffee break at his Microsoft office. His assertion is supported by the data. In 2005 the Center for Immigration Studies released a report on government statistics showing that H-1B employees are paid an average of $13,000 a year less than American workers in the same job in the same state.

Today Microsoft ranks third in the country among companies hiring H-1Bs, so Rennie works with H-1B workers all the time. His anger is not the quasinationalism of Lou Dobbs or the xenophobia of the Minutemen. The rage is not directed at H-1B workers but at people he feels are abusing the program—and chief among them, he says, is Bill Gates.

In early 2007, the richest man in America brought his boyish happy talk to the nation's capital, testifying before the Senate in an attempt to persuade lawmakers to eliminate the government's annual cap on the number of H-1B visas. Almost all the WashTech members I met brought up Gates's testimony, making sure I understood what an atrocity they think it was. Here they are, working as permatemps, and the founder of their company spits out the Great Labor Shortage Lie by telling Congress he can't find qualified full-time workers.

The union published a full-page ad in *Roll Call* to pressure Congress to oppose Gates's H-1B request. The ad was not partisan, which is smart for two reasons. First, rank-and-file tech workers have mixed partisan loyalties, and they are more likely to donate to something bipartisan. Second, the Washington problem on these issues is truly bipartisan. Republicans may be the party of Wall Street, but Democrats—thanks to oodles of tech-industry campaign contributions—have become the party of Silicon Valley. "The people in the Senate were all praising Gates, telling him, Oh, you're such a great guy," Rennie says, his hand balled up into a fist, tapping his knee. "I just couldn't believe some of the stuff that was being said."

In particular, Rennie cites the last of the Fantastic Four—the Great Education Myth. Parroted by just about everybody in business, politics and media, this fairy tale tells us that if everyone just gets a college degree, our problems with outsourcing, stagnant wages and pension cuts will magically vanish. In the white-collar world, this myth says all you have to do is go back to school and you'll be fine. But Census figures show that between 2000 and 2004, earnings of college grads dropped by more than 5 percent. The *Financial Times* reports that "earnings of average US workers with an undergraduate degree have not kept up with gains in productivity in recent decades," primarily because "a change in labor market institutions and norms [has] reduced the bargaining power of most US workers" (translation: the loss of unions has meant less worker leverage). Even *Fortune* concedes that "just maybe the jobs most threatened by outsourcing are no longer those of factory workers with a high school education . . . but those of college-educated desk workers [who] look more outsourceable by the day."

The potentially insurmountable obstacle for WashTech, though, is something it cannot fully control. It can gradually break down the Fantastic Four and update the labor movement's image for its union-averse constituency. But without the intangible of inspiration, it will be having a "fight with a windmill," as Saul Alinsky would say. Those who join the uprising do so because they are tired of a political and economic system that ignores them. But for those folks, like white-collar workers, who may be less political by nature, that feeling of disenfranchisement can serve as a suppressant. Their apolitical, nonconfrontational disposition means that they, more than most others, need an inspiration that proves the value of joining the uprising. And without that inspiration, whatever sympathies they may have are easily quashed by a sense of helplessness.

Rennie sums it up in distinctly Microsoft terms. "It's hard to change things when people turn on the television and see someone like Gates with all the Congressmen fawning all over him." They need to see something else. With the rise of populism in the 2008 election campaign, perhaps they soon will.

DAVID SIROTA is a bestselling author and nationally syndicated newspaper columnist. This article is adopted from his newest book, *The Uprising: An Unauthorized Tour of the Populist Revolt Scaring Wall Street and Washington* (Crown).

Reprinted by permission from the June 23, 2008 issue of *The Nation*. Copyright © 2008 by The Nation. For subscription information, call 1-800-333-8536. Portions of each week's Nation magazine can be accessed at www.thenation.com

Computer Software Engineers

Significant Points

- Computer software engineers are projected to be one of the fastest growing occupations over the 2004–14 period.
- Very good opportunities are expected for college graduates with at least a bachelor's degree in computer engineering or computer science and with practical work experience.
- Computer software engineers must continually strive to acquire new skills in conjunction with the rapid changes that are occurring in computer technology.

Nature of the Work

The explosive impact of computers and information technology on our everyday lives has generated a need to design and develop new computer software systems and to incorporate new technologies into a rapidly growing range of applications. The tasks performed by workers known as computer software engineers evolve quickly, reflecting new areas of specialization or changes in technology, as well as the preferences and practices of employers. Computer software engineers apply the principles and techniques of computer science, engineering, and mathematical analysis to the design, development, testing, and evaluation of the software and systems that enable computers to perform their many applications. (A separate statement on Computer hardware engineers appears elsewhere in the *Handbook.*)

Software engineers working in applications or systems development analyze users' needs and design, construct, test, and maintain computer applications software or systems. Software engineers can be involved in the design and development of many types of software, including software for operating systems and network distribution, and compilers, which convert programs for execution on a computer. In programming, or coding, software engineers instruct a computer, line by line, how to perform a function. They also solve technical problems that arise. Software engineers must possess strong programming skills, but are more concerned with developing algorithms and analyzing and solving programming problems than with actually writing code.

Computer applications software engineers analyze users' needs and design, construct, and maintain general computer applications software or specialized utility programs. These workers use different programming languages, depending on the purpose of the program. The programming languages most often used are C, C++, and Java, with Fortran and COBOL used less commonly. Some software engineers develop both packaged systems and systems software or create customized applications.

Computer systems software engineers coordinate the construction and maintenance of a company's computer systems and plan their future growth. Working with the company, they coordinate each department's computer needs—ordering, inventory, billing, and payroll recordkeeping, for example—and make suggestions about its technical direction. They also might set up the company's intranets—networks that link computers within the organization and ease communication among the various departments.

Systems software engineers work for companies that configure, implement, and install complete computer systems. These workers may be members of the marketing or sales staff, serving as the primary technical resource for sales workers and customers. They also may be involved in product sales and in providing their customers with continuing technical support. Since the selling of complex computer systems often requires substantial customization for the purchaser's organization, software engineers help to explain the requirements necessary for installing and operating the new system in the purchaser's computing environment. In addition, systems software engineers are responsible for ensuring security across the systems they are configuring.

Computer software engineers often work as part of a team that designs new hardware, software, and systems. A core team may comprise engineering, marketing, manufacturing, and design people, who work together until the product is released.

Working Conditions

Computer software engineers normally work in well-lighted and comfortable offices or laboratories in which computer equipment is located. Most software engineers work at least 40 hours a week; however, due to the project-oriented nature of the work, they also may have to work evenings or weekends to meet deadlines or solve unexpected technical problems.

Like other workers who sit for hours at a computer, typing on a keyboard, software engineers are susceptible to eyestrain, back discomfort, and hand and wrist problems such as carpal tunnel syndrome.

As they strive to improve software for users, many computer software engineers interact with customers and coworkers. Computer software engineers who are employed by software vendors and consulting firms, for example, spend much of their time away from their offices, frequently traveling overnight to meet with customers. They call on customers in businesses ranging from manufacturing plants to financial institutions.

As networks expand, software engineers may be able to use modems, laptops, e-mail, and the Internet to provide more technical support and other services from their main office, connecting to a customer's computer remotely to identify and correct developing problems.

Training, Other Qualifications, and Advancement

Most employers prefer to hire persons who have at least a bachelor's degree and broad knowledge of, and experience with, a variety of computer systems and technologies. The usual degree concentration for applications software engineers is computer science or software engineering; for systems software engineers, it is computer science or computer information systems. Graduate degrees are preferred for some of the more complex jobs.

Academic programs in software engineering emphasize software and may be offered as a degree option or in conjunction with computer science degrees. Increasing emphasis on computer security suggests that software engineers with advanced degrees that include mathematics and systems design will be sought after by software developers, government agencies, and consulting firms specializing in information assurance and security. Students seeking software engineering jobs enhance their employment opportunities by participating in internship or co-op programs offered through their schools. These experiences provide the students with broad knowledge and experience, making them more attractive candidates to employers. Inexperienced college graduates may be hired by large computer and consulting firms that train new employees in intensive, company-based programs. In many firms, new hires are mentored, and their mentors have an input into the performance evaluations of these new employees.

For systems software engineering jobs that require workers who have a college degree, a bachelor's degree in computer science or computer information systems is typical. For systems engineering jobs that place less emphasis on workers having a computer-related degree, computer training programs leading to certification are offered by systems software vendors. Nonetheless, most training authorities feel that program certification alone is not sufficient for the majority of software engineering jobs.

Persons interested in jobs as computer software engineers must have strong problem-solving and analytical skills. They also must be able to communicate effectively with team members, other staff, and the customers they meet. Because they often deal with a number of tasks simultaneously, they must be able to concentrate and pay close attention to detail.

As is the case with most occupations, advancement opportunities for computer software engineers increase with experience. Entry-level computer software engineers are likely to test and verify ongoing designs. As they become more experienced, they may become involved in designing and developing software. Eventually, they may advance to become a project manager, manager of information systems, or chief information officer. Some computer software engineers with several years of experience or expertise find lucrative opportunities working as systems designers or independent consultants or starting their own computer consulting firms.

As technological advances in the computer field continue, employers demand new skills. Computer software engineers must continually strive to acquire such skills if they wish to remain in this extremely dynamic field. For example, computer software engineers interested in working for a bank should have some expertise in finance as they integrate new technologies into the computer system of the bank. To help them keep up with the changing technology, continuing education and professional development seminars are offered by employers, software vendors, colleges and universities, private training institutions, and professional computing societies.

Employment

Computer software engineers held about 800,000 jobs in 2004. Approximately 460,000 were computer applications software engineers, and around 340,000 were computer systems software engineers. Although they are employed in most industries, the largest concentration of computer software engineers—almost 30 percent—are in computer systems design and related services. Many computer software engineers also work for establishments in other industries, such as software publishers, government agencies, manufacturers of computers and related electronic equipment, and management of companies and enterprises.

Employers of computer software engineers range from start-up companies to established industry leaders. The proliferation of Internet, e-mail, and other communications systems is expanding electronics to engineering firms that are traditionally associated with unrelated disciplines. Engineering firms specializing in building bridges and powerplants, for example, hire computer software engineers to design and develop new geographic data systems and automated drafting systems. Communications firms need computer software engineers to tap into growth in the personal communications market. Major communications companies have many job openings for both computer software applications engineers and computer systems engineers.

An increasing number of computer software engineers are employed on a temporary or contract basis, with many being self-employed, working independently as consultants. Some consultants work for firms that specialize in developing and maintaining client companies' websites and intranets. About 23,000 computer software engineers were self-employed in 2004.

Job Outlook

Computer software engineers are projected to be one of the fastest-growing occupations from 2004 to 2014. Rapid employment growth in the computer systems design and related services industry, which employs the greatest number of computer software engineers, should result in very good opportunities for those college graduates with at least a bachelor's degree in computer engineering or computer science and practical experience working with computers. Employers will continue to seek computer professionals with strong programming, systems analysis, interpersonal, and business skills. With the software industry beginning to mature, however, and with routine software engineering work being increasingly outsourced overseas, job growth will not be as rapid as during the previous decade.

Employment of computer software engineers is expected to increase much faster than the average for all occupations, as businesses and other organizations adopt and integrate new technologies and seek to maximize the efficiency of their computer systems. Competition among businesses will continue to create an incentive for increasingly sophisticated technological innovations, and organizations will need more computer software engineers to implement these changes. In addition to jobs created through employment growth, many job openings will result annually from the need to replace workers who move into managerial positions, transfer to other occupations, or leave the labor force.

Demand for computer software engineers will increase as computer networking continues to grow. For example, the expanding integration of Internet technologies and the explosive growth in electronic commerce—doing business on the Internet—have resulted in rising demand for computer software engineers who can develop Internet, intranet, and World Wide Web applications. Likewise, expanding electronic data-processing systems in business, telecommunications, government, and other settings continue to become more sophisticated and complex. Growing numbers of systems software engineers will be needed to implement,

safeguard, and update systems and resolve problems. Consulting opportunities for computer software engineers also should continue to grow as businesses seek help to manage, upgrade, and customize their increasingly complicated computer systems.

New growth areas will continue to arise from rapidly evolving technologies. The increasing uses of the Internet, the proliferation of websites, and mobile technology such as the wireless Internet have created a demand for a wide variety of new products. As individuals and businesses rely more on hand-held computers and wireless networks, it will be necessary to integrate current computer systems with this new, more mobile technology. Also, information security concerns have given rise to new software needs. Concerns over "cyber security" should result in businesses and government continuing to invest heavily in software that protects their networks and vital electronic infrastructure from attack. The expansion of this technology in the next 10 years will lead to an increased need for computer engineers to design and develop the software and systems to run these new applications and integrate them into older systems.

As with other information technology jobs, employment growth of computer software engineers may be tempered somewhat as more software development is contracted out abroad. Firms may look to cut costs by shifting operations to lower wage foreign countries with highly educated workers who have strong technical skills. At the same time, jobs in software engineering are less prone to being sent abroad compared with jobs in other computer specialties, because the occupation requires innovation and intense research and development.

Earnings

Median annual earnings of computer applications software engineers who worked full time in May 2004 were about $74,980. The middle 50 percent earned between $59,130 and $92,130. The lowest 10 percent earned less than $46,520, and the highest 10 percent earned more than $113,830. Median annual earnings in the industries employing the largest numbers of computer applications software engineers in May 2004 were as follows:

Software publishers...$79,930
Management, scientific,
  and technical consulting services.......................78,460
Computer systems design and related services.......76,910
Management of companies and enterprises...........70,520
Insurance carriers...68,440

Median annual earnings of computer systems software engineers who worked full time in May 2004 were about $79,740. The middle 50 percent earned between $63,150 and $98,220. The lowest 10 percent earned less than $50,420, and the highest 10 percent earned more than $118,350. Median annual earnings in the industries employing the largest numbers of computer systems software engineers in May 2004 are as follows:

Scientific research and development services.......$91,390
Computer and peripheral equipment
    manufacturing...87,800
Software publishers..83,670
Computer systems design and related services.......79,950
Wired telecommunications carriers........................74,370

According to the National Association of Colleges and Employers, starting salary offers for graduates with a bachelor's degree in computer engineering averaged $52,464 in 2005; offers for those with a master's degree averaged $60,354. Starting salary offers for graduates with a bachelor's degree in computer science averaged $50,820.

According to Robert Half International, starting salaries for software engineers in software development ranged from $63,250 to $92,750 in 2005. For network engineers, starting salaries in 2005 ranged from $61,250 to $88,250.

Related Occupations

Other workers who use mathematics and logic extensively include computer systems analysts, computer scientists and database administrators, computer programmers, computer hardware engineers, computer support specialists and systems administrators, engineers, statisticians, mathematicians, and actuaries.

From *Occupational Outlook Handbook,* 2006/07 Edition. Published by Bureau of Labor Statistics, U.S. Department of Labor. http://www.bls.gov/oco/

How Deep Can You Probe?

Many employers are going online to check out job candidates. But does the practice carry hidden risks?

RITA ZEIDNER

When Mary Willoughby was looking to hire a technology director, she went online to cheek out the leading candidate.

On his page on MySpace, a popular social networking site, the applicant talked at length about his interest in violent films and boasted about his romantic exploits.

Based on what she saw, Willoughby, the human resources director for a New York nonprofit that provides assistance to people with disabilities, decided to keep her search open and ultimately offered the job to someone else.

"It's not that he did anything wrong" Willoughby says of the young man she passed over. "But we're an organization that serves the disabled. We decided that this was not a good fit."

Several high-profile cases of resume fraud, widely reported by the media, underscore the problems that can occur when an applicant is not adequately vetted. Earlier this year, a previously well-regarded Massachusetts Institute of Technology admissions officer was forced to resign after admitting she lied about where she had gone to school. Last year, RadioShack Corp.'s chief executive, David Edmundson, was forced from his job for lying about his credentials.

Eager to keep their own companies' names out of the headlines, many employers are trying to be more vigilant. A recent survey by the Society for Human Resource Management (SHRM) found that nearly half of the HR professionals who responded run a candidate's name through a search engine like Google or Yahoo! before making an offer. About one in five of those HR professionals who conduct such searches said they have disqualified a candidate because of what they uncovered.

Looking for Trouble

Many employers do online background searches to identify fraudsters before they are brought on board. And even if a search turns up nothing negative about a candidate, it may help an employer show due diligence and fend off a negligent hiring charge if relations with a new hire turn ugly later.

Some 15 percent of the HR professionals who responded to the SHRM survey said they check social networking sites like MySpace and its fast-growing competitor Facebook to see what a job candidate has posted. And their ranks are likely to increase: Some 40 percent of the surveys respondents who don't now go to the sites say they are "somewhat likely" or "very likely" to visit them in the next 12 months. In most cases, checking such a site only takes a few moments.

Recruiter Tom Darrow of Talent Connections in Atlanta says he doesn't check such sites when scoping out candidates, but he can understand why employers do. Darrow offers a hypothetical example of a pharmaceutical company concerned about infiltration by radical animal fights advocates. While information about a candidate's attitude toward animal testing might not come up in an interview, or be revealed in a traditional background check, it might be disclosed on a networking site.

"The only downside of checking out the candidate's MySpace page," Darrow says, "is that it takes time."

Recognizing Hidden Risks

But some HR practitioners say they are unnerved by the trend and question whether it is ethical, responsible or even legal for employers to be trolling such sites. "I've had some heated

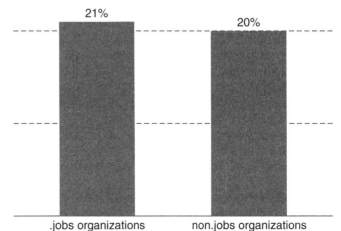

Making the Cut. Respondents who said they eliminated a job candidate based on information discovered from a search engine within the past 12 months.

Source: SHRM 2007 Advances in E-Recruiting: Leveraging the .jobs Domain.

discussions on this with my colleagues," says Willoughby of the Center for Disability Rights in Rochester, N.Y., a member of SHRM's Workplace Staffing and Deployment Special Expertise Panel who has earned SPHR certification.

Inadvertent violations of the federal Fair Credit Reporting Act (FCRA) and related state consumer protection laws are a hidden risk of online screening, according to Les Rosen, a former California deputy district attorney and a founding member of the National Association of Professional Background Screeners, a Morrisville, N.C. based trade group representing more than 500 background investigators.

The FCRA requires employers to notify job applicants and obtain their consent before conducting a background check. And while the law is geared toward obtaining official reports such as criminal histories and driving records, it's a good idea for employers doing online checks to follow the same notification and consent rules, says Rosen, author of *The Safe Hiring Manual* (On Demand Press, 2005) and head of a background screening firm. For a company bent on running Google searches on its potential hires, Rosen recommends that such an inquiry be conducted post-offer and only with the applicant's consent. An employer who changes his mind about a worker after finding disparaging information online generally would not be required to provide an explanation, Rosen says.

Employers also increase their exposure to discrimination claims when they gather too much information about a candidate. Companies suspected of rejecting a candidate based on race, religion or marital status can find themselves being hit with a claim of hiring based on unlawful factors.

Robert E. Capwell, chief knowledge officer at Employment Background Investigations Inc. in Pittsburgh, says if an employer does turn up information that a candidate could claim was used to discriminate against him or her, "You can't turn back the clock."

And just because a hiring official is turned off by the raunchy material someone posts on Facebook or MySpace doesn't mean she can use it to disqualify a candidate. Many states limit the extent to which employers can consider off-duty conduct in making a hiring decision, according to Capwell.

"If [the activity] is not related to the job and it doesn't change how the applicant does [his or her] work, then maybe it shouldn't be considered," says Capwell.

When it comes to a job candidate's political activities, the line for employers is often blurry and may depend on specific circumstances. For example, in the hypothetical case of the pharmaceutical company that is considering a candidate who criticizes animal testing on his Facebook page, "I feel, absolutely, that this is job-related," says Darrow, who maintains that an employer has the right not to hire someone who opposes the way the company does business.

Using networking sites for hiring purposes may also violate these sites' terms, some lawyers say. Both Facebook and MySpace post rules prohibiting the use of information on their sites for commercial purposes. That arguably includes vetting employment candidates. The sites also ban the collection of e-mail addresses and the dissemination of unsolicited e-mails and solicitations—common practices for many recruiters.

RedPrairie's easy-to-use Workforce Management software gives you clear visibility and control over what's happening in every one of your locations. It automatically creates legally compliant schedules, accurately closes payroll, and alerts you when there's a problem so you can take action and avoid penalties. This means there are no more payroll glitches, early clock-ins, missed meal breaks or employees with too many scheduled hours. Sound good? It's even better than you think. Check us out at www.RedPrairie.com.

Some lawyers warn that using social networking sites to vet job candidates may hurt employers by turning off good candidates who don't want the company snooping on them without their consent.

Another reason for employers to exercise caution: There's always the possibility that the information found online about job candidates simply isn't true.

Human resource consultant Becky Strickland of HR Matters in Pueblo, Colo., says she takes any information gleaned from the Internet with a grain of salt. Even an incriminating photo of a job candidate isn't necessarily proof positive that the person has engaged in bad behavior. The photo could have been created by an imposter.

"The Internet is not necessarily a reliable source" Strickland says.

Screening e Screeners

Online databases can be another potential landmine for do-it-yourself screeners. While some legitimate information is accessible to employers over the Internet for a fee, many databases shortcut background screening industry standards. Unbeknownst to their paying clients, some databases rely on incomplete data sources or on information that is out-of-date. Some databases that provide criminal histories don't distinguish between arrest records and convictions. That could be a problem since using arrest records to disqualify an employee is illegal in some states.

"National databases are a tool, but the information always needs to be verified," advises Capwell.

A thorough criminal background check almost always requires a trip to the county courthouse in each of the jurisdictions where the applicant has lived, Capwell says.

To illustrate the problem with large commercial databases, Rosen cites in his book a 2004 study in which a University of Maryland professor obtained the criminal records of 120 Virginia parolees and submitted their names to a popular online background check company. Sixty names came back showing the person had no criminal record, and other reports were so jumbled it was hard to identify specific offenses.

In some cases, database inaccuracies can prompt an employer to take the wrong action. In June, a coalition of labor, privacy and civil rights groups filed a complaint with the Federal Trade Commission urging the agency to investigate four transportation companies that fired 100 railroad workers after conducting criminal background checks. The complaint alleges that at least

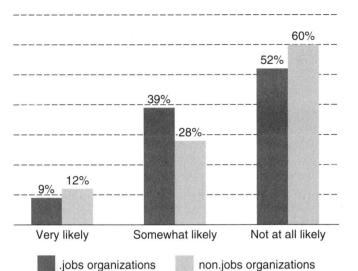

.jobs organizations **non.jobs organizations**

Using Search Engines. Respondents who indicated the likelihood that their organization will begin using search engines to review online information posted by job candidates within the next 12 months.

Source: SHRM 2007 Advances in E-Recruiting: Leveraging the .jobs Domain.

some of the firings were related to database errors. In addition, several of the workers had clean records but were victims of identity theft.

"The ability of an ordinary American to get a job, qualify for credit or even find a place to live depends increasingly on the information collected and stored by massive data aggregators," says Ari Schwartz, deputy director of the Center for Democracy and Technology in Washington, D.C., one of the groups filing the complaint. "If you're using data to make a hiring decision, there's an ethical obligation to tell the individual why you made that decision—especially if the information may not be correct."

Tapping Technology

Notwithstanding the pitfalls of the Interact, technology does provide some relief to those looking for speedy ways to identify falsehoods and root out those hiding a criminal past.

Some system designers are partnering directly with screening companies to ensure that data flows smoothly from an employer's human resource information system to a background screening company.

"If we can get data directly out of an HR system and don't have to read it off a fax or decipher someone's handwriting, we avoid the potential for error and save time," Capwell says. He can then send the information electronically to court researchers anywhere in the country for verification.

Streamlining the process even further, a few large data brokers, including Little Rock, Ark. based Acxiom and Alpharetta, Ga. based ChoicePoint have gotten into the applicant tracking business and are now marketing all-in-one applicant tracking and background checking systems.

Anne Nimke of Pinstripe Talent in Brookfield, Wis., says she depends on SkillSurvey, an online reference collection tool that allows potential employers to send a preselected set of screening questions to candidates' references via e-mail. The tool then scores the responses.

Other resources employers can access online include employment verification tools available on the websites of the Social Security Administration and the Department of Homeland Security.

Employers and background screeners also are increasingly relying on the Internet to obtain the signature necessary to conduct a background check. Many companies get authorization with a click-through process. More-advanced software allows an applicant to scribble a signature by clicking and dragging the mouse.

RITA ZEIDNER is manager of the SHRM Online HR Technology Focus Area.

From *HR Magazine,* October, 2007. Copyright © 2007 by Society for Human Resource Management. Reprinted by permission via the Copyright Clearance Center.

E-Monitoring in the Workplace

Privacy, Legislation, and Surveillance Software

Protecting the corporation while respecting employee privacy— an old puzzle made more complex with new software.

G. Daryl Nord, Tipton F. McCubbins, and Jeretta Horn Nord

"Through advanced computer technology, employers can now continuously monitor employees' actions without the employee even knowing he or she is being 'watched.' The computer's eye is unblinking and ever-present. Sophisticated software allows every minute of the day to be recorded and evaluated [1]."

Increasingly, personnel in institutions worldwide use email and the Internet on a daily basis at work. This daily reliance and dependency on technology has created new issues with respect to employee privacy in the workplace and has added new stress to the employer-employee relationship. Employee privacy, long considered a basic right, is often taken for granted by employees. However, as a result of technological monitoring, this view may be naïve.

According to the annual survey, *Workplace Monitoring and Surveillance Survey 2001* conducted by the American Management Association, more than three-quarters of all major U.S. firms (nearly double the 1997 survey results) are recording and/or reviewing the email messages, telephone calls, Internet connections, and computer files of their employees. Workplace monitoring has existed for a long time in one form or another and will undoubtedly continue to proliferate and become increasingly sophisticated as technology advances. This article examines the employer/employee workplace privacy relationship, identifies the existing federal and state law governing workplace privacy, and discusses the rapidly developing monitoring software market.

Workplace Privacy

Most U.S. citizens are accustomed to the expectation of privacy. Privacy, as defined by the Merriam-Webster dictionary is a: the quality or state of being apart from company or observation; b: freedom from unauthorized intrusion <one's right to *privacy*>. But in the workplace, to what degree can workers expect privacy and protection from observation and unauthorized intrusion? Workers may sometimes expect they have the same privacy rights at the office as they have at home. Others may assume that since they have an account number and

password on their software and email system their individual privacy is protected and secure.

Do you know anyone who occasionally takes a moment out of his or her day to check a stock quote, sports score, or movie listing online at work? As of January 2002, approximately 55 million U.S. adults accessed the Internet at work, up from 43 million in March 2000. Fifty-five percent of those with Internet access at work went online on a typical day in 2001, compared to 50% in 2000, and many were going online more frequently throughout the day than they had in 2001 [10]. More than 72% of Internet users do more than just surf the Web. Popular Internet activities include instant messaging, downloading music, and watching video clips [9]. In another Internet work-related study, Yankelovich Partners discovered that 62% of workers go online at work for personal reasons at least once a day, while about 20% do so 10 or more times a day. In a 2002 study by the Computer Security Institute (CSI), 78% of polled enterprises reported employee abuse of Internet access privileges by workers, including downloading pirated software or pornography, shopping on the Internet, and inappropriate use of email systems. These studies readily show the escalating magnitude of non-work related Internet use at work.

Employers want to make sure their employees are using company time productively and not creating a legal liability for their business as a result of harassing or offensive communications. A recent study revealed that 10% of U.S. companies have received subpoenas resulting from employee email [5]. In addition, employers have security concerns relating to the intentional or accidental sending of sensitive data via email attachments as well as the ongoing concern of viruses entering the business from outside communications. Consequently, employers are monitoring employee's computer and Internet access to a greater degree than in the past. As illustrated in Table 1, the American Management Association surveys conducted from 1999 to 2001 and again in 2005, exposed the growing trend of employer monitoring of employees' computer files, email messaging, and Internet connections [2].

Table 1   Survey Results by AMA on Employee Monitoring

	1999	2000	2001	2005
Storage and review of computer files	21.4%	30.8%	36.1%	50%
Storage and review of email messages	27%	38.1%	46.5%	55%
Monitoring Internet connections	NA	54.1%	62.8%	76%

According to another recent AMA survey, the 2003 E-mail Rules, Policies and Practices Survey, over half (52%) of employers monitor email. Three-fourths of the 1,100 employers surveyed have put written email policies in place. And 22% have terminated an employee for violating email policy [3].

Federal Privacy Legislation in the Workplace

Most U.S.-based employees assume they have a constitutional right to privacy. However, constitutional rights to privacy are generally inferred through the U.S. Constitution's Fourth Amendment's rights to freedom from unreasonable search and seizure. These freedoms usually apply only to state actions. In an employment context, state actions are fairly narrowly limited to protecting federal, state, and municipal employees. Private-sector employees must look elsewhere for protection. Possible sources for such protection from employer snooping include federal legislation and state common law tort actions such as invasion of privacy [4].

The primary piece of federal legislation suggesting employee privacy interest is the Electronic Communications Privacy Act (ECPA). However, there are three exceptions under the ECPA that effectively eliminate any substantial expectation of privacy an employee might have with respect to his/her employer.

Workplace monitoring has existed for a long time in one form or another and will undoubtedly continue to proliferate and become increasingly sophisticated as technology advances.

The first of the ECPA exceptions is the "provider exception." If an employer actually owns and is providing the telephone, email, or Internet services to the employee being monitored, there is little doubt that the employer is protected from employee privacy claims. However, if the employer is merely providing email services through a third-party Internet provider, it is not as clear that the employer would enjoy the same protection. Nevertheless, given the fact the employer is "providing" the provider, coupled with the generous interpretation that most courts have granted employers, there is good reason to believe that even these providers of providers would enjoy protection from employee privacy suits [7].

The second exception is the "ordinary course of business" exception. It really provides an exception to the definition of an electronic device, and therefore excludes the employer's monitoring from the ECPA and the employee protections provided therein. Under this exception the employer may monitor employee communications to ensure such legitimate business objectives as assuring quality control, preventing sexual harassment, and preventing unauthorized use of equipment, such as excessive telephone or email usage.

However, the "course of business" language also implies a limitation on the extent of monitoring in the event the employer discovers he has accessed a personal conversation. In monitoring telephone conversations it is well established that employers can continue to listen only for so long as it takes to determine the conversation is in fact personal. At that point, the employer must cease the surveillance. The case setting the standard for this limitation is a 1983 case dealing with the use of the telephone. A thorough examination of the standard as it applies to email usage has not yet occurred, but a similar application should probably be expected. However, at least one case has suggested that no monitoring of an employee's personal email may be allowed without prior notification [8].

The third exception is the "consent" exception. If at least one party to the communication is either the party who intercepts the communication or gives consent to the interception then the ECPA has not been violated. The "consent" exception apparently applies even when the sender of the intercepted communication has been assured that all email communications would remain confidential and privileged. In *Smyth v. The Pillsbury Company,* Smyth sent his supervisor emails that contained inappropriate and unprofessional comments from Smyth's home computer. The supervisor received the email over Pillsbury's email system. The email included such statements such as "kill the backstabbing . . . " and referred to the company's holiday party as the "Jim Jones Koolaid affair." At a later date the company intercepted these email messages and terminated Smyth's employment based upon their content.

Although the court did not explain exactly how the interception took place, the email messages were apparently retrieved from storage with the supervisor's consent. As a result of the consent, even the prior promise of confidentiality did not provide the employee with privacy protection.

State Privacy Case Law

The common law tort of invasion of privacy is recognized by most states. The Restatement (Second) of Torts §652B defines invasion of privacy as: " . . . intentionally intruding, physically or otherwise, upon the solitude or seclusion of another . . . , if the intrusion would be highly offensive to a reasonable person." Employees have tried to use this tort as a protection for privacy in the workplace. Although it shows some potential for privacy protection, it has generally stumbled over two problems. The first is that the employee must have a reasonable expectation of privacy, and the second is that the intrusion would be highly offensive to the reasonable person.

Along with the ever-increasing exploitation of technology in the workplace has come the capability for employers to see and measure nearly every aspect of company usage.

In *McLaren v. Microsoft* (1999), Microsoft made available to McLaren, as part of his employment, use of an email system owned and administered by Microsoft. McLaren had the right and ability to store email he received either in the server-based "inbox" or in a "personal folder" protected by a personal store password. As part of a harassment investigation, Microsoft decrypted McLaren's personal store password and broke into his personal folder even though it had been specifically requested by McLaren not to do so.

McLaren argued that the password-protected personal folder was basically the same as a locked storage locker provided by a company for employees to store personal items in while at work. It has long been accepted that employees have a legitimate expectation of privacy with regard to such lockers. However, the court rejected this argument. It stated that because the email was first received and stored in the "inbox," which was subject to inspection, McLaren could have no expectation of privacy simply by moving it to a protected folder. How this is different from a telephone call that can only be monitored long enough to determine if it is of a business or personal nature the court did not explain. True, in this case, the fact that the email messages were pertinent to a harassment investigation would make them subject to legitimate business scrutiny. However, the court did not seem to rely on this fact in declaring a blanket open season on email monitoring. Second, although it is possible to distinguish between illicit information being carried through public space from the front door of a business to an employee's locked storage locker and an email message sitting in an inbox before being transferred to a protected personal folder, such distinctions are not so obvious as to deny a need for recognition. However the court seemed sufficiently confident in its analysis that it did not address the issue.

In determining that the intrusion was not highly offensive, the court properly recognized the importance of whether the intrusion was justified. The fact that McLaren was under investigation, and that he had notified Microsoft that the email was relevant to that investigation, clearly support the court's finding that Microsoft's actions were justified. Therefore, they were not highly offensive even though the actions had been specifically forbidden by McLaren and led to his dismissal.

Company Electronic Communications Policy

In a case [11] in which the California Appellant Court ruled in favor of the employer strictly on the basis of a signed electronic communications policy, the court stated that at a minimum the policy should contain a statement that:

1. Electronic communication facilities provided by the company are owned by the company and should be used solely for company business.
2. The company will monitor all employee Internet and email usage. It should state who may review the information, the purposes for which the information may be used, and that the information may be stored on a separate computer [6, 7].
3. The company will keep copies of the Internet and email passwords.
4. The existence of a separate password is not an assurance of the confidentiality of the communication or other "protected" material.

5. The sending of any discriminatory, offensive, or unprofessional message or content is strictly prohibited.
6. The accessing of any Internet site that contains offensive of discriminatory content is prohibited.
7. The posting of personal opinions on the Internet using the company's access is strictly prohibited. This is particularly true of, but not limited to, opinions that are political or discriminatory in nature.
8. Although not included in the court's list, the policy should clearly state potential repercussions to the employee for violating the policy [4].

Legally, these requirements are considered minimum standards that a sound policy should meet. They should be clear and unequivocal, and they should be read and signed by each employee. However, the employer should also remain aware of the employee's normal human desire for reasonable amounts of privacy. Therefore the employer should try to minimize unnecessary intrusion into this privacy expectation in order to reduce the negative impact on employee morale.

Monitoring Software

Along with the ever-increasing exploitation of technology in the workplace has come the capability for employers to see and measure nearly every aspect of company computer usage. The dilemma that employers must resolve is how to balance the obvious benefits of employee use of technological tools with the risks inherent in providing those tools to employees. As stated earlier, many employers have sought to achieve this balance by electronically monitoring the use that their employees make of email, the Internet, and other computer-related activities.

Monitoring software allows employers to see, measure, and manage employees' computer systems, monitors, disks, software, email, and Web and Internet access. The software can automatically archive all collected information into a corporate network server for review at a later time. The list in Table 2 illustrates the many capabilities of typical monitoring software readily available on the market today by companies such as Spectorsoft and DynaComm.

Conclusion

E-monitoring and employee workplace privacy are issues that will continue to present questions and problems for some time to come. In addition, it looks as if there will be ongoing efforts to balance employee workplace privacy with the need for employers to manage and protect company resources from non-productive, non-work related activities. Federal and state legislation governing monitoring and workplace privacy will undoubtedly continue to evolve and be tested in the court systems.

There are many legitimate reasons for organizations to want to know what is occurring on their computer systems. Those reasons range from workplace harassment, to loss of productivity, and even to company sabotage. Therefore, it is easy to understand why it would be prudent for companies to have such a strong incentive to find a healthy balance between employee privacy rights and organizational concerns.

Table 2 Surveillance Capabilities of Monitoring Software on the Market Today

The workplace end user types any keystroke in any window on his/her remote PC, that text appears on the network administrator's screen in real time or archived to a corporate server.

Typed text that is monitored may include email messages, online chat conversations, documents, passwords and all other keystrokes.

The network administrator can view the actual screen of the workplace desktops being monitored.

Internet usage can be monitored in real time and a log file recording of all Internet activity can be made.

A spy module can see and list software running on the remote PC and can view in real time the software applications and run executions.

A record and activity log for all workstations on the local or shared network location can be produced.

Monitoring software provides the ability to take snapshots of a remote PC screen or active window in specified time intervals and save them on the local or shared network location.

The workplace user's system can be turned off, restarted, and actually logged completely off the network.

The network administrator can run programs and execute commands on remote computers, open Web pages or documents, send instant messages for remote users, and terminate remote processes.

Files can be readily copied including logs and screenshots from the desktop computers. The administrator can have the same file access permissions, as a current user has on the workplace computer.

Multiple employee computers can simultaneously be monitored from a single workstation in the LAN.

Workplace surveillance software that runs on monitored computers is hidden and difficult for an employee to locate or even know that the software is present and monitoring their every keystroke. The monitoring software usually cannot be terminated without the network administrator's permission.

References

1. American Civil Liberties Union (ACLU). Workplace Rights on Electronic Monitoring, ACLU online archives; archive.aclu.org/issues/worker/legkit2.html

2. American Management Association, AMA Research: Workplace Monitoring and Surveillance, 1999, 2000, 2001 and 2005; www.amanet.org/research/archive_2001_1999.htm

3. American Management Association, Survey on Workplace E-Mail Reveals Disasters in the Making, May 28, 2003; www.amanet.org/press/amanews/Email_Survey2003.htm

4. Bloom, E., Schachter, M., and Steelman, E. Justice in a Changing World: Competing Interests in the Post 9-11 Workplace: The New Line Between Privacy and Safety. 29 Wm. Mitchell L. Rev. 897 (2003).

5. Crimmins, J. Even federal judges come under surveillance when online. *Chicago Daily Law Bulletin 147,* 159 (Aug. 14, 2001).

6. *Deal v. Spears,* 980 F.2d 1153, 1155-1157 (8th Cir. 1992).

7. DiLuzio, S. Workplace E-Mail: It's Not as Private as You Might Think. 25 Del. J. Corp. L. 741 (2000).

8. Kopp, K. Electronic Communications in the Workplace: E-Mail Monitoring and the Right of Privacy. 8 Seaton Hall Const. L. J. 861 (1998).

9. Neilson//NetRankings, U.S. Online Population Internet Use. (Dec. 18, 2002); www.nielsen-netratings.com/pr/pr_021218.pdf

10. Pew Internet & American Life, Getting Serious Online: As Americans Gain Experience, They Use the Web More at Work, Write Emails with More Significant Content, Perform More Online Transactions, and Pursue More Serious Activities, (Mar. 3, 2002); www.pewinternet.org/reports/toc.asp?Report555

11. *TBG Insurance Services Corporation v. The Superior Court of Los Angeles Co.;* Robert Zieminski, Real Party in Interest, 96 Cal. App. 4th 443; 117 Cal. Rptr. 2d 155 (Cal. App. 2002).

G. DARYL NORD (daryl.nord@okstate.edu) is a professor of Management Science & Information Systems in the William S. Spears School of Business, at Oklahoma State University, Stillwater, OK. **TIPTON F. MCCUBBINS** (tipton.mccubbins@okstate.edu) is an associate professor of Legal Studies in Business in the William S. Spears School of Business, at Oklahoma State University, Stillwater, OK. **JERETTA HORN NORD** (jeretta.nord@okstate.edu) is a professor of Management Science & Information Systems and Associate Dean for Undergraduate Programs in the William S. Spears School of Business, at Oklahoma State University, Stillwater, OK.

From *Communications of the ACM,* 49(8), August 2006, pp. 73–77. Copyright © 2006 by Association for Computing Machinery. Reprinted by permission.

UNIT 4

Computers, People, and Social Participation

Unit Selections

Key Points to Consider

- The overview to this unit mentions de Tocqueville's observation that Americans tend to form civic associations and Putnam's argument that this tendency is declining. Do you think that computing has played any part in the decline? What does Putnam say? What do other scholars say about Putnam's work?

- Ben Franklin's autobiography is considered a classic of American literature. There, he describes several civic associations that he formed in early Philadelphia. What were they?

- Social scientists sometimes say that the likelihood of participating in civic life declines 10 percent for every ten miles one commutes. What is the source for this figure? Is there a similar figure relating civic participation to daily minutes spent online?

- Carr ("Is Google Making Us Stupid?") quotes Friedrich Nietsche on the typewriter: "Your are right, . . ., our writing equipment takes part in forming our thoughts." Use the Internet to find out who Walter J. Ong was. What does he have to say about writing and thought? How about Marshall McLuhan? How did these two early students of media studies know one another?

- Deresiewicz's piece ("The End of Solitude") is a cry from the heart. Do you agree when he says that "If six hours of television a day creates the aptitude for boredom, the inability to sit still, a hundred text messages a day creates the aptitude for loneliness, the inability to be by yourself"?

- Do you read books for pleasure? What about your family?

- Have you been cyberbullied? Were you surprised to learn that ("It's Not Easy to Stand up to Cyberbullies") "there seems to be little that concerned institutions (or their besmirched students) can do to clean up their electronic neighborhoods"? Use the Internet to find instances of cyberbullying in the news and how these have been treated by the courts.

- Would you like the option of tracking your exercise routine via personal sensors and a social networking site?

- Do you prefer viewing your favorite newspaper on the Web or in the print version? What do you gain or lose with each version?

- Do you use e-mail? If so, in what capacity?

Student Website

www.mhhe.com/cls

Internet References

Alliance for Childhood: Computers and Children
http://drupal6.allianceforchildhood.org/computer_position_statement

The Core Rules of Netiquette
http://www.albion.com/netiquette/corerules.html

SocioSite: Networks, Groups, and Social Interaction
http://www.sociosite.net

The early and astute observer of American culture, Alexis de Tocqueville (1805–1859), had this to say about the proclivity of Americans to form civic associations:

> Americans of all ages, all conditions, and all dispositions constantly form associations. . . . The Americans make associations to give entertainments, to found seminaries, to build inns, to construct churches, to diffuse books, to send missionaries to the Antipodes; in this manner they found hospitals, prisons, and schools. If it is proposed to inculcate some truth or to foster some feeling by the encouragement of a great example, they form a society. Wherever at the head of some new undertaking you see the government in France, or a man of rank in England, in the United States you will be sure to find an association. . . . The first time I heard in the United States that a hundred thousand men had bound themselves publicly to abstain from spiritous liquors, it appeared to me more like a joke than a serious engagement, and I did not at once perceive why these temperate citizens could not content themselves with drinking water by their own firesides. . . . Nothing, in my opinion is more deserving of our attention than the intellectual and moral associations of America. . . . In democratic countries the science of association is the mother of science; the progress of all the rest depends upon the progress it has made (Tocqueville, 1945, v. 2, pp. 114–118).

He laid this tendency squarely at the feet of democracy. If all men—we're talking about the first half of the 19th century here—are equal before the law, then, to do any civic good requires that these equal, but individually powerless, men band together.

A century and a half later, we have the technical means to communicate almost instantly and effortlessly across great distances. But we are banding together less. In 1995, Robert D. Putnam made the news with an article, later expanded into a book, called *Bowling Alone* (Putnam 2000). He argued that the civil associations de Tocqueville had noticed so long ago were breaking down. Americans were not joining the PTA, the Boy Scouts, the local garden club, or bowling leagues in their former numbers. Putnam discovered that although more people are bowling than ever, participation in leagues was down by 40 percent since 1980. The consequences for a functioning democracy are severe.

Although the articles in this unit do not directly address the idea of civic participation, one question is the glue that holds them together. Do computers assist or detract from civic life? Another French social observer, Emile Durkheim (1858–1917), argued that a vital society must have members who feel a sense of community. Community is easily evident in preindustrial societies where kinship ties, shared religious belief, and custom reinforce group identity and shared values. Not so in modern societies, particularly in the United States, where a mobile population commutes long distances and retreats each evening to the sanctity and seclusion of individual homes. Contemporary visitors to the United States are struck by the cultural cafeteria available to Americans. They find a dizzying array of religions, beliefs, moral

© Getty Images/Stockbyte

and philosophical perspectives, modes of social interaction, entertainment venues and, now, networked computers. One need only observe a teenager frantically instant-messaging her friends from a darkened bedroom to know that while computer technology has surely given us great things, it has taken away something as well. The capacity to maintain friendships without face-to-face contact, the ability to construct a computer profile that edits anything not in line with one's interests, seems to push society a step closer to self-interested individualism.

Or does it? One can argue that the new communications technologies permit relationships that were never before possible. To cite a large example, moveon.org organized many thousands of people, in a matter of weeks, entirely over the Internet, to oppose the invasion of Iraq in the spring of 2003. Or a smaller one. Immigration, always a wrenching experience, is less wrenching now, since immigrants to the United States can be in daily touch with their families across the globe. Or consider how the virtual bazaar, eBay, surely one of the extraordinary aspects of the Internet, puts Americans in touch with Japanese, Latvians, Montenegrans, peoples whom we might never have known. Recall Postman: "Technology giveth and technology taketh away."

What technology seems to have taken away in the past few years is the ability either to concentrate or to be alone, at least according to the first two articles in this unit. For a contrary view, see Steven Johnson's book, *Everything Bad Is Good for You* (Riverhead, 2005).

One person who is not fretting about the new technologies is Ashley Qualls. She founded WhateverLife.com, a website that supplies designs for MySpace pages. When she was offered $1.5 million "and a car of her choice—as long as the price tag wasn't more than $100,000," the seventeen-year-old promptly dropped out of school to manage her improbable company. Read about it in Chuck Salter's "Girl Power."

It's easy enough for commentators of a certain age to find fault with emerging technologies. Read Negar Azimi's piece,

"Bloggers Against Torture," to get another perspective. Activists in developing nations are turning to blogs to evade tight media controls. The story of Emad Mohamed Ali Mohamed, a young Egyptian bus driver, whose torture at the hands of police had been videotaped and passed around Egyptian blogs, is evidence enough to reverse Postman (Article 1): "Though technology taketh away, it also giveth."

But there's a dark side to blogging. What can you do when you're the innocent victim of a scurrilous blogger, something we now describe with the newly minted term, "cyberbullying"? Not much, as it happens. Read Robert O'Neil's piece ("It's Not Easy to Stand up to Cyberbullies, but We Must") to see why. If we're no longer forming civic associations, we can still go to the gym, each in his or her own ipod-controlled space. Our workouts can be better than ever, thanks to computer technology (see "The Nike Experiment").

A civil society is unimaginable without a free press. Yet in the United States, the readership of newspapers is declining, along with the numbers watching TV news, the very medium that did away with so many afternoon papers not long ago. While TV news has added the aggressive editorializing of Lou Dobbs and Bill O'Reilly, large newspapers have developed websites to generate readership and revenue. "Center Stage" tells the story of several online newsrooms. Here we learn that "with many people posting and without fixed schedules, it is impractical to funnel all content through a copy desk. So a fair amount of copy produced by the Web staff gets little or no editing, and few items get the multiple reads routine in print."

Just when universities thought they had saved money by emailing everything to students, the students began texting and logging in to social networking sites. What's an administrator to do? See "E-Mail Is for Old People" for a peek at how they try to keep up with student taste in electronic communication.

References

Tocqueville, Alexis de. (1945). *Democracy in America.* New York: Vintage Books.

Putnam, Robert D. (2000). *Bowling Alone: The Collapse and Revival of American Community.* New York: Simon & Schuster.

Is Google Making Us Stupid?

What the internet is doing to our brains.

NICHOLAS CARR

"Dave, stop. Stop, will you? Stop, Dave. Will you stop, Dave?" So the supercomputer HAL pleads with the implacable astronaut Dave Bowman in a famous and weirdly poignant scene toward the end of Stanley Kubrick's *2001: A Space Odyssey*. Bowman, having nearly been sent to a deep-space death by the malfunctioning machine, is calmly, coldly disconnecting the memory circuits that control its artificial brain. "Dave, my mind is going," HAL says, forlornly. "I can feel it. I can feel it. I'm afraid."

I can feel it, too. Over the past few years I've had an uncomfortable sense that someone, or something, has been tinkering with my brain, remapping the neural circuitry, reprogramming the memory. My mind isn't going—so far as I can tell—but it's changing. I'm not thinking the way I used to think. I can feel it most strongly when I'm reading. Immersing myself in a book or a lengthy article used to be easy. My mind would get caught up in the narrative or the turns of the argument, and I'd spend hours strolling through long stretches of prose. That's rarely the case anymore. Now my concentration often starts to drift after two or three pages. I get fidgety, lose the thread, begin looking for something else to do. I feel as if I'm always dragging my wayward brain back to the text. The deep reading that used to come naturally has become a struggle.

I think I know what's going on. For more than a decade now, I've been spending a lot of time online, searching and surfing and sometimes adding to the great databases of the Internet. The Web has been a godsend to me as a writer. Research that once required days in the stacks or periodical rooms of libraries can now be done in minutes. A few Google searches, some quick clicks on hyperlinks, and I've got the telltale fact or pithy quote I was after. Even when I'm not working, I'm as likely as not to be foraging in the Web's info-thickets' reading and writing e-mails, scanning headlines and blog posts, watching videos and listening to podcasts, or just tripping from link to link to link. (Unlike footnotes, to which they're sometimes likened, hyperlinks don't merely point to related works; they propel you toward them.)

For me, as for others, the Net is becoming a universal medium, the conduit for most of the information that flows through my eyes and ears and into my mind. The advantages of having immediate access to such an incredibly rich store of information are many, and they've been widely described and duly applauded. "The perfect recall of silicon memory," *Wired*'s Clive Thompson has written, "can be an enormous boon to thinking." But that boon comes at a price. As the media theorist Marshall McLuhan pointed out in the 1960s, media are not just passive channels of information. They supply the stuff of thought, but they also shape the process of thought. And what the Net seems to be doing is chipping away my capacity for concentration and contemplation. My mind now expects to take in information the way the Net distributes it: in a swiftly moving stream of particles. Once I was a scuba diver in the sea of words. Now I zip along the surface like a guy on a Jet Ski.

I'm not the only one. When I mention my troubles with reading to friends and acquaintances—literary types, most of them—many say they're having similar experiences. The more they use the Web, the more they have to fight to stay focused on long pieces of writing. Some of the bloggers I follow have also begun mentioning the phenomenon. Scott Karp, who writes a blog about online media, recently confessed that he has stopped reading books altogether. "I was a lit major in college, and used to be [a] voracious book reader," he wrote. "What happened?" He speculates on the answer: "What if I do all my reading on the web not so much because the way I read has changed, i.e. I'm just seeking convenience, but because the way I THINK has changed?"

Bruce Friedman, who blogs regularly about the use of computers in medicine, also has described how the Internet has altered his mental habits. "I now have almost totally lost the ability to read and absorb a longish article on the web or in print," he wrote earlier this year. A pathologist who has long been on the faculty of the University of Michigan Medical School, Friedman elaborated on his comment in a telephone conversation with me. His thinking, he said, has taken on a "staccato" quality, reflecting the way he quickly scans short passages of text from many sources online. "I can't read *War and Peace* anymore," he admitted. "I've lost the ability to do that. Even a blog post of more than three or four paragraphs is too much to absorb. I skim it."

Anecdotes alone don't prove much. And we still await the long-term neurological and psychological experiments that will provide a definitive picture of how Internet use affects cognition. But a recently published study of online research habits, conducted by scholars from University College London, suggests that we may well be in the midst of a sea change in the way we read and think. As part of the five-year research program, the scholars examined computer logs documenting the behavior of visitors to two popular research sites, one operated by the British Library and one by a U.K. educational consortium, that provide access to journal articles, e-books, and other sources of written information. They found that people using the sites exhibited "a form of skimming activity," hopping from one source to another and rarely returning to any source they'd already visited. They typically read no more than one or two pages of an article or book before they would "bounce" out to another site. Sometimes they'd save a long article, but there's no evidence that they ever went back and actually read it. The authors of the study report:

> It is clear that users are not reading online in the traditional sense; indeed there are signs that new forms of "reading" are emerging as users "power browse" horizontally through titles, contents pages and abstracts going for quick wins. It almost seems that they go online to avoid reading in the traditional sense.

Thanks to the ubiquity of text on the Internet, not to mention the popularity of text-messaging on cell phones, we may well be reading more today than we did in the 1970s or 1980s, when television was our medium of choice. But it's a different kind of reading, and behind it lies a different kind of thinking—perhaps even a new sense of the self. "We are not only *what* we read," says Maryanne Wolf, a developmental psychologist at Tufts University and the author of *Proust and the Squid: The Story and Science of the Reading Brain.* "We are *how* we read." Wolf worries that the style of reading promoted by the Net, a style that puts "efficiency" and "immediacy" above all else, may be weakening our capacity for the kind of deep reading that emerged when an earlier technology, the printing press, made long and complex works of prose commonplace. When we read online, she says, we tend to become "mere decoders of information." Our ability to interpret text, to make the rich mental connections that form when we read deeply and without distraction, remains largely disengaged.

Reading, explains Wolf, is not an instinctive skill for human beings. It's not etched into our genes the way speech is. We have to teach our minds how to translate the symbolic characters we see into the language we understand. And the media or other technologies we use in learning and practicing the craft of reading play an important part in shaping the neural circuits inside our brains. Experiments demonstrate that readers of ideograms, such as the Chinese, develop a mental circuitry for reading that is very different from the circuitry found in those of us whose written language employs an alphabet. The variations extend across many regions of the brain, including those that govern such essential cognitive functions as memory and the interpretation of visual and auditory stimuli. We can expect as well that the circuits woven by our use of the Net will be different from those woven by our reading of books and other printed works.

S ometime in 1882, Friedrich Nietzsche bought a typewriter— a Malling-Hansen Writing Ball, to be precise. His vision was failing, and keeping his eyes focused on a page had become exhausting and painful, often bringing on crushing headaches. He had been forced to curtail his writing, and he feared that he would soon have to give it up. The typewriter rescued him, at least for a time. Once he had mastered touch-typing, he was able to write with his eyes closed, using only the tips of his fingers. Words could once again flow from his mind to the page.

But the machine had a subtler effect on his work. One of Nietzsche's friends, a composer, noticed a change in the style of his writing. His already terse prose had become even tighter, more telegraphic. "Perhaps you will through this instrument even take to

---

Also See

Living with a Computer
(July 1982)

"The process works this way. When I sit down to write a letter or start the first draft of an article, I simply type on the keyboard and the words appear on the screen . . ."
—James Fallows

---

a new idiom," the friend wrote in a letter, noting that, in his own work, his " 'thoughts' in music and language often depend on the quality of pen and paper."

"You are right," Nietzsche replied, "our writing equipment takes part in the forming of our thoughts." Under the sway of the machine, writes the German media scholar Friedrich A. Kittler, Nietzsche's prose "changed from arguments to aphorisms, from thoughts to puns, from rhetoric to telegram style."

The human brain is almost infinitely malleable. People used to think that our mental meshwork, the dense connections formed among the 100 billion or so neurons inside our skulls, was largely fixed by the time we reached adulthood. But brain researchers have discovered that that's not the case. James Olds, a professor of neuroscience who directs the Krasnow Institute for Advanced Study at George Mason University, says that even the adult mind "is very plastic." Nerve cells routinely break old connections and form new ones. "The brain," according to Olds, "has the ability to reprogram itself on the fly, altering the way it functions."

As we use what the sociologist Daniel Bell has called our "intellectual technologies"—the tools that extend our mental rather than our physical capacities—we inevitably begin to take on the qualities of those technologies. The mechanical clock, which came into common use in the 14th century, provides a compelling example. In *Technics and Civilization,* the historian and cultural critic Lewis Mumford described how the clock "disassociated time from human events and helped create the belief in an independent world of mathematically measurable sequences." The "abstract framework of divided time" became "the point of reference for both action and thought."

The clock's methodical ticking helped bring into being the scientific mind and the scientific man. But it also took something away. As the late MIT computer scientist Joseph Weizenbaum observed in his 1976 book, *Computer Power and Human Reason: From Judgment to Calculation,* the conception of the world that emerged from the widespread use of timekeeping instruments "remains an impoverished version of the older one, for it rests on a rejection of those direct experiences that formed the basis for, and indeed constituted, the old reality." In deciding when to eat, to work, to sleep, to rise, we stopped listening to our senses and started obeying the clock.

The process of adapting to new intellectual technologies is reflected in the changing metaphors we use to explain ourselves to ourselves. When the mechanical clock arrived, people began thinking of their brains as operating "like clockwork." Today, in the age of software, we have come to think of them as operating "like computers." But the changes, neuroscience tells us, go much deeper than metaphor. Thanks to our brain's plasticity, the adaptation occurs also at a biological level.

The Internet promises to have particularly far-reaching effects on cognition. In a paper published in 1936, the British mathematician Alan Turing proved that a digital computer, which at the time existed only as a theoretical machine, could be programmed to perform the function of any other information-processing device. And that's what we're seeing today. The Internet, an immeasurably powerful computing system, is subsuming most of our other intellectual technologies. It's becoming our map and our clock, our printing press and our typewriter, our calculator and our telephone, and our radio and TV.

When the Net absorbs a medium, that medium is re-created in the Net's image. It injects the medium's content with hyperlinks, blinking ads, and other digital gewgaws, and it surrounds the content with the content of all the other media it has absorbed. A new e-mail message, for instance, may announce its arrival as we're glancing over the latest headlines at a newspaper's site. The result is to scatter our attention and diffuse our concentration.

The Net's influence doesn't end at the edges of a computer screen, either. As people's minds become attuned to the crazy quilt of Internet media, traditional media have to adapt to the audience's new expectations. Television programs add text crawls and pop-up ads, and magazines and newspapers shorten their articles, introduce capsule summaries, and crowd their pages with easy-to-browse info-snippets. When, in March of this year, *The New York Times* decided to devote the second and third pages of every edition to article abstracts, its design director, Tom Bodkin, explained that the "shortcuts" would give harried readers a quick "taste" of the day's news, sparing them the "less efficient" method of actually turning the pages and reading the articles. Old media have little choice but to play by the new-media rules.

Never has a communications system played so many roles in our lives—or exerted such broad influence over our thoughts—as the Internet does today. Yet, for all that's been written about the Net, there's been little consideration of how, exactly, it's reprogramming us. The Net's intellectual ethic remains obscure.

About the same time that Nietzsche started using his typewriter, an earnest young man named Frederick Winslow Taylor carried a stopwatch into the Midvale Steel plant in Philadelphia and began a historic series of experiments aimed at improving the efficiency of the plant's machinists. With the approval of Midvale's owners, he recruited a group of factory hands, set them to work on various metalworking machines, and recorded and timed their every movement as well as the operations of the machines. By breaking down every job into a sequence of small, discrete steps and then testing different ways of performing each one, Taylor created a set of precise instructions—an "algorithm," we might say today—for how each worker should work. Midvale's employees grumbled about the strict new regime, claiming that it turned them into little more than automatons, but the factory's productivity soared.

More than a hundred years after the invention of the steam engine, the Industrial Revolution had at last found its philosophy and its philosopher. Taylor's tight industrial choreography—his "system," as he liked to call it—was embraced by manufacturers throughout the country and, in time, around the world. Seeking

maximum speed, maximum efficiency, and maximum output, factory owners used time-and-motion studies to organize their work and configure the jobs of their workers. The goal, as Taylor defined it in his celebrated 1911 treatise, *The Principles of Scientific Management,* was to identify and adopt, for every job, the "one best method" of work and thereby to effect "the gradual substitution of science for rule of thumb throughout the mechanic arts." Once his system was applied to all acts of manual labor, Taylor assured his followers, it would bring about a restructuring not only of industry but of society, creating a utopia of perfect efficiency. "In the past the man has been first," he declared; "in the future the system must be first."

Taylor's system is still very much with us; it remains the ethic of industrial manufacturing. And now, thanks to the growing power that computer engineers and software coders wield over our intellectual lives, Taylor's ethic is beginning to govern the realm of the mind as well. The Internet is a machine designed for the efficient and automated collection, transmission, and manipulation of information, and its legions of programmers are intent on finding the "one best method"—the perfect algorithm—to carry out every mental movement of what we've come to describe as "knowledge work."

Google's headquarters, in Mountain View, California—the Googleplex—is the Internet's high church, and the religion practiced inside its walls is Taylorism. Google, says its chief executive, Eric Schmidt, is "a company that's founded around the science of measurement," and it is striving to "systematize everything" it does. Drawing on the terabytes of behavioral data it collects through its search engine and other sites, it carries out thousands of experiments a day, according to the *Harvard Business Review,* and it uses the results to refine the algorithms that increasingly control how people find information and extract meaning from it. What Taylor did for the work of the hand, Google is doing for the work of the mind.

The company has declared that its mission is "to organize the world's information and make it universally accessible and useful." It seeks to develop "the perfect search engine," which it defines as something that "understands exactly what you mean and gives you back exactly what you want." In Google's view, information is a kind of commodity, a utilitarian resource that can be mined and processed with industrial efficiency. The more pieces of information we can "access" and the faster we can extract their gist, the more productive we become as thinkers.

Where does it end? Sergey Brin and Larry Page, the gifted young men who founded Google while pursuing doctoral degrees in computer science at Stanford, speak frequently of their desire to turn their search engine into an artificial intelligence, a HAL-like machine that might be connected directly to our brains. "The ultimate search engine is something as smart as people—or smarter," Page said in a speech a few years back. "For us, working on search is a way to work on artificial intelligence." In a 2004 interview with *Newsweek,* Brin said, "Certainly if you had all the world's information directly attached to your brain, or an artificial brain that was smarter than your brain, you'd be better off." Last year, Page told a convention of scientists that Google is "really trying to build artificial intelligence and to do it on a large scale."

Such an ambition is a natural one, even an admirable one, for a pair of math whizzes with vast quantities of cash at their disposal and a small army of computer scientists in their employ. A fundamentally scientific enterprise, Google is motivated by a desire to use technology, in Eric Schmidt's words, "to solve problems that have never been solved before," and artificial intelligence is the hardest problem out there. Why wouldn't Brin and Page want to be the ones to crack it?

Still, their easy assumption that we'd all "be better off" if our brains were supplemented, or even replaced, by an artificial intelligence is unsettling. It suggests a belief that intelligence is the output of a mechanical process, a series of discrete steps that can be isolated, measured, and optimized. In Google's world, the world we enter when we go online, there's little place for the fuzziness of contemplation. Ambiguity is not an opening for insight but a bug to be fixed. The human brain is just an outdated computer that needs a faster processor and a bigger hard drive.

The idea that our minds should operate as high-speed data-processing machines is not only built into the workings of the Internet, it is the network's reigning business model as well. The faster we surf across the Web—the more links we click and pages we view—the more opportunities Google and other companies gain to collect information about us and to feed us advertisements. Most of the proprietors of the commercial Internet have a financial stake in collecting the crumbs of data we leave behind as we flit from link to link—the more crumbs, the better. The last thing these companies want is to encourage leisurely reading or slow, concentrated thought. It's in their economic interest to drive us to distraction.

Maybe I'm just a worrywort. Just as there's a tendency to glorify technological progress, there's a countertendency to expect the worst of every new tool or machine. In Plato's *Phaedrus,* Socrates bemoaned the development of writing. He feared that, as people came to rely on the written word as a substitute for the knowledge they used to carry inside their heads, they would, in the words of one of the dialogue's characters, "cease to exercise their memory and become forgetful." And because they would be able to "receive a quantity of information without proper instruction," they would "be thought very knowledgeable when they are for the most part quite ignorant." They would be "filled with the conceit of wisdom instead of real wisdom." Socrates wasn't wrong—the new technology did often have the effects he feared—but he was shortsighted. He couldn't foresee the many ways that writing and reading would serve to spread information, spur fresh ideas, and expand human knowledge (if not wisdom).

The arrival of Gutenberg's printing press, in the 15th century, set off another round of teeth gnashing. The Italian humanist Hieronimo Squarciafico worried that the easy availability of books would lead to intellectual laziness, making men "less studious" and weakening their minds. Others argued that cheaply printed books and broadsheets would undermine religious authority, demean the work of scholars and scribes, and spread sedition and debauchery.

As New York University professor Clay Shirky notes, "Most of the arguments made against the printing press were correct, even prescient." But, again, the doomsayers were unable to imagine the myriad blessings that the printed word would deliver.

So, yes, you should be skeptical of my skepticism. Perhaps those who dismiss critics of the Internet as Luddites or nostalgists will be proved correct, and from our hyperactive, data-stoked minds will spring a golden age of intellectual discovery and universal wisdom. Then again, the Net isn't the alphabet, and although it may replace the printing press, it produces something altogether different. The kind of deep reading that a sequence of printed pages promotes is valuable not just for the knowledge we acquire from the author's words but for the intellectual vibrations those words set off within our own minds. In the quiet spaces opened up by the sustained, undistracted reading of a book, or by any other act of contemplation, for that matter, we make our own associations, draw our own inferences and analogies, foster our own ideas. Deep reading, as Maryanne Wolf argues, is indistinguishable from deep thinking.

If we lose those quiet spaces, or fill them up with "content," we will sacrifice something important not only in our selves but in our culture. In a recent essay, the playwright Richard Foreman eloquently described what's at stake:

> I come from a tradition of Western culture, in which the ideal (my ideal) was the complex, dense and "cathedral-like" structure of the highly educated and articulate personality—a man or woman who carried inside themselves a personally constructed and unique version of the entire heritage of the West. [But now] I see within us all (myself included) the replacement of complex inner density with a new kind of self—evolving under the pressure of information overload and the technology of the "instantly available."

As we are drained of our "inner repertory of dense cultural inheritance," Foreman concluded, we risk turning into " 'pancake people'—spread wide and thin as we connect with that vast network of information accessed by the mere touch of a button."

I'm haunted by that scene in *2001*. What makes it so poignant, and so weird, is the computer's emotional response to the disassembly of its mind: its despair as one circuit after another goes dark, its childlike pleading with the astronaut—"I can feel it. I can feel it. I'm afraid"—and its final reversion to what can only be called a state of innocence. HAL's outpouring of feeling contrasts with the emotionlessness that characterizes the human figures in the film, who go about their business with an almost robotic efficiency. Their thoughts and actions feel scripted, as if they're following the steps of an algorithm. In the world of *2001*, people have become so machinelike that the most human character turns out to be a machine. That's the essence of Kubrick's dark prophecy: as we come to rely on computers to mediate our understanding of the world, it is our own intelligence that flattens into artificial intelligence.

From *The Atlantic,* July, 2008. Copyright © 2008 by Nicholas M Carr. Reprinted by permission of Nicholas Carr.

The End of Solitude

WILLIAM DERESIEWICZ

As everyone seeks more and broader connectivity, the still, small voice speaks only in silence.

What does the contemporary self want? The camera has created a culture of celebrity; the computer is creating a culture of connectivity. As the two technologies converge—broadband tipping the Web from text to image, social-networking sites spreading the mesh of interconnection ever wider—the two cultures betray a common impulse. Celebrity and connectivity are both ways of becoming known. This is what the contemporary self wants. It wants to be recognized, wants to be connected: It wants to be visible. If not to the millions, on *Survivor* or *Oprah,* then to the hundreds, on Twitter or Facebook. This is the quality that validates us, this is how we become real to ourselves—by being seen by others. The great contemporary terror is anonymity. If Lionel Trilling was right, if the property that grounded the self, in Romanticism, was sincerity, and in modernism it was authenticity, then in postmodernism it is visibility.

So we live exclusively in relation to others, and what disappears from our lives is solitude. Technology is taking away our privacy and our concentration, but it is also taking away our ability to be alone. Though I shouldn't say taking away. We are doing this to ourselves; we are discarding these riches as fast as we can. I was told by one of her older relatives that a teenager I know had sent 3,000 text messages one recent month. That's 100 a day, or about one every 10 waking minutes, morning, noon, and night, weekdays and weekends, class time, lunch time, homework time, and toothbrushing time. So on average, she's never alone for more than 10 minutes at once. Which means, she's never alone.

I once asked my students about the place that solitude has in their lives. One of them admitted that she finds the prospect of being alone so unsettling that she'll sit with a friend even when she has a paper to write. Another said, why would anyone want to be alone?

To that remarkable question, history offers a number of answers. Man may be a social animal, but solitude has traditionally been a societal value. In particular, the act of being alone has been understood as an essential dimension of religious experience, albeit one restricted to a self-selected few. Through the solitude of rare spirits, the collective renews its relationship with divinity. The prophet and the hermit, the sadhu and the yogi, pursue their vision quests, invite their trances, in desert or forest or cave. For the still, small voice speaks only in silence. Social life is a bustle of petty concerns, a jostle of quotidian interests, and religious institutions are no exception. You cannot hear God when people are chattering at you, and the divine word, their pretensions notwithstanding, demurs at descending on the monarch and the priest. Communal experience is the human norm, but the solitary encounter with God is the egregious act that refreshes that norm. (Egregious, for no man is a prophet in his own land. Tiresias was reviled before he was vindicated, Teresa interrogated before she was canonized.) Religious solitude is a kind of self-correcting social mechanism, a way of burning out the underbrush of moral habit and spiritual custom. The seer returns with new tablets or new dances, his face bright with the old truth.

Like other religious values, solitude was democratized by the Reformation and secularized by Romanticism. In Marilynne Robinson's interpretation, Calvinism created the modern self by focusing the soul inward, leaving it to encounter God, like a prophet of old, in "profound isolation." To her enumeration of Calvin, Marguerite de Navarre, and Milton as pioneering early-modern selves we can add Montaigne, Hamlet, and even Don Quixote. The last figure alerts us to reading's essential role in this transformation, the printing press serving an analogous function in the 16th and subsequent centuries to that of television and the Internet in our own. Reading, as Robinson puts it, "is an act of great inwardness and subjectivity." "The soul encountered itself in response to a text, first Genesis or Matthew and then 'Paradise Lost' or 'Leaves of Grass.'" With Protestantism and printing, the quest for the divine voice became available to, even incumbent upon, everyone.

But it is with Romanticism that solitude achieved its greatest cultural salience, becoming both literal and literary. Protestant solitude is still only figurative. Rousseau and Wordsworth made it physical. The self was now encountered not in God but in Nature, and to encounter Nature one had to go to it. And go to it with a special sensibility: The poet displaced the saint as social seer and cultural model. But because Romanticism also inherited the 18th-century idea of social sympathy, Romantic solitude existed in a dialectical relationship with sociability—if less for Rousseau and still less for Thoreau, the most famous solitary of all, then certainly for Wordsworth, Melville, Whitman, and many others. For Emerson, "the soul environs itself with friends, that it may enter into a grander self-acquaintance or solitude; and it goes alone, for a season, that it may exalt its conversation or society." The Romantic practice of solitude is neatly captured by Trilling's "sincerity": the belief that the self is validated by a congruity of public appearance and private essence, one that stabilizes its relationship with both itself and others. Especially, as Emerson suggests, one beloved other. Hence the famous Romantic friendship pairs: Goethe and Schiller, Wordsworth and Coleridge, Hawthorne and Melville.

Modernism decoupled this dialectic. Its notion of solitude was harsher, more adversarial, more isolating. As a model of the self and its interactions, Hume's social sympathy gave way to Pater's thick wall of personality and Freud's narcissism—the sense that the soul, self-enclosed and inaccessible to others, can't choose but be alone. With exceptions, like Woolf, the modernists fought shy of friendship. Joyce and Proust disparaged it; D.H. Lawrence was wary of it; the modernist friendship pairs—Conrad and Ford, Eliot and Pound, Hemingway and Fitzgerald—were altogether cooler than their Romantic counterparts. The world was now understood as an assault on the self, and with good reason.

The Romantic ideal of solitude developed in part as a reaction to the emergence of the modern city. In modernism, the city is not only more menacing than ever, it has become inescapable, a labyrinth: Eliot's London, Joyce's Dublin. The mob, the human mass, presses in. Hell is other people. The soul is forced back into itself—hence the development of a more austere, more embattled form of self-validation, Trilling's "authenticity," where the essential relationship is only with oneself. (Just as there are few good friendships in modernism, so are there few good marriages.) Solitude becomes, more than ever, the arena of heroic self-discovery, a voyage through interior realms made vast and terrifying by Nietzschean and Freudian insights. To achieve authenticity is to look upon these visions without flinching; Trilling's exemplar here is Kurtz. Protestant self-examination becomes Freudian analysis, and the culture hero, once a prophet of God and then a poet of Nature, is now a novelist of self—a Dostoyevsky, a Joyce, a Proust.

But we no longer live in the modernist city, and our great fear is not submersion by the mass but isolation from the herd. Urbanization gave way to suburbanization, and with it the universal threat of loneliness. What technologies of transportation exacerbated—we could live farther and farther apart—technologies of communication redressed—we could bring ourselves closer and closer together. Or at least, so we have imagined. The first of these technologies, the first simulacrum of proximity, was the telephone. "Reach out and touch someone." But through the 70s and 80s, our isolation grew. Suburbs, sprawling ever farther, became exurbs. Families grew smaller or splintered apart, mothers left the home to work. The electronic hearth became the television in every room. Even in childhood, certainly in adolescence, we were each trapped inside our own cocoon. Soaring crime rates, and even more sharply escalating rates of moral panic, pulled children off the streets. The idea that you could go outside and run around the neighborhood with your friends, once unquestionable, has now become unthinkable. The child who grew up between the world wars as part of an extended family within a tight-knit urban community became the grandparent of a kid who sat alone in front of a big television, in a big house, on a big lot. We were lost in space.

Under those circumstances, the Internet arrived as an incalculable blessing. We should never forget that. It has allowed isolated people to communicate with one another and marginalized people to find one another. The busy parent can stay in touch with far-flung friends. The gay teenager no longer has to feel like a freak. But as the Internet's dimensionality has grown, it has quickly become too much of a good thing. Ten years ago we were writing e-mail messages on desktop computers and transmitting them over dial-up connections. Now we are sending text messages on our cellphones, posting pictures on our Facebook pages, and following complete strangers on Twitter. A constant stream of mediated contact, virtual, notional, or simulated, keeps us wired in to the electronic hive—though contact, or at least two-way contact, seems increasingly beside the point. The goal now, it seems, is simply to become known, to turn oneself into a sort of miniature celebrity. How many friends do I have on Facebook? How many people are reading my blog? How many Google hits does my name generate? Visibility secures our self-esteem, becoming a substitute, twice removed, for genuine connection. Not long ago, it was easy to feel lonely. Now, it is impossible to be alone.

As a result, we are losing both sides of the Romantic dialectic. What does friendship mean when you have 532 "friends"? How does it enhance my sense of closeness when my Facebook News Feed tells me that Sally Smith (whom I haven't seen since high school, and wasn't all that friendly with even then) "is making coffee and staring off into space"? My students told me they have little time for intimacy. And of course, they have no time at all for solitude.

But at least friendship, if not intimacy, is still something they want. As jarring as the new dispensation may be for people in their 30s and 40s, the real problem is that it has become completely natural for people in their teens and 20s. Young people today seem to have no desire for solitude, have never heard of it, can't imagine why it would be worth having. In fact, their use of technology—or to be fair, our use of technology—seems to involve a constant effort to stave off the possibility of solitude, a continuous attempt, as we sit alone at our computers, to maintain the imaginative presence of others. As long ago as 1952, Trilling wrote about "the modern fear of being cut off from the social group even for a moment." Now we have equipped ourselves with the means to prevent that fear from ever being realized. Which does not mean that we have put it to rest. Quite the contrary. Remember my student, who couldn't even write a paper by herself. The more we keep aloneness at bay, the less are we able to deal with it and the more terrifying it gets.

There is an analogy, it seems to me, with the previous generation's experience of boredom. The two emotions, loneliness and boredom, are closely allied. They are also both characteristically modern. The Oxford English Dictionary's earliest citations of either word, at least in the contemporary sense, date from the 19th century. Suburbanization, by eliminating the stimulation as well as the sociability of urban or traditional village life, exacerbated the tendency to both. But the great age of boredom, I believe, came in with television, precisely because television was designed to palliate that feeling. Boredom is not a necessary consequence of having nothing to do, it is only the negative experience of that state. Television, by obviating the need to learn how to make use of one's lack of occupation, precludes one from ever discovering how to enjoy it. In fact, it renders that condition fearsome, its prospect intolerable. You are terrified of being bored—so you turn on the television.

I speak from experience. I grew up in the 60s and 70s, the age of television. I was trained to be bored; boredom was cultivated within me like a precious crop. (It has been said that consumer society wants to condition us to feel bored, since boredom creates a market for stimulation.) It took me years to discover—and my nervous system will never fully adjust to this idea; I still have to fight against boredom, am permanently damaged in this respect—that having nothing to do doesn't have to be a bad thing. The alternative to boredom is what Whitman called idleness: a passive receptivity to the world.

So it is with the current generation's experience of being alone. That is precisely the recognition implicit in the idea of solitude, which is to loneliness what idleness is to boredom. Loneliness is not the absence of company, it is grief over that absence. The lost sheep is lonely; the shepherd is not lonely. But the Internet is as powerful a machine for the production of loneliness as television is for the manufacture of boredom. If six hours of television a day creates the aptitude for boredom, the inability to sit still, a hundred text messages a day creates the aptitude for loneliness, the inability to be by yourself. Some degree of boredom and loneliness is to be expected, especially among young people, given the way our human environment has been attenuated. But technology amplifies those tendencies. You could call your schoolmates when I was a teenager, but you couldn't call them 100 times a day. You could get together with your friends when I was in college, but you couldn't always get together with them when you wanted to, for the simple reason that you couldn't always find them. If boredom is the great emotion of the TV generation, loneliness is the great emotion of the Web generation. We lost the ability to be still, our capacity for idleness. They have lost the ability to be alone, their capacity for solitude.

And losing solitude, what have they lost? First, the propensity for introspection, that examination of the self that the Puritans, and the Romantics, and the modernists (and Socrates, for that matter) placed at the center of spiritual life—of wisdom, of conduct. Thoreau called it fishing "in the Walden Pond of [our] own natures," "bait[ing our] hooks with darkness." Lost, too, is the related propensity for sustained reading. The Internet brought text back into a televisual world, but it brought it back on terms dictated by that world—that is, by its remapping of our attention spans. Reading now means skipping and skimming; five minutes on the same Web page is considered an eternity. This is not reading as Marilynne Robinson described it: the encounter with a second self in the silence of mental solitude.

But we no longer believe in the solitary mind. If the Romantics had Hume and the modernists had Freud, the current psychological model—and this should come as no surprise—is that of the networked or social mind. Evolutionary psychology tells us that our brains developed to interpret complex social signals. According to David Brooks, that reliable index of the social-scientific zeitgeist, cognitive scientists tell us that "our decision-making is powerfully influenced by social context"; neuroscientists, that we have "permeable minds" that function in part through a process of "deep imitation"; psychologists, that "we are organized by our attachments"; sociologists, that our behavior is affected by "the power of social networks." The ultimate implication is that there is no mental space that is not social (contemporary social science dovetailing here with postmodern critical theory). One of the most striking things about the way young people relate to one another today is that they no longer seem to believe in the existence of Thoreau's "darkness."

The MySpace page, with its shrieking typography and clamorous imagery, has replaced the journal and the letter as a way of creating and communicating one's sense of self. The suggestion is not only that such communication is to be made to the world at large rather than to oneself or one's intimates, or graphically rather than verbally, or performatively rather than narratively or analytically, but also that it can be made completely. Today's young people seem to feel that they can make themselves fully known to one another. They seem to lack a sense of their own depths, and of the value of keeping them hidden.

If they didn't, they would understand that solitude enables us to secure the integrity of the self as well as to explore it. Few have shown this more beautifully than Woolf. In the middle of *Mrs. Dalloway,* between her navigation of the streets and her orchestration of the party, between the urban jostle and the social bustle, Clarissa goes up, "like a nun withdrawing," to her attic room. Like a nun: She returns to a state that she herself thinks of as a kind of virginity. This does not mean she's a prude. Virginity is classically the outward sign of spiritual inviolability, of a self untouched by the world, a soul that has preserved its integrity by refusing to descend into the chaos and self-division of sexual and social relations. It is the mark of the saint and the monk, of Hippolytus and Antigone and Joan of Arc. Solitude is both the social image of that state and the means by which we can approximate it. And the supreme image in *Mrs. Dalloway* of the dignity of solitude itself is the old woman whom Clarissa catches sight of through her window. "Here was one room," she thinks, "there another." We are not merely social beings. We are each also separate, each solitary, each alone in our own room, each miraculously our unique selves and mysteriously enclosed in that selfhood.

To remember this, to hold oneself apart from society, is to begin to think one's way beyond it. Solitude, Emerson said, "is to genius the stern friend." "He who should inspire and lead his race must be defended from traveling with the souls of other men, from living, breathing, reading, and writing in the daily, time-worn yoke of their opinions." One must protect oneself from the momentum of intellectual and moral consensus—especially, Emerson added, during youth. "God is alone," Thoreau said, "but the Devil, he is far from being alone; he sees a great deal of company; he is legion." The university was to be praised, Emerson believed, if only because it provided its charges with "a separate chamber and fire"—the physical space of solitude. Today, of course, universities do everything they can to keep their students from being alone, lest they perpetrate self-destructive acts, and also, perhaps, unfashionable thoughts. But no real excellence, personal or social, artistic, philosophical, scientific or moral, can arise without solitude. "The saint and poet seek privacy," Emerson said, "to ends the most public and universal." We are back to the seer, seeking signposts for the future in splendid isolation.

Solitude isn't easy, and isn't for everyone. It has undoubtedly never been the province of more than a few. "I believe," Thoreau said, "that men are generally still a little afraid of the dark." Teresa and Tiresias will always be the exceptions, or to speak in more relevant terms, the young people—and they still exist—who prefer to loaf and invite their soul, who step to the beat of a different drummer. But if solitude disappears as a social value and social idea, will even the exceptions remain possible? Still, one is powerless to reverse the drift of the culture. One can only save oneself—and whatever else happens, one can still always do that. But it takes a willingness to be unpopular.

The last thing to say about solitude is that it isn't very polite. Thoreau knew that the "doubleness" that solitude cultivates, the ability to stand back and observe life dispassionately, is apt to make us a little unpleasant to our fellows, to say nothing of the offense implicit in avoiding their company. But then, he didn't worry overmuch about being genial. He didn't even like having to talk to people three times a day, at meals; one can only imagine what he would have made of text-messaging. We, however, have made of geniality—the weak smile, the polite interest, the fake invitation—a cardinal virtue. Friendship may be slipping from our grasp, but our friendliness is universal. Not for nothing does "gregarious" mean "part of the herd." But Thoreau understood that securing one's self-possession was worth a few wounded feelings. He may have put his neighbors off, but at least he was sure of himself. Those who would find solitude must not be afraid to stand alone.

WILLIAM DERESIEWICZ writes essays and reviews for a variety of publications. He taught at Yale University from 1998 to 2008.

From *The Chronicle Review,* January 30, 2009. Copyright © 2009 by William Deresiewicz. Reprinted by permission.

Girl Power

No rich relatives? no professional mentors? no problem. Ashley Qualls, 17, has built a million-dollar website. She's lol all the way to the bank.

CHUCK SALTER

Late last year, Ian Moray stumbled across a cotton-candy-pink website called Whateverlife.com. As manager of media development at the online marketing company ValueClick Media, he was searching for under-the-radar destinations for notoriously fickle teenagers. Beyond MySpace and Facebook, countless sites come and go in the teen universe, like soon forgotten pop songs. But Whateverlife stood out. It was more authentic somehow. It featured a steady supply of designs for MySpace pages and attracted a few hundred-thousand girls a day. "Clever design, a growing base—that's a no-brainer for us," Moray says.

He approached Ashley Qualls, Whateverlife's founder, about incorporating ads from ValueClick's 450 or so clients and sharing the revenue. At first, she declined. Then a few weeks later she changed her mind. He was in Los Angeles and she was in Detroit, so they arranged everything by phone and email. They still have yet to meet in person.

When did Moray, who's 40, learn that his new business partner was 17 years old?

Pause.

"When our director of marketing told me why FAST COMPANY was calling," says Moray, now ValueClick's director of media development. "I assumed she was a seasoned Internet professional. She knows so much about what her site does, more than people three times her age."

It's like that famous *New Yorker* cartoon. A dog typing away at a computer tells his canine buddy, "On the Internet, nobody knows you're a dog."

At 17 going on 37 (at least), Ashley is very much an Internet professional. In the less than two years since Whateverlife took off, she has dropped out of high school, bought a house, helped launch artists such as Lily Allen, and rejected offers to buy her young company. Although Ashley was flattered to be offered $1.5 million and a car of her choice—as long as the price tag wasn't more than $100,000—she responded, in effect, Whatever.:) "I don't even have my license yet," she says.

Ashley is evidence of the meritocracy on the Internet that allows even companies run by neophyte entrepreneurs to compete, regardless of funding, location, size, or experience—and she's a reminder that ingenuity is ageless. She has taken in more than $1 million, thanks to a now-familiar Web-friendly business model. Her MySpace page layouts are available for the bargain price of . . . nothing. They're free for the taking. Her only significant source of revenue so far is advertising.

According to Google Analytics, Whateverlife attracts more than 7 million individuals and 60 million page views a month. That's a larger audience than the circulations of *Seventeen, Teen Vogue,* and *CosmoGirl!* magazines combined. Although website rankings vary with the methodology, Quantcast, a popular source among advertisers, ranked Whateverlife.com a staggering No. 349 in mid-July out of more than 20 million sites. Among the sites in its rearview mirror: Britannica.com, AmericanIdol.com, FDA.gov, and CBS.com.

And one more, which Ashley can't quite believe herself: "I'm ahead of Oprah!" (Oprah.com: No. 469.) Sure, Ashley is a long way from having Oprah's clout, but she is establishing a platform of her own. "I have this audience of so many people, I can say anything I want to," she says. "I can say, 'Check out this movie or this artist.' It's, like, a rush. I never thought I'd be an influencer." (Attention pollsters: 1,500 girls have added the Join Team Hillary '08 desktop button to their MySpace pages since Ashley offered it in March.)

She has come along with the right idea at the right time. Eager to customize their MySpace profiles, girls cut and paste the HTML code for Whateverlife layouts featuring hearts, flowers, celebrities, and so on onto their personal page and—presto—a new look. Think of it as MySpace clothes; some kids change their layouts nearly as frequently. "It's all about giving girls what they want," Ashley says.

These days, she and her young company are experiencing growing pains. She's learning how to be the boss—of her mother, her friends, developers-for-hire in India. And Whateverlife, one of the first sites offering MySpace layouts specifically for girls, needs to mature as well. "MySpace layouts" was among the top 30 search terms on Google in June. Ashley knows that she needs new content—not just more layouts, but more features, to distinguish Whateverlife from the thousands of sites in the expanding MySpace ecosystem. Earlier this year, she created an online magazine. Cell-phone wallpaper, a new source of revenue at 99 cents to $1.99 a download, is in the works.

Running a growing company without an MBA, not to mention a high-school diploma, is hard enough, but Ashley confronts another extraordinary complication. Business associates may forget that she is 17, but Detroit's Wayne County Probate Court has not. She's a minor with considerable assets—"business affairs that may be jeopardized," the law reads—that need protection in light of the rift her sudden success has caused in an already fractious family. In January, a probate judge ruled that neither Ashley nor her parents could adequately manage her finances. Until she turns 18, next June, a court-appointed conservator is controlling Whaterlife's assets; Ashley must request funds for any expense outside the agreed-upon monthly budget.

The arrangement, she says, affects her ability to react in a volatile industry. "It's not like I'm selling lemonade," she says. Besides, it's her company. If she wants to contract developers or employ her mother, Ashley says, why shouldn't she be able to do it without the conservator's approval?

So the teenager has hired a lawyer. She wants to emancipate herself and be declared an adult. Now. At 17. Why not just sit tight until June? The girl trying to grow up fast can't wait that long.

> I'm doing what everyone says they want to do, "live like there's no tomorrow."
>
> —Ashley in her blog, "The Daily Life of a Simple Kind of Gal," July 1, 2006; 2:43 A.M.

Ashley is different from the recent crop of high-profile teen entrepreneurs. True, her eighth-grade class did vote her "most likely to succeed," but it's safe to say they were predicting 20 or 30 years out, not three years removed from middle school. She created her company almost by accident and without the resources that typically give young novices a leg up. Catherine Cook, 17, started myYearbook.com by teaming up with her older brother, a Harvard grad and Internet entrepreneur. Ben Casnocha, the 19-year-old founder of software company Comcate and author of the new memoir *My Start-Up Life,* is the son of a San Francisco lawyer and has tapped Silicon Valley brains and bank accounts.

But Ashley had no connections. No business professionals in the family. No rich aunt or uncle. In the working-class community of downriver Detroit, south of downtown and the sprawling Ford plant in Dearborn, Michigan, she bounced back and forth between her divorced parents, neither of whom attended college. Her father is a machinist, her mother, until recently, a retail data collector for ACNielsen. "My mom still doesn't understand how I do it," Ashley says. To be fair, she did go to her mother for the initial investment: $8 to register the domain name. Ashley still hasn't spent a dime on advertising.

It all started as a hobby. She began dabbling in website design eight years ago, when she was 9, hogging the family's Gateway computer in the kitchen all day. When she wasn't playing games, she was teaching herself the basics of Web design.

To which her mother, Linda LaBrecque, responded, "Get off that computer. *Now!*" For Ashley's 12th birthday, her mother splurged on an above-ground swimming pool—"just so she'd go outside," LaBrecque says.

Whaterlife just sort of happened, another accidental Web business. Originally, Ashley created the site in late 2004 when she was 14 as a way to show off her design work. "I was the dorky girl who was into HTML," she says. It attracted zero interest beyond her circle of friends until she figured out how to customize MySpace pages. So many classmates asked her to design theirs that she began posting layouts on her site daily, several at first, then dozens.

By 2005, her traffic had exploded; she needed her own dedicated server. Ashley, who had bartered site designs for free Web hosting, couldn't afford the monthly rental, not on her babysitting income. Her Web host suggested Google AdSense, a service that supplies ads to a site and shares the revenue. The greater the traffic, the more money she'd earn.

"She would look up how much she had made," says Jen Carey, 17, one of her closest friends. "It was $50. She thought that was the coolest."

The first check, her first paycheck of any kind, was even cooler: $2,790.

"It was more than I made in a month," her mother says.

"It made me want to do even more designs," Ashley says. But first, she went on a shopping spree at a nearby mall with Bre Newby, her best friend since third grade. Ashley walked out with eight pairs of jeans from J.C. Penney and an armful of other clothes. Without a credit card or a bank account, the 15-year-old paid $600 in cash—the most she'd ever spent.

"Before, I would ask my mom, 'Can I have $10?' and she'd say, 'No, you have to wait a few weeks,'" Ashley recalls.

She hasn't asked since.

In January 2006, a few months after that first payday and six months before her 16th birthday, she withdrew from school. Instead of taking AP English, French, and algebra II, instead of being a straight-A sophomore at Lincoln Park High School, Ashley stayed home to nurture her budding business and take classes through an online high school. "Everybody was shocked," she says. "They asked, 'Are you sure you know what you're doing?' But I had this crazy opportunity to do something different."

That "something different" was Whaterlife. The name came to Ashley in a moment of frustration. After losing a video game to Bre, she dropped the controller and blurted out, "Whatever, life." She liked it instantly. She thought it would be a great name for a website, for "whatever life you lead."

Now her life is centered around working in the basement of the two-story, four-bedroom house that she bought last September for $250,000. It's located in a fenced-off subdivision in the community of Southgate, a couple of blocks removed from Dix Highway, a thoroughfare dotted with body shops and convenience stores. She lives with her mother; her 8-year-old sister, Shelby; three cats; two turtles; a Rottweiler; a hamster; and a fish.

Ashley's home office is the physical embodiment of her website. The business brings in as much as $70,000 a month, but there's not a whiff of corporate convention. It's fun, whimsical, and unabashedly pink. Pink walls. Pink rug. Pink chairs, pillows, and lamp. Even the blue, green, and silver stick-on robots dancing on the wall have tiny pink hearts. It's a teenager's version of the workplace, which earned raves when she posted pictures on MySpace:

"SOO FLIPPING CUTE!"

"OMG I want that office."

"Geez. That's just incredible. I'm what . . . almost ten years your senior and I am inspired by you."

The space reflects Ashley's personality, like everything else about her business. Therein lies one of the main reasons for Whaterlife's success, says Robb Lippitt, whom Ashley considers the only good thing to come out of her legal issues. When her lawyer realized she was running her company alone, he arranged a meeting with Lippitt, the former COO of ePrize, an online promotions outfit that is one of Detroit's fastest-growing companies. Having helped build ePrize to $30 million in annual revenue and 325 employees, he now helps other local entrepreneurs scale the mountain. In April, he became her $200-an-hour consultant and first business mentor.

Since Ashley, his youngest client ever, had never taken a class in accounting or read a business book, she needed a crash course on the basics, such as maintaining two accounts, business and personal. "She was running her business like a piggy bank," says Lippitt, 38.

But he found her to be a quick study and, in many ways, a natural entrepreneur. "She lacks experience, but I was blown away by her instincts," he says. How she makes her layouts compatible with social-networking sites other than MySpace, so her company isn't tied to one site. How she decided to offer her designs as cell-phone wallpaper, creating a new service and revenue stream based on existing inventory. Ashley, he realized, has a vision for Whaterlife that goes beyond a MySpace tools site. It could be a multifaceted community for girls.

Convinced that her fans need help building websites, she hired developers in India to create an easy-to-use application and wrote one-teen-to-another tutorials. After the site builder launched in May, though, she told Lippitt she was disappointed by delays and early bugs. Hiccups were common, he assured her; he expected modest results, maybe a few hundred users. But 28,000 signed up in the first week. "There are CEOs across the country who would be dancing in their offices if they got that reaction," he says.

Ashley is the demographic she's serving, which gives her a powerful advantage over far more experienced adults trying to channel their inner teen or glean clues from focus groups. Her site looks and sounds like something made by a teenager, not something manufactured to look that way.

The risk, of course, is that she could lose touch with her audience as she outgrows it. But Lippitt says she already grasps the importance of understanding her customers, not simply assuming they share her taste. She conducts polls about their favorite stores, celebrities, and *American Idol* contestants. She solicits feedback on new features. And she's thinking of the next step: "I may have to hire people younger than me."

Some days I miss school. I miss the laughter, the lunch lines, the jackass of the class, the evil ass teacher, sometimes I even miss the drama.

August 4, 2006; 1:30 A.M.

On a Wednesday in early June, the gang's all here after school. Well, everyone except Bre. Shayna Bone, 17, and Jen—outfitted in matching Whaterlife T-shirts, featuring row after row of multicolored hearts—sit at a table reviewing their W-4 forms. It's official: The staff is doubling for the summer.

Mike Troutt, 16, who's stretched across a white L-shaped couch, won't be joining them. A past contributor to the Whaterlife magazine, he's working as an apprentice at a local tattoo shop for the summer. He's contemplating where he'll get his first tattoo, he announces. Tomorrow's the big day.

As usual, Ashley is working away at her computer, a new desktop with a touch-screen monitor, one of three computers in her basement. Often, she's up at 7 or working into the wee hours on a "designfest" with Bre, fueled with music and Monster energy drinks.

In just 15 minutes, she creates a layout. Blue and pink streaks on a black background with blocks of pink rap lyrics. Her fingers race across the keyboard as she tries different fonts, sizes, compositions, switching out HTML coding as she talks. "Don't worry," she tells a wary Shayna, "I'll teach you."

Ashley the CEO, who has no fewer than 14 hearts on her business card, is both utterly familiar and a complete mystery to her friends. In some ways, she's the same old "Ash"—or "AshBo," a nickname they coined because she didn't have her own room at one point (Ashley + hobo = AshBo). She still plays *The Sims,* still giggles when Jen laughs like Eddie Murphy, and is still up for silliness, like standing by the road holding a sign that says, Honk if you believe in the Loch Ness Monster, or taking breaks on the swing set down the street.

AshBo looks even younger than 17. She has straight brown hair with light streaks down to the middle of her back. She has a French pedicure, like Jen and her mother. Her clothes are nothing fancy. "I don't need $2,000 shirts," Ashley says. "I'm fine with Target." Or a University of Michigan sweatshirt over a summer dress.

In other ways, she's an alien among normal teens. She can go on about hiring freelance developers, studying site-traffic trends, calculating ad rates, maintaining low overhead (her main operating expense is seven servers). "Sometimes when I talk about the site, my friends just stare at me," she says. She carries a BlackBerry and a Coach bag (a recent birthday present to herself). Her friends tease her about her last ring tone, which consisted of The Donald, someone they couldn't care less about, barking, "This is Donald Trump telling you to have an ego!"

Whaterlife has definitely brought out a bolder side. "One minute, she's joking around with us, and then, 'Oh, guys, hold on, I gotta take this call,'" says Mike. "She turns it on like a light switch." She's no longer the shy 15-year-old who would ask her mother or father to make a difficult phone call. Who didn't know how to respond to advertisers' cold calls. Who didn't know how to negotiate. Now, it's "Is that the best you can do for me?"

"Something clicked," says her mother, who can be direct herself. "She's not letting people walk over her."

At one point, Ashley takes a call upstairs in the kitchen, where a fax machine sits on the countertop. The company that's building the application for her cell-phone wallpaper is on the line. The developer walks her through the latest mock-up, answering Ashley's questions. She's one of those teens who has mastered the art of talking to adults as a peer, of making eye contact rather than looking down or away at a moment's blush.

Her mother, whom Ashley hired recently to keep the books, listens in, hand on hip, a cigarette cocked. Afterward, she asks, "What was he talking about?"

Ashley translates. She'll ask her mother for advice, but she doesn't necessarily take it. "I'm stubborn, like her," she says. Ashley has more leverage than the typical teen. She's the breadwinner. And yet for all her newfound independence, she still needs to be driven everywhere. She hasn't taken driver's ed because she wants to take the class with a friend, not alone.

Occasionally, she feels the tug of her old life, traditions like Lincoln Park's Spirit Week, when she'd paint her cheeks orange and blue, the school colors. More than once, she has returned, just for the day, hanging out in her French teacher's classroom. Ashley wonders if she'll be allowed to participate in graduation. By then, she may have already earned an associate's degree in design, at Henry Ford Community College.

She's determined to bring her friends along for this strange and wonderful ride. They rode in the limo to her over-the-top sweet-16 party at the local Masonic Temple, where guests wore pink Whateverlife rubber bracelets and the door prize was an Xbox. She took Bre on a family vacation to Hawaii, Ashley's first flight. And when the friends go out—tonight it's to Chili's—she picks up the tab.

This summer, she's the boss. One of Ashley's friends had pitched in making layouts last year, but things got a tad awkward when Ashley thought her friend's productivity was dipping. Now she insists they've made up—BFF. But after the misunderstanding, she wrote up employee guidelines. She wanted to spell out her expectations. Lippitt is impressed. She's learning from her mistakes, a challenge for any new entrepreneur.

"I told them I need a minimum of 25 layouts a week to get paid," Ashley says. "It's just business."

> Do I keep my site?
> Do I sell and be set for life?
> God, it's all so overwhelming.
>
> August 4, 2006; 1:30 A.M.

L ast year, Steve Greenberg, the former president of Columbia Records and now the head of indie label S-Curve Records, witnessed the power of Whateverlife. Greenberg discovered Joss Stone, produced the Hanson brothers, and helped make Baha Men's "Who Let the Dogs Out" an unofficial sports anthem. Last year, he decided to promote Jonas Brothers, an unknown pop trio, online instead of on radio. He

turned to Nabbr, a company that had developed a viral widget, a small desktop application that plays videos and can be easily shared with other sites. It's like "a music poster on a bedroom wall," says Mike More, Nabbr's CEO.

The widget made its Internet debut on Whateverlife. While surfing MySpace for leads, More had noticed how many Jonas Brothers fans used Whateverlife layouts. In less than two months, 60,000 fans transferred the Jonas Brothers' three-part video from Whateverlife to their MySpace pages, in effect becoming 60,000 new distribution points. "This teenage girl in the Midwest got more views for our video than YouTube," says Greenberg, 46. "It wasn't even close." The viral campaign encouraged fans to vote for the band on MTV's *Total Request Live,* and the group's song "Mandy" hit No. 4, unheard of without radio play.

Since then, Whateverlife has become one of the primary vehicles for Nabbr's viral campaigns for artists and movies, breaking acts such as the Red Jumpsuit Apparatus and 30 Seconds to Mars, as well as Lily Allen. More's staff sends Ashley signed CDs and photos to pass on to Whateverlife fans, and artists record personal shout-outs to her and Whateverlife that play on her site. She's light years ahead of traditional media such as *Teen Vogue,* More says. "If I were Condé Nast, I'd figure out a way to buy her," he says. "I would."

As previous suitors can attest, that wouldn't be easy. In March 2006, an associate of MySpace cofounder Brad Greenspan approached Ashley with a bid valued at more than $1.5 million. She passed. Three months later, Greenspan's people came back with a second offer: $700,000, a car, and her own Internet show with a marketing budget of $2 million.

Sorry, fellas. "I created this from nothing, and I want to see how far I can take it," Ashley says. "If I wanted to do an Internet show, I could do it on my own. I have the audience."

Until now, she has maintained a remarkably low profile in the offline world. Her scheduled appearance on the "Totally Wired Teen Superstars" panel at Mashup, a teen-marketing conference in July, was to be her first public-speaking appearance—and her first business trip. An even bigger gig is possible: her own reality-TV show. Rick Sadlowski, a TV production executive in Detroit who worked with Eminem when he was still Marshall Mathers, is eager to pitch the idea to MTV. Ashley is mulling it over.

Move over, Paris Hilton. It's Whateverlife: The Not-So Simple Life.

> Got evaluated by my therapist for emancipation—
> need to get a few teachers' written letters; should
> be cool.
>
> April 7, 2007; 9:53 P.M.

I n February 2006, following a falling-out with her mother, Ashley moved in with her father and older brother. With her business booming, she says, she began supporting them—groceries, bills, rent, renovations. At first, she didn't mind. One of the benefits of Whateverlife was the ability to take care of her family in a way she'd never imagined, certainly not when she was a child overhearing arguments about unpaid bills. Ashley says she bought her brother a used car and paid her grandmother's taxes. The insurance through Whateverlife covered her mother's back surgery. But in August, Ashley moved back in with her mother. She hasn't spoken to her father since. Or to her brother, who later filed (then withdrew) a petition to become her conservator. "I used to trust easily," Ashley says. "I've learned to be careful."

When her brother took his name off a joint bank account with her, Lincoln Park Community Credit Union petitioned the probate court to assign a conservator. After several months, the judge tapped attorney Alan May. He has 40 years' worth of experience with conservatorships, but Ashley's situation makes the case unique in his career. Although May's role is protecting Ashley's interests, it hasn't always felt that way to her, not when she hasn't had complete control over the money she made. But she says, "I don't want this to come across like a war."

Until recently, though, the tension was undeniable. Ashley was unhappy having to get May's approval for expenses such as her mother's nearly $500-a-week pay. May declined to discuss the case, but in papers filed last spring with the court, he characterized LaBrecque as uncooperative and evasive.

"They're making me out to be the bad guy," Ashley's mother says. LaBrecque, 42, had little growing up herself. Her father worked on the assembly line at General Motors until he died of a heart attack at 42, leaving his wife to raise six kids on Social Security. "It was rough but we survived," she says. "I feel so lucky my daughter doesn't have to live the life I lived."

In mid-July, seven months after being assigned a conservator, Ashley finally sat down with everybody for the first time: her mother, her lawyer, her consultant, her guardian ad litem, and her conservator. She says that she feels much better about the situation.

But that doesn't change the fact that she wants to be on her own. The typical conservatorship case involves a minor with an inheritance or an elderly person who has lost his faculties. "It's unusual to be emancipated to run your own business," says Darren Findling, Ashley's lawyer. "But she's the perfect candidate—an Internet superstar who happens to be a minor."

For now, she's trying to block all this out and concentrate on her business.

On Thursday, while her friends are slaving through exams, Ashley meets with Lippitt for two hours. They couldn't appear more different. He's a low-key, analytical sort with a law degree. Lives on the other side of town, in the Tony Bloomfield Hills suburb. Drives a black Lexus, a rarity on her block. As an entrepreneur, though, she relates to him better than anyone else right now.

"I know, I'm always jumping on 10,000 things," Ashley says and then pitches her latest brainstorm, her own social-networking application for girls.

"Hmm," he says. "How do you think the reaction of MySpace would be?"

A teenage CEO, Lippitt is learning, is even more easily distracted and more fearless than an adult entrepreneur. "Failure is an abstract concept to her, and I want it to stay that way," he says. When he was a teenager, his father lost his body shop and had to start over, attending law school in his forties.

Lippitt urges Ashley to prioritize and think about profits as well as design. As clever as her site-building tool is, it doesn't allow a way to run ads on the pages it creates. "You're leaving revenue on the table," he tells her.

At times, Lippitt has to remind himself that she's only 17. "Even if she could go a lot faster, I don't know if that's the best thing for her," he says. "She's already in the adult world doing adult things. I'm reluctant to drive her away from living an important and fun time in her life."

But he's not shy about pushing her when she needs it. Today, he tells her it's time to consider approaching companies to advertise. So far, she has relied largely on Google AdSense, which supplies ads in exchange for what she says is a 40% cut. The direct model is not only potentially more lucrative but also allows her to target brands more suited to teens than, say, Microsoft Office 2007. "I'm not sure that's a good fit," he says of the software ad placed by ValueClick.

Ashley is excited about the idea. And a little nervous. She'll need a sales presentation, a company logo, and ad rates. Eventually, she may want to hire a sales rep, a job she'd never heard of until Lippitt described it. More important, she'll need to sell herself to name-brand companies. "If she can combine 'I'm 17' with a little more about her business, I think she's unstoppable," Lippitt says.

This could be the next growth spurt for Ashley and What everlife. It's scary, sure, but she's getting used to the demands and challenges of "this crazy opportunity." She's learning, stretching, getting that much-needed seasoning.

She and Lippitt brainstorm about which brands would resonate with girls like her. This is the fun part. No petitions. No regrets. No family feud. Just a 17-year-old and her big dreams in a pink, pink, pink world full of promise. And if they don't come true? Well, there's always college.

From *Fast Company*, September 2007, pp. 104–112. Copyright © 2007 by Mansueto Ventures LLC. Reprinted by permission.

Bloggers against Torture

Negar Azimi

The video that circulated on Egyptian blogs this winter showed Emad Mohamed Ali Mohamed, a 21-year-old bus driver, lying on the floor stripped naked from the waist down—his hands bound behind his back and his legs held in the air. He screams and begs as he is sodomized with a stick while those around him, whose faces are not visible to us, taunt him.

Hours earlier, Ali Mohamed (known among friends as Emad al-Kabir) had been picked up by two plain-clothes police officers in Bulaq alDaqrur, a roughish slum in Giza, across the river from downtown Cairo's crumbling Europeanate area. The young man's offense was venturing to break up a scuffle between police officers and his cousin. Despite the inhospitable treatment he endured, al-Kabir was released thirty-six hours later with no charges to speak of. After all, torture of this variety is commonplace. Protesting its manifestations, or questioning the logic behind it, is usually met with a shrug, even contemptuous indifference.

And so, when it was announced in late December that the two police officers who had supervised the abuse, Capt. Islam Nabih and Cpl. Reda Fathi, had been detained and their case transferred to a criminal court for investigation, it seemed that something had changed. With the simple act of uploading the video to a blog, a web impresario known as Demagh MAK had unleashed a storm of attention both at home and abroad around the case of the diminutive, soft-spoken bus driver. (A still image from the video is reproduced on this page and on this magazine's cover.) A link to the video, passed around among activists and journalists and posted on YouTube (until it was removed for graphic content), was finally picked up by the more intrepid Egyptian independent papers as well as Arab satellite channels such as Al Jazeera and Dream TV. Even a handful of jihadi websites chimed in, fuming about the excesses of the infidel Egyptian regime. Within days, the video had taken on a life of its own.

Watching the revelations unfold, one couldn't help but think there was more to come. Sure enough, before long another leak— also spread via blogs—revealed a man (later identified as Ah med Gad) receiving sharp slaps to the face from a belligerent officer. And then came the jarring image of a young woman, ostensibly a murder suspect, pleading for mercy while suspended from a stick held across two chairs, in what seemed a throwback to a medieval interrogation method. Whoever was behind the camera, presumably a police officer, seemed to relish the ability to capture the scene: As the woman screams "Please, ya basha!" (a sign of prostration) over and over, the camera moves in and out, making use of the zoom function with abandon.

Indeed, this may be just the beginning. Wael Abbas, a Cairo-based blogger who was among the first to post the torture videos, has received nearly a dozen additional videos since the beginning of December. Most have been forwarded anonymously, and most, like al-Kabir's, were captured with simple cellphone cameras.

I met Abbas in late December in Cairo, just as the stir created by the al-Kabir video was reaching its peak. "We know people get raped, beaten all the time. And who's going to stick up for a bus driver? But now it's public, and everyone is talking. The government has to do something. They've lost face," he explained.

While the capacity of the web to jump-start democracy has been exaggerated, blogs have enormous potential as an advocacy tool.

Bloggers in the developing world have long been the subject of romantic odes in the Western press (give a young man a blog and he will start a revolution). While the capacity of digital technologies to jump-start democracy has often been exaggerated, recent events in Egypt demonstrate blogs' enormous potential as an advocacy tool and, more broadly, as an alternative source of news. Here, a number of bloggers seem to have cracked into a hitherto tightly sealed state monopoly on information dissemination, breaking stories in many cases before the mainstream press.

In this neighborhood, the official press dominates circulation numbers—with a single state-controlled paper producing up to 1 million copies a day, while the whole of the independent press puts out 10,000–40,000, according to Arab Press Freedom Watch. Though a handful of independent papers, such as *Al-Dustour* (whose editor, Ibrahim Issa, faces charges of "insulting the president") and *Al Masry Al Youm* (whose writers have faced similar charges), have managed to push the bounds of what is allowable in the public sphere, until recently it would have been unheard of to take on such subjects as torture carried out by officials without being summarily shut down.

But things are changing. In many cases blogs, working hand in hand with the modest independent press as well as satellite television channels ("We are the children of Al Jazeera," one blogger recently told me), have broken a number of big stories—from sectarian strife in Alexandria to state-sponsored violence during the last parliamentary elections, and even the type of routine crackdowns that occur during demonstrations. Together these forces have not only created an alternative source of information but have increasingly managed to shame the government into punishing those responsible for abuses. Since the leak of the notorious "slaps" video, the officer charged with the abuse of Gad, for example, has been suspended while his case is under investigation. The Interior Ministry, meanwhile, has publicly called for the identification of the pleading woman hanging from the stick, as well as the officers who carried out that abuse.

Still, whatever happens to the perpetrators of the recent spate of leaked abuses, torture will likely remain routine in Egypt for the time being. The sort of roughing up that takes place in dark alleys, security checkpoints and dingy police stations daily—normally targeting ordinary citizens—continues to pass unquestioned. Not only are torture and abuse tolerated; in the security services violence is broadly valued as a sign of authority, strength, bravado. It is not uncommon for lower-level officers to get promotions for such theatrics. In fact, the original video of al-Kabir appears to have circulated for months (the abuse was carried out in January 2006) among police officers and taxi drivers, Abu Ghraib–style, before it was leaked to the public. The images were likely shared for bragging purposes—and to serve as a sort of warning to those who would dare to tread on police turf, as al-Kabir had. It's hardly surprising that, following the video's wide circulation and al-Kabir's statements on a satellite television channel about his experience, he received a torrent of phone calls demanding his silence and threatening both him and his family.

This is not the first time that bloggers in this country have roused the ire of the authorities. Last spring at least six bloggers were arrested in connection with demonstrations in solidarity with senior judges demanding independence of the judiciary from the executive branch. Although the bloggers were not explicitly picked up for their writings, their arrests revealed the deep links between electronic activism and the street at large. In Egypt in particular, blogging as a phenomenon was not born in a vacuum but rather has emerged as an extension of existing popular movements—whether it is the country's modest street opposition movement, Kifaya, or even the banned Muslim Brotherhood, which has equally embraced the web and the blogosphere (just look at ikhwanweb.net). Together with e-mail and text messaging, blogging has undeniably changed the way activism is carried out.

Alaa Abd El Fattah, a 24-year-old who blogs with his wife at manalaa.net and also runs omraneya.net, an aggregator for more than 1,500 Egyptian blogs (with 2,000 in queue), was among the detained last spring—held for forty-six days on various charges ranging from insulting the president to obstructing traffic to inciting citizens to topple the regime. As he was leaving state security upon his release one official took him aside, making it clear that he was an avid reader of blogs.

"The people they targeted at the time of the judges' demonstrations used the Internet to mobilize. We've gotten as far as we have as a movement because we're linked to the street. We spread word of demonstrations through blogs, we organize and gain supporters through them, we publicize abuses at protests. Kifaya even started as a petition on the Internet," El Fattah tells me. He counts himself among the self-proclaimed "geeks" who helped make building a community of bloggers a possibility in Egypt and ultimately made the Egyptian blogosphere a success story in the region.

Another young blogger, Mohamed al-Sharkawi, was arrested twice during the judges' demonstrations. On his blog, he had not only supported the striking judges but also posted strident editorials critical of President Hosni Mubarak. In detention, he was blindfolded, beaten and molested with a rolled-up cardboard tube. When I met him in January at his rooftop apartment, he recalled the experience. "All I remember is three voices hanging above me: 'Why are you attending demonstrations? Why did you write on your blog that we treated you badly in prison? Do you think you'll become a star?'" When I asked al-Sharkawi what he would do if the authorities eventually shut down his blog, which he continues to update daily, he replied, "I'll set up another one. They have nearly killed me already—what more can they do?"

But how threatening, we may wonder, can a handful of bloggers be—and how much of a threat could they be to the twenty-five-year-and-running rule of a leader like Mubarak? After all, many of them are simply tech-savvy twenty somethings recently out of university. And besides, how big a role can bloggers play in a country in which they number just over 3,000—a mere fraction of whom write political content?

Hossam el-Hamalawy runs arabawy.org, a blog that has been central to documenting what he has dubbed Egypt's very own Videogate. "We're exploding," he tells me. "The government didn't see it coming, and it's creating a domino effect. You read bloggers in Tunisia, Yemen, Libya, and they take pride in the Egyptian gains. Once you get this far, there's no going back. You can't take the plug out." As recently as January 2005, there were only about thirty blogs in the country. "My dream is that one day there will be a blogger with a digital camera in every street in Egypt."

Exploding or not, this sort of electronic activism defies facile definitions. No longer simply an upper- or middle-class phenomenon, blogging has become an outlet for expression among a broad spectrum of people. Some bloggers post exclusively from Internet cafes (those without PCs), some are without a university education, many are women. Today there is a blogger in every urban center in Egypt—from the stark Sinai Peninsula to Mansoura in the Nile Delta. Most write in Arabic. Recently one blogger went so far as to set up a site devoted to bringing attention to police brutalities taking place in the Sinai following bouts of terrorism (hundreds, even thousands of Bedouins have been disappeared by state security, often locked away and abused with impunity). Other blogs broach the sensitive subject of how the country's religious minorities are treated—particularly the Copts, who make up Egypt's Christian community. Blogs have also been a crucial space for engaging such uncomfortable topics as sexuality, race and beyond. Suddenly, the (improvised) Arabic word *mudawena*, signifying a blogger, has found its way into the lexicon.

The turning point in Egypt in particular, if one were to identify one, may go back to May 2005. Under pressure from his Western patrons to engage in what is casually referred to as "reform," President Mubarak had called for a referendum vote on a constitutional amendment that would provide for the country's first multiparty elections. The proposed amendment, however, was dismissed by many within the country as little more than window dressing to appease the United States, an empty gesture at best. Protests calling for boycotts of the vote on referendum day devolved into a melee marked by hundreds of men—many of them hired government thugs—harassing and sexually abusing women who had gathered on downtown streets. While the government vehemently denied allegations of sexual abuse (dismissing the "fantasies" and "fabrications" of a few "creative minds"), images shot by both participants and observers on small digital cameras and phones wound up on blogs like Wael Abbas's in the following days—making it virtually impossible to explain away the accusations. Since that time, blogs have become a repository for everything from stories about striking ambulance workers threatening to commit suicide to debates about corruption in the health sector to accounts of camel butchers shouting obscenities at parliamentary speaker Fathi Sorour. In other words, these are stories that would never see the light of day given the conventions and dictates of the state press.

For good reason, the government is growing jittery about blogging. At the moment, at least one blogger, Abdul Kareem Nabeil Suleiman (who goes by the Internet name Kareem Amer), remains in solitary confinement, awaiting trial for his criticisms of Islam in general and conservative Al-Azhar University, where he was once a student, in particular. The charges against him include "defaming the president of Egypt." One Coptic blogger, Hala Helmy Botros (she goes by the Internet name Hala El Masry), who has written at length about persecution of the Coptic minority, clearly went too far recently; the computers at an Internet cafe she once frequented have been confiscated. (Proprietors of Internet cafes are often given lists of people who may not use their services, checking ID is de rigueur and prominent signs announce "No entry to political or sexual sites by order of the State Security.") And on January 8 a reporter from Al Jazeera named Howeida Taha was detained as she was leaving the country. Taha had tapes in hand for work on a forthcoming documentary on torture; she had recorded testimonies of victims and had amassed various videos of police brutality. Al Jazeera, for its part, announced on its Arabic-language website that Egyptian prosecutors had accused the journalist of "filming footage that harms the national interest of the country, possessing and giving pictures contradicting the truth, and giving a wrong description of the situation in the country."

There are additional signs that the government campaign against electronic activism may be escalating. The Interior Ministry has been pursuing this campaign through a special unit called the Department for Confronting Computer and Internet Crime. Thanks to a 2006 court ruling, websites can be shut down if they are deemed a threat to national security. Some of the country's more active political bloggers, such as Abbas and al-Sharkawi, are regularly trailed, harassed and intimidated by state security. And the official press has been launching rhetorical attacks against bloggers at large, accusing them of "spreading malicious rumors about Egypt," "working for the Americans," "engaging in satanic sexual fantasy" and so on.

Middle Eastern bloggers are engaging in a sort of citizen journalism that stands, in its own modest way, to alter the political terrain.

Across the Middle East bloggers are engaging in a sort of citizen journalism that stands, in its own modest way, to alter the political terrain. In Bahrain they have clamored for freedom of expression on the web, also having played a large role in pushing for female participation in that country's parliamentary elections. Earlier this year Bahraini bloggers used Google Earth satellite maps to juxtapose the vast wealth of the ruling family against increasingly destitute areas, exposing the rampant inequities in the Gulf kingdom at large

(imagine palace meets slum). The Google Earth site was shut down for three days until international attention seemed to shame the Bahraini government into lifting the ban. In Lebanon blogs provided a home for reactions to last summer's war, along with documentation of its ravages. In Qaddafi's Libya blogs persist, though a number of political bloggers have been imprisoned, and in one especially sordid case a writer covering government corruption had his fingers chopped off before he was murdered—presumably a sign to others who would consider following his lead. And this is to say nothing of Iran, where Internet activity is so significant that despite restrictions, Farsi has cracked the top ten represented languages in the global blogosphere.

But where, you may ask, are the Western governments that have lent such impassioned rhetorical support to the democratic aspirations of citizens of the Middle East since 9/11? In Egypt, the US government in particular has undeniably played some role in creating openings for activists, bloggers among them. But today that commitment seems to have ebbed, the enthusiasm for democracy promotion dampened by the prospect of Islamist groups like the Muslim Brotherhood, Hamas and Hezbollah gaining power via elections throughout the region.

And so when Secretary of State Condoleezza Rice passed through Cairo on one leg of a Middle East tour in January, she made it crystal clear that her Administration had opted to favor stability over rocking the boat. She uttered hardly a whisper about the events of recent weeks (torture revelations, jailed bloggers) or the country's dismal human rights record in general. At a news conference in the historic city of Luxor, Rice intoned, "Obviously the relationship with Egypt is an important strategic relationship—one that we value greatly." On previous trips to the country, Rice had been more confrontational, raising issues such as the importance of free and fair elections, the need for an independent judiciary and even the country's subpar treatment of its political prisoners. This time around, however, there was not a peep about anything that could compromise the postcard image of Egypt as a reliably moderate, pro-Western Arab regime. As the US government's grandiose plan to democratize the region stumbles—and Iraq in particular (which was to be the jewel in the crown of this new Middle East) slips further into pandemonium—even the requisite lip service to reform has all but disappeared. The noose on local democracy activists, in the meantime, tightens.

Just days before the Secretary of State's visit, in what seemed an uncanny twist of fate, al-Kabir, the young bus driver, was sentenced to three months in prison. The charge: "resisting authorities." While the police officers responsible for his abuse will face a trial in March, his lawyer and human rights groups expressed concern that al-Kabir would face further torture in prison. His bizarre sentence seemed to signal that little may have changed, despite the glimmer of hope offered by the media frenzy of the past weeks. Indeed, as the ruling was announced, it seemed that for the Egyptian regime as well as the US government that readily accommodates it, it was back to business as usual.

NEGAR AZIMI is senior editor of *Bidoun,* an arts and culture magazine based in New York.

Reprinted by permission from the February 19, 2007 issue of *The Nation.* Copyright © 2007 by The Nation. For subscription information, call 1-800-333-8536. Portions of each week's Nation magazine can be accessed at www.thenation.com

It's Not Easy to Stand up to Cyberbullies, but We Must

Robert M. O'Neil

A decade ago, the Supreme Court proclaimed the Internet a "unique and wholly new medium—a vast platform from which to address and hear from a worldwide audience of millions of readers, viewers, researchers, and buyers." Academe fully shared that sense of promise and excitement. Even at that time, the justices were hardly naïve about the lurking presence of offensive material in cyberspace; the court's first major case about free speech online, *Reno v. American Civil Liberties Union,* did, after all, involve regulation of sexually explicit imagery. But the general impression of the Internet was apparently sufficiently benign that the court was ready to confer full First Amendment protection on a new medium.

Little did we anticipate how different that rosy view might seem today, especially from the vantage point of the college campus. Several troubling developments have occurred within the past months, the most recent in April, in the aftermath of "Cedar Fest," a street festival held near Michigan State University. The event devolved into a melee, and the local police declared their intent to investigate and possibly to file criminal charges for incitement against the authors of Facebook postings publicizing the event.

A second incident involves the 2006 suicide of Megan Meier, a 13-year-old in Missouri. The details emerged last fall: She was apparently driven to kill herself by taunts and cruel messages from an adult neighbor posing as another teenager on MySpace. On May 15, a federal grand jury indicted the woman—the mother of Megan's former friend—on one count of conspiracy and three counts of accessing a computer without authorization and via interstate commerce to obtain information to inflict emotional distress.

Although the victim's young age might leave college students unimpressed about their potential liability for digital harassment, lawmakers in at least two states have recently sponsored "cyberbullying" laws that, to quote the proposed Missouri legislation, would impose criminal liability on the basis of "intent to coerce, intimidate, harass, or cause substantial emotional distress." The legal response to Megan Meier's tragedy could affect electronic messages in higher education as well.

Both of those troubling events are as novel as they are disturbing, and both pose legal and policy issues for higher education.

At the heart of the problem lies a profound difference between electronic and print messages.

In 1996, Congress enacted Section 230 of the Communications Decency Act, which provides immunity from legal liability for messages posted by anyone other than the operator or proprietor of a site or service. Thus a person who has been indisputably defamed in cyberspace may recover damages only if the message was personally posted by the blog or site operator, or if the prospective plaintiff can somehow discover the identity of the typically anonymous or pseudonymous author. The readiness of state courts to compel bloggers and sites to "unmask" authors in response to such claims varies widely, and offers at best an unreliable avenue of potential redress for the libel victim.

The presence of such a barrier goes far to explain why victims are frustrated, as most poignantly illustrated by Juicy Campus, a campus-gossip website. The victims of Juicy Campus have seen job prospects vanish and collegial esteem abate overnight as the direct result of scurrilous charges about dishonesty, promiscuity, or other attacks on their characters. Yet the website, which is divided into more than 60 message boards dedicated to individual colleges and universities, is wholly beyond reach of college officers. Student leaders at a number of institutions have publicly condemned Juicy Campus, while others have urged their fellow students to boycott the site and have even obtained classmates' pledges never to visit it.

Pepperdine University complained to Google, Juicy Campus's ad network, and it removed the site from its network, although Juicy Campus simply joined another ad network and the postings continued unabated. New Jersey officials have begun an inquiry into possible violations of the state's consumer-fraud laws, but Juicy Campus's founder insists the site makes no claims that are actionable.

Others have fought back by bombarding the site with content intended to crash it or at least slow it down, but no long-term effects seem to have resulted. Indeed, a recent *Chronicle* account notes that "students on dozens of campuses continue to post to the site enthusiastically, calling each other names. Many others wish it would stop, but even some of them are reading to see whose name appears next."

The prospect of criminal liability for inflammatory Internet postings may, however, pose different issues. East Lansing police, for example, may be able to identify the author or authors of the messages that apparently triggered the recent riot at Michigan State. The "unmasking" process should be simpler in that context. Service providers and site proprietors will readily identify the author of a credible threat when asked to do so by law-enforcement agencies, and would probably be far more responsive to an incitement charge than to a private libel suit.

Even if the inciter or inciters can be identified, however, liability is far from clear. Nearly 40 years ago, the Supreme Court established a clear and highly protective standard for culpable advocacy that remains unimpaired even by developments after September 11, 2001: A provocative speaker may not under the First Amendment be punished "except where such advocacy is directed to inciting or producing imminent lawless action and is likely to incite or produce such action." Several years later the justices added an important corollary: The charged statements must be "addressed to [a particular] person or group" and must be "intended to produce, and likely to produce, imminent disorder."

How those standards may apply to Internet advocacy is complex. Any communication other than inflammatory face-to-face statements would typically fall well short of "incitement." In cyberspace, anything less direct or "addressed" than a person-to-person e-mail message, or possibly a catalytic message posted in a small, closed chat room or newsgroup, would almost certainly fail to meet the Supreme Court's appropriately high standards for incitement.

Finally, the prospect of liability—either civil or criminal—for damaging another person's reputation, or inflicting even graver harm through electronic messages, remains highly problematic under U.S. law (other legal systems, though, may be more protective of individual interests, as an invasion-of-privacy suit just filed against Facebook by a group of Canadian law students suggests).

Tort law has long allowed recovery for intentional infliction of emotional distress, although only when there is clear proof of intent, of impact, and of a specifically directed (if not face-to-face) message. Libel suits are always chancy, especially for anyone who may be deemed a "public figure," and there is a risk that a plaintiff's reputation might suffer more in the course of seeking vindication.

Institutional sanctions may occasionally avail, but beyond such appeals to higher standards of student expression, there seems remarkably little that concerned institutions (or their besmirched students) can do to clean up their electronic neighborhoods.

ROBERT M. O'NEIL is founding director of the Thomas Jefferson Center for the Protection of Free Expression, a former president of the University of Virginia, and a professor emeritus of law at UVa.

From *The Chronicle of Higher Education,* by Robert M. O'Neil, July 11, 2008. Copyright © 2008 by The Chronicle of Higher Education. Reproduced with permission. This article may not be published, reposted, or redistributed without the express permission of The Chronicle of Higher Education.

The Nike Experiment: How the Shoe Giant Unleashed the Power of Personal Metrics

MARK MCCLUSKY

On June 6, 2008, Veronica Noone attached a small sensor to her running shoes and headed out the door. She pressed start on her iPod and began keeping track of every step she took. It wasn't a long run—just 1.67 miles in 18 minutes and 36 seconds, but it was the start of something very big for her.

Since that day, she's run 95 more times, logging 283.8 miles in about 48 hours on the road. She's burned 28,672 calories. And her weight, which topped 225 pounds when she was pregnant, has settled in at about 145.

Noone knows all of that thanks to the sensor system, called Nike+. After each run, she can sync her iPod to the Nike+ website and get a visual representation of the workout—a single green line. Its length shows how far she's gone, and the peaks and valleys reflect her speed.

For a self-described "stat whore," there's something powerfully motivating about all the data that Nike+ collects. "It just made running so much more entertaining for me," says Noone, who blogs at ronisweigh.com. "There's something about seeing what you've done, how your pace changes as you go up and down hills, that made me more motivated."

Noone is now running four times a week and just did her first 10-mile race. She's training for a half marathon and hoping to do a full marathon by the end of the year. And she attributes much of her newfound fitness to the power of data. "I can log in to Nike+ and see what I've done over the past year," she says. "That's really powerful for me. When I started, I was running shorter and slower. But I can see that progression. I don't have to question what I've done. The data is right there in white and green."

Noone has joined the legion of people, from Olympic-level athletes to ordinary folks just hoping to lower their blood pressure, who are plugging into a data-driven revolution. And it goes way beyond Nike+. Using a flood of new tools and technologies, each of us now has the ability to easily collect granular information about our lives—what we eat, how much we sleep, when our mood changes.

And not only can we collect that data, we can analyze it as well, looking for patterns, information that might help us change both the quality and the length of our lives. We can live longer and better by applying, on a personal scale, the same quantitative mindset that powers Google and medical research. Call it Living by Numbers—the ability to gather and analyze data about yourself, setting up a feedback loop that we can use to upgrade our lives, from better health to better habits to better performance.

Few things illustrate the power and promise of Living by Numbers quite as clearly as the Nike+ system. By combining a dead-simple way to amass data with tools to use and share it, Nike has attracted the largest community of runners ever assembled—more than 1.2 million runners who have collectively tracked more than 130 million miles and burned more than 13 billion calories.

With such a huge group, Nike is learning things we've never known before. In the winter, people in the US run more often than those in Europe and Africa, but for shorter distances. The average duration of a run worldwide is 35 minutes, and the most popular Nike+ Powersong, which runners can set to give them extra motivation, is "Pump It" by the Black Eyed Peas.

The company couldn't have gathered all that information, and gained all those insights, if it hadn't reconfigured how runners approach their sport. Nike has done more than create a successful product; it has fundamentally changed the way more than a million people think about exercise.

A brown plastic box, emblazoned with Nike's iconic Swoosh logo, sits on the conference room table at the company's headquarters in Beaverton, Oregon. It's a clunky thing, the size of a thick paperback book, with a waist strap and two ports on the front that look like miniature speakers, lending it the air of a shrunken mid-'80s boom box.

It was called the Nike Monitor, and it was the company's first attempt to sell runners a product that would tell them how far and fast they had run. The ports on the front weren't speakers—they were sonar detectors that would calculate a runner's speed, which would then be announced over a pair of headphones. The Monitor had to be strapped to the runner's waist facing forward.

It may have been a good idea, but it was utterly impractical. Less than two years after its 1987 launch, the Monitor was dropped from Nike's product lineup.

How Nike+ Works

Michael Tchao, head of Nike's Techlab, laughs. "You can imagine that this device, a little big, maybe not the most fashionable, wasn't the huge runaway success we had hoped. But even 20 years ago, we were experimenting in this space."

Despite Nike's shoe-centric business, its experiments in electronics continued. It launched a line of sports watches, made heart rate monitors, and even entered into an agreement with Philips to market an MP3 player. And Nike engineers constantly tinkered with what they referred to as a "smart shoe," a sneaker with built-in sensors that would automatically record the length and speed of your runs.

But a smart shoe, they realized, wasn't enough—you needed a device to save the data. By late 2004 the engineers started to notice that most of the runners they saw on Nike's campus were sporting white earbuds. The Apple iPod, which debuted in 2001, had mushroomed in popularity, with sales doubling every quarter. "Most runners were running with music already," says Nike president and CEO Mark Parker. "We thought the real opportunity would come if we could combine music and data."

Nike engineers started to brainstorm. They cooked up various demos, even sketching a shoe with an embedded iPod. Finally, Parker picked up the phone and called a friend who worked at Apple—CEO Steve Jobs. After that call, teams from both companies got together at Nike headquarters. "We talked about the idea of Nike+ and actually had a little storyboard that showed it," says Tchao, who worked at Apple for 10 years before joining Nike. "Steve called it 'the speedometer for sports,' and we thought that was an interesting way to describe it. People drove around in cars before speedometers, and today you can't imagine driving without one."

Both companies saw profit potential if they could develop the system together, so the Nike and Apple teams each took on different parts of the project. Apple refined the sensor that Nike had prototyped, making it smaller and more durable. Nike focused on the shoes and the interface for the Web and the iPod. It created a simple system based around the idea of setting goals.

If a runner wants to run 5 miles, they enter that distance and press start. During the run, voice prompts let the runner know how fast they're moving, how far they've gone, and how much farther they need to go. At the end of the run, the user presses stop and the data is saved on the iPod. The next time they sync their iPod, the workout data is automatically uploaded to NikePlus.com, which adds the current information to the history of all their runs.

The basic science that allowed Nike and Apple to capture this information is low tech, introduced in a 40-year-old study published by biomechanical researcher Richard Nelson at Penn State. Nelson filmed a mix of 16 freshman and varsity athletes at the university running at various speeds, on smooth and sloped surfaces. What he found was both simple and powerful—the amount of time a runner's foot is in contact with the ground is inversely proportional to how fast he's running and unaffected by slope or stride length. That means if you know how long that

---

Capture

The shoe sensor's accelerometer measures the amount of time a runner's foot is on the ground, which is inversely proportional to speed. Transmitting at 2.4 GHz, the sensor sends data to a receiver that's either attached to an iPod nano or built into the second-gen iPod touch.

Sync

After the workout, the iPod is synced to a computer running iTunes, which automatically sends the data, including start time, duration, and distance, to the Nike+ servers, formatted in a specially structured XML file that can also be read by third-party and open source apps.

Share

Users can access their run history at NikePlus.com, browse through a graph that shows all their activity, and then drill down to details about each workout. If they need more motivation, they can enter challenges or set individualized goals, like running 100 miles in a month.

---

contact lasts, you can make a pretty good guess as to how fast the runner is going.

"People in biomechanics knew about this, but they felt it wasn't good enough for the lab, because it's accurate to plus or minus 5 percent," says Mario Lafortune, director of Nike's Sport Research Lab. "But for an application like Nike+ it's tremendously accurate."

The Nike+ sensor consists of just three parts. There's an accelerometer that detects when your foot hits and leaves the ground, calculating that all-important contact time. There's a transmitter that sends the information to a receiver, one that's either clipped onto an iPod nano or built into the second-generation iPod touch. And there's the battery. That's what Nike+ is.

What's more interesting is what Nike+ *isn't*. There's no GPS that automatically tracks your routes—if you want to map your run, you have to do it manually on the Nike site. There's no heart rate monitor, so even though you know how far and how fast you've traveled, you don't know what level of cardiovascular exertion it required. "We really wanted to separate ourselves from that sort of very technical, geeky side of things," Tchao says. "Everyone understands speed and distance."

In other words, Nike+ isn't a perfect tool; it wasn't designed to be. But it's good enough, and more crucially, it's simple. Nike learned a huge lesson from Apple: The iPod wasn't a massive hit because it was the most powerful music player on the market but because it offered the easiest, most streamlined user experience.

But that simple, dual-variable tracking can lead to novel insights, especially once you have so many people feeding in data: The most popular day for running is Sunday, and most Nike+ users tend to work out in the evening. After the holidays, there's a huge increase in the number of goals that runners set; this past January, they set 312 percent more goals than the month before.

There's something even deeper. Nike has discovered that there's a magic number for a Nike+ user: five. If someone uploads only a couple of runs to the site, they might just be trying it out. But once they hit five runs, they're massively more likely to keep running and uploading data. At five runs, they've gotten hooked on what their data tells them about themselves.

I n the mid-1920s at Western Electric's manufacturing plant in Cicero, Illinois, the management began an experiment. The lighting in an area occupied by one set of workers was increased so there was better illumination to help them see the telephone relays they were building. Perhaps not surprisingly, workers who had more light were able to assemble relays faster.

Other changes were then made: Employees were given rest breaks. Their productivity increased. They were allowed to work shorter hours. Again, they were more efficient during those hours.

But then something weird happened. The lighting was cut back to normal . . . and productivity still went up. In fact, just about every change the company made had only one effect: increased worker productivity. After months of tinkering, the work conditions were returned to the original state, and workers built more relays than they did in the exact same circumstances at the start of the experiment.

What was happening? Why was it that no matter what the Hawthorne plant managers did, the workers just performed better? Researchers puzzled over the results, and some still doubt the details of the experiment's protocols. But the study gave rise to what's known in sociology as the Hawthorne effect.

The gist of the idea is that people change their behavior—often for the better—when they are being observed (which is why it's sometimes called the observer effect). Those workers at Western Electric didn't build more relays because there was more or less light or because they had more or fewer breaks. The Hawthorne effect posits that they built more relays simply because they knew someone was keeping track of how many relays they built.

When you lace up your running shoes outfitted with the Nike+ sensor and fire up your iPod, you're both the researcher and the subject—a self-contained experimental system. And what you're likely to find is that the Hawthorne effect kicks in. You're actively observing yourself, and just that fact not only provides information you can act on but also may modify your behavior. That's the power of Living by Numbers.

Keeping track of our lives is nothing new. Athletes have kept training logs to quantify and analyze their workouts. Counting calories has long been a popular and effective way to lose weight.

In the past, that required two steps. First, there was the recording of the information, then the actual effort to modify behavior. In study after study, this extra work turned out to be a huge burden. Compliance fell, and the outcome suffered: People would stop monitoring their caloric intake, fail to change it, and fail to lose weight. Make the data-gathering easy and you remove one of the barriers to meaningful improvement in our lives.

With Nike+ and other tools, that first step has become almost effortless. Dieters don't have to calculate the caloric content of meals manually; they can just log in to FitDay to enter the information in an online food diary. Keeping a training log doesn't mean busting out a pen and paper at the end of a run. It's as simple as listening to music on an iPod while exercising.

But the power of self-tracking is even more profound. It's not just that collecting this data can help us change our behavior all on its own. Using the immensely powerful tools now becoming available, we can set up positive feedback loops: We keep track of something, see how the data matches up with what we'd like to have happen, and then use that knowledge to modify our actions.

The effect of feedback on attempts to change behavior is well established. A 2001 study in the *American Journal of Health Behavior* showed that personalized feedback increased the effectiveness of everything from smoking-cessation programs to interventions for problem drinkers to exercise programs. Feedback is important and powerful; it works.

That feedback can be internal, too, because when we start to do things to make ourselves more healthy, our bodies react. When obese people lose as little as 7 percent of their body weight, the levels of adiponectin in their blood goes up—reducing their risk of developing type 2 diabetes. Or consider the five-run threshold that Nike has seen in the data. It might be that runners not only like the information they get; they might be getting positive feedback from their body after five runs as well.

Think of it this way: It used to be that to lose weight, you'd keep a diary of everything you ate. Stepping on a scale is easy enough and gives one data point—about the system's output, not its inputs. But develop a system that allows you to track not only your weight but also what you eat, how you exercise, even how you're feeling, and suddenly you can start to pull things together. You can see how all those variables interact and then put that information to use.

We tend to think of our physical selves as a system that's simply too complex to comprehend. But what we've learned from companies like Google is that if you can collect enough data, there's no need for a grand theory to explain a phenomenon. You can observe it all through the numbers. Everything is data. *You* are your data, and once you understand that data, you can act on it.

O n August 31, 2008, thousands of runners lined up for a 10K race in Taipei. And in Melbourne, Australia. In Istanbul and Munich, in Paris and New York, in Austin and at Nike headquarters. In 25 cities, Nike organized what it dubbed the Human Race. But if you weren't in one of these locations, you could still participate—by running 10 kilometers on your own and uploading the data to Nike+ . That day, 779,275 people participated both at the race sites and virtually, together running more than 4 million miles.

Gathering and connecting such a large community unlocks another powerful effect of Living by Numbers—the feedback loop that comes not from you but from the world around you. Simply put, other people can tell you to go out and run.

It's one thing if some company tells me that I'm slacking off, like when Nike+ sends an email reminding me to get out and exercise. It's a whole different thing if people whose opinion I care about get on my case. Nike+ lets a user create a goal—one that other people can see. Let's say I pledge to run 100 miles this month. I can then enter the email addresses of people I'd like to cheer me on—my wife, my mother, my boss. As I sync up after each run, the data is uploaded to the site, and my support group is updated on my progress. The hope is that they'll use whatever techniques they can to try to motivate me. (One imagines praise, guilt, and threats, in that order.)

Again, Nike is tapping into well-known science here—the power of communities. Nicholas Christakis, a researcher at Harvard Medical School, has been examining how social networks influence our behavior. For instance, in a network of more than 12,000 people in Framingham, Massachusetts, he found that smoking behavior tends to cluster: People quit smoking in groups, as part of a team effort; as more of them stop, the remaining smokers find themselves moving to the margins of the social network. Those community ties have direct effects on people's behavior.

Competition can be another great motivator. Nike+ has a feature that sets up challenges for a group of runners, from just two friends to the entire massive community. Software developer and Nike+ runner Cabel Sasser compares the system to a videogame. "Like any good online game, you can challenge your friends," wrote Sasser on his blog. "First to 100 miles? Fastest 5-mile time? Your call. These challenges wind up being incredibly inspiring . . . Logging in after a long run, uploading your data, and seeing where you are in the standings is a pretty awesome way to wrap up your exercise. And more important, sitting around the house, wondering what to do, thinking about jogging, and then realizing that if you don't go jogging tonight you're going to lose points and slip in the standings—now that's true videogame motivation."

As Nike has slowly added features to Nike+ , a small group of outside software makers have raced forward, showing how the system might grow and morph over time. Open source projects like Neki + + and Running Tracker give you control over your data, allowing you to download and analyze it directly, without going through Nike's site. Since the data is exported from the iPod in a standardized format, it's relatively easy for other services to manipulate. Users have hooked Nike+ into other social networks—Twiike automatically posts your run data to Twitter whenever you sync it.

In a stance that's uncommon for a company that has historically relied on patented technology like its Air cushioning system, Nike seems to be genuinely excited to see these tools sprout up. After all, the more apps out there, the more Nike+ gear the company can sell. "The more we can open up Nike+ , the better," says Stefan Olander, who oversees digital content for the Nike+ site. "The only reason to close it out is because you actually don't believe that you have a strong enough product for others to want to take it and do good things with it." So far, Nike hasn't officially released a software kit to allow developers to hook directly into Nike+ , but that's likely to come.

"The open sourcing piece hasn't been developed yet," says Nike CEO Parker, "but that's part of our plan moving forward. The technology here is still in its infancy."

The challenge Nike faces is that it's a hardware company, one that owes its success to deep understanding of cushioning foam and biomechanics. The genius of Nike+ isn't the hardware, no matter how clever and easy to use it might be. The genius is the software—the deeper insight it allows and the connections with others it helps make.

So while some athletes would like to see more features, like heart rate monitoring (the company says that it is looking into it for a next-generation product), that's almost beside the point. If Nike wants to make Nike+ into the universal platform where athletes track their workout data, it has to find new, unexpected ways to collect and share it effortlessly.

Nike has always tried to meet the physical needs of athletes with shoes and equipment, but Nike+ does something very different. Nike+ is about creating, and then meeting, a psychological need. "What Nike+ taught us about was context," says Trevor Edwards, Nike vice president of global brand management. "It lets the product live beyond its physical use."

There's a purity about running. All you need are a set of legs and lungs and the effort required to move forward, faster. For most runners, it's an intensely individual experience—you and the road or trail. The world shrinks, and you focus on yourself in isolation.

Of course, another word for *isolation* is *boredom.* For a lot of people, there's something excruciating about exercise—it's right up there with balancing your checkbook, visiting your in-laws, and flossing your teeth. That was the case with Rick Law. "I used to complain about how inactive I was and wish there was an interesting way to become more physically active," says Law, who works as a technology manager at Thomson Reuters in Fort Worth, Texas. In 2007, Law's wife gave him a Nike+ system for Christmas, hoping it would motivate him.

It did. The first run Law did was just over 10 minutes long, not even a mile. But day after day, he'd head out in the morning before going to the office, putting in the work to get stronger and faster. Soon he was up to 3 miles, then 8, then 10.

By tracking his effort—enhancing an analog experience with digital technology—Law found that running could be as interesting as his work. When you're Living by Numbers, what happens after the run becomes as important as the run itself. Law got feedback as he ran and enjoyed the sense of accomplishment that came from charting his progress as he got more and more fit.

For many Nike+ users, doing their exercise becomes inextricable from measuring it. Again and again, they tell you that without their unit, running is mundane, like listening to a symphony through laptop speakers "Forgetting my Nike+ sensor, or my iPod battery being dead, just takes the life out of my run," Law says.

A couple of weeks before Christmas 2008, Law ran the Dallas White Rock Half Marathon. "It was an endurance struggle for me," Law says. "But in a year, I went from the couch to a half marathon." He finished the 13.1 miles in two hours, 26 minutes, 28 seconds. Now, Law is training for the Chicago Marathon in October, tracking a new goal. All told, he's spent 75 hours and 27 minutes on the road, and he's put in 428.8 miles. And counting.

Senior editor **MARK MCCLUSKY** (mark_mcclusky@wired.com) wrote about performance-enhancing drugs in issue 15.01.

From *Wired,* July 2009. Copyright © 2009 by Wired. Reprinted by permission.

Center Stage

The Internet has become an integral part of the way newspapers distribute their content, a phenomenon that's only going to increase. AJR's senior editor takes a firsthand look at four papers' Web operations.

CARL SESSIONS STEPP

It's only 9 A.M. and today's Houston Chronicle has barely hit people's doorsteps, but Sylvia Wood, the Chronicle's online local news editor, already is working a breaking, and heartbreaking, story.

A 15-year-old boy has been killed playing with a pistol with three friends. As seems so common, the boys thought the gun was unloaded. They pulled the trigger once. A harmless click. The second time, the ninth grader was shot in the chest.

Wood has posted a brief on chron.com. She has a Chronicle reporter on the way to the scene and is scrambling to locate a yearbook photo of the victim. She's also juggling two more spot stories while around her, in a newsroom as quiet as a library, print colleagues shuffle in sipping from their Starbucks cups and grunting their good mornings.

The chance for error probably soars. On the other hand, you can correct those errors immediately and forever.

It is a scene repeated more and more often as mainstream newsrooms adjust to becoming two worlds in one. The roller-coaster rhythm of print—the steady early climb followed by the precipitous plunge to deadline—is being joined, and may soon be overtaken, by the Web's all-out, all-day, all-night news cycle. Like the arrival of a gigantic planet next door, online newsrooms have begun exerting a culture-changing gravitational pull.

What do online newsrooms look like? How do they work? How are they affecting their print neighbors? I recently visited online newsrooms of various sizes and interviewed journalists within and outside the online world. The results were enlightening, and sometimes surprising.

First, at places large enough to have separate online newsrooms, they look similar to their print counterparts, except they are cleaner, quieter and younger. You see the usual rows of desks grouped into pods, with executives occupying glass offices. But things tend to look newer and sleeker, with carpet still unstained. There seem to be more twentysomethings. And because Web journalists mostly post copy gathered by others, there is less reporting going on and thus less noise.

Organizationally, online newsrooms are arranged by section. But you also find TV studios and mysterious hideaways where technical wizardry takes place (one at washingtonpost.com is known as The Cave). Titles vary. Online journalists are as likely to be called producers or news directors as editors.

A vital difference: With many people posting and without fixed schedules, it is impractical to funnel all content through a copy desk. So a fair amount of copy produced by the Web staff gets little or no editing, and few items get the multiple reads routine in print.

Design isn't a daily concern. Most homepages have a standard look, with a low-tech tool or template that lets editors post easily. Covering breaking news—especially crime, a role that had been appropriated by broadcast—is making a comeback. The running spot-news blog seems especially popular.

Most striking are two clear, probably transforming trends: a move toward merging online and print newsrooms, and a surge toward producing news almost around the clock. These changes may well revolutionize newsrooms, and they raise important questions. Who will produce the volumes of copy required? How will quality be monitored without the overlapping layers of editing? What will be stressed in hiring? How will all this affect the enduring and ingrained newsroom culture?

To explore all this, a good place to start is the sprawling operations of the Houston Chronicle and chron.com.

Dean Betz, chron.com's online news editor and in effect its managing editor, is hurrying to the newsroom's 4 P.M. meeting when he encounters, in an elevator, Dudley Althaus, a Mexico City correspondent on a home visit.

The reporter has heard the paper wants him to start a blog. Betz nods. The reporter wonders how you balance news and opinion in a blog. Let's discuss it with your editor, Betz replies. In the hallway, the Chronicle's reader representative, James Campbell, buttonholes Betz. He's already blogging. They chat about it as they enter the news meeting, a huge affair involving more than 35 people. Betz sets up an online connection projected onto a big screen.

He's called on right away by Editor Jeff Cohen. Betz describes what chron.com and its competitors have been posting.

Some key financial reports are due today, and Cohen presses for quick online publication. "We have got to be getting these stories up the second they come in," Cohen says. Then he announces, to predictable titters, that the website will be partnering in some unspecified way with a local Web-based dating service.

From blogs to business data to dating, Web activity is seizing center stage in Houston.

Betz, 44, says the goal is "making the newspaper and the website one thing. That's the only way newspapers have any chance of making things work—not thinking they are newspaper companies, but that they are news companies."

Editor Cohen, 51, is a convert. His print newsroom has about 350 staffers, and the paper's daily circulation is about 520,000. As at most newspapers, circulation and penetration have dropped, but Cohen says "we have more than made up for it on the Web." With 20 editorial staffers, the website draws some 2.9 million unique viewers a month and makes a profit. "It's obvious you have to start devoting more of your resources to the Web," Cohen says.

For now, most Web staffers work from the paper's 10th floor. Only Sylvia Wood sits in the fifth-floor city room. But all that is going to change.

Cohen opens a binder to show his online goals for 2006: to generate more content from readers, develop more Spanish content and "further integrate the Web and the newsroom."

He leads a brisk tour of space being remodeled to bring Web journalists onto the newsroom floor. "In order for it to be clear what we're doing," he says, "they've got to be close—in sight, in mind, not out of sight, out of mind."

Environmental reporter Dina Cappiello, 32, understands. "Psychologically, the physical presence says, 'This is important. This isn't going to be an afterthought.'"

The one Web editor inside the newsroom, Wood, sits with other assistant city editors at the center of the action. Here, she says, "You're pretty much clued in as to what the reporters are doing."

Wood, 39, works a 7 A.M. to 4 P.M. shift. She takes a handoff from an overnight editor, sits in on the morning news meeting, trolls early for updates and spot news, and tries to post about eight local items a day. "My goal," Wood says, "is to get as much as we can up before the 12 o'clock news."

The morning flurry stems in part from the fact that visits to chron.com spike as people arrive at work. The entire morning paper "rolls over" onto the Web around 12:30 A.M., but the site evolves all day. There are updates and Web-only features from sports and entertainment as well as news, plus numerous discussion forums and blogs by staff members and readers.

TV News Online

The police chase breaks out at 2:20 P.M., just as Jim Thompson, KHOU-TV's website manager, is saying, "Our bread and butter is immediacy, breaking news, delivering content as it happens."

On cue, both Channel 11, a CBS affiliate, and its partner, KHOU.com, go straight to live chase video from the station's helicopter. Web Deputy Editor Michelle Homer streams it online, while KHOU reporters provide TV voice-over. The chase runs live for more than an hour until its dramatic end. The runaway driver crashes into a car occupied by a grandmother, mother and 8-month-old girl. As cameras roll and police close in, the mother leaps from her car and pounds furiously on the offending vehicle.

With about 350,000 unique visitors a month and a full-time staff of four, Belo-owned KHOU.com is smaller than its Houston Chronicle competitor. But it aggressively tracks local news, especially stories with hot video.

The KHOU newsroom resembles a small newspaper, with reporters' desks lining one side. The room is dominated by a power triangle: the TV assignment desk, the TV producers' pod and the Web pod, which benefits from the proximity. "Anyone who has worked in a newsroom knows," Thompson says, "that about 50 percent of what you get you overhear."

The police chase electrifies the room. All four assignment desk editors are simultaneously barking into phones and pounding keyboards. A news meeting comes to a standstill as Executive News Director Keith Connors follows the action. Thompson's group staffs the website six days a week, changing the lead story at least every three hours or so. The set-up is similar to newspaper sites, but far more preoccupied with video.

"If on TV we don't get video, we don't have a story," Thompson, 38, says. "So whenever a story breaks, our team is out the door. And that plays great for the website."

The Web also lends itself to footage that might not suit TV, Thompson says. "We don't want it to be a polished TV stand-up. We want it to be rough and raw. We want you the viewer to know what's it's like to be there. Sometimes it's not going to be pretty, but it's going to be the fastest, most accurate news you can get."

Connors plans to double the Web staff this year. "To be in this game, you have to get in totally," he says. "We are not wading in the kiddie pool. We need to jump totally in."

—Carl Sessions Stepp

Legal reporter Mary Flood, 52, a Web enthusiast who has covered Enron-related stories for three years, says she has filed as many as 12 updates a day from important court cases. "It's simultaneously made things more exciting and more exhausting," she says.

Online Favorites

Most viewed newspaper websites in February

Unique Visitors

nytimes.com	12,702,000
USAToday.com	10,372,000
washingtonpost.com	8,244,000
latimes.com	4,865,000
SFGate.com (San Francisco Chronicle)	4,602,000
wsj.com (Wall Street Journal)	3,937,000
Boston.com (Boston Globe)	3,525,000
nydailynews.com	3,026,000
chicagotribune.com	2,942,000
chron.com (Houston Chronicle)	2,916,000

Source: *Nielsen//NetRatings.*

Wood, Flood and practically everyone else acknowledge that with speed and continuous posting come risks. "The chance for error probably soars," says Flood, who urges sources to look for mistakes and alert her. "On the other hand, you can correct those errors immediately and forever."

Most Web content does get edited, although blurbs, headlines and short items may be posted directly by one person, and some contributors' blogs are unedited.

Cohen stresses that "I would prefer to have it completely accurate, vetted and dead-solid perfect rather than racing to get it up. If there are five editors that read every story before the newspaper version, there may be just two or three who vet it for the website. But still they are acutely aware of the accuracy issues."

Scott Clark, 46, the website's vice president and editor, says Web producers want better quality control. They consult wire service veterans about handling the fast pace. "We're jumping into stories in progress, and we get things wrong, the natural errors that come from the fog of news," Clark says. "We talk about knowing when to 'vague it up' and wait for the facts to settle. People on the Web recognize that they're seeing a flow and not the newspaper end product. They expect to come back and see that the story has changed. But the standards of journalism on the Web are the same as in print."

Almost everybody also agrees that the 24-7 cycle stretches resources.

Science writer Eric Berger, 32, is another big Web fan. As a reporter and SciGuy blogger, his is a familiar byline online. He tells about covering the launch of the shuttle Discovery last July. He rose before dawn and blogged from 4:55 A.M. through the 9:39 A.M. launch until 11 A.M., then wrote a print story for the next morning's front page. He isn't complaining, Berger stresses, but it's clear the Web adds work.

Reporter Cappiello underlines the point. "Industrywide, not just here, the Web requires more labor," she says. "I'm a little concerned how a reporter who covers cops is going to not only file, file, file for the Web, but report the print story and do the Sunday enterprise story."

Cohen does foresee his Web staff growing this year. Still, extra work and all, these journalists and others increasingly welcome the chance to revitalize their work. Blogging has been a big incentive; all those writers who wanted to be columnists now have the chance. You still encounter some skeptics, but it seems that a corner has been turned.

"There are people who think this is a ridiculous extension of their job," Flood says. "I look at this as my new job. It's the future of news. I love it."

This will also be the year of print-online integration at USA Today, where Editor Ken Paulson wants "a single 24-hour news organization." He's even moved the site's top executive, Kinsey Wilson, to the paper's masthead as an executive editor. For now, the online newsroom still occupies it own floor in USA Today's gleaming McLean, Virginia, skyscraper. But Paulson says that "culturally, we're merged," and over the coming months many sports, business, features and other online staffers will move side by side with their print counterparts.

On the day I visit, the Web staff is gathering for its 8:15 A.M. "cabinet meeting," so called because the nine editors huddle around a row of metal filing cabinets.

USAToday.com staffs its homepage around the clock, although less gets posted once the newspaper's contents are uploaded by midnight. Today's homepage editor, Brett Molina, 30, has been on duty since 6 A.M., updating stories about a mine fire and an Osama bin Laden tape.

The news meeting, one of several daily, resembles the typical print get-together, except more attention goes to multimedia and special effects. For example, Chet Czarniak, 55, the online managing editor who presides, expresses concern about live coverage of the mining disaster. "If raw video comes in," he warns, "be careful what we use."

Another exchange highlights the costs and benefits of immediacy. An editor has spotted what he calls a classic dumb headline, "Flawed coin was a mistake." Unlike in a print edition where it would live forever, the head is quickly rewritten.

With more than 10 million unique visitors a month, USAToday.com has 75 editorial staffers, with a funky combination of titles, some from print, some from broadcast. They face an unusual mission, since they don't produce local news. Their national audience spills over several time zones. Viewers come for assorted news, sports and the special packages and surprises associated with the USA Today brand.

USAToday.com puts less emphasis on breaking-news updates from its reporters than on special stories, imaginative packaging and Web-only features. "I'd rather have their 'breaking analysis' than chasing the basics," says Executive Producer Jody Brannon, 46. "What we're trying to do online," she adds, "is celebrate a new way of storytelling that leverages our expertise in visuals, graphics and multimedia." For example, video editor David Freer, 22, is fixing up an on-site TV studio and plans to "pump up this site" with video.

The action seems nonstop, with the homepage changing at least every 15 or 20 minutes. "The pace is just incredible," Czarniak says. "Saturday at 11 P.M. is just as important as Monday at 11 A.M. Speed to market is vital. It's not even a deadline a minute. There are constant deadlines. Our train is always leaving the station."

News Editor Randy Lilleston, 46, sees print people learning "broadcast sensibilities." "Stories are not permanent," he says. "They evolve. The story you read now is not the same as the one you'll read in two hours."

Lilleston, too, worries about balancing accuracy and speed. "Do you get the vetting you get in a newspaper? No, you do not," he says. But he adds crisply, "I reject the idea that online is an excuse for sloppiness. One of my goals is to knock down the idea that it is OK to be temporarily wrong. It is not OK."

Lilleston sees progress toward online safeguards. For example, most items posted directly are short, so typos and errors may be relatively easy to spot. Without a copy desk, editors are expected to turn to the person sitting next to them for a "second set of eyes." They constantly read behind one another, before and after postings.

News Director Patty Michalski, 33, who oversees the homepage, advises, "Get it right the first time. If it means taking two seconds longer, so be it." Michalski also stresses those small but all-important headlines, subheads (known as "chatter") and blurbs. Those few words often determine readership. She pushes posters to seek suggestions from others and to consider "anything to make it a teensy bit more specific."

Across the sites I visited, editors are emphasizing journalistic skills over technical know-how. A few years ago, Czarniak says, hiring priorities were something like 60 percent technical skills, 40 percent journalistic. "Now we're going the other way. The tools are much improved. It's easier to publish now. What we're looking for most are people who know good storytelling."

Even at USA Today, where the newspaper helped revolutionize design, the look of the homepage remains relatively constant. Too much change, says Brannon, "complicates the experience for the user." Except for mammoth stories, the homepage sticks to two or three "standard looks," with templates for easy posting.

Nor did I find many signs of the totally converged reporter, prowling for news with notebook, tape recorder and digital camera and wearing a videocam as headgear. Increasingly, reporters do take photos and provide audio, and some sites are experimenting with giving reporters, especially abroad, cell phones that allow video feeds. But few yet have the time, or capability, to function as multimedia do-it-alls. "I've seen their video," laughs video editor Freer, "and I don't like it."

For now, the big step is consolidation, a culture shock in itself. Czarniak says merging makes sense for production, quality and content. "The ultimate vision is that there are conversations about content among everyone," he says. "You're not concerned about the platform. You're concerned about how to tell the story."

Other major papers are moving toward consolidation, including the New York Times and the Los Angeles Times. But merging news operations can be complicated. In some places, the print newsroom is unionized while the online newsroom is not. Sometimes more than one corporate structure is involved. Besides, independence has its own advantages.

So not everyone is consolidating. A prime exception is washingtonpost.com, located across the Potomac River, in Virginia, four miles from its print sibling.

Technically, it's a separate company: Washington Post-Newsweek Interactive. Post Ombudsman Deborah Howell, in a column last December titled "The Two Washington Posts," quoted Post Co. CEO Donald Graham as saying that, while the two versions obviously must cooperate, each is a full-time, stand-alone operation.

The action seems nonstop, with the homepage changing at least every 15 or 20 minutes.

Many Web staffers privately believe being closer would help. But there also is a sense that separate status lets the website flourish outside the shadow of the magisterial printed Post.

Whether it is the Web or print or handhelds, the future is giving people news when they want it and how they want it.

In February, the Newspaper Association of America named washingtonpost.com as the best overall news site among large publications.

Staff members also point out that coordination by phone, e-mail and instant messaging is easy. In addition, a seven-person Continuous News Desk inside the Post's print newsroom provides copy and liaison.

Here, too, the online newsroom resembles that of a newspaper, except that the architecture is more modernistic, the tones more subdued. It's a jeans and sneakers environment, but less rowdy than many city rooms.

Executive Editor and Vice President Jim Brady, 38, says he sometimes feels like an insurance office, and he goads people to walk rather than e-mail across the room.

A big challenge, Brady says, is "getting a newsroom to move at lightning speed." But he sees somewhat less pressure here because, with stories constantly being posted, "there isn't the big run-up to deadline and then a sigh of relief."

The site, with about 65 full-time editorial staff and 20 to 24 part-timers, received 8.2 million unique visitors in February, according to Nielsen//NetRatings. About 80 percent are not from the Washington area, so the homepage is "bifurcated." A computer reads the ZIP codes of incoming viewers and directs them to either the local or the national homepage.

Dominating the room is the newsdesk, a semicircular command center occupied by a homepage editor, breaking news producer and photo editor. They work facing 10 monitors tuned to local and national news and weather. Two people have overnight duty, but the action picks up with the 5:30 A.M. arrival of a dayside homepage editor. Regular news meetings take place at 7 A.M., noon, 3 P.M. and 7 P.M.

Deputy Editor Meghan Collins Sullivan, 31, oversees the homepage and what she calls "the constant decision-making process." Rarely do more than a few minutes pass between updates, and the site gets frequent feeds from the Continuous News Desk's writers and other Post reporters. "There's a different sense of urgency here because we are on constant deadline," Sullivan says. "We don't have a limited amount of space. We have an infinite amount. So you can always be doing new things."

Sullivan and homepage editor Kenisha Malcolm, 28, convene the noon news meeting, similar to those at other websites. On this day, about 15 people take part, including, via conference call from the Post, Lexie Verdon, 51, from Continuous News. There's the usual discussion of upcoming stories, plus attention to audio, video, special features and the explosively popular blogs and online discussions.

Brady's second in command, Editor Howard Parnell, 45, grew up in nearby Falls Church, Virginia, and delivered the Post as a kid. He spent more than a decade working in print and the past 11 years online. Parnell agrees that the biggest difference online is the 24-7 pace. But he also sees across-the-board similarities.

"The managing people part is similar," he says, "and the emphasis on storytelling, on getting it right, and, just as it was in my newspaper days, the idea that this is a public trust."

Consolidation's not that big an issue at the Daily Times in Salisbury, Maryland, where the "online newsroom" consists pretty much of City Editor Joe Carmean posting from his desk when he has time.

This morning's Web lead is about the newspaper itself, where a press breakdown has delayed delivery for hours. Papers are being printed at another Gannett paper up the road, and many won't be delivered until after lunch. With regular carriers unavailable, Executive Editor Greg Bassett and other honchos have been drafted to run delivery routes. The phone is ringing ceaselessly, and people wander into the lobby scouting for copies.

Ironically, the print version's front page can be found only one place this morning: on the website (delmarva.com), which regularly links to a pdf version of page one.

Bassett, 45, in the office since 4 A.M. and out on his route since 9, finally makes it back around 2 P.M., having just delivered his last 50 copies to subscribers at a local jail. He edits his hometown paper, which is unusual in this mobile age. In fact, he was born in the hospital directly across the street.

The paper has 28 editorial staffers, about 29,000 in circulation and 130,000 unique Web visitors a month. It's a small, community-oriented operation, but Bassett sees the future as clearly as anyone else, and he embraces the Web's potential.

"We write for online and update for print," he recites, echoing a refrain heard often around Gannett. "The only time I'm happy is when I have a newspaper in front of me and a tuna sandwich in my hand. But my 9-year-old son is going to get all his news from his cell phone."

When corporate executives solicited his training priorities for this year, Bassett specified "how to set up a 24-hour newsroom" and "how to write for online."

For now, only a handful of newsroom staffers can post, including Bassett, Carmean and Managing Editor Erick Sahler. More are being trained, and Bassett hopes to hire a full-time "online champion" this year.

Contents from the paper and several affiliated weeklies are automatically uploaded through Gannett's Digital Production Center, and Gannett provides additional Web packages. Wire news is also automatically updated. The website does relatively little with local sports, has no discussion groups or blogs (though one is planned), and offers only occasional audio. Its emphasis is on breaking news.

Like his counterparts at larger papers, Bassett pushes reporters toward feeding the Web quickly.

Around noon the day I visit, a reporter files a short piece on a morning meeting. City Editor Carmean scans it, then calls the writer. "Just one quick question," he says, and then peppers him with seven questions. (Editors are like that.) A few minutes later, Carmean calls up the Web template, types in a headline and subhead and posts the story.

Sahler, 39, sees the Web as a vehicle for once again competing with broadcast to cover wrecks, fires and early meetings.

"If there is a murder, before I could be content to wait for the cops to gather information because I was only thinking of publishing for tomorrow," says reporter Ben Penserga, 27. "Now I have to grab what I can for the Web."

The managing people part is similar, and the emphasis on storytelling, on getting it right, and, just as it was in my newspaper days, the idea that this is a public trust.

Carmean concedes that Web duties lengthen his day by about two hours, but he claims not to mind. "Sure it's long hours, and there are a lot of time-consuming elements," he says. "But I want to do it. I want this stuff on the Web. I want to reach a younger audience. There is no second place in journalism."

Back at the Houston Chronicle, Sylvia Wood has, before noon, posted a yearbook photo of the ninth grader and a staff-written story on the shooting. Now she is racing after other stories.

It is easy to imagine the time, coming soon, when the 24-hour Web cycle dominates the newsroom tempo, work flow and culture. It will bring new excitement, but giant demands for resources in a time of cutbacks and thin reserves. It may also bring serious quality-control issues. Print journalism's credibility has long been connected to its layers of editing.

As for tomorrow's journalists, they will more likely be identified by their function than by their medium. As newsrooms turn into diversified information retailers, the biggest distinction may be between those who develop the content and those who distribute it, via print, broadcast, the Internet or other channels.

Eventually, many editors foresee consolidated newsrooms with a single chain of command and few distinctions between print and online. For now, most aren't leaping quite that far.

First comes the physical merger. That will bring both groups into side-by-side cooperation but maintain, at least at first, their separate identities. After that, who knows?

"The endgame," says Chronicle Editor Jeff Cohen, "is to have all our excellent journalists producing content, and air traffic controllers putting it on the various platforms."

Or, as Sylvia Wood says: "Whether it is the Web or print or handhelds, the future is giving people news when they want it and how they want it."

Senior Editor **CARL SESSIONS STEPP** (cstepp@jmail.umd.edu) teaches at the Philip Merrill College of Journalism at the University of Maryland. He wrote about newspapers' increased interest in short-form narratives in AJR's August/September 2005 issue.

From *American Journalism Review,* April/May 2006, pp. 48–53. Copyright © 2006 by the Philip Merrill College of Journalism at the University of Maryland, College Park, MD 20742-7111. Reprinted with permission.

E-Mail Is for Old People

As students ignore their campus accounts, colleges try new ways of communicating.

Dan Carnevale

Maurice Johnson, a freshman studying interior design at Harcum College, spends hours each day online, both for work and play. One thing he rarely does, though, is open his campus e-mail account. "I check it about every other month," he says.

Moe, as his friends call him, has his own fashion label and regularly corresponds with other designers through his MySpace page. He chats with friends through instant messaging. He also has a few commercial e-mail accounts that he checks daily.

But his Harcum account lies dormant. Not only does he prefer other means of communication, but the college e-mail addresses—created by a combination of a student's first and last names plus part of the student's identification number—are too complicated to give out to friends or to check online. "I don't like the Harcum e-mail," he says. "It's too confusing."

Mr. Johnson is not alone in his disdain for campus e-mail. College officials around the country find that a growing number of students are missing important messages about deadlines, class cancellations, and events sent to them by e-mail because, well, the messages are sent to them by e-mail.

In response, some institutions require that students check their college e-mail accounts so they do not miss announcements, holding students responsible for official information that comes through that medium. Other institutions are attempting to figure out what technology students are using to try to reach them there.

A 2005 report from the Pew Internet and American Life Project called "Teens and Technology" found that teenagers preferred new technology, like instant messaging or text messaging, for talking to friends and use e-mail to communicate with "old people." Along the same lines, students interviewed for this article say they still depend on e-mail to communicate with their professors. But many of the students say they would rather send text messages to friends, to reach them wherever they are, than send e-mail messages that might not be seen until hours later.

Students have not given up on e-mail altogether. In fact, a survey of more than 1,300 students at the University of Illinois at Chicago earlier this year found that 86 percent of them still use campus e-mail regularly. Eszter Hargittai, an assistant professor of communication studies and sociology at Northwestern University who conducted the survey, says students often ignore messages coming from their colleges, considering them a form of spam.

Brian Niles, chief executive officer of TargetX, a company that helps colleges use technology to recruit new students, says colleges need to branch out and find new ways to connect with students.

"It's not that they don't read e-mail," Mr. Niles says. "It's that they have their own world, and you need to know how to reach them in that world."

'Big Family'

Harcum, a two-year college outside Philadelphia, enrolls about 900 students. It is the type of institution where the college president's wife can be found tending to the plants in front of campus buildings. "Harcum's a very big family," says Lisa A. Mixon, assistant director of public relations and marketing.

Ms. Mixon created the college's MySpace page (http://myspace.com/harcumcollege) after she realized that many students were missing important messages. They were paying no attention to the college e-mail newsletter. They were not even showing up for ice-cream socials—and everyone likes ice cream.

It seemed clear that students were not ignoring their MySpace pages, though. Some students here have more than one such page. Some have MySpace pages for their pet snakes.

A key feature of MySpace and other social-networking sites is the ability to link with another user by designating him or her a "friend." Friends are able to send each other messages and announcements, and view pictures and items that are blocked from other users.

After the college put up its site in August, Ms. Mixon searched online for Harcum students with MySpace pages and found more than 200 of them. She contacted the students individually, over the course of a few weeks, and asked each of them to become a friend of the college. So far, more than 160 have said yes.

Joseph J. Diorio, Harcum's director of public relations and marketing, who admits that he relies on Ms. Mixon to keep him "hip," says he finds the online service to be a good way for the college and its students to get to know each other better.

Using MySpace is like "being able to walk into a residence hall and everybody's door is open," says Mr. Diorio. "We knew that's where students were going."

Harcum keeps its MySpace page lively, with photos of students on the campus. Officials have also posted a picture of a cartoon rabbit with the caption: "College prepares you for the real world, which also sucks."

"We thought, What the heck, it's not the official Harcum Web page," Mr. Diorio says.

A student also writes a weekly blog for the college MySpace page. Current blog posts include some complaints about cafeteria food interjected in discussions about forthcoming events. Ms. Mixon plans to invite additional students to write for the blog, letting them vent honestly about anything on their minds.

Reaching Students

As some students reduce their use of e-mail in favor of other means of communication, colleges are trying new technologies to reach them. Among the new techniques:

Cellphone Text Messages

Students live and die by their cellphones. A few colleges now provide information, including snow closures and sports scores, to students instantly, wherever they are.

Instant Messages

Some professors now make themselves available to students via instant-messaging software, especially during office hours. And some admissions counselors use it to answer questions from prospective students faster, and through a medium in which many students are most comfortable.

MySpace and Facebook

Some colleges have begun using the popular social-networking services to provide information to their students, including calendars of events, deadlines, and other announcements. College officials also use the services to present a lighter side of an institution— something different from the stuffy main Web page.

"They like Harcum," she says, "but they'd be honest about things they didn't like."

'Not as Formal'

In addition, the Harcum MySpace page includes dates of important events, such as volleyball games and alumni weekends. It also allows students to pose general questions to college officials, if they are not sure whom they need to talk to. "If they have a question and they can't get to the right person," Ms. Mixon says, "they have someplace to go."

Ashley M. Elliott, a veterinary-technology student in her second year at Harcum, says the Harcum MySpace page shows the college is making an effort to reach students. "It's down to the student's level," she says. "It's not as formal as the website."

Becoming MySpace friends with a college may seem lame to some students. But Steven J. Arnone, another veterinary-technology student in his second year at Harcum, wants to convince his classmates that all the cool kids are doing it.

"I'm spreading the word that it's not stupid," Mr. Arnone says. "To be honest, I'm proud. It's like slapping a college sticker on the back of your car."

The MySpace service asks users to rank their friends, which could put Harcum in the awkward position of seeming to play favorites. Ms. Mixon says she picks the college's top friends randomly. "I just keep rotating them," she says.

She says that the college may have a contest to determine who deserves to be listed as Harcum's favorite friend, possibly judging how much school spirit a student displays on his or her MySpace page.

While Harcum has convinced a good portion of its student population to be its friends, some friends are closer than others.

"I'm a friend, but I've never actually been to the site," says Shay Curry, who is in her first year studying early-childhood education at Harcum.

Ms. Curry says she felt obligated to befriend Harcum when the request came in—even though the invitation did not indicate that it was mandatory to do so.

Matthew J. Roane, a Harcum psychology major who has four e-mail accounts, says he never uses his Harcum account or the college MySpace page. He finds out about announcements and events the old-fashion way—from printed fliers.

Trying Too Hard?

Just because students use new means of communication does not mean that colleges should, however.

Some students at the University of Maryland at College Park, for instance, say they would rather keep talking to professors and campus officials through e-mail.

"I like to separate my personal life from my school life," says Amanda J. Heilman, a freshman studying animal sciences at the university.

Emily Diehl, another freshman majoring in animal sciences, agrees. "It would be weird if all your professors had Facebook," she says.

But even the students who use their campus e-mail accounts will sometimes not open messages that appear to be from the college.

"These students are walking spam filters," says Paul Lehmann, the director of student activities at Utica College. "They are masters of multiple forms of communication and have perfected the skill of cutting through the multiple forms of communication that they are bombarded with to find what they are interested in and want to reply to."

The result, he says, is that no matter how important the message from the college, students will often choose to ignore it.

"Students receive multiple 'official' messages a day, with information that runs the gamut of importance," says Stephanie Dupaul, director of undergraduate business admissions at Southern Methodist University's business school. "A reminder that there is a free movie in the student center on Friday night hits their in boxes with the same level of urgency as an announcement of registration deadlines or changes in official university policies."

Pennsylvania State University has been trying different ways to use technology to reach students, including podcasts, RSS feeds, and Web video clips.

The university's latest attempt is to use cellphone text messaging, by setting up a service that can blast announcements to students using the technology.

Subscribers to the service can let the university know what types of messages they want to receive. Many choose to get updates on emergency announcements, such as school closures, and some also want to be notified about upcoming concerts or sports scores, which are available seconds after a Nittany Lions game has ended.

Bill Mahon, assistant vice president for university relations at Penn State, says many students use text messaging more than e-mail. So administrators expected the plan to be popular with the students.

"We thought maybe in a year we'd get 2,000 people," Mr. Mahon says of the program, which started in August. "As it turns out, in the first three weeks or so we have 1,000 subscribers."

Mr. Mahon says the service will really come in handy in the winter, when snow can create havoc on campus. And the service has already proved useful, he says. Not long ago, a road near the campus was closed because of an oil spill. Penn State officials were able to let subscribers know immediately, so they could plan an alternate route.

"In the old days, we couldn't do that," Mr. Mahon says. "We just let thousands of people drive on that road to find policemen sending them in a different direction."

Not all students want the cell-phone service, he says. It is best to give them many options. "The key is, you can't do just one thing," he says.

Web Portals

Harrisburg University of Science and Technology, a new institution that began enrolling students last year, has already run into difficulties communicating with students.

Because many students do not check their e-mail, officials are creating a Web portal for students. James B. Young, associate vice president for information services at the university, says the portal will be a place that lets students register for courses and find out about upcoming events, and that provides other services.

But, he says, it will be much more informal than the main university Web page. He hopes to put a "youthful edge to it."

"We're brand new and we're pushing habits early," Mr. Young says. "Hopefully MyHU will become an indispensable space."

The University of South Carolina Upstate, on the other hand, is sticking with campus e-mail accounts. Officials have informed students that e-mail is the official means of communication and that they must check it.

In the past, any student could send a message via campus e-mail to the entire student population. Students used the capability to find roommates and for other informal matters, but it also led to many unwanted messages for students.

"So they stopped checking it," says Laura Puckett-Boler, assistant vice chancellor for student and diversity affairs. "They were missing announcements."

So the university set up an electronic newsletter, called E-blast, that is sent out once a week with students' informal announcements and requests. Now only certain administrators can send bulk e-mail.

Despite the requirement, not everybody on the campus uses their university e-mail accounts, she says. But students manage to get by, either by forwarding the information to another account, or just learning what they need to know through friends.

"They're still responsible for the information," Ms. Puckett-Boler says. "Students figure out what to do."

From *The Chronicle of Higher Education*, by Dan Carnevale, October 6, 2006, pp. A27–A29. Copyright © 2006 by The Chronicle of Higher Education. Reproduced with permission. This article may not be published, reposted, or redistributed without the express permission of The Chronicle of Higher Education.

Societal Institutions: Law, Politics, Education, and the Military

Unit Selections

Key Points to Consider

- The overview to this unit mentions that civil institutions were overlooked in the excitement after the collapse of the former Soviet Union. Find on the Internet and read Francis Fukuyama's essay, "The End of History." Do you agree with his arguments? Does computing have any role to play in the development of civil institutions?

- Use the Internet to find out if commentators have anything to say about the difficulty of managing complex weaponry in outposts around the globe.

- How has high-tech weaponry fared in the Iraq war?

- Do you read political blogs? Why would someone read a political blog rather than *The New Statesman* (on the right) or *The Nation* (on the left)?

- Do you e-mail your professors? Under what circumstances?

- Do your professor's allow you to cite *Wikipedia* in your papers? Why or why not?

- Find out as much as you can about Fair Use. When Google digitized copyrighted books ("Google & the Future of Books"), was it violating Fair Use? What about your professors who distribute photocopies of articles?

Student Website
www.mhhe.com/cls

Internet References

ACLU: American Civil Liberties Union
http://www.aclu.org

Information Warfare and U.S. Critical Infrastructure
http://www.twurl.com/twurled_world/ullman/cover.htm

Living in the Electronic Village
http://www.rileyis.com/report

United States Patent and Trademark Office
http://www.uspto.gov

World Intellectual Property Organization
http://www.wipo.org

After the collapse of the Soviet Union, many Americans believed that democracy and a market economy would develop in short order. Commentators seemed to have taken a cue from Francis Fukuyama's imposingly entitled essay, "The End of History," that appeared in *The National Interest* in 1989. "What we may be witnessing," he wrote, is "not just the end of the Cold War, or the passing of a particular period of post-war history, but . . . the universalization of Western liberal democracy as the final form of human government." Fukuyama, deputy director of the State Department's planning staff in the elder Bush administration, hedged a bit. He was careful to argue that the victory of liberal capitalism "has occurred primarily in the realm of ideas or consciousness and is as yet incomplete in the real or material world."

We have grown wiser since those heady times. The events of September 11 showed Americans, in the most brutal fashion, that not everyone shares their values. More important, the political and economic chaos that has been so much a part of Russian life since the collapse of the Soviet Union has led many commentators to conclude that liberal democracy and a market economy require more than "the realm of ideas or consciousness." They need, above all else, institutions that govern political and economic relationships. They require mechanisms for business contracts and land use, courts to adjudicate disputes, government agencies to record titles and regulate resources, and, not just a mechanism but a tradition of representative government. In a phrase, democracy and a market economy require the institutions of civil society.

We in the United States and Western Europe have long traditions of civil society, in some cases reaching back hundreds of years. The French sociologist, Emile Durkheim (1858–1917), hoped that as traditional societies gave way to urban industrial societies, rule by contract and law would provide the glue for social cohesion. To a very large extent this has been the case in the United States. The room in which I am writing is part of a house that sits on a small piece of property that belongs to me. I am confident that my title to this property is part of the public record. Were someone to appear on my doorstep with a claim to my property, a procedure exists to adjudicate our dispute. If I do not personally understand the rule, I can hire a lawyer, a specialist in civil procedures, to make my case before an independent judiciary.

Strictly speaking, the military is not part of civil society. Yet, since civilians control the U.S. military by constitutional mandate, we can consider it a civil institution without stretching the meaning of the term terribly. On the eve of the Iraq war in April 2003, *BusinessWeek Online* ran a pair of articles illustrating what one called the "doctrine of digital warfare," a doctrine that stresses air power, agile ground forces, and computer communication over lethal firepower and a large infantry. Sophisticated military systems take years to develop and deploy. Despite some tough-going in Iraq, the U.S. commitment to a high-tech battle field has not waned. Steve Featherstone ("The Coming Robot Army") describes the Army's Future Combat System "as the costliest program in history." The individual soldier is still part of the vision, "but he has been reconfigured as a sort of plug-and-play

© U.S. Air Force photo by Mr. Gerald Sonnenberg

warrior, a node in what is envisioned as a sprawling network of robots, manned vehicles, ground sensors, satellites, and command sensors." Featherstone's piece makes it clear that military hardware is the result of a partnership between the engineering talent of the private sector and the very deep pockets of the American military.

While students and others with access to free broad-band Internet service have been giving the music industry headaches for the past few years, it is Google itself that has been causing the publishers to lie awake nights. Google has been busily digitizing books from several large research libraries. Some of these are still protected by copyright. Check out Google Books and see for yourself. Robert Darnton ("Google & the Future of Books") presents a balanced view of this effort. His is an important voice, since he directs the Harvard library, one of the largest in the country, and a good example of the kind of civil institution that has undergone enormous change with the introduction of networked computers. One of those changes is the nature of the archive itself. At least until paper rots—rather sooner than we might like, given the number of books printed on paper made from wood pulp—the contents of traditional libraries is available to anyone with eyes to see. Not so with the digital library, as Steve Kolowich points out ("Archiving Writers' Work in the Age of E-Mail"). John Updike's papers recently arrived at Harvard on floppy disk.

A civil society is unimaginable without a free press. Yet in the United States, the readership of newspapers is declining, along with the numbers watching TV news, the very medium that did away with so many afternoon papers not long ago. Donna Shaw's piece ("Wikipedia in the Newsroom") illustrates a new issue that newspapers face, one that college students face as well. As much as all of us use *Wikipedia,* it's not quite proper to cite it in polite circles.

Education is yet another piece of civil society. U.S. students in public schools study the mechanism of government, recite the Pledge of Allegiance, and learn to revere the sacred texts of American democracy, the Declaration of Independence, the Constitution, and the Bill of Rights. One task of U.S. public education is to instill a common ideal of citizenship into a diverse and changing population. The contribution of computing to education—if not always uncontroversial—has been substantial. From educational software, to wired college campuses, to Internet-mediated distance education, computing has been a part of education since the introduction of personal computers in the early eighties. If you throw in mass, standardized testing, an enterprise nearly unthinkable without computers, computing has been a part of U.S. education since the 1950s. Over the past decade, students have become increasingly comfortable e-mailing their professors. As "E-Mail in Academia" argues, studies have shown that there is a relationship between a student's success and "the quality of one-on-one communication between teacher and student." This article reports on a formal study of academic e-mail use at the University of North Carolina.

The Coming Robot Army

Introducing America's future fighting machines.

STEVE FEATHERSTONE

A small gray helicopter was perched on the runway, its rotors beating slowly against the shroud of fog and rain blowing in from the Chesapeake Bay. Visibility was poor, but visibility did not matter. The helicopter had no windows, no doors, and, for that matter, no pilot. Its elliptical fuselage looked as if it had been carved out of wood and sanded smooth of detail. It hovered above the runway for a moment, swung its blind face toward the bay, and then dissolved into the mist.

The helicopter was the first among a dozen unmanned aerial vehicles (UAVs) scheduled to fly during the annual Association for Unmanned Vehicle Systems International conference in Baltimore. The live demonstration area at Webster Field, a naval air facility located seventy miles south of Washington, D.C., was laid out along the lines of a carnival midway. Big defense contractors and small engineering firms exhibited the latest military robots under white tents staked out alongside an auxiliary runway. Armed soldiers kept watch from towers and strolled through the throng of military officers and industry reps. I took a seat among rows of metal chairs arrayed in front of a giant video screen, which displayed a live feed from the helicopter's surveillance camera. There was little to see except clouds, so the announcer attempted to liven things up.

"Yesterday we saw some boats out there," he said, with an aggressive enthusiasm better suited to a monster-truck rally. "They didn't know they were being targeted by one of the newest UAVs!" Next, two technicians from AeroVironment, Inc., jogged onto the airfield and knelt in the wet grass to assemble what appeared to be a remote-controlled airplane. One of them raised it over his shoulder, leaned back, and threw it into the air like a javelin. The airplane—called the Raven—climbed straight up, stalled, dipped alarmingly toward the ground, and then leveled off at two hundred feet, its tiny electric motor buzzing like a mosquito. The screen switched to show the Raven's video feed: a bird's-eye view of the airstrip, at one end of which a large American flag flapped limply on a rope strung between two portable cranes next to an inflatable Scud missile launcher.

"A lot of the principles we use here are taken from the model industry," an AeroVironment spokesman told the announcer

as the Raven looped around the field. The U.S. military has purchased more than 3,000 Ravens, many of which have been deployed in Iraq and Afghanistan, but apparently none of the military officers present had ever seen one land. At the end of the Raven's second flight, the crowd went silent as the tiny plane plummeted from the sky and careered into the ground, tearing off its wings. The technicians scrambled to the crash site, stuck the wings back on, and held the Raven triumphantly above their heads.

"It's designed that way," the spokesman explained.

"Hey, if you can't fix it with duct tape," the announcer said, "it's not worth fixing, am I right?"

Other teams took the field to demonstrate their company's UAVs. The sheer variety of aircraft and their launching methods—planes were slung from catapults and bungee cords, shot from pneumatic guns and the backs of pickup trucks, or simply tossed by hand into the air—testified to the prodigious growth in demand for military robots since the terrorist attacks of September 11, 2001, and the subsequent "global war on terrorism." In his opening conference remarks, Rear Admiral Timothy Heely compared the embryonic UAV market with aviation in the first decades of the twentieth century, when the Wright brothers built planes in their workshop and dirigibles carried passengers. "It's all out there," he said. "You don't want to throw anything away."

Weaponized robots are the ultimate "force multiplier"—they can do the most damage with less people

It started to drizzle again. The military officers sought refuge under a catered VIP tent decorated with red, white, and blue bunting while the rest of us scattered in all directions. I headed to the unmanned ground vehicle (UGV) tent located at the far end of the runway. The tent's interior was dim; the air, sticky and hot. Tables stocked with brochures and laptops lined the vinyl walls. Robots rested unevenly on the grass. This was the first year UGVs were allowed demonstration time at the conference, and company reps were eager to show what their robots could do. A rep from iRobot, maker of the popular Roomba robotic vacuum cleaner, flipped open a shiny metal briefcase that contained an LCD monitor and a control panel studded with switches and buttons for operating the PackBots, a "man-packable" tracked robot not much bigger than a telephone book. Hundreds of PackBots have already been deployed in Iraq.

"If you can operate a Game Boy, you're good," the rep said.

A Raytheon engineer fired up an orange robot that looked like a track loader used in excavation. The only difference was a solid black box containing a radio receiver on top of the cage where the human driver normally sat. It rumbled out of the tent onto the airfield, followed by a camera crew.

"It's a Bobcat," the announcer shouted. "It's a *biiig* Bobcat!"

The Bobcat rolled up to a steel garbage bin containing a "simulated Improvised Explosive Device," hoisted it into the air with a set of pincers, and crumpled it like a soda can. A Raytheon spokesman listed all the things the tricked-out Bobcat could do, such as breach walls.

"You could also crush things like a car if you wanted to," he added.

"I never thought of crushing something," the announcer said. "But yeah, this would do very nicely."

After the Bobcat had dispatched the mangled garbage bin and returned to the tent, I asked a Raytheon engineer if the company had thought about arming it with machine guns. "Forget the machine guns," he said dismissively. "We're going lasers."

Military robots are nothing new. During World War II, Germans sent small, remote-controlled bombs on tank treads across front lines; and the United States experimented with unmanned aircraft, packing tons of high explosives into conventional bombers piloted from the air by radio (one bomber exploded soon after takeoff, killing Joseph Kennedy's eldest son, and the experiment was eventually shelved). But in a war decided by the maneuver of vast armies across whole continents, robots were a peculiar sideshow.

The practice of warfare has changed dramatically in the past sixty years. Since Vietnam, the American military machine has been governed by two parallel and complementary trends: an aversion to casualties and a heavy reliance on technology. The Gulf War reinforced the belief that technology can replace human soldiers on the battlefield, and the "Black Hawk down" incident in Somalia made this belief an article of faith. Today, any new weapon worth its procurement contract is customarily referred to as a "force multiplier," which can be translated as doing more damage with less people. Weaponized robots are the ultimate force multiplier, and every branch of the military has increased spending on new unmanned systems.

At $145 billion, the Army's Future Combat Systems (FCS) is the costliest weapons program in history, and in some ways the most visionary as well. The individual soldier is still central to the FCS concept, but he has been reconfigured as a sort of plug-and-play warrior, a node in what is envisioned as a sprawling network of robots, manned vehicles, ground sensors, satellites, and command centers. In theory, each node will exchange real-time information with the network, allowing the entire system to accommodate sudden changes in the "battle space." The fog of war would become a relic of the past, like the musket, swept away by crystalline streams of encrypted data. The enemy would not be killed so much as deleted.

FCS calls for seven new unmanned systems. It's not clear how much autonomy each system will be allowed. According to *Unmanned Effects (UFX): Taking the Human Out of the Loop*, a 2003 study commissioned by the U.S. Joint Forces Command, advances in artificial intelligence and automatic target recognition will give robots the ability to hunt down and kill the enemy with limited human supervision by 2015. As the study's title suggests, humans are the weakest link in the robot's "kill chain"—the sequence of events that occurs from the moment an enemy target is detected to its destruction.

At Webster Field, the latest link in the military's increasingly automated kill chain was on display: the Special Weapons Observation Reconnaissance Detection System, or SWORDS. I squatted down to take a closer look at it. Despite its theatrical name, SWORDS was remarkably plain, consisting of two thick rubber treads, stubby antennae, and a platform mounted with a camera and an M240 machine gun—all painted black. The robot is manufactured by a company named Foster-Miller, whose chief representative at the show was Bob Quinn, a slope-shouldered, balding man with bright blue eyes. Bob helped his engineer to get SWORDS ready for a quick demo. Secretary of the Army Francis Harvey, the VIP of VIPs, was coming through the UGV tent for a tour.

"The real demonstration is when you're actually firing these things," Bob lamented. Unfortunately, live fire was forbidden at Webster Field, and Bob had arrived too late to schedule a formal demonstration. At another conference two months before, he had been free to drive SWORDS around all day long. "I was going into the different booths and displays, pointing my gun, moving it up and down like the sign of the cross. People were going like this"—he jumped back and held up his hands in surrender—"then they would follow the robot back to me because they had no idea where I was. And that's the exact purpose of an urban combat capability like this."

Sunlight flooded into the tent as Secretary Harvey parted the canopy, flanked by two lanky Rangers in fatigues and berets. Bob ran his hand over his scalp and smoothed his shirt. It was sweltering inside the tent now. Beneath the brim of his tan baseball cap, Secretary Harvey's face was bright red and beaded with sweat. He nodded politely, leaning into the verbal barrage of specifications and payloads and mission packages the reps threw at him. When he got to SWORDS, he clasped his hands behind his back and stared down at the robot as if it were a small child. Someone from his entourage excitedly explained the various weapons it could carry.

Bob had orchestrated enough dog-and-pony shows to know that technology doesn't always impress men of Secretary Harvey's age and position. "We don't have it in the field yet," Bob interrupted, going on to say that SWORDS wasn't part of any official procurement plan. It was a direct result of a "bootstrap effort" by real soldiers at Picatinny Arsenal in New Jersey who were trying to solve real problems for their comrades in the field. "And soldiers love it," he added.

On the long bus ride back to Baltimore, I sat behind Master Sergeant Mike Gomez, a Marine UAV pilot. "All we are are battery-powered forward observers," he joked. Mike was biased against autonomous robots that could fire weapons or drop bombs with minimal, if any, human intervention. There were too many things that could go wrong, and innocent people could be killed as a result. At the same time, he wasn't opposed to machines that were "going to save Marines, save time, save manpower, save lives."

It wasn't the first time that day I'd heard this odd contradiction, and over the next three days I'd hear it again and again. It was as if everyone had rehearsed the same set of talking points. Robots will take soldiers out of harm's way. Robots will save lives. Allow robots to pull the trigger? No way, it'll never happen. But wasn't the logical outcome of all this fancy technology an autonomous robot force, no humans required save for those few sitting in darkened control rooms half a world away? Wasn't the best way to save lives—American lives, at least—to take humans off the battlefield altogether? Mike stared out the bus window at the passing traffic.

"I don't think that you can ever take him out," he said, his breath fogging the tinted glass. "What happens to every major civilization? At some point they civilize themselves right out of warriors. You've got sheep and you've got wolves. You've got to have enough wolves around to protect your sheep, or else somebody else's wolves are going to take them out."

Coming from a career soldier, Mike's views of war and humanity were understandably romantic. To him, bad wolves weren't the real threat. It was the idea that civilization might be able to get along without wolves, good or bad, or that wolves could be made of titanium and silicon. What would happen to the warrior spirit then?

Scores of scale-model UAVs dangled on wires from the ceiling of the exhibit hall at the Baltimore Convention Center, rotating lazily in currents of air-conditioning. Models jutted into the aisles, their wings canted in attitudes of flight. Company reps blew packing dust off cluster bombs and electronic equipment. They put out bowls of candy and trinkets. Everywhere I looked I saw ghostly black-and-white images of myself, captured by dozens of infrared surveillance cameras mounted inside domed gimbals, staring back at me from closed-circuit televisions.

In addition to cameras, almost every booth featured a large plasma monitor showing a continuous video loop of robots blowing up vehicles on target ranges, or robots pepper-spraying intruders, robots climbing stairs, scurrying down sewer pipes, circling above battlefields and mountain ranges. These videos were often accompanied by a narrator's bland voice-over, muttered from a sound system that rivaled the most expensive home theater.

I sat down in the concession area to study the floor map. An engineer next to me picked at a plate of underripe melon and shook his head in awe at the long lines of people waiting for coffee. "Four or five years ago it was just booths with concept posters pinned up," he said. "Now the actual stuff is here. It's amazing."

At the fringes of the exhibit hall, I wandered through the warrens of small companies and remote military arsenals squeezed side-by-side into 10 × 10 booths. I followed the screeching chords of thrash metal until I stood in front of a television playing a promotional video featuring a robot called Chaos. Chaos was built by Autonomous Solutions, a private company that had been spun out of Utah State University's robotics lab. In the video, it clambered over various types of terrain, its four flipper-like tracks chewing up dirt and rocks and tree bark. The real thing was somewhat less kinetic. A Chaos prototype lay motionless on the floor in front of the television. I nudged it with my foot and asked the company's young operations manager what it was designed to do.

"Kick the pants off the PackBot," he said, glancing around nervously. "No, I'm kidding."

A few booths down I encountered a group of men gathered around a robot the size of a paperback book. Apparently, it could climb walls by virtue of a powerful centrifuge in its belly. A picture showed it stuck to a building outside a second-story window, peering over the sill. But the rep holding the remote-control box kept ramming the robot into a cloth-draped wall at the back of his booth. The robot lost traction on the loose fabric and flipped over on its back, wheels spinning. A rep from the neighboring booth volunteered use of his filing cabinet. The little robot zipped across the floor, bumped the cabinet, and, with a soft whir, climbed straight up the side. When it got to the top it extended a metal stalk bearing a tiny camera and scanned the applauding crowd.

I continued along the perimeter, trying to avoid eye contact with the reps. Since it was the first day of the show, they were fresh and alert, rocking on their heels at the edges of their booths, their eyes darting from name badge to name badge in search of potential customers. I picked up an M4 carbine resting on a table in the Chatten Associates booth. The gun's grip had been modified to simulate a computer mouse. It had two rubber keys and a thumb stick for operating a miniature radio-controlled tank sporting an assault rifle in its turret.

"You'll need this," said Kent Massey, Chatten's chief operating officer. He removed a helmet from a mannequin's head and placed it on mine. Then he adjusted the heads-up display, a postage stamp-sized LCD screen that floated in front of my right eye. The idea behind the setup was that a soldier could simultaneously keep one eye on the battlefield while piloting the robot via a video feed beamed back to his heads-up display. He never had to take his finger off the trigger.

I blinked and saw a robot's-eye view of traffic cones arranged on a fluorescent green square of artificial turf. I turned my head first to the left, then to the right. The gimbal-mounted camera in the tank mimicked the motion, swiveling left, then right. I pushed the thumb stick on the carbine's pistol grip. The tank lurched forward, knocking down a cone.

"Try not to look at the robot," Kent advised.

I turned my back to him and faced the aisle. It was difficult for me to imagine how the soldier of the future would manage both the stress of combat and the information overload that plagues the average office worker. Simply driving the tank made me dizzy, despite Kent's claims that Chatten's head-aiming system increased "situational awareness" and "operational efficiency" by 400 percent. Then again, I wasn't Army material. I was too old, too analog. As a Boeing rep would later explain to me, they were "building systems for kids that are in the seventh and eighth grades right now. They get the PDAs, the digital things, cell phones, IM."

As I crashed the tank around the obstacle course, conventioneers stopped in the aisle to determine why I was pointing a machine gun at them. I aimed the muzzle at the floor.

"The one mission that you simply cannot do without us is armed reconnaissance," Kent said over my shoulder. "Poke around a corner, clear a house . . . We lost thirty-eight guys in Fallujah in exactly those kinds of circumstances, plus a couple hundred wounded. If [the robot] gets killed, there's no letter to write home."

Robots have always been associated with dehumanization and, more explicitly, humanity's extinction. The word "robot" is derived from the Czech word for forced labor, "*robota*," and first appeared in Karel Capek's 1920 play, R.U.R (*Rossum's Universal Robots*), which ends with the destruction of mankind.

This view of robots, popularized in such movies as the *Terminator* series, troubles Cliff Hudson, who at the time coordinated robotics efforts for the Department of Defense. I ran into Cliff on the second day of the show, outside Carnegie Mellton's National Robotics Engineering Center's booth. Like the scientists in R.U.R., Cliff saw robots as a benign class of mechanized serfs. Military robots will handle most of "the three Ds: dull, dangerous, dirty-type tasks," he said, such as transporting supplies, guarding checkpoints, and sniffing for bombs. The more delicate task of killing would remain in human hands.

"I liken it to the military dog," Cliff said, and brought up a briefing given the previous day by an explosive-ordnance disposal (EOD) officer who had just returned from Iraq. The highlight of the briefing was an MTV-style video montage of robots disarming IEDs. It ended with a soldier walking away from the camera, silhouetted against golden evening sunlight, his loyal robot bumping along the road at his heels. Cliff pressed his hands together. "It's that partnership, it's that team approach," he said. "It's not going to replace the soldier. It's going to be an added capability and enhancer."

Adjacent to where we stood talking in the aisle was a prototype of the Gladiator, a six-wheeled armored car about the size of a golf cart, built by Carnegie Mellon engineers for the Marines. It was one mean enhancer. The prototype was equipped with a machine gun, but missiles could be attached to it as well.

"If you see concertina wire, you send this down range," Cliff said, maintaining his theme of man/robot cooperation. "And then the Marines can come up behind it. It's a great weapon." Despite its capabilities, the Gladiator hadn't won the complete trust of the Marines. "It's a little unstable," Cliff admitted. "Most people are uncomfortable around it when the safety is removed."

Reps proffering business cards began circling around Cliff and his entourage, sweeping me aside. Jörgen Pedersen, a young engineer with thin blond hair and a goatee, watched the scene with bemused detachment, his elbows propped on the Gladiator's turret. Jörgen had written the Gladiator's fire-control software.

"How safe is this thing?" I asked him.

"We wanted it to err on the side of safety first," Jörgen said. "You can always make something more *un*safe." In the early stages of the Gladiator's development, Jörgen had discovered that its communications link wasn't reliable enough to allow machine-gun bursts longer than six seconds. After six seconds, the robot would stop firing. So he reprogrammed the fire-control system with a fail-safe.

"You may have great communications here," Jörgen said, touching the Gladiator with his fingertips. "But you take one step back and you're just on the hairy edge of where this thing can communicate well."

The integrity of data links between unmanned systems and their operators is a major concern. Satellite bandwidth, already in short supply, will be stretched even further as more robots and other sophisticated electronics, such as remote sensors, are committed to the battlefield. There's also the possibility that radio signals could be jammed or hijacked by the enemy. But these problems are inherent to the current generation of teleoperated machines: robots that are controlled by humans from afar. As robots become more autonomous, fulfilling missions according to pre-programmed instructions, maintaining constant contact with human operators will be unnecessary. I asked Jörgen if robots would someday replace soldiers on the battlefield. He reiterated the need for a man in the loop.

"Maybe that's because I'm short-sighted based on my current experiences," he said. "Maybe the only way that it could happen is if there's no other people out on that field doing battle. It's just robots battling robots. At that point, it doesn't matter. We all just turn on the TV to see who's winning."

It is almost certain that robot deployment will save lives, both military and civilian. And yet the prospect of robot-on-human warfare does present serious moral and ethical, if not strictly legal, issues. Robots invite no special consideration under the laws of armed conflict, which place the burden of responsibility on humans, not weapons systems. When a laser-guided bomb kills civilians, responsibility falls on everyone involved in the kill chain, from the pilot who dropped the bomb to the commander who ordered the strike. Robots will be treated no differently. It will become vastly more difficult, however, to assign responsibility for noncombatant deaths caused by mechanical or programming failures as robots are granted greater degrees of autonomy. In this sense, robots may prove similar to low-tech cluster bombs or land mines, munitions that "do something that they're not supposed to out of the control of those who deploy them, and in doing so cause unintended death and suffering," according to Michael Byers, professor of global politics and international law at the University of British Columbia.

As robots become more autonomous, constant contact with human operators will be unnecessary.

The moral issues are perhaps similar to those arising from the use of precision-guided munitions (PGMs). There's no doubt that PGMs greatly limit civilian casualties and collateral damage to civilian infrastructure such as hospitals, electrical grids, and water systems. But because PGM strikes are more precise compared with dropping sticks of iron bombs from B-52s, the civilian casualties that often result from PGM strikes are considered necessary, if horribly unfortunate, mistakes. One need look no further than the PGM barrage that accompanied the ground invasion of Iraq in 2003. "Decapitation strikes" aimed at senior Iraqi leaders pounded neighborhoods from Baghdad to Basra. Due to poor intelligence, none of the fifty known strikes succeeded in finding their targets. In four of the strikes forty-two civilians were killed, including six members of a family who had the misfortune of living next door to Saddam Hussein's half brother.

It's not difficult to imagine a similar scenario involving robots instead of PGMs. A robot armed only with a machine gun enters a house known to harbor an insurgent leader. The robot opens fire and kills a woman and her two children instead. It's later discovered that the insurgent leader moved to a different location at the last minute. Put aside any mitigating factors that might prevent a situation like this from occurring and assume that the robot did exactly what it was programmed to do. Assume the commander behind the operation acted on the latest intelligence, and that he followed the laws of armed conflict to the letter. Although the deaths of the woman and children might not violate the laws of armed conflict, they fall into a moral black hole where no one, no human anyway, is directly responsible. Had the innocents of My Lai and Haditha been slain not by errant men but by errant machines, would we know the names of these places today?

More troubling than the compromised moral calculus with which we program our killing machines is how robots reduce even further the costs, both fiscal and human, of the choice to wage war. Robots do not have to be recruited, trained, fed, or paid extra for combat duty. When they are destroyed, there are no death benefits to disburse. Shipping them off to hostile lands doesn't require the expenditure of political capital either. There will be no grieving robot mothers pitching camp outside the president's ranch gates. Robots are, quite literally, an off-the-shelf war-fighting capability—war in a can.

This bloodless vision of future combat was best captured by a billboard I saw at the exhibition, in the General Dynamics booth. The billboard was titled "Robots as Co-Combatants," and two scenes illustrated the concept in the garish style of toy-model-box art. One featured UGVs positioned on a slope near a grove of glossy palm trees. In the distance, a group of mud-brick buildings resembling a walled compound was set against a barren mountain range. Bright red parabolas traced the trajectories of mortar shells fired into the compound from UGVs, but there were no explosions, no smoke.

The other scene was composed in the gritty vernacular of television news footage from Iraq. A squad of soldiers trotted down the cracked sidewalk of a city street, past stained concrete facades and terraces awash in glaring sunlight. A small, wingless micro-UAV hovered above the soldiers amid a tangled nest of drooping telephone lines, projecting a cone of white light that suggested an invisible sensor beam. And smack in the foreground, a UGV had maneuvered into the street, guns blazing. In both scenes, the soldiers are incidental to the action. Some don't even carry rifles. They sit in front of computer screens, fingers tapping on keyboards.

On the last day of the show, I sat in the concession area, chewing a stale pastry and scanning the list of the day's technical sessions. Most were dry, tedious affairs with such titles as "The Emerging Challenge of Loitering Attack Missiles." One session hosted by Foster-Miller, the company that manufactures the SWORDS robot, got my attention: "Weaponization of Small Unmanned Ground Vehicles." I filled my coffee cup and hustled upstairs.

I took a seat near the front of the conference room just as the lights dimmed. Hunched behind a podium, a Foster-Miller engineer began reading verbatim from a PowerPoint presentation about the history of SWORDS, ending with a dreary bullet-point list cataloguing the past achievements of the TALON robot, SWORDS's immediate predecessor.

"TALON has been used in most major, major . . ." The engineer faltered.

"Conflicts," someone in the audience stage-whispered. I turned to see that it was Bob Quinn. He winked at me in acknowledgment.

"Conflicts," the engineer said. He ended his portion of the talk with the same video montage that had inspired Cliff Hudson to compare robots to dogs. TALON robots were shown pulling apart tangles of wire connected to IEDs, plucking at garbage bags that had been tossed on the sides of darkened roads, extracting mortar shells hidden inside Styrofoam cups. Bob Quinn took the podium just as the final shot in the montage, that of the soldier walking down the road with his faithful TALON robot at his heels, faded on the screen behind him. The lights came up.

"The 800-pound gorilla, or the bully in the playpen, for weaponized robotics—for all ground-based robots—is Hollywood," Bob said. The audience stirred. Bob strolled off the dais and stood in the aisle, hands in his pockets. "It's interesting that UAVs like the Predator can fire Hellfire missiles at will without a huge interest worldwide. But when you get into weaponization of ground vehicles, our soldiers, our safety community, our nation, our world, are not ready for autonomy. In fact, it's quite the opposite."

Bob remained in the aisle, narrating a series of PowerPoint slides and video clips that showed SWORDS firing rockets and machine guns, SWORDS riding atop a Stryker vehicle,

SWORDS creeping up on a target and lobbing grenades at it. His point was simple: SWORDS was no killer robot, no Terminator. It was a capable weapons platform firmly in the control of the soldiers who operated it, nothing more. When the last video clip didn't load, Bob stalled for time.

"We've found that using Hollywood on Hollywood is a good strategy to overcome some of the concerns that aren't apparent with UAVs but are very apparent with UGVs," he said. Last February a crew from the History Channel had filmed SWORDS for an episode of *Mail Call*, a half-hour program hosted by the inimitable R. Lee Ermey, best known for his role as the profane drill sergeant in the movie *Full Metal Jacket*. Ermey's scowling face suddenly appeared onscreen, accompanied by jarring rock music.

"It's a lot smarter to send this robo-soldier down a blind alley than one of our flesh-and blood warriors," Ermey shouted. "It was developed by our troops in the field, not some suit in an office back home!"

Ermey's antic mugging was interspersed with quick cutaways of SWORDS on a firing range and interviews with EOD soldiers.

"The next time you start thinking about telling the kids to put away that video game, think again!" Ermey screamed. He jabbed his finger into the camera. "Some day they could be using those same kinds of skills to run a robot that will save their bacon!"

"That's a good way to get off the stage," Bob said. He was smiling now, soaking in the applause. "I think armed robots will save soldiers' lives. It creates an unfair fight, and that's what we want. But they will be teleoperated. The more as a community we focus on that, given the Hollywood perceptions, the better off our soldiers will be."

Downstairs in the exhibit hall, I saw that Boeing had also learned the value of Hollywood-style marketing. I had stopped by the company's booth out of a sense of obligation more than curiosity: Boeing is the lead contractor for FCS. While I was talking to Stephen Bishop, the FCS business-development manager, I noticed a familiar face appear on the laptop screen behind him.

"Is that—MacGyver?"

Stephen nodded and stepped aside so that I could get a better view of the laptop. The face did indeed belong to Richard Dean Anderson, former star of the television series *MacGyver* and now the star of a five-minute promotional film produced by Boeing. Judging by the digital special effects, the film probably cost more to make than what most companies had spent on their entire exhibits. Not coincidentally, the film is set in 2014, when the first generation of FCS vehicles are scheduled for full deployment. An American convoy approaches a bridge near a snowy mountain pass somewhere in Asia, perhaps North Korea. The enemy mobilizes to cut the Americans off, but they are detected and annihilated by armed ground vehicles and UAVs.

At the center of this networked firestorm is Richard Dean Anderson, who sits inside a command vehicle, furrowing his brow and tapping a computer touchscreen. As the American forces cross the bridge, a lone enemy soldier hiding behind a

boulder fires a rocket at the lead vehicle and disables it. The attack falters.

"I do not have an ID on the shooter!" a technician yells. Anderson squints grimly at his computer screen. It's the moment of truth. Does he pull back and allow the enemy time to regroup, or does he advance across the bridge, exposing his forces to enemy fire? The rousing martial soundtrack goes quiet.

"Put a 'bot on the bridge," Anderson says.

A dune-buggy-like robot darts from the column of vehicles and stops in the middle of the bridge in a heroic act of self-sacrifice. The lone enemy soldier takes the bait and fires another missile, destroying the robot and unwittingly revealing his position to a micro-UAV loitering nearby. Billions of dollars and decades of scientific research come to bear on this moment, on one man hiding behind a snow-covered boulder. He is obliterated.

"Good job," Anderson sneers. "Now let's finish this."

The film ends as American tanks pour across the bridge into enemy territory. The digitally enhanced point of view pulls back to reveal the FCS network, layer by layer, vehicle by vehicle, eighteen systems in all, until it reaches space, the network's outer shell, where a spy satellite glides by.

"Saving soldiers' lives," Stephen said, glancing at his press manager to make sure he was on message. I commended the film's production values. Stephen seemed pleased that I'd noticed. "Three-stars and four-stars gave it a standing ovation at the Pentagon last November," he told me.

"You can't argue with MacGyver," I said.

"Because it's all about saving soldiers' lives," Stephen said. "Works for congressmen, works for senators, works for the grandmother in Nebraska."

Later that summer I visited Picatinny Arsenal, "Home of American Firepower," in New Jersey, to see a live-fire demonstration of the SWORDS robot. SWORDS was conceived at Picatinny by a small group of EOD soldiers who wanted to find a less dangerous way to "put heat on a target" inside caves in Afghanistan. Three years later, SWORDS was undergoing some final tweaks at Picatinny before being sent to Aberdeen Proving Ground for its last round of safety tests. After that, it would be ready for deployment.

"As long as you don't break my rules you'll be fine," said Sergeant Jason Mero, motioning for us to gather around him. Sgt. Mero had participated in the initial invasion of Iraq, including the assault on Saddam International Airport. He had buzzed sandy brown hair, a compact build, and the brusque authority common to non-commissioned officers. He told us exactly where we could stand, where we could set up our cameras, and assured us that he was there to help us get what we needed. Other than the "very, very loud" report of the M240 machine gun, there was little to worry about.

"The robot's not going to suddenly pivot and start shooting everybody," he said, without a hint of irony.

A crew from the Discovery Networks' Military Channel dragged their gear onto the range. They were filming a special on "Warbots," and the producer was disappointed to learn that the SWORDS robot mounted with a formidable-looking M202 grenade launcher wasn't operable. He would have to make do with the less telegenic machine-gun variant. The producer, Jonathan Gruber, wore a canvas fishing hat with the brim pulled down to the black frames of his stylish eyeglasses. Jonathan gave stage directions to Sgt. Mero, who knelt in the gravel next to SWORDS and began describing how the loading process works.

"Sergeant, if you could just look to me," Jonathan prompted. "Good. So, is a misfeed common?"

"No, not with this weapon system," Sgt. Mero said. "It's very uncommon." "My questions are cut out," Jonathan said. "So if you could repeat my question in the answer? So, you know, 'Misfeeds are not common . . .'"

"Mis—" Sgt. Mero cleared his throat. His face turned red. "However, misfeeds are not common with the M240 bravo."

"Okay, great, I'm all set for now, thanks."

The firing range was scraped out of the bottom of a shallow gorge, surrounded on all sides by trees and exposed limestone. Turkey vultures circled above the ridge. The weedy ground was littered with spent shell casings and scraps of scorched metal. Fifty yards from where I sat, two human silhouettes were visible through shoulder-high weeds in front of a concrete trap filled with sand. Sgt. Mero hooked a cable to SWORDS's camera, then flipped a red switch on the control box. I felt the M240's muzzle blast on my face as SWORDS lurched backward on its tracks, spilling smoking shells on the ground.

A cloud of dust billowed behind the silhouettes. Sgt. Mero fired again, then again. With each burst, recoil pushed SWORDS backward, and Sgt. Mero, staring at the video image on the control box's LCD screen, readjusted his aim. I could hear servos whining. When Sgt. Mero finished the ammunition belt, he switched off SWORDS and led us downrange to the targets.

"So, um, Sergeant?" Jonathan said. "As soon as you see our camera you can just start talking."

"As you see, the M240—"

"And Sergeant?" Jonathan interrupted. "I don't think you have to scream. You can just speak in a normal voice. We're all close to you."

"The problem with a heavy machine gun is, obviously, there's going to be a lot of spray," Sgt. Mero said, bending down to pick up one of the silhouettes that had fallen in the weeds. "Our second guy over here that we actually knocked down—he didn't get very many bullets, but he actually got hit pretty hard."

Through the weeds I spotted the SWORDS robot squatting in the dust. My heart skipped a beat. The machine gun was pointed straight at me. I'd watched Sgt. Mero deactivate SWORDS. I saw him disconnect the cables. And the machine gun's feed tray was empty. There wasn't the slightest chance of a misfire. My fear was irrational, but I still made a wide circle around the robot when it was time to leave.

Within our lifetime, robots will give us the ability to wage war without committing ourselves to the human cost of actually fighting a war. War will become a routine, a program. The great nineteenth-century military theorist Carl von Clausewitz understood that although war may have rational goals, the conduct of war is fundamentally irrational and unpredictable. Absent fear, war cannot be called war. A better name for it would be target practice.

Back on the firing line, Sgt. Mero booted up SWORDS and began running it around the range for the benefit of the cameras. It made a tinny, rattling noise as it rumbled over the rocks. A Discovery crewman waddled close behind it, holding his camera low to the ground. He stumbled over a clump of weeds, and for a second I thought he was going to fall on his face. But he regained his balance, took a breath, and ran to catch up with the robot.

"I think I'm good," Jonathan said after the driving demonstration. "Anything else you want to add about this?"

"Yeah," Sgt. Mero said, smiling wryly. "It kicks *ass*. It's *awesome*." In repentance for this brief moment of sarcasm, Sgt. Mero squared his shoulders, looked straight into the camera, and began speaking as if he were reading from cue cards. "These things are amazing," he said breathlessly. "They don't complain, like our regular soldiers do. They don't cry. They're not scared. This robot here has no fear, which is a good supplement to the United States Army."

"That's great," Jonathan said.

Steve Featherstone is a writer and photographer in Syracuse, New York. His last article for *Harper's Magazine*, "The Line Is Hot," appeared in the December 2005 issue.

From *Harper's Magazine*, February 2007, pp. 43–46, 48–52. Copyright © 2007 by Harper's Magazine. Reprinted by permission.

Google & the Future of Books

ROBERT DARNTON

How can we navigate through the information landscape that is only beginning to come into view? The question is more urgent than ever following the recent settlement between Google and the authors and publishers who were suing it for alleged breach of copyright. For the last four years, Google has been digitizing millions of books, including many covered by copyright, from the collections of major research libraries, and making the texts searchable online. The authors and publishers objected that digitizing constituted a violation of their copyrights. After lengthy negotiations, the plaintiffs and Google agreed on a settlement, which will have a profound effect on the way books reach readers for the foreseeable future. What will that future be?

No one knows, because the settlement is so complex that it is difficult to perceive the legal and economic contours in the new lay of the land. But those of us who are responsible for research libraries have a clear view of a common goal: we want to open up our collections and make them available to readers everywhere. How to get there? The only workable tactic may be vigilance: see as far ahead as you can; and while you keep your eye on the road, remember to look in the rearview mirror.

When I look backward, I fix my gaze on the eighteenth century, the Enlightenment, its faith in the power of knowledge, and the world of ideas in which it operated—what the enlightened referred to as the Republic of Letters.

The eighteenth century imagined the Republic of Letters as a realm with no police, no boundaries, and no inequalities other than those determined by talent. Anyone could join it by exercising the two main attributes of citizenship, writing and reading. Writers formulated ideas, and readers judged them. Thanks to the power of the printed word, the judgments spread in widening circles, and the strongest arguments won.

The word also spread by written letters, for the eighteenth century was a great era of epistolary exchange. Read through the correspondence of Voltaire, Rousseau, Franklin, and Jefferson—each filling about fifty volumes—and you can watch the Republic of Letters in operation. All four writers debated all the issues of their day in a steady stream of letters, which crisscrossed Europe and America in a transatlantic information network.

I especially enjoy the exchange of letters between Jefferson and Madison. They discussed everything, notably the American Constitution, which Madison was helping to write in Philadelphia while Jefferson was representing the new republic in Paris. They often wrote about books, for Jefferson loved to haunt the bookshops in the capital of the Republic of Letters, and he frequently bought books for his friend. The purchases included Diderot's *Encyclopédie,* which Jefferson thought that he had got at a bargain price, although he had mistaken a reprint for a first edition.

Two future presidents discussing books through the information network of the Enlightenment—it's a stirring sight. But before this picture of the past fogs over with sentiment, I should add that the Republic of Letters was democratic only in principle. In practice, it was dominated by the wellborn and the rich. Far from being able to live from their pens, most writers had to court patrons, solicit sinecures, lobby for appointments to state-controlled journals, dodge censors, and wangle their way into salons and academies, where reputations were made. While suffering indignities at the hands of their social superiors, they turned on one another. The quarrel between Voltaire and Rousseau illustrates their temper. After reading Rousseau's *Discourse on the Origins of Inequality* in 1755, Voltaire wrote to him, "I have received, Monsieur, your new book against the human race. . . . It makes one desire to go down on all fours." Five years later, Rousseau wrote to Voltaire. "Monsieur, . . . I hate you."

The personal conflicts were compounded by social distinctions. Far from functioning like an egalitarian agora, the Republic of Letters suffered from the same disease that ate through all societies in the eighteenth century: privilege. Privileges were not limited to aristocrats. In France, they applied to everything in the world of letters, including printing and the book trade, which were dominated by exclusive guilds, and the books themselves, which could not appear legally without a royal privilege and a censor's approbation, printed in full in their text.

One way to understand this system is to draw on the sociology of knowledge, notably Pierre Bourdieu's notion of literature as a power field composed of contending positions within the rules of a game that itself is subordinate to the dominating forces of society at large. But one needn't subscribe to Bourdieu's school of sociology in order to acknowledge the connections between literature and power. Seen from the perspective of the players, the realities of literary life contradicted the lofty ideals of the Enlightenment. Despite its principles, the Republic of Letters, as it actually operated, was a closed world, inaccessible to the underprivileged.

Yet I want to invoke the Enlightenment in an argument for openness in general and for open access in particular.

If we turn from the eighteenth century to the present, do we see a similar contradiction between principle and practice—right here in the world of research libraries? One of my colleagues is a quiet, diminutive lady, who might call up the notion of Marion the Librarian. When she meets people at parties and identifies herself, they sometimes say condescendingly, "A librarian, how nice. Tell me, what is it like to be a librarian?" She replies, "Essentially, it is all about money and power."

We are back with Pierre Bourdieu. Yet most of us would subscribe to the principles inscribed in prominent places in our public libraries. "Free To All," it says above the main entrance to the Boston Public Library; and in the words of Thomas Jefferson, carved in gold letters on the wall of the Trustees' Room of the New York Public Library: "I look to the diffusion of light and education as the resource most to be relied on for ameliorating the condition promoting the virtue and advancing the happiness of man." We are back with the Enlightenment.

Our republic was founded on faith in the central principle of the eighteenth-century Republic of Letters: the diffusion of light. For Jefferson, enlightenment took place by means of writers and readers, books and libraries—especially libraries, at Monticello, the University of Virginia, and the Library of Congress. This faith is embodied in the United States Constitution. Article 1, Section 8, establishes copyright and patents "for limited times" only and subject to the higher purpose of promoting "the progress of science and useful arts." The Founding Fathers acknowledged authors' rights to a fair return on their intellectual labor, but they put public welfare before private profit.

How to calculate the relative importance of those two values? As the authors of the Constitution knew, copyright was created in Great Britain by the Statute of Anne in 1710 for the purpose of curbing the monopolistic practices of the London Stationers' Company and also, as its title proclaimed, "for the encouragement of learning." At that time, Parliament set the length of copyright at fourteen years, renewable only once. The Stationers attempted to defend their monopoly of publishing and the book trade by arguing for perpetual copyright in a long series of court cases. But they lost in the definitive ruling of *Donaldson* v. *Becket* in 1774.

When the Americans gathered to draft a constitution thirteen years later, they generally favored the view that had predominated in Britain. Twenty-eight years seemed long enough to protect the interests of authors and publishers. Beyond that limit, the interest of the public should prevail. In 1790, the first copyright act—also dedicated to "the encouragement of learning"—followed British practice by adopting a limit of fourteen years renewable for another fourteen.

How long does copyright extend today? According to the Sonny Bono Copyright Term Extension Act of 1998 (also known as "the Mickey Mouse Protection Act," because Mickey was about to fall into the public domain), it lasts as long as the life of the author plus seventy years. In practice, that normally would mean more than a century. Most books published in the twentieth century have not yet entered the public domain. When it comes to digitization, access to our cultural heritage generally ends on January 1, 1923, the date from which great numbers of books are subject to copyright laws. It will remain there—unless private interests take over the digitizing, package it for consumers, tie the packages up by means of legal deals, and sell them for the profit of the shareholders. As things stand now, for example, Sinclair Lewis's *Babbitt,* published in 1922, is in the public domain, whereas Lewis's *Elmer Gantry,* published in 1927, will not enter the public domain until 2022.[1]

To descend from the high principles of the Founding Fathers to the practices of the cultural industries today is to leave the realm of Enlightenment for the hurly-burly of corporate capitalism. If we turned the sociology of knowledge onto the present—as Bourdieu himself did—we would see that we live in a world designed by Mickey Mouse, red in tooth and claw.

Does this kind of reality check make the principles of Enlightenment look like a historical fantasy? Let's reconsider the history. As the Enlightenment faded in the early nineteenth century, professionalization set in. You can follow the process by comparing the *Encyclopédie* of Diderot, which organized knowledge into an organic whole dominated by the faculty of reason, with its successor from the end of the eighteenth century, the *Encyclopédie méthodique,* which divided knowledge into fields that we can recognize today: chemistry, physics, history, mathematics, and the rest. In the nineteenth century, those fields turned into professions, certified by PhDs and guarded by professional associations. They metamorphosed into departments of universities, and by the twentieth century they had left their mark on campuses—chemistry housed in this building, physics in that one, history here, mathematics there, and at the center of it all, a library, usually designed to look like a temple of learning.

Along the way, professional journals sprouted throughout the fields, subfields, and sub-subfields. The learned societies produced them, and the libraries bought them. This system worked well for about a hundred years. Then commercial publishers discovered that they could make a fortune by selling subscriptions to the journals. Once a university library subscribed, the students and professors came to expect an uninterrupted flow of issues. The price could be ratcheted up without causing cancellations, because the libraries paid for the subscriptions and the professors did not. Best of all, the professors provided free or nearly free labor. They wrote the articles, refereed submissions, and served on editorial boards, partly to spread knowledge in the Enlightenment fashion, but mainly to advance their own careers.

The result stands out on the acquisitions budget of every research library: the *Journal of Comparative Neurology* now costs $25,910 for a year's subscription; *Tetrahedron* costs $17,969 (or $39,739, if bundled with related publications as a *Tetrahedron* package); the average price of a chemistry journal is $3,490; and the ripple effects have damaged intellectual life throughout the world of learning. Owing to the skyrocketing cost of serials, libraries that used to spend 50 percent of their acquisitions budget on monographs now spend 25 percent or less. University presses, which depend on sales to libraries, cannot cover their costs by publishing monographs. And young scholars who depend on publishing to advance their careers are now in danger of perishing.

Fortunately, this picture of the hard facts of life in the world of learning is already going out of date. Biologists, chemists, and physicists no longer live in separate worlds; nor do historians, anthropologists, and literary scholars. The old map of the campus no longer corresponds to the activities of the professors and students. It is being redrawn everywhere, and in many places the interdisciplinary designs are turning into structures. The library remains at the heart of things, but it pumps nutrition throughout the university, and often to the farthest reaches of cyberspace, by means of electronic networks.

The eighteenth-century Republic of Letters had been transformed into a professional Republic of Learning, and it is now open to amateurs—amateurs in the best sense of the word, lovers of learning among the general citizenry. Openness is operating everywhere, thanks to "open access" repositories of digitized articles available free of charge, the Open Content Alliance, the Open Knowledge Commons, OpenCourseWare, the Internet Archive, and openly amateur enterprises like Wikipedia. The democratization of knowledge now seems to be at our fingertips. We can make the Enlightenment ideal come to life in reality.

At this point, you may suspect that I have swung from one American genre, the jeremiad, to another, utopian enthusiasm. It might be possible, I suppose, for the two to work together as a dialectic, were it not for the danger of commercialization. When businesses like Google look at libraries, they do not merely see temples of learning. They see potential assets or what they call "content," ready to be mined. Built up over centuries at an enormous expenditure of money and labor, library collections can be digitized en masse at relatively little cost—millions of dollars, certainly, but little compared to the investment that went into them.

Libraries exist to promote a public good: "the encouragement of learning," learning "Free To All." Businesses exist in order to make money for their shareholders—and a good thing, too, for the public good depends on a profitable economy. Yet if we permit the commercialization of the content of our libraries, there is no getting around a fundamental contradiction. To digitize collections and sell the product in ways that fail to guarantee wide access would be to repeat the mistake that was made when publishers exploited the market for scholarly journals, but on a much greater scale, for it would turn the Internet into an instrument for privatizing knowledge that belongs in the public sphere. No invisible hand would intervene to correct the imbalance between the private and the public welfare. Only the public can do that, but who speaks for the public? Not the legislators of the Mickey Mouse Protection Act.

You cannot legislate Enlightenment, but you can set rules of the game to protect the public interest. Libraries represent the public good. They are not businesses, but they must cover their costs. They need a business plan. Think of the old motto of Con Edison when it had to tear up New York's streets in order to get

at the infrastructure beneath them: "Dig we must." Libraries say, "Digitize we must." But not on any terms. We must do it in the interest of the public, and that means holding the digitizers responsible to the citizenry.

It would be naive to identify the Internet with the Enlightenment. It has the potential to diffuse knowledge beyond anything imagined by Jefferson; but while it was being constructed, link by hyperlink, commercial interests did not sit idly on the sidelines. They want to control the game, to take it over, to own it. They compete among themselves, of course, but so ferociously that they kill each other off. Their struggle for survival is leading toward an oligopoly; and whoever may win, the victory could mean a defeat for the public good.

Don't get me wrong. I know that businesses must be responsible to shareholders. I believe that authors are entitled to payment for their creative labor and that publishers deserve to make money from the value they add to the texts supplied by authors. I admire the wizardry of hardware, software, search engines, digitization, and algorithmic relevance ranking. I acknowledge the importance of copyright, although I think that Congress got it better in 1790 than in 1998.

But we, too, cannot sit on the sidelines, as if the market forces can be trusted to operate for the public good. We need to get engaged, to mix it up, and to win back the public's rightful domain. When I say "we," I mean we the people, we who created the Constitution and who should make the Enlightenment principles behind it inform the everyday realities of the information society. Yes, we must digitize. But more important, we must democratize. We must open access to our cultural heritage. How? By rewriting the rules of the game, by subordinating private interests to the public good, and by taking inspiration from the early republic in order to create a Digital Republic of Learning.

What provoked these jeremianic-utopian reflections? Google. Four years ago, Google began digitizing books from research libraries, providing full-text searching and making books in the public domain available on the Internet at no cost to the viewer. For example, it is now possible for anyone, anywhere to view and download a digital copy of the 1871 first edition of *Middlemarch* that is in the collection of the Bodleian Library at Oxford. Everyone profited, including Google, which collected revenue from some discreet advertising attached to the service, Google Book Search. Google also digitized an ever-increasing number of library books that were protected by copyright in order to provide search services that displayed small snippets of the text. In September and October 2005, a group of authors and publishers brought a class action suit against Google, alleging violation of copyright. Last October 28, after lengthy negotiations, the opposing parties announced agreement on a settlement, which is subject to approval by the U.S. District Court for the Southern District of New York.[2]

The settlement creates an enterprise known as the Book Rights Registry to represent the interests of the copyright holders. Google will sell access to a gigantic data bank composed primarily of copyrighted, out-of-print books digitized from the research libraries. Colleges, universities, and other organizations will be able to subscribe by paying for an "institutional license" providing access to the data bank. A "public access license" will make this material available to public libraries, where Google will provide free viewing of the digitized books on one computer terminal. And individuals also will be able to access and print out digitized versions of the books by purchasing a "consumer license" from Google, which will cooperate with the registry for the distribution of all the revenue to copyright holders. Google will retain 37 percent, and the registry will distribute 63 percent among the rightsholders.

Meanwhile, Google will continue to make books in the public domain available for users to read, download, and print, free of charge. Of the seven million books that Google reportedly had digitized by November 2008, one million are works in the public domain; one million are in copyright and in print; and five million are in copyright but out of print. It is this last category that will furnish the bulk of the books to be made available through the institutional license.

Many of the in-copyright and in-print books will not be available in the data bank unless the copyright owners opt to include them. They will continue to be sold in the normal fashion as printed books and also could be marketed to individual customers as digitized copies, accessible through the consumer license for downloading and reading, perhaps eventually on e-book readers such as Amazon's Kindle.

After reading the settlement and letting its terms sink in—no easy task, as it runs to 134 pages and 15 appendices of legalese—one is likely to be dumbfounded: here is a proposal that could result in the world's largest library. It would, to be sure, be a digital library, but it could dwarf the Library of Congress and all the national libraries of Europe. Moreover, in pursuing the terms of the settlement with the authors and publishers, Google could also become the world's largest book business—not a chain of stores but an electronic supply service that could out-Amazon Amazon.

An enterprise on such a scale is bound to elicit reactions of the two kinds that I have been discussing: on the one hand, utopian enthusiasm; on the other, jeremiads about the danger of concentrating power to control access to information.

Who could not be moved by the prospect of bringing virtually all the books from America's greatest research libraries within the reach of all Americans, and perhaps eventually to everyone in the world with access to the Internet? Not only will Google's technological wizardry bring books to readers, it will also open up extraordinary opportunities for research, a whole gamut of possibilities from straightforward word searches to complex text mining. Under certain conditions, the participating libraries will be able to use the digitized copies of their books to create replacements for books that have been damaged or lost. Google will engineer the texts in ways to help readers with disabilities.

Unfortunately, Google's commitment to provide free access to its database on one terminal in every public library is hedged with restrictions: readers will not be able to print out any copyrighted text without paying a fee to the copyright holders (though Google has offered to pay them at the outset); and a single

terminal will hardly satisfy the demand in large libraries. But Google's generosity will be a boon to the small-town, Carnegie-library readers, who will have access to more books than are currently available in the New York Public Library. Google can make the Enlightenment dream come true.

But will it? The eighteenth-century philosophers saw monopoly as a main obstacle to the diffusion of knowledge—not merely monopolies in general, which stifled trade according to Adam Smith and the Physiocrats, but specific monopolies such as the Stationers' Company in London and the booksellers' guild in Paris, which choked off free trade in books.

Google is not a guild, and it did not set out to create a monopoly. On the contrary, it has pursued a laudable goal: promoting access to information. But the class action character of the settlement makes Google invulnerable to competition. Most book authors and publishers who own U.S. copyrights are automatically covered by the settlement. They can opt out of it; but whatever they do, no new digitizing enterprise can get off the ground without winning their assent one by one, a practical impossibility, or without becoming mired down in another class action suit. If approved by the court—a process that could take as much as two years—the settlement will give Google control over the digitizing of virtually all books covered by copyright in the United States.

This outcome was not anticipated at the outset. Looking back over the course of digitization from the 1990s, we now can see that we missed a great opportunity. Action by Congress and the Library of Congress or a grand alliance of research libraries supported by a coalition of foundations could have done the job at a feasible cost and designed it in a manner that would have put the public interest first. By spreading the cost in various ways—a rental based on the amount of use of a database or a budget line in the National Endowment for the Humanities or the Library of Congress—we could have provided authors and publishers with a legitimate income, while maintaining an open access repository or one in which access was based on reasonable fees. We could have created a National Digital Library—the twenty-first-century equivalent of the Library of Alexandria. It is too late now. Not only have we failed to realize that possibility, but, even worse, we are allowing a question of public policy—the control of access to information—to be determined by private lawsuit.

While the public authorities slept, Google took the initiative. It did not seek to settle its affairs in court. It went about its business, scanning books in libraries; and it scanned them so effectively as to arouse the appetite of others for a share in the potential profits. No one should dispute the claim of authors and publishers to income from rights that properly belong to them; nor should anyone presume to pass quick judgment on the contending parties of the lawsuit. The district court judge will pronounce on the validity of the settlement, but that is primarily a matter of dividing profits, not of promoting the public interest.

As an unintended consequence, Google will enjoy what can only be called a monopoly—a monopoly of a new kind, not of railroads or steel but of access to information. Google has no serious competitors. Microsoft dropped its major program to digitize books several months ago, and other enterprises like the Open Knowledge Commons (formerly the Open Content Alliance) and the Internet Archive are minute and ineffective in comparison with Google. Google alone has the wealth to digitize on a massive scale. And having settled with the authors and publishers, it can exploit its financial power from within a protective legal barrier; for the class action suit covers the entire class of authors and publishers. No new entrepreneurs will be able to digitize books within that fenced-off territory, even if they could afford it, because they would have to fight the copyright battles all over again. If the settlement is upheld by the court, only Google will be protected from copyright liability.

Google's record suggests that it will not abuse its double-barreled fiscal-legal power. But what will happen if its current leaders sell the company or retire? The public will discover the answer from the prices that the future Google charges, especially the price of the institutional subscription licenses. The settlement leaves Google free to negotiate deals with each of its clients, although it announces two guiding principles: "(1) the realization of revenue at market rates for each Book and license on behalf of the Rightsholders and (2) the realization of broad access to the Books by the public, including institutions of higher education."

What will happen if Google favors profitability over access? Nothing, if I read the terms of the settlement correctly. Only the registry, acting for the copyright holders, has the power to force a change in the subscription prices charged by Google, and there is no reason to expect the registry to object if the prices are too high. Google may choose to be generous in it pricing, and I have reason to hope it may do so; but it could also employ a strategy comparable to the one that proved to be so effective in pushing up the price of scholarly journals: first, entice subscribers with low initial rates, and then, once they are hooked, ratchet up the rates as high as the traffic will bear.

Free-market advocates may argue that the market will correct itself. If Google charges too much, customers will cancel their subscriptions, and the price will drop. But there is no direct connection between supply and demand in the mechanism for the institutional licenses envisioned by the settlement. Students, faculty, and patrons of public libraries will not pay for the subscriptions. The payment will come from the libraries; and if the libraries fail to find enough money for the subscription renewals, they may arouse ferocious protests from readers who have become accustomed to Google's service. In the face of the protests, the libraries probably will cut back on other services, including the acquisition of books, just as they did when publishers ratcheted up the price of periodicals.

No one can predict what will happen. We can only read the terms of the settlement and guess about the future. If Google

makes available, at a reasonable price, the combined holdings of all the major U.S. libraries, who would not applaud? Would we not prefer a world in which this immense corpus of digitized books is accessible, even at a high price, to one in which it did not exist?

Perhaps, but the settlement creates a fundamental change in the digital world by consolidating power in the hands of one company. Apart from Wikipedia, Google already controls the means of access to information online for most Americans, whether they want to find out about people, goods, places, or almost anything. In addition to the original "Big Google," we have Google Earth, Google Maps, Google Images, Google Labs, Google Finance, Google Arts, Google Food, Google Sports, Google Health, Google Checkout, Google Alerts, and many more Google enterprises on the way. Now Google Book Search promises to create the largest library and the largest book business that have ever existed.

Whether or not I have understood the settlement correctly, its terms are locked together so tightly that they cannot be pried apart. At this point, neither Google, nor the authors, nor the publishers, nor the district court is likely to modify the settlement substantially. Yet this is also a tipping point in the development of what we call the information society. If we get the balance wrong at this moment, private interests may outweigh the public good for the foreseeable future, and the Enlightenment dream may be as elusive as ever.

Notes

1. The Copyright Term Extension Act of 1998 retroactively lengthened copyright by twenty years for books copyrighted after January 1, 1923. Unfortunately, the copyright status of books published in the twentieth century is complicated by legislation that has extended copyright eleven times during the last fifty years. Until a congressional act of 1992, rightsholders had to renew their copyrights. The 1992 act removed that requirement for books published between 1964 and 1977, when, according to the Copyright Act of 1976, their copyrights would last for the author's life plus fifty years. The act of 1998 extended that protection to the author's life plus seventy years. Therefore, all books published after 1963 remain in copyright, and an unknown number—unknown owing to inadequate information about the deaths of authors and the owners of copyright—published between 1923 and 1964 are also protected by copyright. See Paul A. David and Jared Rubin, "Restricting Access to Books on the Internet: Some Unanticipated Effects of U.S. Copyright Legislation," *Review of Economic Research on Copyright Issues,* Vol. 5, No. 1 (2008).

2. The full text of the settlement can be found at www.googlebooksettlement.com/agreement.html. For Google's legal notice concerning the settlement, see page 35 of this issue of *The New York Review.*

From *The New York Review of Books,* February 12, 2009. Copyright © 2009 by New York Review of Books. Reprinted by permission.

Archiving Writers' Work in the Age of E-Mail

STEVE KOLOWICH

L eslie Morris is used to handling John Updike's personal effects. For decades, Mr. Updike had been sending a steady stream of manuscripts and papers to Harvard University's Houghton Library, where Ms. Morris serves as a curator.

But in late February, several weeks after the iconic writer died, some boxes arrived with unexpected contents: approximately 50 three-and-a-half and five-and-a-quarter-inch floppy disks—artifacts from late in the author's career when he, like many of his peers, began using a word processor.

The floppies have presented a bit of a problem. While relatively modern to Mr. Updike—who rose to prominence back when publishers were still using Linotype machines—the disks are outmoded and damage-prone by today's standards. Ms. Morris, who curates modern books and manuscripts, has carefully stored them alongside his papers in a temperature-controlled room in the library "until we have a procedure here at Harvard on how to handle these materials."

Harvard isn't the only university puzzling over new media from old—and not-so-old—masters. Emory University recently received four laptops, an external hard drive, and a Palm Treo personal digital assistant from Salman Rushdie. The University of Texas at Austin recently acquired a series of Zip disks and a laptop containing Norman Mailer's files.

"Once we learned how to preserve paper, we were good," says Naomi L. Nelson, interim director of the manuscript, archives, and rare-book library at Emory University's Robert W. Woodruff Library. "That really hasn't changed a lot. With computers it's a whole different ballgame."

Still, three things are becoming clear. First, these trappings of the digital age will transform the way libraries preserve and exhibit literary collections. Second, universities are going to have to spend money on new equipment and training for their archivists. And finally, scholars will be able to learn more about writers than they ever have before.

In with the Old

Personal computers and external storage devices have been around for more than a quarter-century, but only now, as the famous literary figures of the 20th century begin to pass away, are these technologies showing up on archivists' doorsteps.

According to Ms. Morris, the Updike papers will be the first in the Houghton catalog to have a "significant magnetic-media component," and she realizes that old floppy disks are just the tip of the iceberg. The great American novelists of the digital era—the ones who own BlackBerrys, use Gmail, Facebook, and Twitter, and compose only on computer screens—will soon begin shipping their hard drives off to university libraries.

What happens then is something much on the minds of Matthew G. Kirschenbaum (The Chronicle, August 17, 2007) and Douglas L. Reside. Both Mr. Kirschenbaum, associate director of the Maryland Institute for Technology in the Humanities at the University of Maryland, and Mr. Reside, an assistant director at the institute, possess the collection of skills that may eventually be required of all 21st-century curators. In addition to holding doctorates in English, they are computer experts.

The institute, located in an austere warren of offices in the basement of the university's McKeldin Library, houses a mix of sleek new machines and clunky old ones. An easy office-chair roll away from his newest computer sits Mr. Kirschenbaum's oldest one: a small, gray box known as the Apple II. Mr. Reside's office contains similar artifacts, including a Commodore 64 gaming console.

Amid the institute's state-of-the-art machines, these ridiculous-looking antiques are stark reminders of how rapidly computer technology has evolved, producing one of the major challenges of preservation in the digital age: compatibility.

The problem with the dizzying pace of computer evolution is that new machines are often incapable of learning old tricks—even if the tricks are not really that old. For instance, most new computers don't come with floppy-disk drives. And while Harvard will surely procure machines that can safely read Mr. Updike's disk-based papers, what if those papers were trapped inside an even older storage device—say, something resembling a Commodore 64 game cartridge? Future archivists must have the skills to retrieve them.

Brave New World

Archivists must also know how to transfer their data to new machines, since old machines can survive for only so long before their circuits give out.

That, Ms. Nelson says, calls for people with intimate knowledge of how the new stuff works, plus the resourcefulness to retrofit modernity's round holes to accommodate antiquity's square pegs. "We're still going to need people who are experts in the history of the book, people who study handwriting, organize paper collections, handle obsolete video formats, traditional photography. . . . We're going to do everything we've been doing, and then we're going to be doing this."

Ms. Nelson understands this better than most: While Mr. Updike's floppy disks at Harvard probably contain simple text documents, the digital devices Mr. Rushdie donated to Emory contain entire ecosystems of data.

Writers today do a lot more on computers than they used to, and modern devices hold a lot more information about their users than old ones did. The laptop (and now the mobile device) has become the locus of social life as correspondence has migrated from letters and phone calls to e-mail and text chatting. Recreational reading and research have also increasingly moved to the Web.

Since a laptop logs basically everything its user does, preserving these data environments will allow the scholars of the future unprecedented insight into the minds of literary geniuses. "It's basically like giving someone the keys to your house," says Mr. Kirschenbaum.

The influence of authors' environments on their writing has always interested scholars. Marcel Proust, for example, is known to have been heavily influenced by the paintings he surrounded himself with when he penned the novel *Remembrance of Things Past,* between 1909 and 1922. Imagine if Proust had been writing 100 years later, on a laptop: What else we might be able to learn about his creative process.

The implications for scholarship are tremendous, Mr. Kirschenbaum says. Take a great digital-era author: "You could potentially look at a browser history, see that he visited a particular website on a particular day and time," he says. "And then if you were to go into the draft of one of his manuscripts, you could see that draft was edited at a particular day and hour, and you could establish a connection between something he was looking at on the Web with something that he then wrote."

In some cases, computer forensics can even hint at an author's influences beyond the screen. Mr. Reside recently mined data from old equipment belonging to Jonathan Larson, the late composer and playwright who earned a Pulitzer Prize posthumously for the musical *Rent.* In an early draft, Larson had a character suggest that the moonlight coming through the window is really "fluorescent light from the Gap." In the final draft, the lyric was "Spike Lee shooting down the street."

"From the time stamp on the digital files," Mr. Reside says, "I learned that the lyric was changed in the spring of 1992 . . . when, I believe, Spike Lee was shooting *Malcolm X* in New York City."

A Deluge of Data

That is really just scratching the surface. Imagine how mapping the content of an author's Facebook profile, MySpace page, Flickr account, or Twitter feed might help scholars dissect that author's life and letters. The social-media generation has developed a habit of casually volunteering biographical information. When the great authors of that generation emerge, scholars may be pleased to find plenty of fodder for study already on the public record.

But that is where things get tricky. Information that lives inside a writer's personal hardware—like the data on Mr. Updike's floppy disks or Mr. Rushdie's hard drives—may not have physical dimensions, but it is at least attached to a single device that is owned by somebody. "It's physically here," says Mr. Kirschenbaum, gesturing toward a shelf of Apple Classic computers, donated to the Maryland institute by the poet Deena Larsen. "I can wrap my arms around it."

Not so with e-mail and social-media content. These are not programs run on individual computers; they are Web-based services, hosted remotely by companies like Facebook and Google. The content exists in an ethereal mass of data known in information-technology circles as "the cloud." There, Mr. Kirschenbaum says, "you get into this wilderness of competing terms of service."

With more and more information being stored on the Web, it is no longer clear who owns what.

For example, in February, Facebook rewrote its terms of service to stake a claim on all content that users put on their profiles. After a backlash, the company hastily backed off and reiterated that users own their own profile content. But the case is a reminder of the fluidity and ambiguity of ownership laws in the dawning era of shared media.

"Consumers don't really know their rights here, and many are so wowed with the convenience that they aren't asking themselves the tough questions yet," says Susan E. Thomas, digital archivist at the University of Oxford's Bodleian Library. "Right now we can collect boxes from the attic, but if the family request a cloud service to transfer the archive of their loved one to the Bodleian Library, will that happen? We haven't tried it yet, so I can't tell you."

"That's sort of the brick wall that every archivist knows they're hurtling toward at 100 miles per hour," says Mr. Kirschenbaum.

No Manual

Many other questions also remain unanswered. For example, how much information is too much? A 20th-century author's personal papers might be of manageable quantity—say, what she was able to store in her attic. Digital storage, on the other hand, is cheap, easy, and virtually unlimited. Mining, sorting, and archiving every bit of data stored in author's computers could become a chore of paralyzing tedium and diminishing value.

At present, researchers are wary of discarding anything. "The work of an author over their entire lifetime is such a fraction of the space you have on a server hard disk, so there's no reason to throw any of that away," says Mr. Kirschenbaum. However, he added, unless scholars are able to find what they want in that sea of data, it is not worth archiving in the first place.

The good news is that as computers are logging more data, reference technology is growing more sophisticated. And Ms. Nelson suggests that the new tools for interacting with born-digital artifacts—including a wiki functionality that could allow researchers to annotate materials and share their insights with others—may not be too far away.

New tools and new training, however, mean new money. Richard Ovenden, associate director of Oxford's Bodleian Library, says the speed at which universities adopt digital curation may depend on their willingness to divert funds from more traditional areas. And that could be at a slower pace than the speed of technological invention itself.

From *The Chronicle of Higher Education,* by Steve Kolowich, April 10, 2009. Copyright © 2009 by The Chronicle of Higher Education. Reproduced with permission. This article may not be published, reposted, or redistributed without the express permission of The Chronicle of Higher Education.

Wikipedia in the Newsroom

While the line "according to Wikipedia" pops up occasionally in news stories, it's relatively rare to see the user-created online encyclopedia cited as a source. But some journalists find it very valuable as a road map to troves of valuable information.

DONNA SHAW

When the Las Vegas Review-Journal published a story in September about construction cranes, it noted that they were invented by ancient Greeks and powered by men and donkeys.

Michigan's Flint Journal recently traced the origins of fantasy football to 1962, and to three people connected to the Oakland Raiders.

And when the Arizona Republic profiled a controversial local congressman in August, it concluded that his background was "unclear."

What all three had in common was one of the sources they cited: Wikipedia, the popular, reader-written and -edited online encyclopedia. Dismissed by traditional journalism as a gimmicky source of faux information almost since it debuted in 2001, Wikipedia may be gaining some cautious converts as it works its way into the mainstream, albeit more as a road map to information than as a source to cite. While "according to Wikipedia" attributions do crop up, they are relatively rare.

To be sure, many Wikipedia citations probably sneak into print simply because editors don't catch them. Other times, the reference is tongue-in-cheek: The Wall Street Journal, for example, cited Wikipedia as a source for an item on "turducken" (a bizarre concoction in which a chicken is stuffed into a duck that is stuffed into a turkey) in a subscriber e-mail update just before Thanksgiving. In the e-mail, the Journal reporter wrote that some of his information was "courtesy of Wikipedia's highly informative turducken entry. As my hero Dave Barry says, 'I'm not making this up. Although, I'll admit that somebody on Wikipedia might have.'"

And when Time Inc. Editor-in-Chief John Huey was asked how his staffers made sure their stories were correct, he jokingly responded, "Wikipedia."

It's unclear if many newsrooms have formal policies banning Wikipedia attribution in their stories, but many have informal ones. At the Philadelphia Inquirer, which cited Wikipedia in an article about the death of television personality Tom Snyder last July, Managing Editor Mike Leary recently sent an e-mail to staff members reminding them they are never to use Wikipedia "to verify facts or to augment information in a story." A news database search indicates that "according to Wikipedia" mentions are few and far between in U.S. papers, and are found most frequently in opinion columns, letters to the editor and feature stories. They also turn up occasionally in graphics and information boxes.

Such caution is understandable, as for all its enticements, Wikipedia is maddeningly uneven. It can be impressive in one entry (the one on

the Naval Battle of Guadalcanal includes 138 endnotes, 18 references and seven external links) and sloppy in another (it misspells the name of AJR's editor). Its topics range from the weighty (the Darfur conflict) to the inconsequential (a list of all episodes of the TV series "Canada's Worst Handyman"). Its talk pages can include sophisticated discussions of whether fluorescent light bulbs will cause significant mercury pollution or silly minutiae like the real birth date of Paris Hilton's Chihuahua. Some of its commentary is remarkable but some contributors are comically dense, like the person who demanded proof that 18th-century satirist Jonathan Swift wasn't serious when he wrote that landlords should eat the children of their impoverished Irish tenants.

Hubble Smith, the Review-Journal business reporter who wrote the crane story, says he was simply looking for background on construction cranes for a feature on the Las Vegas building boom when the Wikipedia entry popped up during a search. It was among the most interesting information he found, so he used it. But after his story went to the desk, a copy editor flagged it.

"He said, 'Do you realize that Wikipedia is just made up of people who contribute all of this?'" Smith recalls. "I had never used it before." The reference was checked and allowed to remain in the story.

Indeed, the primary knock against Wikipedia is that its authors and editors are also its users—an unpaid, partially anonymous army, some of whom insert jokes, exaggeration and even outright lies in their material. About one-fifth of the editing is done by anonymous users, but a tight-knit community of 600 to 1,000 volunteers does the bulk of the work, according to Wikipedia cofounder Jimmy Wales. Members of this group can delete material or, in extreme cases, even lock particularly outrageous entries while they are massaged.

The extent of the potential for misinformation became clearer in August, when a new tool called WikiScanner (wikiscanner .virgil.gr/) began providing an ingenious database to identify propagandists and hoaxers. It gave Wikipedia critics plenty of new ammunition, as it revealed that among those surreptitiously rewriting entries were employees of major corporations, politicians and the CIA trying to make their bosses look better. And then there was the John Seigenthaler Sr. episode, in which someone edited the prominent retired journalist's Wikipedia biography to insinuate that he briefly had been a suspect in the assassinations of John and Robert F. Kennedy. In an op-ed piece for USA Today in 2005, Seigenthaler, who once worked for Bobby Kennedy and was one of his pallbearers, railed against Wikipedia, calling it "a flawed and irresponsible research tool." (A Nashville man later admitting inserting the material as a joke aimed at a coworker, and apologized.)

No one is more aware of such pitfalls than the leadership of Wikipedia, whose online disclaimer reminds users that "anyone with an Internet connection" can alter the content and cautions, "please be advised that nothing found here has necessarily been reviewed by people with the expertise required to provide you with complete, accurate or reliable information." An even more blunt assessment appears in the encyclopedia's "Ten things you may not know about Wikipedia" posting: "We do not expect you to trust us. It is in the nature of an ever-changing work like Wikipedia that, while some articles are of the highest quality of scholarship, others are admittedly complete rubbish." It also reminds users not to use Wikipedia as a primary source or for making "critical decisions."

Wales says it doesn't surprise him to hear that some journalists are cautiously trying it out. "I think that people are sort of slowly learning how to use Wikipedia, and learning its strengths and its weaknesses," he says. "Of course, any reasonable person has to be up front that there are weaknesses. . . . On the other hand, there are lots of sources that have weaknesses." Wales thinks the encyclopedia's best journalistic use is for background research rather than as a source to be quoted.

Wales, a board member and chairman emeritus of the nonprofit Wikimedia Foundation Inc., which owns Wikipedia, says the company constantly strives to improve its product. "Right now we're tightly focused on making sure that, for example, the biographies are well sourced," he says. The foundation is also developing new tools "to block people who are misbehaving," including one for new German-language Wikipedia users that will vet their contributions. If it works, Wales says, it can be rolled out for Wikipedia encyclopedias in other languages.

He also defends the right of Wikipedia—and perhaps even reporters—to have a little fun. "I subscribe to Google alerts and I saw that turducken [item in the Wall Street Journal e-mail] and I thought, well, what other source would you use? Britannica doesn't cover this nonsense," he says.

There are still plenty of journalists who aren't convinced of Wikipedia's worth, among them the denizens of testycopyeditors .org, where contributors to the online conversation have names like "crabby editor" and "wordnerdy." Asked his opinion of Wikipedia, Phillip Blanchard, the Washington Post copy editor who started testycopyeditors, responds, "I'm not sure what I could add, beyond 'don't use it' and 'it's junk.' "

While the Post has no written policy against it, "I can't imagine a circumstance under which a fact would be attributed to Wikipedia," says Blanchard, who works on the financial desk. " 'According to Wikipedia' has appeared only a couple of times in the Washington Post, once in a humor column and once in a movie review."

Gilbert Gaul, a Pulitzer Prize-winning reporter at the Post, describes himself as a "dinosaur in the changing world" when it comes to rules about sourcing stories. Wikipedia, he says, doesn't meet his personal test—for one thing, "there is no way for me to verify the information without fact-checking, in which case it isn't really saving me any time." He prefers to do his own research, so he can "see and touch everything," rather than rely on the mostly anonymous content of Wikipedia.

"I like much of the new technology. . . . But to me rules, borders, guidelines and transparency matter a lot," Gaul said in an e-mail interview. "I need and want to be able to trust the people I am reading or chatting with. If I can't, what is the point?"

Other journalists, though, are at least somewhat won over by what can be an impressive feature: those sometimes lengthy Wikipedia citations that lead to other, more authoritative sources. David Cay Johnston, a Pulitzer-winning reporter for the New York Times, says

he recently looked up "thermodynamics" to see where it led him, and found that Wikipedia's entry listed numerous references from reliable sources.

"I have a solid understanding of the concept, but once we get into fine points, I have nothing beyond my skepticism as a reporter to judge the accuracy, validity and reliability of what is there," he says. "However, this entry appears to be useful as a source guide. It has names of researchers whose books were published by eminent organizations, and you can take that as a quick way to find sources. So as a tip sheet, as a road map to reliable sources, Wikipedia seems valuable."

Jim Thomsen, a copy editor at the Kitsap Sun in Bremerton, Washington, has no problem with attributing information to the online encyclopedia in certain cases. "If I see something in Wikipedia I might want to cite for background and context for a story, I trace back the cites to their original sources," Thomsen said in an e-mail interview. "If I feel the origins are solid, I'll use the info.

For a student who just uses a search engine and they use the first thing that pops up . . . this undermines the kind of thing we're trying to teach them.

"I know there's been a lot of hullabaloo about people with agendas seeding Wikipedia with slanted or even false information, but as I see it, that sort of stuff can be easily sniffed out—by looking at the cites, and tracking them back. No cites? Fuhgeddaboudit. The bottom line is that Wikipedia can be a great tool as a central Clearinghouse for contextual information. But not a single syllable there should be taken at face value."

The Los Angeles Times is one of many newspapers that have allowed an occasional "according to Wikipedia" in their pages in the last several months. One was in a commentary piece about Barack Obama; another appeared in a staff-written story about a professional "man in the street" who managed to be interviewed repeatedly. The reference in the latter story drew rapid fire on testycopyeditors.org, with comments including "Shame on the Los Angeles Times" and "No, no, a thousand times no."

Melissa McCoy, the Times' deputy managing editor in charge of copy desks, says the paper occasionally allows Wikipedia attribution. "We're certainly not going to use Wikipedia as a standalone news source, but we're not going to exclude it if it takes us somewhere," she says. "If a reporter spots something in there and it makes them do an extra phone call, it's silly" not to use it.

There's no unanimity about Wikipedia among academic experts, who have engaged in vigorous debates about the online encyclopedia. While many professors refuse to allow students to cite it, it has attracted some prominent defenders, including historians and scientists who have analyzed its content.

"If a journalist were to find something surprising on Wikipedia and the journalistic instincts suggested it was correct, the journalist might add that as an unsubstantiated Wiki-fact and invite Comment," says Cathy Davidson, a professor at Duke University and cofounder of HASTAC (Humanities, Arts, Science, and Technology Advanced Collaboratory, www.hastac.org), a network of researchers developing new ways to collect and share information via technology. "Perhaps an online version of the printed piece, for example, might include a blog inviting people to comment on the Wiki-fact. It may be that there would be Wikifacts online that were not in the printed piece. In other words, why not use the new technologies available to expand knowledge in all kinds of ways?"

Journalists also should consider, Davidson says, whether some of the sources they deem reliable have their own inadequacies. For example, when she recently researched the origins of calculus, she found that standard Western histories generally credited England's Isaac Newton and Germany's Gottfried Wilhelm Leibniz. But Wikipedia went much further, tracing the discovery of basic calculus functions back to the Egyptians in 1800 BC, and then to China, India and Mesopotamia—all hundreds of years before the Europeans.

So while journalists should be cautious no matter what resources they use, "What Wikipedia does reveal to those in the Euro-American world is knowledge which most of our sources, even the most scholarly, have, in the past, neglected because it did not fit in our intellectual genealogies, in our history of ideas," Davidson says.

In December 2005, the science journal Nature published a survey of several experts about the content of comparable Wikipedia and online Encyclopedia Britannica entries. In a conclusion hotly disputed by Britannica, Nature said that Wikipedia "comes close to Britannica in terms of the accuracy of its science entries," in that the average Wikipedia article contained four errors to Britannica's three. Britannica's 20-page response said that "almost everything about the journal's investigation . . . was wrong and misleading . . . the study was so poorly carried out and its findings so error-laden that it was completely without merit." The company further asserted that Nature had misrepresented its own data—its numbers, after all, showed that Wikipedia had a third more inaccuracies than Britannica—and asked for "a full and public retraction of the article." Nature stood by its story.

"The Nature piece profoundly undermined the authority upon which Britannica depends," says Gregory Crane, editor in chief of the Perseus Digital Library at Tufts University. He is a recent convert to the pro-Wikipedia camp, calling it "the most important intellectual phenomenon of the early 21st century."

He recognizes its faults, especially when Wikipedians write about controversial topics. So "people have to do some critical thinking," Crane says, by evaluating their sources, "whether it's Wikipedia or the New York Times."

In an article he wrote in 2005, Crane acknowledged that Wikipedia "is an extreme case whose success so far has shocked skeptical scholars." But he noted as well that other, more mainstream reference works had similar foundations—for example, the Oxford English Dictionary was written over a period of 70 years by thousands of people, including "an inmate at an asylum for the criminally insane."

A 2006 analysis by another scholar and Wikipedia fan, George Mason University historian Roy Rosenzweig, found some inaccuracies, omissions, uneven writing and even plagiarism in selected entries. But his comparison of several Wikipedia biographies against comparable entries in two other encyclopedias found that Wikipedia "roughly matches" Microsoft's Encarta in accuracy while still falling short of the Oxford University Press' American National Biography Online. "This general conclusion is supported by studies comparing Wikipedia to other major encyclopedias," wrote Rosenzweig, who was director of the university's Center for History and New Media until his death last year.

Still, many if not most in the academic community think that Wikipedia, if used at all, should be no more than a secondary source, and they frequently tell their students as much. For Cornell University professor Ross Brann, that position was reinforced in early 2007, after the outing of a salaried Wikipedia employee and editor who called himself "Essjay" and claimed to be a tenured professor with doctorates in theology and canon law. Turns out he had seriously padded his résumé: The New Yorker discovered after interviewing Essjay that he was actually a 24-year-old community college dropout. To Brann, a professor of Judeo-Islamic Studies and director of graduate studies for the Department of Near Eastern Studies, the incident confirmed that Wikipedia could not be trusted as a primary source.

"I just tell students, 'Do not use Wikipedia, do not cite it, do not go there for my classes.' We're trying to teach them how to use sources, how to evaluate different sources, and I think that in general, although obviously a wonderful resource, for a student who just uses a search engine and they use the first thing that pops up . . . this undermines the kind of thing we're trying to teach them," Brann says.

Brann notes that Wikipedia's popularity probably has a lot to do with the fact that its entries so frequently pop up first, because that's the nature of search engines. "Many of them just work by the multiplicity of uses, others by virtue of ad arrangements—somebody is deciding for you what you're going to look at," he says.

And what about college journalists, a group that has never known life without computers? A news database search suggests that they are just as reluctant to cite Wikipedia as their professional colleagues. In August, for example, the University of Iowa newspaper, the Daily Iowan, used the WikiScanner database to determine that thousands of Wikipedia entries had been made or modified by people using the campus computer network. Some involved obvious but harmless enough vandalism: "Hawkeyes Rule" was inserted into text about the college's football stadium; less generously, a former university president was called an "eater of monkey brains," according to the paper's story.

Jason Brummond, editor in chief of the Daily Iowan, says he considers Wikipedia a good initial source, "but you go from there to find what most people would consider a more reputable source." Reporters in his newsroom generally understand that, he adds.

Brummond thinks the age of the journalist doesn't necessarily have that much to do with accepting Wikipedia: "It's more a personal awareness of how Wikipedia works."

In September, the University of Kansas student newspaper ran an editorial calling upon Wikipedia to do a better job of restoring "adulterated pages," noting that "despite a thousand recitations by our professors that Wikipedia is not a genuine source, students trust the site to give them accurate information." Nevertheless, Erick Schmidt, editor of the University Daily Kansan, says he doesn't rely much on Wikipedia, in part because his reporters write mostly about college and community issues. Plus, "we're taught to be cautious of things and skeptical," he says.

Schmidt rejects the notion that college students uncritically accept Wikipedia because they are infatuated with all things Internet. "We don't want to move things to technology because we think it's cool or paper is lame," he says. "But honestly, we are pressed for time, and if technology speeds things up . . . that's why we're being drawn to it."

For his part, Wales maintains that the more people use Wikipedia, the more they'll come to understand and accept it. His conclusion, he says, "comes from people who have used the site for a long time and know, 'I have to be careful'. . . which is what good reporting is supposed to be about anyway."

But whatever the verdict on Wikipedia, one thing should not change, says the New York Times' Johnston: "No matter who your sources are, when you sign your name, you are responsible for every word, every thought, every concept."

Contributing writer **DONNA SHAW** (shaw@tcnj.edu) has written about front-page ads, hyperlocal websites and Pulitzer Prizes for *AJR*.

From *American Journalism Review*, February/March 2008, pp. 40–45. Copyright © 2008 by the Philip Merrill College of Journalism at the University of Maryland, College Park, MD 20742-7111. Reprinted with permission.

E-Mail in Academia

Expectations, Use, and Instructional Impact

An exploration of e-mail communication between faculty and students at UNC Chapel Hill identified issues surrounding the use of e-mail to advance instructional outcomes.

MEREDITH WEISS AND DANA HANSON-BALDAUF

"The more elaborate our means of communication, the less we communicate," claimed theologian and educator Joseph Priestly.[1] Born in 1733, Priestly could hardly have imagined the Internet, e-mail, and instant messaging, although his prophetic statement presaged a dilemma now faced on college campuses worldwide. The popularity of and reliance on emergent computer-mediated communication technologies such as instant messaging, blogs, and social networks have arguably widened the generation gap between faculty and traditional undergraduate students. Marc Prensky defined this generational technology divide by coining the terms *digital natives* and *digital immigrants*. He wrote,

> The single biggest problem facing education today is that our Digital Immigrant instructors, who speak an outdated language (that of the pre-digital age), are struggling to teach a population that speaks an entirely new language.[2]

The purpose of the study reported here was to explore differences between professors (digital immigrants) and undergraduate students (digital natives) at the University of North Carolina at Chapel Hill regarding their expectations and use of e-mail and its perceived impact on instructional outcomes and student success. The ubiquitous nature of e-mail presents an ideal opportunity to investigate its use along this generational divide. Additionally, the study of e-mail practice and perception in the context of higher education might foster more meaningful scholarly communication between teacher and student and, in turn, positively impact instructional outcomes and student success.

Literature Review

Regardless of the context and medium, the process of communication is complicated and multifaceted. Over the years, many have sought to better understand and explain the phenomenon. Ernest Pascarella, for example, has spent much of his career exploring faculty and student communication and its impact on academic achievement and the college experience. Although not set within the context of the digital environment, his studies reveal a strong association between student outcomes and the degree and quality of one-on-one communication between teacher and student.[3] These outcomes reflect positive trends in academic achievement, personal growth (both intellectual and developmental), the degree of effort extended to studies, student connection and satisfaction with academic coursework and the institute, attrition, and attainment of educational and career goals.[4]

How does Pascarella's work fit within the context of a digital instructional environment? Recently, Robert Duran, Lynne Kelly, and James Keaten[5] investigated faculty use and perception of communication via e-mail in correspondence with students. They found that faculty (*n* = 257) received more than two times the number of e-mails they produced (faculty received an average of 15.15 e-mails per week compared to 6.72 e-mails per week they sent). Excuses for late work or missed class sessions were the most cited reasons for student-initiated e-mail communication. Despite some faculty dissatisfaction (*n* = 13, or 21 percent) with the amount of time and effort spent on e-mail communication, faculty overall perceived benefits (a mean of 3.05 on a 5-point scale) and liabilities (2.95) as roughly equal. Faculty found they could communicate better with reticent students (3.25) and relay pertinent and timely course information to classes using e-mail.

A 2003 study conducted by Michael Russell and his colleagues found that teachers use technology, including e-mail, more for preparation and work-related communication, and less often for instructional purposes.[6] Interestingly, this finding seemed especially true among less experienced teachers, despite their self-reported high levels of comfort using technology. In John Savery's 2002 study, however, 90 percent of faculty surveyed reported using e-mail five times or more per semester for instructional use.[7]

Unfortunately, terms such as "instructional purposes" and "instructional use" are not consistently defined across studies. Studies in 2001 and 2004 identified the concept of *cognitive presence* in computer-mediated instruction,[8] which we propose should be present for an instructional use of e-mail. Cognitive presence is defined as an atmosphere of inquiry and higher-order learning that supports critical thinking, reflection, knowledge construction, collaboration, and discourse.

Numerous studies further address the general use of e-mail, particularly in the corporate environment. These studies focus on e-mail etiquette,[9] appropriate behavior, norms, and conventions,[10] development of user expectations,[11] e-mail management and system design,[12] user productivity,[13] and e-mail training.[14] Though these studies investigated how e-mail is used and managed, studies related to e-mail use in the specific context of faculty-student communication and enhanced learning are limited and warrant further investigation.

Purpose of the Study

This study aimed to explore e-mail practice in academia between professors and undergraduate students in relation to their expectations and use of e-mail, along with its perceived impact on instructional outcomes and student success. Additional areas of investigation included survey participants' emotions regarding e-mail use and their formal e-mail training experiences.

The study addressed three questions:

1. What do faculty and students perceive as appropriate e-mail use in their communications with one another?
2. How do faculty and students actually use e-mail in communicating with one another?
3. Does e-mail communication have a perceived positive impact on learning, grades, and faculty-student familiarity?

Methodology

The study employed an exploratory quantitative and qualitative research design using an electronic survey tool. Two surveys were developed and administered to faculty and undergraduate students, respectively, in the fall of 2006. Each survey had approximately 74 parallel questions, presented in a mostly closed-question format. Participants had opportunities to provide comments regarding their responses on select survey questions.

Use of an electronic survey tool enabled gathering information from a large population in a systematic, efficient (both time and cost), and comparable manner. Additionally, participants could complete the survey at a convenient time and place. Prior to administering the survey, a pilot survey checked for clarity of wording and time it would take participants to complete the actual survey.

Each survey consisted of four components:

• Introduction,
• Demographics,
• Style (referring to self-reported e-mail behaviors), and
• Perceived style (referring to a respondent's impression of another's e-mail behavior).

The introduction functioned as a filtering tool to eliminate participants who did not meet study specifications. Part-time students and faculty were not included in this study, for example, nor were faculty with titles other than assistant, associate, or full professor. In addition, participants were instructed to respond only in terms of their e-mail communications surrounding on-campus undergraduate courses (distance education interactions were excluded).

The student survey demographic section collected information about gender, age, ethnicity, residency status, class status, and major. The faculty survey demographic section collected information about gender, age, ethnicity, professorship status level, years teaching, and academic discipline.

The final two sections of both surveys collected core information regarding e-mail attitudes, perceptions, expectations, and behaviors. The style section investigated participant e-mail use in regard to the construction of e-mails, frequency of use, behaviors, responsiveness, attitudes, and expectations. The section on perceived style collected information about how participants viewed their counterparts' attitudes and expectations.

Survey Implementation

The survey was administered through a computer-mediated tool and promoted through the UNC Mass E-mail System, which distributes e-mail messages to the entire university community. The incentive for participating in the survey was the chance to win a $20 gift certificate to a local shopping mall. Means of participant identification were limited to IP addresses (collected as standard procedure with the survey tool) and an optional submission of an e-mail address to participate in the drawing to win the gift certificate.

Participants

Participants were recruited from a pool of UNC Chapel Hill undergraduate students and faculty from all disciplines. Access to this pool of participants was achieved through the UNC Mass E-mail System.

Only full-time undergraduate students and full-time on-campus faculty serving in an on-campus instructional role to undergraduate students were included in the study. This allowed the samples to more accurately reflect a clear distinction between what Prensky refers to as digital natives and digital immigrants, given that the majority of undergraduates are between the ages of 17 and 21.

Procedure

An introductory e-mail outlining the intent of the study directed participants to the survey link. Individuals who consented to participate and who met the specified requirements were asked to respond to a total of 73 questions (74 for faculty). With the exception of the introductory questions, which were designed to ensure that participants met the guidelines for the study, participants had the option of not responding to questions. Many of the questions also permitted comments.

Access to the survey remained open for one week. Participants were informed that the results of the study would be made available to the UNC Chapel Hill community.

Analysis of Data

After closing access to the survey site, we compiled data from both the faculty and student surveys and organized it by category and parallel questions. Coding of data occurred on questions in which respondents could indicate multiple answers. Data was cross-tabulated using descriptive statistics, performing a chi square analysis and using Fisher's exact test, when appropriate, to determine statistical significance.

Results

The UNC Chapel Hill undergraduate faculty population of 1,818 represents more than 60 disciplines. Of the 97 faculty who participated in the study, 56 met the study's specifications; 25 respondents did not teach undergraduate students, and 16 were not ranked as assistant, associate, or full professor. Roughly 43 percent of faculty participants identified themselves as full professors, 38 percent as associate professors, and 20 percent as assistant professors. The average age for a UNC faculty member is approximately 50 years,[15] which is consistent with our survey participants because the majority of our faculty responders were between the ages of 41 and 60.

Of the UNC undergraduate student population, 178 participated in the study. Of those, 166 met study specifications, with roughly 4 percent freshmen, 30 percent sophomores, 24 percent juniors, and 41 percent seniors. Approximately 87 percent were under 22 years of age, and 12 percent were between the ages of 22 and 25. In regard to residency, 79 percent of student participants were in-state, 20 percent out-of-state, and 1 percent international. Table 1 summarizes the demographics of the study participants.

Appropriate E-Mail Use

Research question 1 asked, what do faculty and students perceive as appropriate e-mail use in communicating with one another? As Table 2 shows, both faculty and students generally agree on appropriate use of e-mail correspondence, although faculty are less likely to view lecture clarification as an appropriate use. Faculty additionally reported that providing career advice over e-mail was appropriate.

Faculty respondents provided additional information in open-ended questions regarding their perception of how e-mail can best be used. Comments included:

It is not a substitute for office hours, nor am I willing to answer long substantive questions in e-mail. It is an efficient way to communicate with simple questions and schedule/remind/inform about in-depth opportunities for learning.

I prefer e-mails for some purposes (like excuses for absences) and not for others (like answers that will take a long time to formulate in writing).

I think students should primarily use e-mail to inform the instructor of valid excuses for missing class/assignments, getting clarifications on assignments, or setting up appointments. I think students should meet with instructors during office hours for lecture clarifications, questions about grading, advising, and meeting with prospective instructors.

The comments above seem to offer a possible explanation for student dissatisfaction. Students complained about incomplete explanations and brevity:

The professor not taking the time to thoughtfully read my e-mail. Often they will read parts, and assume one thing and respond to what they assume my concern/question is.

Professors usually send very short e-mails in response to my long ones and don't answer all of my questions.

Too often professors will pop back a quick response when I have sent a well thought out but e-mailed [set of] questions. The habit of writing quick e-mails overrides the original goal of communication. When I e-mail a professor, I don't expect to have a 3 or 4 e-mail conversation; I think out my question in detail hoping they will do the same with their response.

It seems the two groups have different expectations for the appropriate use of e-mail.

Note that while these comments suggest a faculty preference for face-to-face meetings in regard to substantive information inquiry, students might not know this. Furthermore, although survey results indicate that majorities of students (93 percent) and faculty (82 percent) feel that e-mail is an appropriate venue for lesson clarification, communication expectations surrounding substantive e-mail conversations need clarification.

Actual E-Mail Use

Research question 2 asked, how do faculty and students actually use e-mail in communicating with one another? Both faculty (72 percent) and students (78 percent) concur that e-mail use is encouraged as appropriate for coursework correspondence. Forty-one percent of faculty indicated that they provide e-mail behavior expectations to their students at the beginning of the semester; another 39 percent indicated that although they did not extend these expectations to their students, they are open to the possibility; and 20 percent felt that providing e-mail behavior expectations was unnecessary. Fifty-seven percent of student respondents indicated that they would prefer to know faculty e-mail behavior expectations in advance. One student respondent noted,

Table 1 E-Mail Study Participants

	Faculty	Students
Gender		
Female	50%	80%
Male	50%	20%
Ethnicity*		
American Indian or Alaska Native	2%	3%
Asian	2%	11%
Black or African American	2%	14%
Hispanic	0%	5%
White	96%	73%
Other	2%	2%
Range in Age		
Less than 22	0%	87%
22–25	0%	12%
26–30	0%	1%
31–40	14%	1%
41–50	25%	1%**
51–60	34%	**
61+	25%	**

* Participants could choose multiple ethnicities.
** One percent of student participants were over 41 years old.

Table 2 Perceived Appropriate Use of E-mail

	Faculty believe it is appropriate for students to use e-mail for:	Students believe it is appropriate for faculty to use e-mail for:
Assignment clarification	94%	99%
Question asking/ answering	92%	93%
Excuses (missed classes, assignments, etc.)	94%	N/A
Lecture clarification	82%	93%
Relationship building	58%	66%

I think it is fine that every professor has different standards/ expectations about e-mail formality, but they should all make it clear at the beginning of the semester.

Both faculty and students agree that the primary purpose for using e-mail to communicate with one another relates to general housekeeping functions such as assignment clarification, explanations for missed classes or assignments, and question asking and answering. In open-text responses, faculty also reported using e-mail to send out course announcements, items of possible interest, guidance for research, reminders, and feedback on drafts of student work. Students responded that they also used e-mail to set appointments with professors, discuss assignment performance, and request grade clarification (see Table 3).

Table 3 Faculty and Student Use of E-mail Communication

	Faculty use e-mail for:	Students use e-mail for:
Assignment clarification	87%	83%
Excuses (missed classes, assignments, etc.)	78%*	58%
Question asking/answering	83%	83%
Lecture clarification	46%	28%
Relationship building	26%	13%

* Responding to student excuses

In regard to the amount of e-mail, a number of student respondents expressed some frustration:

I respond to all my e-mails the first time I receive them. I will forget to respond if I read them and log out of the session.

I just have to return e-mails as soon as I check them so that I don't forget; also so that my inbox isn't flooded (which it always is).

Faculty respondents had similar frustrations:

I think you should have asked if the increasing volume of e-mails from students is posing a problem for the faculty, who are having to spend hours extra a week in answering e-mails, but get no credit for this in their departments or in the university—the answer is a resounding YES!!!

I would like students to ask themselves if the question can wait until my next office hours. I'm simply too busy to reply to all of the e-mails I get from students.

I would like for them not to ask questions that require long, thoughtful answers. I get hundreds of e-mails a day and am swamped with work. If they need that kind of answer they should talk to me after class or come to office hours (which almost no one does any more).

Results from the study seem to validate faculty frustration in regard to the large amount of e-mail messages they receive. Ninety-four percent of student respondents indicated that they e-mail their professors between one and 10 times a month. With an average class size of 30 students, that equates to a minimum of 30 e-mails a month per class, with the potential for 300 e-mails a month per class. Note also that approximately 5 percent of undergraduate classes at UNC have an enrollment of more than 100 students per instructor.[16]

Perceived Impact of E-Mail

Research question 3 asked, does e-mail communication have a perceived positive impact on learning, grades, and the faculty-student relationship? As Table 4 shows, both students and faculty agree that increased e-mail communication contributes to learning and teacher-student relationships. Students, however, more often believe that it leads to higher grades.

Little narrative information was available regarding improved learning and grades as a result of increased e-mail communication between faculty and students. Respondents had much to say, however, about the idea of e-mail communication and relationship building. As students noted:

Faculty should express some interest in getting to know the student academically/personally more often, and I think e-mail is a good way to get started.

I wish that they would become more personal with students, ask questions and try to get to know the student.

On the flip side, professors indicated:

Relationship building and career advice should be done in person, but setting up appointments for this by e-mail is fine.

I think e-mail communication is great, convenient, and helpful in many ways, but I am concerned that it replaces face-to-face contact with me in too many instances. Fewer students come to office hours because of e-mail, and I think that is a potential problem, especially for students who aren't doing as well in the class as they could be.

It was not clear from survey results whether the increased amount of e-mail communication correlates with a decrease in faculty office hour visits.

When questioned about their views on whether student-faculty e-mail communication was formal or informal, the majority of faculty and students believe it can be either. Analysis of data, however, found a significant difference ($p = 0.0$) in the beliefs held by faculty and students in regard to the other being "too friendly" in communicating via e-mail. Fifty-three percent of faculty members believe that students are often or sometimes too friendly, while only 5 percent of students feel this way about faculty. Perhaps students—as digital natives brought up in an Internet world filled with opportunities for online relationship building—are simply more seasoned in developing online relationships and more apt to view computer-mediated conversations as a means to that end.

Two additional survey components captured interesting results: apprehension about using e-mail to communicate with faculty and reactions to the idea of formal e-mail training.

Apprehension. Clearly, faculty at UNC underestimate student apprehension about initiating e-mail communications with professors. While 35 percent of faculty indicated they perceive students to be apprehensive, 66 percent of student respondents indicated that they were apprehensive. In contrast, 100 percent of faculty responders said they did not feel apprehensive the first time they e-mail a student, while 13 percent of student responders reported believing their professors are at least sometimes apprehensive in initiating e-mail communication. Nonetheless, several students noted comfort using e-mail over other forms of communication. For example:

Because I am shy and don't like to speak on the phone first, I prefer e-mails so I can really think out my message and construct what I want to say so I can avoid miscommunication or sending a garbled message on my part. So I typically use e-mail as a communication mode more than office hours or anything.

Another student noted that the more casual an e-mail conversation, the less intimidating it is for the student to respond:

I noticed my computer science professors are much more casual in their e-mails to me. (Don't always use a lot of formality, sometimes don't use complete sentences, address me by my first name, and sign with their first name.) I like this better than the more formal e-mails I have received from other professors because it makes it less intimidating for me to write them back, and it makes me more comfortable with communicating with them via e-mail.

A student also noted that e-mail is often used when a student is anxious about speaking in front of his/her peers:

E-mail is a method of communication that can reduce anxiety for a student who needs additional help or who wants to express an idea without the judgment of peers.

Table 4 Perceived Positive Impact of Increased E-mail

	Faculty	**Students**
Learning	50%	67%
Grades	6%	30%
Relationships	49%	68%

E-Mail Training. Both students (43 percent) and faculty (64 percent) believe e-mail training would benefit others, but neither group indicates a strong desire for their own personal training in e-mail use. Only 14 percent of faculty and 31 percent of students indicated interest. Faculty's major objection seemed to be time:

> Nice idea. Yet another of those desirable things (like training on using PowerPoint or other computer programs) that I'd love but absolutely don't have time for.

One student was enthusiastic about the possibility:

> Please!!!! I'm so bad at e-mail etiquette, and I can't handle the sheer number of e-mails. I would love to attend training on using e-mail productively.

Other students noted,

> I do not think that real training is necessary; if professors do receive a lot of lazily-composed e-mails, perhaps a few guidelines on the matter, presented at the beginning of the course, would suffice.

> It sounds interesting, but I would have to be convinced that it is relevant and necessary in my life.

Limitations and Implications for Future Research

This exploratory study examined e-mail communication between faculty and students. The primary limitation of the study is sample size. Before results can be generalized to other institutions, further research conducted in multiple academic institutions is necessary to confirm, expand, or revise findings and propagate development of a model of best practice for instructional e-mail use in academia to enhance learning.

We also believe that future studies would benefit from a more-even gender distribution, relative to enrollment, among student responders. It is not clear why female students responded at higher rates than male students in this initial study.

Another limitation of the study was the exclusion of other instructional members of the academic community such as graduate students, adjunct professors, and practitioner instructors, as well as those participating in distance education courses.

It is also prudent to consider the possibility of survey bias in terms of those who chose to participate in the survey. If, as Presky notes, digital immigrants (in this situation, professors) lack a proclivity toward technology use, many might not have read the e-mail calling for participation or might have chosen not to participate in the web-based survey. Future studies, therefore, might benefit from including an alternate method of information gathering for those who are averse to e-mail or Internet interaction.

Discussion

Without question, e-mail has grown to be a viable and indispensable means of information exchange in academia. Results of this initial study unfortunately indicate that e-mail has yet to reach its full potential as a meaningful instructional tool for inquiry and higher-order learning. Survey results and narrative responses, however, offer insight into possibilities for expanding the role and functionality of e-mail as an instructional tool.

We propose that professors can greatly improve e-mail communication and alleviate frustration simply by taking a few minutes at the beginning of each semester to set clear expectations and guidelines for e-mail use. Survey responses indicate that both faculty and students believe this initiative would be helpful. Topics to address during this discussion might include apprehension about using e-mail, appropriate use of e-mail communication, hours during which faculty will respond to e-mail, formality of the communication, grammar standards for the messages, information necessary to include in messages, ways faculty prefer to be addressed and to address students in return, expectations of responsiveness, and appropriate subject lines (see Table 5).

We believe e-mail communication has the potential to greatly enhance learning. As survey results indicate, faculty and students agree that increased e-mail communication can have a positive impact on learning. To realize this impact, though, e-mail communication between professor and student must be seen as an extension of instruction. A paradigm shift from viewing e-mail communication solely as suited for housekeeping functions to viewing it as a means to further scholarly discourse and cognitive challenge is needed.

We suggest that appropriate e-mail use be reframed into an instructional conversation. Students, for example, might be encouraged to ask substantive questions over e-mail without expecting answers. A professor might instead respond with a series of questions or suggest a different angle from which the student could begin to research the answer. The professor might also bring a student's e-mail question to the classroom for discussion or post it on an online discussion board for class collaboration. If this type of exchange is a clearly set expectation at the beginning of the semester, both parties will benefit. Faculty will not feel burdened to answer all questions, and students would not expect them to. Instead, students will be challenged to find their own answers, leading to a truly scholarly exploration that extends the classroom experience.

Finally, as our study revealed, many students feel uneasy or intimidated when initiating face-to-face conversations with faculty; they prefer using e-mail to ask questions or relay information. It is important for faculty to recognize this. Addressing these issues, conveying a sense of openness and availability, and engaging students in positive one-on-one conversations may alleviate some of these feelings and create richer and more meaningful scholarly interactions in the classroom and digital environment.

Conclusion

The ubiquitous use of e-mail in academia coupled with the strong relationship between student achievement and faculty-student one-on-one communication necessitates continued exploration of the influence of instructional e-mail correspondence. It is also a compelling reason for faculty to proficiently, thoughtfully, and strategically craft their e-mail messages to students. In doing so, faculty may increase the scope of their influence, establish a cognitive online presence, and extend scholarly dialogue and thought. Additionally, we propose that the development, communication, and adherence to agreed-upon e-mail expectations, norms, and guidelines would improve communications, lessen faculty and student frustrations, and alleviate student anxiety.

Table 5 Suggested Expectations and Guidelines for E-Mail Use

Topic	Expectations and Guidelines
Apprehension	Shared expectations and guidelines can ease student apprehension about communicating with the professor over e-mail.
	Assuage student fears about approaching the professor with questions in person, during or outside of class.
Appropriate uses	Housekeeping, such as assignment clarification, excuses, question asking/answering, announcements.
	Instructional, such as lecture clarification and question asking/answering. Explain guidelines for such requests.
	Mentoring, such as relationship building and career advice.
Inappropriate uses	Debating grades. Under what circumstances if any is this appropriate over e-mail?
	Long, substantive question asking with the expectation of an e-mail "answer."*
	When is e-mail an inappropriate substitute for office hours or in-class discussion?
Concluding an e-mail	Should students always end with a thank you or some acknowledgment?
	Would faculty prefer students only respond when further action is requested (to avoid e-mail overload)?
E-mail hours	When the professor will or will not respond to e-mail.
Emoticons**	Does the professor appreciate and feel comfortable with their use?
	Will faculty use them when communicating with students? Does this help students understand tone?
Formality	How formal or informal the professor believes e-mail communications should be.
	Does this depend on the context of the message? Or how well the professor and student know each other?
	What does the professor perceive as "too informal" or "too formal" when it comes to e-mail communication with students?
	Appropriate tone.
Grammar, etc.	Are proper grammar, spelling, and complete sentences expected all the time?
	Are one-word answers acceptable?
Information to include	Full name, course, section, semester, etc.
Proper address	How the professor prefers to be addressed.
	How the professor plans to address students.
Responsiveness expectations	The amount of time a student should expect to wait before receiving a response.
	The amount of time the professor expects to wait to receive a student's response.
Subject line	What constitutes an acceptable subject line? One word? Complete description?

* It might be appropriate to set the expectation that the professor will either respond in such a way to aid the student in researching the answer or bring the question to the classroom or online discussion board for class collaboration.

** Groups of keyboard characters that typically represent a facial expression or emotion.

Achieving these goals requires instruction in e-mail use, however. Despite objections to attending e-mail training, both faculty and students agree that it would be beneficial—for each other. By raising awareness of the association between student success and one-on-one communication with faculty in an environment where e-mail serves as one of the primary methods of contact, we hope that both faculty and students will begin to see the value of e-mail training and become more willing to attend. Moreover, we believe it is critical for faculty to realize that learning how to better use e-mail can save them time, assuage a number of their current frustrations, and alleviate student communication concerns.

Clearly, unless training options are flexible in method of delivery, efficient, and relevant to each audience, high attendance will be a challenge. We believe, however, that faculty trained in the optimal use of e-mail can better expand and reframe the use of e-mail communication to enhance teaching and learning and thereby improve student outcomes.

Endnotes

1. John W. Severinghaus, "Priestley, the Furious Free Thinker of the Enlightenment, and Scheele, the Taciturn Apothecary of Uppsala," *Acta Anaesthesiologica Scandinavica,* vol. 46, no. 1 (January 2002), pp. 2–9, http://www.blackwell-synergy.com/toc/aas/46/1

2. Marc Prensky, "Digital Natives, Digital Immigrants," *On the Horizon,* vol. 9, no. 5 (October 2001), pp. 1–6, http://www.marcprensky.com

3. Ernest T. Pascarella and Patrick T. Terenzini, *How College Affects Students: Findings and Insights from Twenty Years of Research* (San Francisco, CA: Jossey-Bass, 1991).

4. For a review of the literature of a number of Pascarella's studies, see Mark A. Lamport, "Student-Faculty Informal Interaction and the Effect on College Student Outcomes:

A Review of the Literature," *Adolescence,* vol. 28, no. 112 (Winter 1993), pp. 971–991.

5. Robert L. Duran, Lynne Kelly, and James A. Keaten, (2005). "College Faculty Use and Perceptions of Electronic Mail to Communicate with Students," *Communication Quarterly,* vol. 53, no. 2 (2005), pp. 159–176.

6. Michael Russell, Damian Bebell, Laura O'Dwyer, and Kathleen O'Connor, "Examining Teacher Technology Use: Implications for Preservice and Inservice Teacher Preparation," *Journal of Teacher Education,* vol. 54, no. 4 (September 2003), pp. 297–311, http://jte.sagepub.com/content/vol54/issue4

7. John R. Savery, "Faculty and Student Perceptions of Technology Integration in Teaching," *Journal of Interactive Online Learning,* vol. 1, no. 2 (Fall 2002), http://www.ncolr .org/jiol/issues/showissue.cfm?volID=1&IssueID=3

8. See the studies by D. Randy Garrison, Terry Anderson, and Walter Archer, "Critical Thinking, Cognitive Presence, and Computer Conferencing in Distance Education," *American Journal of Distance Education,* vol. 15, no. 1 (2001), pp. 7–23, http://www.ajde.com/Contents/vol15_1.htm; and Heather Kanuka and D. Randy Garrison, "Cognitive Presence in Online Learning," *Journal of Computing in Higher Education,* vol. 15, no. 2 (March 2004), pp. 30–49, http://www.jchesite.org/vol152 .html

9. Virginia Shea, *Netiquette* (San Francisco: Albion Books, 1994).

10. Uta Pankoke-Babtz and Phillip Jeffrey, "Documented Norms and Conventions on the Internet," *International Journal of Human-Computer Interaction,* vol. 14, no. 2 (2002), pp. 219–235, http://www.informatik.uni-trier.de/ ley/db/ journals/ijhci/ijhci14.html

11. Joshua R. Tyler and John C. Tang, "When Can I Expect an E-Mail Response: A Study of Rhythms in E-Mail Usage," *Proceedings of the 2003 Eighth European Conference on Computer-Supported Cooperative Work,* held September 14–18, 2003, in Helsinki, Finland (Springer Publishing, 2003), pp. 239–258, http://www.ecscw.org/2003.htm; and Laura A.

Dabbish, Robert E. Kraut, Susan Fussell, and Sara Kiesler, "Understanding E-Mail Use: Predicting Action on a message," *Proceedings of the SIGCHI Conference on Human Factors in Computing Systems,* held April 2–7, 2005, in Portland, Oregon (New York: ACM Press, 2005), pp. 691–700, http://portal.acm .org/citation.cfm?id=1055068

12. Victoria Bellotti, Nicholas Ducheneaut, Mark Howard, and Ian Smith, "Taking E-Mail to Task: The Design and Evaluation of a Task Management Centered E-Mail Tool," *Proceedings of the SIGCHI Conference on Human Factors in Computing Systems,* held April 5–10, 2003, in Ft. Lauderdale, Florida (New York: ACM Press, 2003), pp. 345–352, http://portal.acm.org/citation .cfm?id=642672

13. Guy Vollmer and Katrin Gabbner, "Quality Improvement of E-Mail Communication in Work Groups and Organizations by Reflection," *Proceedings of the 2005 International ACM SIGGROUP Conference on Supporting Group Work,* held at Sanibel Island, Florida (New York: ACM Press, 2005), pp. 124–127, http://portal.acm.org/citation.cfm?id=1099225

14. Anthony Burgess, Thomas Jackson, and Janet Edwards, "E-Mail Training Significantly Reduces E-Mail Defects," *International Journal of Information Management,* vol. 25, no. 1 (2005), pp. 71–83, http://www.elsevier.com/wps/find/ journaldescription.cws_home/30434/description#description

15. University of North Carolina, "UNC: Academic: Facts and Figures," 2006, accessed November 20, 2006, at http:// admissions.unc.edu/academics/factsandfigures.htm

16. University of North Carolina, "Undergraduate Admissions: FAQs," 2007, accessed November 4, 2007, at http://www .admissions.unc.edu/faq/studying.htm#average

Meredith Weiss (mlweiss@e-mail.unc.edu) is Associate Dean for Administration, Finance, and Information Technology in the UNC School of Law. Both she and **Dana Hanson-Baldauf** (hansonda@ e-mail.unc.edu) are PhD candidates in the School of Information and Library Science, University of North Carolina at Chapel Hill.

From *EDUCAUSE Quarterly,* January/March 2008. Copyright © 2008 by Meredith Weiss. Reprinted by permission.

UNIT 6
Risk and Avoiding Risk

Unit Selections

Key Points to Consider

- The overview to this unit mentions Michael Crichton's novel, *Prey.* The physicist Freeman Dyson reviews this novel in the February 13, 2002, issue of *The New York Review of Books.* Do you agree with what he has to say about the threats that technology holds for us?

- Who is Kevin Mitnick? Where does he work now? What does this say about the way we view white-collar crime in the United States?

- Who is Robert Tappan Morris? His family history is interesting. Why?

- Do you feel safe giving your credit card number to merchants over the Web? Find out how (or if) your number is protected from criminals who might intercept traffic between you and the merchants.

- This unit includes an article on the use of the Internet to spread rumors. Do you agree with the editor's decision to include this article under the heading "Risk and Avoiding Risk"?

- How many of the rumors described in Article 31 have you heard? That article was published in 2004. Name two others that have surfaced since then.

- Use the Internet to learn about the Y2K scare.

Student Website
www.mhhe.com/cls

Internet References

AntiOnline: Hacking and Hackers
http://www.antionline.com/index.php

Copyright & Trademark Information for the IEEE Computer Society
http://computer.org/copyright.htm

Electronic Privacy Information Center (EPIC)
http://epic.org

Internet Privacy Coalition
http://www.epic.org/crypto

Center for Democracy and Technology
http://www.cdt.org/crypto

Survive Spyware
http://reviews.cnet.com/4520-3688_7-6456087-1.html

If literature and film are guides, we in the United States and Western Europe have tangled feelings about technology. On the one hand, we embrace each technical marvel that enters the marketplace. On the other, a world in which machines have gained the upper hand is a cultural staple. Not long ago, Michael Crichton's novel, *Prey,* frightened us with killer robots that evolved by natural selection to inhabit bodies, snatch souls, and take over the world. Teenagers around the country are still watching the handsome couple from *The Matrix,* Neo and Trinity, take on technology run amuck. This time, our creations farm humankind and harvest their capacity to produce energy. More recently, *Children of Men* creates a world, torn by war, in which there has not been a human birth in twenty years.

As it happens, we have good reason to worry about technology, especially computer technology, but the risks are more prosaic. They include privacy intrusions, software that cannot be made error free, and deliberate sabotage. We even have grounds to fear that much of our cultural heritage, now digitized, will be inaccessible when the software used to encode it becomes obsolete. These are issues that concern practicing computer scientists and engineers. *The Communications of the ACM,* the leading journal in the field, has run a column for many years called Inside Risks, dedicated to exploring the unintended consequences of computing. Another ACM journal, *Software Engineering Notes,* devotes a large part of each issue to chronicling software failures.

Anyone who has spent time looking at Internet news sources knows that they can sometimes be unreliable. Paul Hitlin's "False Reporting on the Internet and the Spread of Rumors" examines Internet coverage of the Vince Foster suicide along with other stories to understand just why this is so. During the 2008 campaign season, circulating e-mails claimed that President Obama is a Muslim who studied in a fundamentalist Muslim school while a child in Jakarta, and that Hillary Clinton snubbed a group of women whose children died in combat. More recently, "birther" activists claim that Mr. Obama was born in Kenya (or Indonesia, depending on the source), and so is not the legal President, this despite official protest to the contrary from the Hawaii Department of Health.

When a great part of the tide of information that arrives in our mailboxes each day is simply false, what are we to do? The idea that an informed citizenry is essential to a functioning democracy has been around since the middle of the 18th century. How those citizens are to be informed is the crux of the matter. Jefferson himself was sometimes distrustful of newspapers, and no less a figure than Thomas Paine said that there is a "difference between error and licentiousness" (Brown 1997, p. 89). The question then as now is who judges which is which. This leads to the most important question of all: Would our free-wheeling culture be better served by a constrained media, including e-mail? Read the articles and decide for yourself.

Just as Internet news sources cut two ways, so also does the government's ability to amass data. On the one hand, had various government agencies communicated more efficiently, the terrorist attacks of 2001 might have been prevented. On the

© Image 100/CORBIS

other hand, read "A Growing Watch List" to learn about Maher Ahar, a Canadian imprisoned in Syria at the behest of the U.S. government. Although Ahar has since been cleared of terrorism charges and awarded compensation of $9 million, he is still not free to fly to the United States. His name seems to appear on the Terrorist Identities Datamart Environment, a list that is "a storehouse for data about individuals that the intelligence community believes might harm the United States." Why it appears there is a secret.

Those who remember Y2K remember countless news stories about the interconnectedness of computers and our increasing dependence upon them. The global communication network is vastly larger now. Since 1995, the number of Internet users around the world has grown from none to about a quarter of the world's population. Interconnected computer systems are not just more pervasive than they were a few years ago, their dispersion and our dependence on them make them more vulnerable. Greg Bruno's primer on cyber warfare ("The Evolution of Cyber Warfare") underscores the risks. The techniques of cyber war include denial of service attacks in which there is a coordinated effort to flood servers with requests for data, invasion of communications networks, and malicious programs implanted into computers to disrupt or steal information. One U.S. response, D5, "an all-encompassing term that embraces the ability to deceive, deny, disrupt, degrade, and destroy an enemy's computer information systems," comes with risks of its own, according to retired lieutenant colonel William Astore (Article 28). Not least of which is a threat to privacy.

Oh for the old days, when the government was all privacy advocates had to worry about. In the world of networked computers, e-commerce, and social networking, we blithely hand over vulnerable data to who knows whom? To take a simple example, imagine that you're a gmail subscriber. You may well think you have deleted private messages, but they are stored on a server, who knows where for who knows how long, with access by who knows whom? See Simson Garfinkel's excellent piece (Article 29) for the details.

To change pace a little, have you ever read those pages that you must agree to before a software publisher allows you to install its product? Essentially, they exempt the manufacturer from any liability resulting from its use. Imagine such a thing with your car or your dishwasher. Imagine signing an agreement that says the manufacturer is not liable for either, no matter what happens. Much commercial software is simply too complex to be fully tested. "The Software Wars" is an insider's look into the process of software development. The view is not reassuring.

What is a reasonable person to make of all of this? People around the world are actively trying to disrupt Internet traffic. Thieves get hold of computer-generated lists of names, lists presumably compiled so that government agencies could better serve their clients. Our digital records are disintegrating even as we digitize more and more of them. Political debate appears to be reaching new lows, as unattributed allegations swarm through the Internet. The government compiles massive databases about terrorism and catches the innocent in its nets. Disruption of the global communications network could be catastrophic, as financial markets and global supply chains collapse. One strives for the equanimity of Neil Postman: "Technology giveth and technology taketh away."

Reference

Brown, R. (1997). *The Strength of a People: The Ideal of an Informed Citizenry in America 1650-1970*. Chapel Hill, NC: The University of North Carolina Press.

A Growing Watch List

Data on both U.S. citizens and foreigners flow from a massive clearinghouse.

Karen DeYoung

Each day, thousands of pieces of intelligence information from around the world—field reports, captured documents, news from foreign allies and sometimes idle gossip—arrive in a computer-filled office in McLean, Va., where analysts feed them into the nation's central list of terrorists and terrorism suspects.

Called TIDE, for Terrorist Identities Datamart Environment, the list is a storehouse for data about individuals that the intelligence community believes might harm the United States. It is the wellspring for watch lists distributed to airlines, law enforcement, border posts and U.S. consulates, created to close one of the key intelligence gaps revealed after Sept. 11, 2001: the failure of federal agencies to share what they knew about al-Qaeda operatives.

But in addressing one problem, TIDE has spawned others. Ballooning from fewer than 100,000 files in 2003 to about 435,000, the growing database threatens to overwhelm the people who manage it. "The single biggest worry that I have is long-term quality control," says Russ Travers, in charge of TIDE at the National Counterterrorism Center in McLean. "Where am I going to be, where is my successor going to be, five years down the road?"

TIDE has also created concerns about secrecy, errors and privacy. The list marks the first time foreigners and U.S. citizens are combined in an intelligence database. The bar for inclusion is low, and once someone is on the list, it is virtually impossible to get off it. At any stage, the process can lead to "horror stories" of mixed-up names and unconfirmed information, Travers acknowledges.

The watch lists fed by TIDE, used to monitor everyone entering the country or having even a casual encounter with federal, state and local law enforcement, have a higher bar. But they have become a source of irritation—and potentially more serious consequences—for many U.S. citizens and visitors.

In 2004 and 2005, misidentifications accounted for about half of the tens of thousands of times a traveler's name triggered a watch-list hit, the Government Accountability Office reported in September. Congressional committees have criticized the process, some charging that it collects too much information about Americans, others saying it is ineffective against terrorists. Civil rights and privacy groups have called for increased transparency.

"How many are on the lists, how are they compiled, how is the information used, how do they verify it?" asks Lillie Coney, associate director of the Washington-based Electronic Privacy Information Center. Such information is classified, and individuals barred from traveling are not told why.

Republican Sen. Ted Stevens of Alaska said last year that his wife had been delayed repeatedly while airlines queried whether Catherine Stevens was the watch-listed Cat Stevens. The listing referred to the Britain-based pop singer who converted to Islam and changed his name to Yusuf Islam. The reason Islam is not allowed to fly to the United States is secret.

So is the reason Maher Arar, a Syrian-born Canadian, remains on the State Department's consular watch list. Detained in New York while enroute to Montreal in 2002, Arar was sent by the U.S. government to a year of imprisonment in Syria. Canada, the source of the initial information about Arar, cleared him of all terrorism allegations last September—three years after his release—and has since authorized $9 million in compensation.

TIDE is a vacuum cleaner for both proven and unproven information, and its managers disclaim responsibility for how other agencies use the data. "What's the alternative?" Travers says. "I work under the assumption that we're never going to have perfect information—fingerprints, DNA—on 6 billion people across the planet. . . . If someone actually has a better idea, I'm all ears."

The electronic journey a piece of terrorism data takes from an intelligence outpost to an airline counter is interrupted at several points for analysis and condensation.

President Bush ordered the intelligence community in 2003 to centralize data on terrorism suspects, and U.S. agencies at home and abroad now send everything they collect to TIDE. It arrives electronically as names to be added or as additional information about people already in the system.

The 80 TIDE analysts get "thousands of messages a day," Travers says, much of the data "fragmentary," "inconsistent" and "sometimes just flat-out wrong." Often the analysts go back to the intelligence agencies for details. "Sometimes you'll get sort of corroborating information," he says, "but many times you're not going to get much. What we use here, rightly or wrongly, is a reasonable-suspicion standard."

Each TIDE listee is given a number, and statistics are kept on nationality and ethnic and religious groups. Some files include aliases and sightings, and others are just a full or partial name, perhaps with a sketchy biography. Sunni and Shiite Muslims are the fastest-growing categories in a database whose entries include Saudi financiers and Colombian revolutionaries. U.S. citizens—who Travers says make up less than 5 percent of listings—are included if an "international terrorism nexus" is established. A similar exception for the administration's warrantless wiretap program came under court challenge from privacy and civil rights advocates.

Every night at 10, TIDE dumps an unclassified version of that day's harvest—names, dates of birth, countries of origin and passport information—into a database belonging to the FBI's Terrorist Screening Center. TIDE's most sensitive information is not included. The FBI adds data about U.S. suspects with no international ties for a combined daily total of 1,000 to 1,500 new names.

Between 5 and 6 A.M., a shift of 24 analysts drawn from the agencies that use watch lists begins a new winnowing process at the center's Crystal City, Va., office. The analysts have access to case files at TIDE and the original intelligence sources, says the center's acting director, Rick Kopel.

Decisions on what to add to the Terrorist Screening Center master list are made by midafternoon. The bar is higher than TIDE's; total listings were about 235,000 names as of last fall, according to Justice Department Inspector General Glenn A. Fine. The bar is then raised again as agencies decide which names to put on their own watch lists: the Transportation Security Administration's "no-fly" and "selectee" lists for airlines; Consular Lookout and Support System at the State Department; the Interagency Border and Inspection System at the Department of Homeland Security; and the Justice Department's National Crime Information Center. The criteria each agency use are classified, Kopel says.

Some information may raise a red flag for one agency but not another. "There's a big difference between CLASS and no-fly," Kopel says, referring to State's consular list. "About the only criteria CLASS has is that you're not a U.S. person. . . . Say 'a Mohammed from Syria.' That's useless for me to watch-list here in the United States. But if I'm in Damascus processing visas . . . that might be enough for someone to . . . put a hold on the visa process."

All of the more than 30,000 individuals on the TSA's no-fly list are prohibited from entering an aircraft in the United States. People whose names appear on the longer selectee list—those the government believes merit watching but does not bar from travel—are supposed to be subjected to more intense scrutiny.

With little to go on beyond names, airlines find frequent matches. The screening center agent on call will check the file for markers such as sex, age and prior "encounters" with the list. The agent might ask the airlines about the passenger's eye color, height or defining marks, Kopel says. "We'll say, 'Does he have any rings on his left hand?' and they'll say, 'Uh, he doesn't have a left hand.' Okay. We know that [the listed person] lost his left hand making a bomb."

If the answers indicate a match, that "encounter" is fed back into the FBI screening center's files and ultimately to TIDE. Kopel says the agent never tells the airline whether the person trying to board is the suspect. The airlines decide whether to allow the customer to fly.

TSA receives thousands of complaints each year, such as this one released to the Electronic Privacy Information Center in 2004 under the Freedom of Information Act: "Apparently, my name is on some watch list because everytime I fly, I get delayed while the airline personnel call what they say is TSA," wrote a passenger whose name was blacked out. Noting that he was a high-level federal worker, he asked what he could do to remove his name from the list.

The answer, Kopel says, is little. A unit at the screening center responds to complaints, he says, but will not remove a name if it is shared by a terrorism suspect. Instead, people not on the list who share a name with someone listed can be issued letters instructing airline personnel to check with the TSA to verify their identity. The GAO reported that 31 names were removed in 2005.

A recent review of the entire terrorist Screening Center database was temporarily abandoned when it proved too much work even for the night crew, which generally handles less of a workload. But the no-fly and selectee lists are being scrubbed to emphasize "people we think are a danger to the plane, and not for some other reason they met the criteria," Kopel says.

A separate TSA system that would check every passenger name against the screening center's database has been shelved over concern that it could grow into a massive surveillance program. The Department of Homeland Security was rebuked by Congress in December for trying to develop a risk-assessment program to profile travelers entering and leaving the United States based on airline and financial data.

Kopel insisted that private information on Americans, such as credit-card records, never makes it into the screening center database and that "we rely 100 percent on government-owned information."

The center came in for ridicule last year when CBS's "60 Minutes" noted that 14 of the 19 Sept. 11 hijackers were listed—five years after their deaths. Kopel defends the listings, saying that "we know for a fact that these people will use names that they believe we are not going to list because they're out of circulation—either because they're dead or incarcerated. . . . It's not willy-nilly. Every name on the list, there's a reason that it's on there."

From *The Washington Post National Weekly Edition*, April 2–8, 2007. Copyright © 2007 by Washington Post Writers Group. Reprinted by permission via PARS International Corp.

The Evolution of Cyber Warfare

Greg Bruno

Introduction

In the spring of 2007, when Estonian authorities moved a monument to the Red Army from the center of its capital city, Tallinn, to the outskirts of town, a diplomatic row erupted with neighboring Russia. Estonian nationalists regard the army as occupiers and oppressors, a sentiment that dates to the long period of Soviet rule following the Second World War, when the Soviet Union absorbed all three Baltic states. Ethnic Russians, who make up about a quarter of Estonia's 1.3 million people, were nonetheless incensed by the statue's treatment and took to the streets in protest. Estonia later blamed Moscow for orchestrating the unrest; order was restored only after U.S. and European diplomatic interventions. But the story of the "Bronze Statue" did not end there. Days after the riots the computerized infrastructure of Estonia's high-tech government began to fray, victimized by what experts in cybersecurity termed a coordinated "denial of service" attack. A flood of bogus requests for information from computers around the world conspired to cripple (*Wired*) the websites of Estonian banks, media outlets, and ministries for days. Estonia denounced the attacks as an unprovoked act of aggression from a regional foe (though experts still disagree on who perpetrated it—Moscow has denied any knowledge). Experts in cybersecurity went one step further: They called it the future of warfare.

Cyber Warfare: The New Frontier

The attack on Estonia's "paperless government" (BBC) was one of the most publicized hacks in recent computing history. But it wasn't the first case of cyber espionage, nor the most egregious. It's the "tip of the iceberg of the quantity and quality of attacks that are going on," says O. Sami Saydjari, president of the Cyber Defense Agency, a security consultant, and a former Pentagon computer security expert. Israel, India, Pakistan, and the United States have all been accused of launching similar attacks on adversaries.

> **"Chinese [cyber warfare] capabilities have evolved from defending networks from attack to offensive operations against adversary networks."**
>
> —Richard P. Lawless,
> U.S. Deputy Under Secretary for Defense

China, however, may be the most active. Washington has accused the Chinese of hacking into government computer networks at the U.S. Departments of State, Commerce, and Defense—in some instances making off with data. But accusations of Chinese cyber-meddling reached a crescendo in June 2007, when, according to the *Financial Times,* hackers broke into a Pentagon network that serves the Office of the Secretary of Defense, briefly shutting it down. Chinese electronic espionage has also been suspected against British companies (Rolls Royce is one example), as well as government agencies in France, Germany, South Korea, and Taiwan. "Chinese capabilities in this area have evolved from defending networks from attack to offensive operations against adversary networks," Deputy Undersecretary for Defense Richard P. Lawless told (PDF) a House committee in June 2007. China, like Russia, denies the accusations. Both countries argue any attacks originating from IP addresses inside their countries have been directed by rogue citizens, not their governments. Western targets, however, continue to accuse the Chinese of ratcheting up their cyber attack capabilities.

> **"Our ability to penetrate into enemy computer networks, our ability to exploit communication networks, to manipulate digital information, is real."**
>
> —William M. Arkin, Defense Analyst

U.S. Cyber Warfare on the Offensive

The United States, of course, is no innocent bystander. William M. Arkin, a defense analyst who writes the Early Warning blog for the *Washington Post,* says "our ability to penetrate into enemy computer networks, our ability to exploit communication networks, to manipulate digital information, is real," but little is known about the precise nature of Washington's offensive capabilities. Some details, however, have leaked. For instance, in March 2004 the Pentagon announced the formation of an Information Operations team—the Network Attack Support Staff—to streamline the military's cyber attack capabilities (PDF).

The aim, senior military officials said at the time, was to create an "interface between the combatant commanders and the intelligence community."

Arkin, who has reported on cybersecurity issues for over two decades, says the U.S. military also has technologies capable of penetrating and jamming enemy networks, including the classified "Suter" system of airborne technology. According to *Aviation Week,* Suter has been integrated into unmanned aircraft and "allows users to invade communications networks, see what enemy sensors see, and even take over as systems administrator so sensors can be manipulated into positions so that approaching aircraft can't be seen." Some speculate the Israeli military used the capability during its air raid on a Syrian construction site in September 2007. The United States made use of nascent capabilities in the 1999 Kosovo War (MSNBC.com), and built on those lessons in Iraq (Wired).

Cyber-Warfare Tactics

Other cyber tactics are less sophisticated. The attack that temporarily brought down Estonian networks began with a flood of bogus messages targeting government servers, called a "denial of service" attack. The approach harnesses "botnets"—massive networks of interconnected computers—to bombard targeted networks with information requests while masking the location of the primary attacker. James Lewis, a security expert with the Center for Strategic and International Studies (CSIS), says hackers in the Estonia example likely took control of tens of thousands of computers around the world without the knowledge of their owners and directed them at the government's servers. The result, he says, was a relatively minor attack that was nearly impossible to trace (PDF).

Another technique is the use of "malware," "spyware," and other malicious programs imbedded into computer systems to steal information without user knowledge. The software is designed to hide undetected and siphon information from its host—everything from secrets stored on personal computers to Pentagon military mainframes. A December 2007 analysis of U.S. Air Force cyber vulnerabilities (PDF) notes much of the Pentagon's operating systems are off-the-shelf components manufactured overseas, due to cheaper costs. But pinching pennies has potentially opened U.S. military networks to intrusion. "Foreign countries could place hidden components inside the computers, making the computers vulnerable for attack and/or spying," the analysis concludes.

Less common but far more worrisome are cyber attacks aimed at critical infrastructure—like nuclear-power-plant control systems, banks, or subways. In March 2007 the Department of Energy's Idaho Lab conducted an experiment to determine whether a power plant could be compromised by hacking alone. The result—a smoking, self-combusting diesel generator incapacitated by nothing more than keystrokes—sent shivers (CNN) through the private sector. The worries were apparently well-founded. In January 2008 a CIA analyst told U.S. utilities that hackers had succeeded in infiltrating electric companies in undisclosed locations outside the United States and, in at least one instance, shut off power to multiple cities. The hackers then demanded money (AP). "The [U.S.] government is scrambling to

try and protect its own systems, to try and check the Chinese from reading government email," says economist Scott Borg, director of the U.S. Cyber Consequences Unit, a nonprofit research institute that studies cyber threats. "But the focus probably needs to be critical infrastructure. That's what we need to defend."

Patching the Holes

On paper the U.S. government appears to agree. For over a decade government-sanctioned studies have delved into the subject; the Pentagon published a report on "Information Warfare-Defense" (PDF) in 1996, when public use of the Internet was still in its infancy. Saydjari says all of these studies reached the same conclusion: "The threat and vulnerabilities to our national infrastructure is serious, it's getting worse, and it's getting worse at an increasingly fast rate." But only recently has the concern been a constant focus of attention for the security and intelligence communities. Part of the attention deficit lies with the difficulty in defining the cyber threat. A 2006 Air Force task force termed cyberspace "a warfighting domain bounded by the electromagnetic spectrum," but air force officials acknowledge "a full understanding of the domain is years away."

> **"Our information infrastructure . . . increasingly is being targeted for exploitation and potentially for disruption or destruction by a growing array of state and non-state adversaries."**
>
> —Michael McConnell, Director of National Intelligence

What is understood is how potentially devastating the loss of cyberspace dominance could be to U.S. interests. In his annual threat assessment to Congress delivered in February 2008, Director of National Intelligence Michael McConnell discussed "cyber threats" before talking about the war in Afghanistan. "Our information infrastructure . . . increasingly is being targeted for exploitation and potentially for disruption or destruction by a growing array of state and non-state adversaries," McConnell said. "We assess that nations, including Russia and China, have the technical capabilities to target and disrupt" the United States' information infrastructure.

The Pentagon, too, has acknowledged the threat to its infrastructure. The Defense Department is considering banning nonofficial traffic (*Federal Computer Week*) from its servers, and the U.S. Air Force is creating a Cyber Command to defend Pentagon networks. "When we talk about the speed range and flexibility of air power, the thing that enables this for us is the fact of our cyber-dominance," Air Force Gen. Robert Elder told United Press International.

The recent flurry of high-level pronouncements also comes amid a renewed funding commitment from Washington. In November 2007 the Bush administration called on the National Security Agency to coordinate with the Department of Homeland Security to protect government and civilian communication networks from hackers. The $144 million plan, unveiled quietly in White House budget documents (PDF), aims to enhance "civilian agency cybersecurity and strengthen defenses to combat terrorism." In January 2008 President George W. Bush signed two presidential directives calling for the creation of a comprehensive national cybersecurity initiative. According to an article by the *Wall Street Journal,* the White House's 2009 budget request takes the program exponentially further, with an estimated $6 billion request to build a secretive system to protect U.S. communications networks. Details of the proposed program remain classified, angering some civil libertarians who fear monitoring of civilian networks could infringe on privacy rights. Rep. Bennie G. Thompson (D-MS), chairman of the House Homeland Security Committee, has called for the program to be put on hold (PDF) until Congress can adequately review it.

Measuring the Threat

Cyber experts don't dispute that electronic espionage is a vexing problem, or that the United States is a prime target. But they do disagree on how pervasive such attacks are, who is behind them, and how disruptive they may prove to be. According to a tally by the Heritage Foundation, a conservative Washington think tank, the hackers may already be winning: In 2007 the Department of Homeland Security logged an estimated 37,000 attempted breaches of private and government computer systems, and over 80,000 attacks on Pentagon systems. Some hacks "reduced the U.S. military's operational capabilities," the report says (PDF).

Economist Borg says the biggest threat from cyber attacks may be economic. He estimates a shutdown of electric power to any sizable region for more than ten days would stop over 70 percent of all economic activity in that region. "If you can do that with a pure cyber attack on only one critical infrastructure, why would you bother with any traditional military attack?" CSIS' Lewis takes a less alarmist view. "The U.S. is a very big set of targets, and some of our important networks are very secure. So you could inflict damage on the U.S. but it wouldn't be crippling or decisive," he says. "I've seen people who say a cyber attack could turn the United States into a third-world nation in a matter of minutes. That's silly. We have to be realistic about this."

From *Backgrounder,* February 27, 2008. Copyright © 2008 by Foreign Affairs. Reprinted by permission.

Geeks and Hackers, Uncle Sam's Cyber Force Wants You!

WILLIAM J. ASTORE

Recently, while I was on a visit to *Salon.com,* my computer screen momentarily went black. A glitch? A power surge? No, it was a pop-up ad for the U.S. Air Force, warning me that an enemy cyber-attack could come at any moment—with dire consequences for my ability to connect to the Internet. It was an *Outer Limits* moment. Remember that eerie sci-fi show from the early 1960s? The one that began in a blur with the message, "There is nothing wrong with your television set. Do not attempt to adjust the picture. *We* are controlling transmission . . ." It felt a little like that.

And speaking of Air Force ads, there's one currently running on TV and on the Internet that starts with a bird's eye view of the Pentagon as a narrator intones, "This building will be attacked 3 million times today. Who's going to protect it?" Two Army colleagues of mine nearly died on September 11, 2001, when the third hijacked plane crashed into the Pentagon, so I can't say I appreciated the none-too-subtle reminder of that day's carnage. Leaving that aside, it turns out that the ad is referring to cyber-attacks and that the cyber protector it has in mind is a new breed of "air" warrior, part of an entirely new Cyber Command run by the Air Force. Using the latest technology, our cyber elite will "shoot down" enemy hackers and saboteurs, both foreign and domestic, thereby dominating the realm of cyberspace, just as the Air Force is currently seeking to dominate the planet's air space—and then space itself "to the shining stars and beyond."

Part of the Air Force's new "above all" vision of full-spectrum dominance, America's emerging cyber force has control fantasies that would impress George Orwell. Working with the Defense Advanced Research Projects Agency (DARPA), the Department of Homeland Security, and other governmental agencies, the Air Force's stated goal is to gain access to, and control over, any and all networked computers, anywhere on Earth, at a proposed cost to you, the American taxpayer, of $30 billion over the first five years.

Here, the Air Force is advancing the now familiar Bush-era idea that the only effective defense is a dominating offense. According to Lani Kass, previously the head of the Air Force's Cyberspace Task Force and now a special assistant to the Air Force Chief of Staff, "If you're defending in cyber [space], you're already too late. Cyber delivers on the original promise of air power. If you don't dominate in cyber, you cannot dominate in other domains."

Such logic is commonplace in today's Air Force (as it has been for Bush administration foreign policy). A threat is identified, our vulnerability to it is trumpeted, and then our response is to spend tens of billions of dollars launching a quest for total domination. Thus, on May 12 of this year, the Air Force Research Laboratory posted an official "request for proposal" seeking contractor bids to begin the push to achieve "dominant cyber offensive engagement." The desired capabilities constitute a disturbing militarization of cyberspace:

> "Of interest are any and all techniques to enable user and/or root access to both fixed (PC) or mobile computing platforms. Robust methodologies to enable access to any and all operating systems, patch levels, applications and hardware. . . . technology . . . to maintain an active presence within the adversaries' information infrastructure completely undetected. . . . any and all techniques to enable stealth and persistence capabilities. . . . capability to stealthily exfiltrate information from any remotely-located open or closed computer information systems . . ."

Stealthily infiltrating, stealing, and exfiltrating: Sounds like cyber-cat burglars, or perhaps invisible cyber-SEALS, as in that U.S. Navy "empty beach at night" commercial. This is consistent with an Air Force-sponsored concept paper on "network-centric warfare," which posits the deployment of so-called "cyber-craft" in cyberspace to "disable terminals, nodes or the entire network as well as send commands to 'fry' their hard drives." Somebody clever with acronyms came up with D5, an all-encompassing term that embraces the ability to deceive, deny, disrupt, degrade, and destroy an enemy's computer information systems.

No one, it seems, is the least bit worried that a single-minded pursuit of cyber-"destruction"—analogous to that "crush . . . kill . . . destroy" android on the 1960s TV series *Lost in Space*—could create a new arena for that old cold war nuclear acronym MAD (mutually assured destruction), as America's enemies and rivals seek to D5 our terminals, nodes, and networks.

Here's another less-than-comforting thought: America's new Cyber Force will most likely be widely distributed in basing terms. In fact, the Air Force prefers a "headquarters" spread across several bases here in the United States, thereby cleverly tapping the political support of more than a few members of Congress.

Finally, if, after all this talk of the need for "information dominance" and the five Ds, you still remain skeptical, the Air Force has prepared an online "What Do You Think?" survey and quiz (paid for, again, by you the taxpayer, of course) to silence naysayers and cyberspace appeasers. It will disabuse you of the notion that the Internet is a somewhat benign realm where cooperation of all sorts, including the international sort, is possible. You'll learn, instead, that we face nothing but ceaseless hostility from cyber-thugs seeking to terrorize all of us everywhere all the time.

Of Ugly Babies, Icebergs and Air Force Computer Systems

Computers and their various networks are unquestionably vital to our national defense—indeed, to our very way of life—and we do need to be able to protect them from cyber attacks. In addition, striking at an enemy's ability to command and control its forces has always been part of warfare. But spending $6 billion a year for five years on a mini-Manhattan Project to atomize our opponents' computer networks is an escalatory boondoggle of the worst sort.

Leaving aside the striking potential for the abuse of privacy, or the potentially destabilizing responses of rivals to such aggressive online plans, the Air Force's militarization of cyberspace is likely to yield uncertain technical benefits at inflated prices, if my experience working on two big Air Force computer projects counts for anything. Admittedly, that experience is a bit dated, but keep in mind that the wheels of procurement reform at the Department of Defense (DoD) do turn slowly, when they turn at all.

Two decades ago, while I was at the Space Surveillance Center in Cheyenne Mountain, the Air Force awarded a contract to update our computer system. The new system, known as SPADOC 4, was, as one Air Force tester put it, the "ugly baby." Years later, and no prettier, the baby finally came on-line, part of a Cheyenne Mountain upgrade that was hundreds of millions of dollars over budget. One Air Force captain described it in the following way:

"The SPADOC system was . . . designed very poorly in terms of its human machine interface . . . [leading to] a lot of work arounds that make learning the system difficult. . . . [Fortunately,] people are adaptable and they can learn to operate a poorly designed machine, like SPADOC, [but the result is] increased training time, increased stress for the operators, increased human errors under stress and unused machine capabilities."

My second experience came a decade ago, when I worked on the Air Force Mission Support System or AFMSS. The idea was to enable pilots to plan their missions using the latest tools of technology, rather than paper charts, rulers, and calculators. A sound idea, but again botched in execution.

The Air Force tried to design a mission planner for every platform and mission, from tankers to bombers. To meet such disparate needs took time, money, and massive computing power, so the Air Force went with Unix-based SPARC platforms, which occupied a small room. The software itself was difficult to learn, even counterintuitive. While the Air Force struggled, year after year, to get AFMSS to work, competitors came along with PC-based flight planners, which provided 80 percent of AFMSS's functionality at a fraction of the cost. Naturally, pilots began clamoring for the portable, easy-to-learn PC system.

Fundamentally, the whole DoD procurement cycle had gone wrong—and there lies a lesson for the present cyber-moment. The Pentagon is fairly good at producing decent ships, tanks, and planes (never mind the typical cost overruns, the gold-plating, and so on). After all, an advanced ship or tank, even deployed a few years late, is normally still an effective weapon. But a computer system a few years late? That's a paperweight or a doorstop. That's your basic disaster. Hence the push for the DoD to rely, whenever possible, on COTS, or commercial-off-the-shelf, software and hardware.

Don't get me wrong: I'm not saying it's only the Pentagon that has trouble designing, acquiring and fielding new computer systems. Think of it as a problem of large, by-the-book bureaucracies. Just look at the FBI's computer debacle—attempting (for years) to install new systems that failed disastrously—or, for that matter the ever more imperial Microsoft's struggles with Vista.

Judging by my past experience with large-scale Air Force computer projects, that $30 billion will turn out to be just the tip of the cyber-war procurement iceberg and, while you're at it, call those "five years" of development ten. Shackled to a multi-year procurement cycle of great regulatory rigidity and complexity, the Air Force is likely to struggle but fail to keep up with the far more flexible and creative cyber world, which almost daily sees the fielding of new machines and applications.

Loving Big "Cyber" Brother

Our military is the ultimate centralized, bureaucratic, hierarchical organization. Its tolerance for errors and risky or "deviant" behavior is low. Its culture is designed to foster obedience, loyalty, regularity, and predictability, all usually necessary in handling frantic life-or-death combat situations. It is difficult to imagine a culture more antithetical to the world of computer developers, programmers and hackers.

So expect a culture clash in militarized cyberspace—and more taxpayers' money wasted—as the Internet and the civilian computing world continue to outpace anything the DoD can muster. If, however, the Air Force should somehow manage to defy the odds and succeed, the future might be even scarier.

After all, do we really want the military to dominate cyberspace? Let's say we answer "yes" because we love our big "Above All" cyber-brother. Now, imagine you're Chinese or Indian or Russian. Would you really cede total cyber-dominance to the United States without a fight? Not likely. You would simply launch—or intensify—your own cyber war efforts.

Interestingly, a few people have surmised that the Air Force's cyber-war plans are so outlandish they must be bluster—a sort of warning shot to competitors not to dare risk a cyber attack on the United States, because they'd then face cyber obliteration.

Yet it's more likely that the Air Force is quite sincere in promoting its $30 billion "mini-Manhattan" cyber-war project. It has its own private reasons for attempting to expand into a new realm (and so create new budget authority as well). After all, as a service, it's been somewhat marginalized in the War on Terror. Today's Air Force is in a flat spin, its new planes so expensive that relatively few can be purchased, its pilots increasingly diverted to "fly" Predators and Reapers—unmanned aerial vehicles—its top command eager to ward off the threat of future irrelevancy.

But even in cyberspace, irrelevancy may prove the name of the game. Judging by the results of previous U.S. military-run computer projects, future Air Force "cyber-craft" may prove more than a day late and billions of dollars short.

WILLIAM J. ASTORE, a retired lieutenant colonel (USAF), has taught at the Air Force Academy and the Naval Postgraduate School. He currently teaches at the Pennsylvania College of Technology. A regular contributor to TomDispatch, he is the author of *Hindenburg: Icon of German Militarism* (Potomac, 2005). His email is wastore at pct.edu

Reprinted by permission from the June 5, 2008 issue of *The Nation*. Copyright © 2008 by The Nation. For subscription information, call 1-800-333-8536. Portions of each week's Nation magazine can be accessed at www.thenation.com

Privacy Requires Security, Not Abstinence: Protecting an Inalienable Right in the Age of Facebook

SIMSON GARFINKEL

I'd be a fool to include my Social Security number in this article: doing so would leave me vulnerable to all manner of credit fraud, scams, and even criminal arrest. All of this would surely happen because a few bad people would read the article, write down my SSN, and pretend to be me.

We know a lot more about the use and abuse of SSNs today than we did back in 2002. That was the year the California state legislature passed SB 1386, the first U.S. law requiring that consumers be notified when computer systems holding their personal information are "breached" or that information is otherwise compromised. Because of SB 1386, we learned in 2005 that ChoicePoint—a company most Americans had never heard of—had somehow sold detailed credit histories on more than 163,000 consumers directly to identity thieves (more than 800 people suffered direct losses as a result). And in 2007, we learned that identity thieves had broken into the computer systems of the discount retailer TJX and stolen more than 45 million credit-card numbers.

We've also learned that governments are equally bad at securing personal information, as demonstrated by the half-million records breached at the Oklahoma Department of Human Services, the eight million records reportedly exposed at the Virginia Department of Health Professions, and the 26.5 million records stolen (along with a laptop and portable hard drive) from a work-from-home employee of the U.S. Department of Veterans Affairs.

All these cases, and many more, paint a disturbing picture of what is really threatening privacy in America today.

Privacy matters. Data privacy protects us from electronic crimes of opportunity—identity theft, stalking, even little crimes like spam. Privacy gives us the right to meet and speak confidentially with others—a right that's crucial for democracy, which requires places for political ideas to grow and mature. Absolute privacy, also known as solitude, gives us space to grow as individuals. Who could learn to write, draw, or otherwise create if every action, step, and misstep were captured, immortalized, and evaluated? And the ability to conduct transactions in privacy protects us from both legal and illegal discrimination.

Until recently, people who wanted to preserve their privacy were urged to "opt out" or abstain from some aspects of modern society. Concerned about having your purchases tracked by a credit-card company? Use cash. Concerned that E-ZPass records might be used against you in a lawsuit? Throw coins at that toll booth. Don't want to show your ID at the airport? Drive. Don't want your location tracked minute by minute? Turn off your cell phone. And be in a minority: faced with the choice of convenience or privacy, Americans have overwhelmingly chosen the former. Companies like TJX haven't even suffered from allowing their customers' personal data to be leaked.

Now, however, abstinence no longer guarantees privacy. Of course, it never really did. But until the past two decades it was always possible to keep some private information out of circulation. Today, although you can avoid the supermarket savings card, the market will still capture your face with its video cameras. You can use cash, but large cash transactions are reported to the federal government. You can try to live without the Internet—but you'll be marginalized. Worse, you won't be able to participate in the public debate about how your privacy is wasting away—because that debate is happening online. And no matter what you do, it won't prevent your information from being stored in commercial networked systems.

In this environment, the real problem is not that your information is out there; it's that it's not protected from misuse. In other words, privacy problems are increasingly the result of poor security practices. The biggest issue, I've long maintained, is that decision makers don't consider security a priority. By not insisting on secure systems, governments and corporations alike have allowed themselves to get stuck with insecure ones.

Consider the humble Social Security number. As a privacy advocate, I always chafe when people ask me for my "social." As a security professional, I am deeply disturbed that a number designed as an identifier—for the single specific purpose of tracking individuals' earnings to calculate Social Security benefits—has come to be used as a verifier of identity for countless other purposes. Providing my SSN should not "prove" that I am who I say I am any more than providing my name or address does. But in the absence of any better system, this number has become, in the words of Joanne McNabb, chief of California's Office of Privacy Protection, the "key to the vault for identity thieves."

Yes, privacy as we know it is under attack—by a government searching for tax cheats and terrorists; by corporations looking for new customers; by insurance companies looking to control costs; and even by nosy friends, associates, and classmates. Collectively, we made things worse by not building strong privacy and security guarantees into our information systems, our businesses, and our society. Then we went and networked everything, helping both legitimate users and criminals. Is it any wonder things turned out this way?

All of a sudden, we have a lot of work to do.

But while our current privacy issues feel as new as Twitter, the notion of privacy as a right is old. Americans have always expected this fight to be maintained, even as technology opened ever more powerful tools for its subversion. The story of privacy in America is the story of inventions and the story of fear; it is best told around certain moments of opportunity and danger.

The Constitution

The word privacy doesn't appear in the U.S. Constitution, but courts and constitutional scholars have found plenty of privacy protections in the restriction on quartering soldiers in private homes (the Third Amendment); in the prohibition against "unreasonable searches and seizures" (the Fourth Amendment); and in the prohibition against forcing a person to be "a witness against himself" (the Fifth Amendment). These provisions remain fundamental checks on the power of government.

Over time, however, the advance of technology has threatened privacy in new ways, and the way we think about the concept has changed accordingly.

Back in 1890 two Boston lawyers, Samuel Warren and Louis Brandeis, wrote an article in the Harvard Law Review warning that the invasive technologies of their day threatened to take "what is whispered in the closet" and have it "proclaimed from the house-tops." In the face of those threats, they posited a direct "right to privacy" and argued that individuals whose privacy is violated should be able to sue for damages.

Warren and Brandeis called privacy "the right to be let alone" and gave numerous examples of ways it could be invaded. After more than a century of legal scholarship, we've come to understand that these examples suggest four distinct kinds of invasion: intrusion into a person's seclusion or private affairs; disclosure of embarrassing private facts; publicity that places a person in a "false light"; and appropriation of a person's name or likeness.

In our world, "intrusions into a person's seclusion or private affairs" might describe someone's hacking into your computer system. Consider the case of Patrick Connolly, a U.S. military contractor accused of victimizing more than 4,000 teenagers by breaking into their computers and threatening to make their pictures and videos public unless they sent him sexually explicit photos and videos of themselves. You can also be intruded upon in many lesser ways: when companies force advertisements onto your screen, for example, or make pop-ups appear that you

need to close. It's intrusive for a telemarketer to call you during dinner. That's why programs that block Internet advertisements and the federal government's "do not call" list are both tightly seen as privacy-protecting measures.

The desire to prevent the disclosure of embarrassing private facts, meanwhile, is one of the driving forces behind the privacy regulations of the Health Insurance Portability and Accountability Act (HIPAA). Because of this law and the regulations deriving from it, a health-care provider cannot disclose information in your medical records unless you give explicit permission. Another law, the Video Privacy Protection Act of 1988, makes it illegal for Netflix to disclose the movies you rent.

"False light" is a problem we still don't know how to address online. It's all too easy on today's Internet to attack a person's reputation with anonymously posted false statements. And even though free-speech advocates invariably say that the antidote to bad speech is more speech, experience has shown that this remedy is less effective in the age of Google. For example, two years ago AutoAdmit, an online message board for law students and lawyers, was sued by two female Yale Law students who said they'd been unable to obtain summer associate positions because vile and malicious sexual comments about them appeared whenever someone searched for their names.

Using a name or likeness without permission is at the heart of most "sexting" cases that reach the newspapers. Journalists often focus on the fact that teens are willingly sending sexy or downright pornographic photos of themselves to their boyfriends or girlfriends. But the real damage happens when a recipient forwards one of these photos to friends. That is, the damage is caused by the appropriation, not the receipt.

The fact that a dusty *Harvard Law Review* article corresponds so closely with the online privacy problems we face today suggests that even though technology is a driving factor in these privacy invasions, it's not the root source. The source is what sits in front of the computer's screen, not behind it.

For another example, consider electronic surveillance. Although e-mail and telephones give the appearance of privacy, sensitive electronic communications have always been an attractive target. Wiretapping was employed by both sides during the Civil War, prompting some states to pass laws against it. But it was the invention of the microphone and the telephone that brought the possibility of electronic surveillance into the homes of ordinary Americans. This shifted the action in U.S. privacy law from information to communication.

In 1928, in a case called *Olmstead v. United States,* the Supreme Court heard the appeal of a Seattle bootlegger whose phones had been tapped by federal agents. The agents had not trespassed or broken any laws to install the wiretaps, but they didn't have a search warrant either, as would have been required for a physical search of Roy Olmstead's property.

Brandeis, who had been appointed to the court by Woodrow Wilson in 1916, was appalled. "Whenever a telephone line is tapped, the privacy of the persons at both ends of the line is invaded, and all conversations between them upon any subject, and although proper, confidential and privileged, may be overheard," he wrote in his opinion. Alas, it was a dissent. By a 5–4 majority, the court found in favor of the government: search warrants were not required for eavesdropping on electronic communications, because "there was no searching." Olmstead went to prison, federal agents got the right to wiretap without a warrant, and that's how the law stood for another 39 years, until the case was overturned by a more liberal court in 1967.

It's comforting to know that U.S. law eventually gets things right with respect to privacy—that is the power of our republic, after all. But it's also troubling how long it sometimes takes. A lot of injustice can happen while we wait for the law to accommodate advances in technology.

The Computer

Consumer data banks as we know them today—big repositories of personal information, indexed by name and specifically constructed for the purpose of sharing information once regarded as "private"—didn't start with computers. But computers certainly helped.

One of today's largest consumer reporting firms was started in 1899, when two brothers created the Retail Credit Company—now known as Equifax—to track the creditworthiness of Atlanta grocery and retail customers. Businesses were encouraged to report which of their customers reliably paid their bills and which did not. Retail Credit collected the information, published it in a book, and sold copies.

Retail Credit and other consumer reporting firms maintained paper files until the 1960s. When they finally started to computerize, they came head to head with a Columbia University political-science professor named Alan Westin.

Westin had uncovered countless cases in which people had been denied credit, insurance, housing, even jobs, because of errors in consumer files—records that many victims didn't even know existed. He feared that computerization would make credit data banks much more widely used, with ominous consequences unless they were properly regulated. In the computer age, he said, privacy is no longer just the right to be left alone; it involves people's right "to determine for themselves when, how, and to what extent information about them is communicated to others." Possession of personal information, Westin said, should not give corporations unlimited rights to use that information.

Westin's research sparked numerous congressional investigations and got him invited to testify before Congress. People were entitled to view their own records, he said. And they needed a way to dispute the records and force an investigation if they thought there was an error.

Retail Credit and others protested that they would be stymied and bankrupted by a flood of requests. And Westin's definition of privacy could put different parties' rights in clear conflict—taken to its extreme today, it would mean that an ex-lover could order you to remove his or her name from your address book and delete all those old e-mails. But Westin and the other privacy advocates won the day, and Congress passed the Fair Credit Reporting Act of 1970. A Nixon administration advisory committee then developed the Code of Fair Information Practice, a guiding set of principles that underlies the majority of U.S. privacy laws passed since.

This code is surprisingly straightforward. There should be no secret data banks; individuals must be able to view their records;

there must be a way to correct errors; organizations maintaining data banks must make sure they're reliable and protect them from unauthorized access; and information collected for one purpose must not be used for other purposes.

For example, the Video Privacy Protection Act was passed after Judge Robert Bork's video rental records were obtained by the Washington, DC, weekly City Paper in an attempt to dig up embarrassing information while the U.S. Senate was debating his 1987 nomination to the Supreme Court. The Driver's Privacy Protection Act of 1994 was passed after actress Rebecca Schaeffer was murdered in 1989 by a crazed fan, who had hired a private investigator to track down her address. The investigator was able to get the information through the California Department of Motor Vehicles, which had required Schaeffer to provide her home address when she applied for a license.

In both cases, Congress acted to prevent personal information from being reused in certain ways without permission. Score two for the updated concept of privacy.

The Internet

In the 1980s and early 1990s, while lawmakers in Europe and Canada passed comprehensive privacy legislation complete with commissioners and enforcement mechanisms, the United States adopted a piecemeal approach. Some databases had legally mandated privacy guarantees; others didn't. Wiretapping required a warrant—except when companies taped employees for the purpose of "improving customer service." But even if policies weren't consistent, they basically covered most situations that arose.

Then came the Internet's explosive growth—a boon to community, commerce, and surveillance all at the same time. Never before had it been so easy to find out so much, so quickly. But while most Internet users soon became dependent on services from companies like Yahoo and Google, few realized that they themselves were the product these companies were selling.

All activity on the Internet is mediated—by software on your computer and on the remote service; by the remote service itself; and by the Internet service providers that carry the data. Each of these mediators has the ability to record or change the data as it passes through. And each mediator has an incentive to exploit its position for financial gain.

Thousands of different business models bloomed. Companies like Doubleclick realized that they could keep track of which Internet users went to which websites and integrate this information into vast profiles of user preferences, to be used for targeting ads. Some ISPs went further and inserted their own advertisements into the user's data stream. One e-mail provider went further still: it intercepted all the e-mail from Amazon .com to its users and used those messages to market its own online clearinghouse for rare and out-of-print books. Whoops. That provider was eventually charged with violating the Federal Wiretap Act. But practically every other intrusive practice was allowed by the law and, ultimately, by Congress, which was never able to muster the will to pass comprehensive Internet privacy legislation.

It's not that Congress was shy about regulating the Internet. It's just that congressional attention in the 1990s was focused on shielding children from online pornography—through laws eventually found unconstitutional by the Supreme Court, because they also limited the rights of adults. The one significant piece of Internet privacy legislation that Congress did manage to pass was the Children's Online Privacy Protection Act (COPPA), which largely prohibited the intentional collection of information from children 12 or younger.

Instead, it fell mostly to the Federal Trade Commission to regulate privacy on the Internet. And here the commission used one primary tool: the FTC Act of 1914 (since updated), which prohibits businesses from engaging in "unfair or deceptive acts or practices." The way this works in connection with online privacy is that companies write "privacy policies" describing what they do with personal information they obtain from their customers. Companies that follow their policies are fine—even if they collect your information and publish it, sell it, or use it to send e-mail or for "any other lawful purpose" (and the law is pretty tolerant). The only way for companies to get in trouble is to claim that they will honor your privacy in a specific manner and then do something different.

Hearings were held at the end of the Clinton administration to pass some online privacy legislation with real teeth. I testified in favor of strong regulations at one of those hearings, but sitting next to me at the witness table were powerful business interests who argued that regulation would be expensive and hard to enforce. The legislation didn't go anywhere. Business groups saw this outcome as the triumph of their "market-based" approach: consumers who weren't happy with a company's privacy stance could always go elsewhere. Privacy activists winced, knowing that legislation would be unlikely to pass if the Republicans won in 2000. We had no idea how right we were.

9/11: The First National Scare of the Computer Age

The terrorist attacks of September 11, 2001, changed the terms of the debate. Suddenly, the issue was no longer whether Congress should protect consumer privacy or let business run wild. Instead, the question became: Should Congress authorize the Bush administration to use the formidable power of state surveillance to find terrorists operating inside the United States and stop them before they could carry out their next attack?

The administration itself had no doubts. Where laws protecting privacy got in the way of its plans to prevent attacks, it set out to change those laws. The pinnacle of this effort was the USA Patriot Act, signed on October 26, 2001, which dramatically expanded government power to investigate suspected terrorism. In the months that followed, representatives for the administration repeatedly denounced those who complained about threats to privacy and liberty; they were, said Attorney General John Ashcroft, "giv[ing] ammunition to America's enemies."

It was a strong, simple, and remarkably effective message—so effective that we know of only a few cases in which Congress pushed back. The first and most public such case involved a Department of Defense research project called Total Information Awareness (TIA).

Soon renamed Terrorism Information Awareness, TIA was the brainchild of the Defense Advanced Research Projects Agency's newly created Information Awareness Office, which was run by retired admiral John Poindexter (a former national security advisor) and his deputy, Robert L. Popp. The idea, which drew heavily on both men's earlier work in undersea surveillance and antisubmarine warfare, was to use new advances in data mining and transactional analysis to catch terrorists while they were planning their attacks.

One way to find submarines is to wire the ocean with listening sensors and then to try to filter the sounds of the sea to reveal the sounds of the subs. The terrorist problem is similar, Poindexter explained at the 2002 DARPATech conference. The key difference is that instead of being in an ocean of water, the terrorists were operating in an ocean of data and transactions. "We must find terrorists in a world of noise, understand what they are planning, and develop options for preventing their attacks," he said in his published remarks.

The approach isn't so far-fetched. Consider that the 1995 Oklahoma City bombing used explosives made of fertilizer and fuel oil, delivered in a rented Ryder truck. One way to stop similar plots in advance might be to look for people other than farmers who are purchasing large quantities of fertilizers used in making bombs—with extra points if the person (or one of his friends) has also rented a moving truck.

That task will be made a bit easier when stores that sell ammonium nitrate are registered with the Department of Homeland Security (a federal law to that effect was passed in 2007). Still: even when we have such registration, the prevention of an attack using fertilizer will require real-time purchase information from every fertilizer seller in the United States.

While I was a graduate student at MIT during the summer of 2003, I got a job working on the TIA project, because I thought that data mining would be a way to objectively look through mountains of personal information without compromising privacy. Congress, however, opposed TIA on the grounds that it treated everyone in the country as a suspect, and because it feared that a massive data surveillance system might be used for purposes other than catching terrorists. This prospect was not so hypothetical: in 1972 Richard Nixon had ordered the IRS to investigate his political opponents, including major contributors to George McGovern's presidential campaign. (Many believe that opposition to TIA was also a kind of payback against Poindexter, who had been convicted of lying to Congress in the Iran-Contra scandal of the 1980s but had his conviction overturned on appeal.) Congress defunded the program in 2003.

TIA was never more than a research project. But other initiatives were moving ahead at the same time.

For example, in 2002 officials from the Transportation Security Administration asked JetBlue Airways to provide detailed passenger information to Torch Concepts, a company in Huntsville, AL, that was developing a data mining system even more invasive than the one envisioned by DARPA. JetBlue was eager to help: five million passenger records were transferred. The records, which included passenger names, addresses, phone numbers, and itineraries, were then combined, or "fused," with a demographic database purchased from a marketing services company called Acxiom. That second database specified passengers' gender, income, occupation, and Social Security number; whether they rented or owned their home; how many years they had lived at their current address; how many children they had; how many adults lived in their household; and how many vehicles they owned.

Torch Concepts identified "several distinctive travel patterns" in the data and concluded that "known airline terrorists appear readily distinguishable from the normal JetBlue passenger patterns," according to a company PowerPoint presentation unearthed by travel writer and privacy activist Edward Hasbrouck and publicized by Wired News on September 18, 2003. A media uproar ensued, but a 2004 report from the Department of Homeland Security ultimately concluded that no criminal laws had been broken, because JetBlue provided the data directly to Torch and not to the federal government. (JetBlue did violate its own privacy policy, however.)

Another data fusion project launched in the wake of 9/11 was the Multistate Anti-Terrorism Information Exchange (Matrix), which was also shut down amid privacy concerns. According to a report by the DHS Privacy Office, the system was designed to allow law enforcement agencies in different states to easily search one another's computers, although the system "was over-sold as a pattern analysis tool for anti-terrorism purposes." The report found that Matrix was late in forming its privacy policy and that it "lacked adequate audit controls." Public support fell off, states pulled out, and the project was terminated.

Since then, a number of states and cities have partnered with DHS to create so-called "fusion centers," with the goal of helping sensitive information flow between federal, state, and even local law enforcement agencies. There were 58 fusion centers around the country by February 2009, according to the department's website, and DHS spent more than $254 million to support them between 2004 and 2007.

Few details of what actually happens at these centers have been made public. But in April 2008, Jack Tomarchio, then the department's principal deputy undersecretary for intelligence and analysis, told the Senate Committee on Homeland Security and Governmental Affairs that information from two U.S. fusion centers had been passed to a foreign government, which set up a terrorism investigation as a result. "DHS received a letter expressing that country's gratitude for the information," he testified. "This information would not have been gleaned without state and local participation."

At least in the eyes of the Bush administration, sacrificing the privacy of Americans to the security of the country had proved well worthwhile. But now the pendulum is swinging back, showing once again that our republic values privacy and will act to protect it from abuses—eventually.

Facebook

Here's a koan for the information age: Why do so many privacy activists have Facebook pages?

Originally conceived as a place for Harvard undergraduates to post their photos and cell-phone numbers—information that Harvard, because of privacy concerns, wasn't putting online back in 2003—Facebook has grown to be the fourth-most-popular "website" in the world, according to the Web services firm Alexa.

But Facebook is really a collection of applications powered by private information: a smart address book that friends and business contacts update themselves; a (mostly) spam-free messaging system; a photo-sharing site. And on Facebook, developers write seamlessly integrated applications.

These applications are troubling from a privacy perspective. Say you want to complete one of those cool Facebook surveys. Click a button and you'll be taken to a page with the headline "Allow Access?" Then you'll be told that using the application allows it to "pull your profile information, photos, your friends' info, and other content that it requires to work." How much information? There's no way to be sure, really—perhaps everything you've put into Facebook.

The roughly one in five Internet users who spend an average of 25 minutes each day on Facebook implicitly face a question every time they type into a Facebook page: Do they trust the site's security and privacy controls? The answer is inevitably yes.

That's the reason privacy activists are on Facebook: it's where the action is. It's easy to imagine a future where most personal messaging is done on such platforms. Activists and organizations that refuse to take part might find themselves irrelevant.

It was in a similar context that Scott McNealy, then CEO of Sun Microsystems, famously said, "You have zero privacy anyway. Get over it." In January 1999, McNealy was trying to promote a new technology for distributed computing that Sun had cooked up—an early version of what we might call "cloud computing" today—and reporters were pestering him about how the system would protect privacy. Four and a half years later, he told the San Francisco Chronicle, "The point I was making was someone already has your medical records. Someone has my dental records. Someone has my financial records. Someone knows just about everything about me."

Today it's not just medical and financial records that are stored on remote servers—it's everything. Consider e-mail. If you download it from Post Office Protocol (POP) accounts, as most Internet users still did in 1999, the mail is copied to your computer and then deleted from your ISP's servers. These days, however, most people use Web mail or the Internet Message Access Protocol (IMAP), which leaves a copy on the server until it is explicitly deleted. Most people don't know where that server is—it's just somewhere "in the cloud" of the Internet.

Services like Facebook, Gmail, and Google Docs are becoming wildly popular because they give users the freedom to access their data from home and from work without having to carry it back and forth. But leaving your data on some organization's servers creates all sorts of opportunities for mishap. The organization might have a bad employee who siphons out data for personal profit. Cyberthieves might break into its servers and try to steal lots of people's data at the same time. Or a hacker might specifically target your data and contact the organization, claiming to be you. All these are security threats—security threats that become privacy threats because it's your data.

Where We Are Now

I have spent a good part of my professional life looking for ways to make computer systems more secure, and I believe that many of the problems we face today are not only tractable—many of them have already been solved. The threat of data theft by insiders can he mitigated by paying employees enough, auditing their work, limiting the amount of authority that any one employee has, and harshly punishing any individual who abuses the employer's trust. Computer systems can be made immune to buffer-overflow attacks, one of the most common security vulnerabilities in recent years, by programming them in modern languages like Java and Python instead of 1980s standards like C and C++. We really do know how to build secure systems. Unfortunately, these systems cost more to develop, and using them would require us to abandon the ones we already have—at least for our critical applications.

But one fundamental problem is harder to solve: identifying people on the Internet. What happens if somebody impersonating you calls up a company and demands access to your data?

If Google or Yahoo were storefronts, they would ask to see a state-issued ID card. They might compare a photo of you that they took when you opened the account with the person now standing in their lobby. Yes, there are phony IDs, and there are scams. Nevertheless, identification technology works pretty well most of the time in the physical world.

It turns out that we essentially have the technology to solve this problem in the digital world as well. Yet the solutions that have been developed aren't politically tenable—not only because of perceived costs but also, ironically, because of perceived privacy concerns.

I understand these fears, but I think they are misplaced. When someone can wreak havoc by misappropriating your personal data, privacy is threatened far more by the lack of a reliable online identification system than it would be by the introduction of one. And it is likely that it would cost society far more money to live with poor security than to address it.

I believe that we will be unable to protect online privacy without a strong electronic identity system that's free to use and backed by the governments of the world—a true passport for online access. One of the fundamental duties of government is to protect the internal security of the nation so that commerce can take place. For hundreds of years, that has meant creating identification documents so that people can prove their citizenship and their identity. But the U.S. government has abdicated its responsibility in the online world, and businesses have made up their own systems—like asking for your Social Security number and address, and perhaps your favorite color.

The difficulty of identifying people in the electronic world is a problem for every single company, every single organization, every single website. And it is especially a problem for Facebook and Google, because at a very basic level, they don't know who their customers are. When you open an account at a bank, U.S. law requires that you prove your identity with some state-issued identification. Bank accounts are linked to an actual identity. But electronic accounts like those on Facebook and

Google aren't. They project an identity, but they aren't linked, really, to anything. That's a real problem if some hacker takes over your Gmail account and you need to get it back.

One solution would be to make driver's licenses and other state-issued IDs usable online by adding electronic chips. Just imagine: no more passwords to access your bank account, to buy something at Amazon, or to bid on eBay. Just insert your card. And if you lost the card, you could report it missing and get a new one. Instantly, all your online accounts would recognize the new credential and refuse to honor the old one.

Similar proposals have been made in the past: in the 1990s the U.S. Postal Service began working toward a system called the "U.S. Card." But the project never really got off the ground—party because the technology wasn't quite ready, but also because of significant public opposition. In fact, in the United States every attempt to improve identification credentials has provoked significant public opposition. Many privacy activists see mandatory ID cards as one of the hallmarks of a police state. And many state governments fear the costs.

Though a stronger identification system would undoubtedly harm some citizens through errors, I think the opposition is unfortunate. We're already being identified every time we use an online banking service, or make an online purchase, or even use Facebook. We're just being identified through ad hoc, broken systems that are easy for bad guys to exploit. If we had a single strong identity system, we could adopt legislation to protect it from inappropriate use. A California law enacted in 2003, for example, prevents bars, car dealers, and others from collecting information swiped from a driver's license for any purpose other than age verification or license authentication.

For more than 100 years, American jurisprudence has recognized privacy as a requirement for democracy, social relations, and human dignity. For nearly 50, we've understood that protecting privacy takes more than just controlling intrusions into your home; it also requires being able to control information about you that's available to businesses, government, and society at large. Even though Americans were told after 9/11 that we needed to choose between security and privacy, it's increasingly clear that without one we will never have the other.

We need to learn how to protect privacy by intention, not by accident. Although technology can help, my belief is that such protections need to start with clearly articulated polices. Just as Nixon created the Environmental Protection Agency to protect our environment, we need some kind of Privacy Protection Agency to give our rights a fighting chance. Our piecemeal approach is no longer acceptable.

SIMSON GARFINKEL is an associate professor at the naval postgraduate school in Monterey, CA, the views expressed in this article are those of the author and do not necessarily reflect the views of the U.S. Government or the Department of Defense.

From *Technology Review*, August 2009. Copyright © 2009 by Technology Review. Reprinted by permission via Copyright Clearance Center.

The Software Wars

Why You Can't Understand Your Computer

PAUL DE PALMA

On a bright winter morning in Philadelphia, in 1986, my downtown office is bathed in sunlight. I am the lead programmer for a software system that my firm intends to sell to the largest companies in the country, but like so many systems, mine will never make it to market. This will not surprise me. If the chief architect of the office tower on whose twenty-sixth floor I am sitting designed his structure with the seat-of-the-pants cleverness that I am using to design my system, prudence would advise that I pack my business-issue briefcase, put on my business-issue overcoat, say good-bye to all that sunlight, and head for the front door before the building crumbles like a Turkish high-rise in an earthquake.

But I am not prudent; nor am I paid to be. Just the opposite. My body, on automatic pilot, deflects nearly all external stimuli. I can carry on a rudimentary conversation, but my mind is somewhere else altogether. In a book-length profile of Ted Taylor, a nuclear-weapons designer, that John McPhee wrote for *The New Yorker*, Dr. Taylor's wife tells McPhee a wonderful story about her husband. Mrs. Taylor's sister visits for the weekend. Taylor dines with her, passes her in the hall, converses. He asks his wife on Monday morning—her sister having left the day before—when she expects her sister to arrive. Mrs. Taylor calls this state "metaphysical absence." You don't have to build sophisticated weaponry to experience it. When my daughter was younger, she used to mimic an old John Prine song. "Oh my stars," she sang, "Daddy's gone to Mars." As you will see, we workaday programmers have more in common with weapons designers than mere metaphysical absence.

My mind reels back from Mars when a colleague tells me that the *Challenger* has exploded. The *Challenger*, dream child of NASA, complex in the extreme, designed and built by some of the country's most highly trained engineers, is light-years away from my large, and largely uninspired, piece of data-processing software. If engineering were music, the *Challenger* would be a Bach fugue and my system "Home on the Range." Yet despite the differences in technical sophistication, the software I am building will fail for many of the same reasons that caused the *Challenger* to explode seconds after launch nearly twenty years ago.

Software's unreliability is the stuff of legend. *Software Engineering Notes,* a journal published by the ACM, the largest professional association of computer scientists, is known mostly for the tongue-in-cheek catalogue of technical catastrophes that appears at the beginning of each issue. In the March 2001 issue—I picked this off my shelf at random—you can read about planes grounded in L.A. because a Mexican air-traffic controller keyed in too many characters of flight description data, about a New York database built to find uninsured drivers, which snared many of the insured as well, about Florida eighth graders who penetrated their school's computer system, about Norwegian trains that refused to run on January 1, 2001, because of a faulty Year 2000 repair. The list goes on for seven pages and is typical of a column that has been running for many years.

People often claim that one of every three large-scale software systems gets canceled midproject. Of those that do make it out the door, three-quarters are never implemented: some do not work as intended; others are just shelved.

People often claim that one of every three large-scale software systems gets canceled midproject. Of those that do make it out the door, three-quarters are never implemented: some do not work as intended; others are just shelved. Matters grow even more serious with large systems whose functions spread over several computers—the very systems that advances in networking technology have made possible in the past decade. A few years ago, an IBM consulting group determined that of twenty-four companies surveyed, 55 percent built systems that were over budget; 68 percent built systems that were behind schedule; and 88 percent of the completed systems had to be redesigned. Try to imagine the same kind of gloomy numbers for civil engineering: three-quarters of all bridges carrying loads below specification; almost nine of ten sewage treatment plants, once completed, in need of redesign; one-third of highway projects canceled because technical problems have grown beyond the capacity of engineers to solve them. Silly? Yes. Programming has miles to go before it earns the title "software engineering."

In civil engineering, on the other hand, failures are rare enough to make the news. Perhaps the best-known example is the collapse of the Tacoma-Narrows Bridge. Its spectacular failure in 1940, because of wind-induced resonance, was captured on film and has been a staple of physics courses ever since. The collapse of the suspended walkway in the Kansas City Hyatt Regency in 1981 is a more recent example. It failed because structural engineers thought that verifying the design of connections joining the walkway segments was the job of their manufacturer. The manufacturer had a different recollection. The American Society of Civil Engineers quickly adopted a protocol for checking shop designs. These collapses are remarkable for two related reasons. First, bridge and building failures are so rare in the United States that when they do occur we continue to talk about them half a century later. Second, in both cases, engineers correctly determined the errors and took steps not to repeat them. Programmers cannot make a similar claim. Even if the cause of system failure is discovered, programmers can do little more than try not to repeat the error in future systems. Trying not to repeat an error does not compare with building well-known tolerances into a design or establishing communications protocols among well-defined players. One is exhortation. The other is engineering.

None of this is new. Responding to reports of unusable systems, cost overruns, and outright cancellations, the NATO Science Committee convened a meeting of scientists, industry leaders, and programmers in 1968. The term *software engineering* was invented at this conference in the hope that, one day, systematic, quantifiable approaches to software construction would develop. Over the intervening years, researchers have created a rich set of tools and techniques, from design practices to improved programming languages to techniques for proving program correctness. Sadly, anyone who uses computers knows that they continue to fail regularly, inexplicably, and, sometimes, wonderfully—*Software Engineering Notes* continues to publish pages of gloomy tales each quarter. Worse, the ACM has recently decided not to support efforts to license software engineers because, in its words, "there is no form of licensing that can be instituted today assuring public safety." In effect, software-engineering discoveries of the past thirty years may be interesting, but no evidence suggests that understanding them will improve the software-development process.

As the committee that made this decision surely knows, software-engineering techniques are honored mostly in the breach. In other words, business practice, as much as a lack of technical know-how, produces the depressing statistics I have cited. One business practice in particular ought to be understood. The characteristics of software often cited as leading to failure—its complexity, its utter plasticity, its free-floating nature, unhampered by tethers to the physical world—make it oddly, even paradoxically, similar to the practice of military procurement. Here is where the *Challenger* and my system, dead these twenty long years, reenter the story.

I n the mid-eighties I worked for a large management-consulting firm. Though this company had long employed a small group of programmers, mostly to support in-house systems, its software-development effort and support staff grew substantially, perhaps by a factor of ten, over a period of just a few years. A consulting firm, like a law firm, has a cap on its profits. Since it earns money by selling time, the number of hours its consultants can bill limits its revenue. And there is a ceiling to that. They have to eat and sleep, after all. The promise of software is the promise of making something from nothing. After development, only the number of systems that can be sold limits return on investment. In figuring productivity, the denominator remains constant. Forget about unhappy unions, as with cars and steel; messy sweatshops, as with clothing and shoes; environmental regulations, as with oil and petrochemicals. Software is a manufacturer's dream. The one problem, a very sticky problem indeed, is that it does not wear out. The industry responds by adding features, moving commercial software one step closer to military systems. More on this later. For now, just understand that my company, like so many others under the influence of the extraordinary attention that newly introduced personal computers were receiving at the time, followed the lure of software.

My system had one foot on the shrinking terra firma of large computers and the other in the roiling, rising sea of microcomputers. In fact, mine was the kind of system that three or four years earlier would have been written in COBOL, the language of business systems. It perhaps would have used a now obsolete database design, and it would have gone to market within a year. When told to build a similar system for a microcomputer, I did what I knew how to do. I designed a gray flannel system for a changing microcomputer market.

Things went along in a predictable if uninspired way until there was a shift in management. These changes occur so frequently in business that I had learned to ignore them. The routine goes like this. Everyone gets a new organization chart. They gather in conference rooms for mandatory pep talks. Then life goes on pretty much as before. Every so often, though, management decisions percolate down to the geeks, as when your manager arrives with a security officer and gives you five minutes to empty your desk, unpin your *Dilbert* comics, and go home. Or when someone like Mark takes over.

When that happened, I assumed falsely that we would go back to the task of producing dreary software. But this was the eighties. Junk bonds and leveraged buyouts were in the news. The arbitrageur was king. Business had become sexy. Mark, rumor had it, slept three hours a night. He shuttled between offices in New York, Philadelphia, and Montreal. Though he owned a house in Westchester County, now best known as the home of the Clintons, he kept an apartment in Philadelphia, where he managed to spend a couple of days each week. When Mark, the quintessential new manager ("My door is always open"), arrived, we began to live like our betters in law and finance. Great bags of bagels and cream cheese arrived each morning. We lunched in trendy restaurants. I, an erstwhile sixties radical, began to ride around in taxis, use my expense account, fly to distant cities for two-hour meetings. Life was sweet.

During this time, my daughter was an infant. Her 4:00 A.M. feeding was my job. Since I often had trouble getting back to sleep, I sometimes caught an early train to the office. One of these mornings my office phone rang. It was Mark. He sounded relaxed, as if finding me at work before dawn was no more surprising than bumping into a neighbor choosing apples at Safeway. This was a sign. Others followed. Once, Mark organized a dinner for our team in a classy hotel. When the time came for his speech, Mark's voice rose like Caesar's exhorting his troops before the Gallic campaign. He urged us to bid farewell to our wives and children. We would, he assured us, return in six months with our shields or upon them. I noticed then that a few of my colleagues were in evening dress. I felt like Tiresias among the crows. When programmers wear tuxedos, the world is out of joint.

Suddenly, as if by magic, we went from a handful of programmers producing a conventional system to triple that number, and the system was anything but conventional. One thing that changed was the programming language itself. Mark decided that the system would be splashier if it used a database-management system that had recently become commercially available for mainframes and was promised, shortly, for microcomputers. These decisions—hiring more people to meet a now unmeetable deadline; using a set of new and untested tools—represented two of the several business practices that have been at the heart of the software crisis. Frederick Brooks, in his classic book, *The Mythical Man-Month,* argues from his experience building IBM's System 360 operating system that any increased productivity achieved by hiring more people gets nibbled at by the increased complexity of communication among them. A system that one person can develop in thirty days cannot be developed in a single day by thirty people. This simple truth goes down hard in business culture, which takes, as an article of faith, the idea that systems can be decreed into existence.

The other practice, relying on new, untested, and wildly complex tools, is where software reigns supreme. Here, the tool was a relational database-management system. Since the late sixties, researchers have realized that keeping all data in a central repository, a database, with its own set of access techniques and backup mechanisms, was better than storing data with the program that used it. Before the development of database-management systems, it was common for every department in a company to have its own data, and for much of this data to overlap from department to department. So in a university, the registrar's office, which takes care of student records, and the controller's office, which takes care of student accounts, might both have copies of a student's name and address. The problem occurs when the student moves and the change has to be reported to two offices. The argument works less well for small amounts of data accessed by a single user, exactly the kind of application that the primitive microcomputers of the time were able to handle. Still, you could argue that a relational database-management system might be useful for small offices. This is exactly what Microsoft Access does. But Microsoft Access did not exist in 1986, nor did any other relational database-management system for microcomputers. Such systems had only recently become available for mainframes.

Something unique to software, especially new software: no experts exist in the sense that we might speak of an expert machinist, a master electrician, or an experienced civil engineer. There are only those who are relatively less ignorant.

One company, however, an infant builder of database-management systems, had such software for minicomputers and was promising a PC version. After weeks of meetings, after an endless parade of consultants, after trips to Washington, D.C., to attend seminars, Mark decided to go with the new product. One of these meetings illustrates something unique to software, especially new software: no experts exist in the sense that we might speak of an expert machinist, a master electrician, or an experienced civil engineer. There are only those who are relatively less ignorant. On an early spring evening, we met in a conference room with a long, polished wood table surrounded by fancy swivel chairs covered in gorgeous, deep purple fabric. The room's walls turned crimson from the setting sun. As the evening wore on, we could look across the street to another tower, its offices filled with miniature Bartlebys, bent over desks, staring into monitors, leafing through file cabinets. At the table with representatives from our company were several consultants from the database firm and an independent consultant Mark had hired to make sure we were getting the straight scoop.

Here we were: a management-consulting team with the best, though still less than perfect, grasp of what the proposed system was supposed to do, but almost no grasp of the tools being chosen; consultants who knew the tools quite well, but nothing about the software application itself, who were fully aware that their software was still being developed even as we spoke; and an independent consultant who did not understand either the software or its application. It was a perfect example of interdependent parasitism.

My company's sin went beyond working with complex, poorly understood tools. Neither the tools nor our system existed. The

database manufacturer had a delivery date and no product. Their consultants were selling us a nonexistent system. To make their deadline, I am confident they hired more programmers and experimented with unproven software from still other companies with delivery dates but no products. And what of *those* companies? You get the idea.

No one in our group had any experience with this software once we adopted it. Large systems are fabulously complex. It takes years to know their idiosyncrasies. Since the introduction of the microcomputer, however, nobody has had years to develop this expertise. Because software does not wear out, vendors must consistently add new features in order to recoup development costs. That the word processor you use today bears almost no resemblance to the one you used ten years ago has less to do with technological advances than with economic realities. Our company had recently acquired a smaller I company in the South. This company owned a mini computer for which a version of the database software had already been released. Mark decided that until the PC database was ready for release, we could develop our system on this machine, using 1,200-baud modems, a modem about one-fiftieth as fast as the one your cable provider tells you is too slow for the Web, and a whole lot less reliable.

Let me put this all together. We had a new team of programmers who did not understand the application, using ersatz software that they also did not understand, which was running on a kind of machine no one had ever used before, using a remote connection that was slow and unstable.

Weeks before, I had begun arguing that we could never meet the deadline and that none of us had the foggiest idea of how to go about building a system with the tools we had. This was bad form. I had been working in large corporations long enough to know that when the boss asks if something can be done, the only possible response is "I'm your boy." Business is not a Quaker meeting. Mark didn't get to be my boss by achieving consensus. I knew that arguing was a mistake, but somehow the more I argued, the more I became gripped by a self-righteous fervor that, while unattractive in anyone (who likes a do-gooder?), is suicide in a corporate setting. Can-do-ism is the core belief. My job was to figure out how to extend the deadline, simplify the requirements, or both—not second-guess Mark. One afternoon I was asked if I might like to step down as chief architect and take over the documentation group. This was not a promotion.

Sitting in my new cubicle with a Raskolnikovian cloud over my head, I began to look more closely at the database-management system's documentation. Working with yet another consultant, I filled a paper database with hypothetical data. What I discovered caused me to win the argument but lose the war. I learned that given the size of the software itself and the amount of data the average client would store, along with the overhead that comes with a sophisticated database, a running system would fill a microcomputer hard disk, then limited to 30 megabytes, several times over. If, by some stroke of luck, some effort of will, some happy set of coincidences that I had yet to experience personally, we were able to build the system, the client would run up against hardware constraints as soon as he tried to use it. After weeks of argument, my prestige was slipping fast. I had already been reduced to writing manuals for a system I had designed. I was the sinking ship that every clearheaded corporate sailor had already abandoned. My triumphant revelation that we could not build a workable system, even if we had the skill to do so, was greeted with (what else?) complete silence.

L ate in 1986 James Fallows wrote an article analyzing the *Challenger* explosion for the *New York Review of Books*. Instead of concentrating on the well-known O-ring problem, he situated the failure of the *Challenger* in the context of military procurement, specifically in the military's inordinate fondness for complex systems. This fondness leads to stunning cost overruns, unanticipated complexity, and regular failures. It leads to Osprey aircraft that fall from the sky, to anti-missile missiles for which decoys are easy to construct, to FA-22 fighters that are fabulously over budget. The litany goes on. What these failures have in common with the *Challenger* is, Fallows argues, "military procurement disease," namely, "over-ambitious schedules, problems born of too-complex design, shortages of spare parts, a 'can-do' attitude that stifles embarrassing truths ('No problem, Mr. President, we can lick those Viet Cong'), and total collapse when one component unexpectedly fails." Explanations for this phenomenon include competition among the services; a monopoly hold by defense contractors who are building, say, aircraft or submarines; lavish defense budgets that isolate military purchases from normal market mechanisms; the nature of capital-intensive, laptop warfare where hypothetical justifications need not—usually cannot—be verified in practice; and a little-boy fascination with things that fly and explode. Much of this describes the software industry too.

Fallows breaks down military procurement into five stages:

The Vegematic Promise, wherein we are offered hybrid aircraft, part helicopter, part airplane, or software that has more features than could be learned in a lifetime of diligent study. Think Microsoft Office here.

The Rosy Prospect, wherein we are assured that all is going well. I call this the 90 percent syndrome. I don't think I have ever supervised a project, either as a software manager overseeing professionals or as a professor overseeing students, that was not 90 percent complete whenever I asked.

The Big Technical Leap, wherein we learn that our system will take us to regions not yet visited, and we will build it using tools not yet developed. So the shuttle's solid-fuel boosters were more powerful than any previously developed boosters, and bringing it all back home, my system was to use a database we had never used before, running on a computer for which a version of that software did not yet exist.

The Unpleasant Surprise, wherein we learn something unforeseen and, if we are unlucky, calamitous. Thus, the shuttle's heat-resistant tiles, all 31,000 of them, had to be installed at the unexpected rate of 2.8 days per tile, and my system gobbled so much disk space that there was scarcely any room for data.

The House of Cards, wherein an unpleasant surprise, or two, or three, causes the entire system to collapse. The Germans flanked the Maginot Line, and in my case, once we learned that our reliance on a promised database package outstripped operating-system limits, the choices were: one, wait for advances in operating systems; two, admit a mistake, beg for forgiveness, and resolve to be more prudent in the future; or, three, push on until management pulls the plug.

In our case, the first choice was out of the question. We were up against a deadline. No one knew when, or if, the 30 MB disk limit would be broken. The second choice was just as bad. The peaceable kingdom will be upon us, the lamb will lie down with the lion, long before you'll find a hard-driving manager admitting an error. These guys get paid for their testosterone, and for men sufficiently endowed, in the famous words of former NASA flight director Gene Kranz, "failure is not an option." We were left with the third alternative, which is what happened. Our project was canceled. Inside the fun house of corporate decision making, Mark was promoted—sent off to manage a growing branch in the South. The programmers left or were reassigned. The consultant who gave me the figures for my calculations was fired for reasons that I never understood. I took advantage of my new job as documentation chief and wrote an application to graduate school in computer science. I spent the next few years, while a student, as a well-paid consultant to our firm.

Just what is it about software, even the most conventional, the most mind-numbing software, that makes it similar to the classiest technology on the planet? In his book *Trapped in the Net,* the Berkeley physicist turned sociologist, Gene Rochlin, has this to say about computer technology:

> Only in a few specialized markets are new developments in hardware and software responsive primarily to user demand based on mastery and the full use of available technical capacity and capability. In most markets, the rate of change of both hardware and software is dynamically uncoupled from either human or organizational learning logistics and processes, to the point where users not only fail to master their most recent new capabilities, but are likely to not even bother to try, knowing that by the time they are through the steep part of their learning curve, most of what they have learned will be obsolete.

To give a homey example, I spent the last quarter hour fiddling with the margins on the draft copy of this article. Microsoft Word has all manner of arcane symbols—Exacto knives, magnifying glasses, thumbtacks, globes—plus an annoying little paper clip homunculus that pops up, seemingly at random, to offer help that I always decline. I don't know what any of this stuff does. Since one of the best-selling commercial introductions to the Microsoft Office suite now runs to nearly a thousand pages, roughly the size of Shakespeare's collected works, I won't find out either. To the untrained eye, that is to say, to mine, the bulk of what constitutes Microsoft Word appears to be useful primarily to brochure designers and graphic artists. This unused cornucopia is not peculiar to Microsoft, nor even to microcomputer software. Programmers were cranking out obscure and poorly documented features long before computers became a consumer product.

Though the medium on which it is stored might decay, the software itself, because it exists in the same ethereal way as a novel, scored music, or a mathematical theorem, lasts as long as the ability to decode it.

But why? Remember the nature of software, how it does not wear out. Adding features to a new release is similar, but not identical, to changes in fashion or automobile styling. In those industries, a change in look gives natural, and planned, obsolescence a nudge. Even the best-built car or the sturdiest pair of jeans will eventually show signs of wear. Changes in fashion just speed this process along. Not so with software. Though the medium on which it is stored might decay, the software itself, because it exists in the same ethereal way as a novel, scored music, or a mathematical theorem, lasts as long as the ability to decode it. That is why Microsoft Word and the operating systems that support it, such as Microsoft Windows, get more complex with each new release.

But this is only part of the story. While software engineers at Oracle or Microsoft are staying up late concocting features that no one will ever use, hardware engineers at Intel are inventing ever faster, ever cheaper processors to run them. If Microsoft did not take advantage of this additional capacity, someone else would. Hardware and software are locked in an intricate and pathological dance. Hardware takes a step. Software follows. Hardware takes another step, and so on. The result is the Vegematic Promise. Do you want to write a letter to your bank? Microsoft Word will work fine. Do you need to save your work in any one of fifteen different digital formats? Microsoft Word will do the job. Do you want to design a Web page, lay out a brochure, import clip art, or include the digitally rendered picture of your dog? The designers at Microsoft have anticipated your needs. They were able to do this because the designers at Intel anticipated theirs. What no one anticipated was the unmanageable complexity of the final product from the user's perspective and the stunning, internal complexity of the product that Microsoft brings to market. In another time, this kind of complexity would have been reserved for enterprises of true consequence, say the Manhattan Project or the *Apollo* missions. Now the complexity that launched a thousand ships, placed men on the moon, controlled nuclear fission and fusion, the complexity that demanded of its designers years of training and still failed routinely, sits on my desk. Only this time, developers with minimal, often informal, training, using tools that change before they master them, labor for my daughter, who uses the fruits of their genius to chat with her friends about hair, makeup, and boys.

As I say, accelerating complexity is not just a software feature. Gordon Moore, one of Intel's founders, famously observed, in 1965, that the number of transistors etched on an integrated circuit board doubled every year or so. In the hyperbolic world of computing, this observation, altered slightly for the age of microprocessors, has come to be called Moore's Law: the computing power of microprocessors tends to double every couple of years. Though engineers expect to reach physical limits sometime in the first quarter of this century, Moore has been on target for the past couple dozen years. As a related, if less glamorous example, consider the remote control that accompanies electronic gadgetry these days. To be at the helm of your VCR, TV, DVD player, stereo (never mind lights, fans, air-conditioning, and fireplace), is to be a kind of Captain Kirk of home and hearth. The tendency, the Vegematic Promise, is to integrate separate remote controls into a single device. A living room equipped with one of these marvels is part domicile, part mission control. I recently read about one fellow who, dazzled by the complexity of integrated remotes, fastened his many devices to a chunk of four-by-four with black electrical tape. I have ceded operation of my relatively low-tech equipment to my teenage daughter, the only person in my house with the time or inclination to decipher its runic symbols.

But software is different in one significant way. Hardware, by and large, works. When hardware fails, as early versions of the Pentium chip did, it is national news. It took a computer scientist in Georgia doing some fairly obscure mathematical calculations to uncover the flaw. If only software errors were so well hidden. Engineers, even electrical engineers, use well-understood, often off-the-shelf, materials with well-defined limits. To offer a simple example, a few years ago I taught a course in digital logic. This course, standard fare for all computer science and computer engineering majors, teaches students how to solve logic problems with chips. A common lab problem is to build a seven-segment display, a digital display of numbers, like what you might find on an alarm clock. Students construct it using a circuit board and chips that we order by the hundreds. These chips are described in a catalogue that lists the number and type of logical operations encoded, along with the corresponding pins for each. If you teach software design, as I do, this trespass into the world of the engineer is instructive. Software almost always gets built from scratch. Though basic sorting and string manipulation routines exist, these must be woven together in novel ways to produce new software. Each programmer becomes a craftsman with a store of tricks up his sleeve. The more experienced the programmer, the more tricks.

To be fair, large software-development operations maintain libraries of standard routines that developers may dip into when the need arises. And for the past ten years or so, new object-oriented design and development techniques have conceived of ways to modularize and standardize components. Unfortunately, companies have not figured out how to make money by selling components, probably for the same reason that the music industry is under siege from Napster's descendants. If your product is only a digital encoding, it can be copied endlessly at almost no cost. Worse, the object-oriented programming paradigm seems often to be more complex than a conventional approach. Though boosters claim that programmers using object-oriented techniques are more productive and that their products are easier to maintain, this has yet to be demonstrated.

Software is peculiar in another way. Though hardware can be complex in the extreme, software obeys no physical limits. It can be as feature-rich as its designers wish. If the computer's memory is too small, relatively obscure features can be stored on disk and called into action only when needed. If the computer's processor is too slow, just wait a couple of years. Designers want your software to be very feature-rich indeed, because they want to sell the next release, because the limits of what can be done with a computer are not yet known, and, most of all, because those who design computer systems, like the rich in the world of F. Scott Fitzgerald, are different from you and me. Designers love the machine with a passion not constrained by normal market mechanisms or even, in some instances, by managerial control.

On the demand side, most purchases are made by institutions, businesses, universities, and the government, where there is an obsessive fear of being left behind, while the benefits, just as in the military, are difficult to measure. The claims and their outcomes are too fuzzy to be reconciled. Since individual managers are rarely held accountable for decisions to buy yet more computing equipment, it should not surprise you that wildly complex technology is being underused. Thus: computer labs that no one knows what to do with, so-called smart classrooms that are obsolete before anyone figures out how to use them, and offices with equipment so complicated that every secretary doubles as a systems administrator. Even if schools and businesses buy first and ask questions later, *you* don't have to put up with this. You could tell Microsoft to keep its next Windows upgrade, your machine is working very nicely right now, thank you. But your impertinence will cost you. Before long, your computer will be an island where the natives speak a language cut off from the great linguistic communities. In a word, you will be isolated. You won't be able to buy new software, edit a report you wrote at work on your home computer, or send pictures of the kids to Grandma over the Internet. Further, a decision to upgrade later will be harder, perhaps impossible, without losing everything your trusted but obsolete computer has stored. This is what Rochlin means when he writes that hardware and software are "dynamically uncoupled from either human or organizational learning." To which I would add "human organizational need."

What if the massively complex new software were as reliable as hardware usually is? We still wouldn't know how to use it, but at least our screens wouldn't lock up and our projects wouldn't be canceled midstream. This reliability isn't going to happen, though, for at least three reasons. First, programmers love complexity, love handcrafted systems, with an ardor that most of us save for our spouses. You have heard about the heroic hours worked by employees of the remaining Internet start-ups. This is true, but true only partly so that young men can be millionaires by thirty. There is something utterly beguiling about programming a computer. You lose track of time, of space even. You begin eating pizzas and forgetting to bathe. A phone call is an unwelcome intrusion. Second, nobody can really oversee a programmer's work, short of reading code line by line. It is simply too complex for anyone but its creator to understand, and even for him it will be lost in the mist after a couple of weeks. The 90 percent syndrome is a natural consequence. Programmers, a plucky lot, always think that they are further along than they are.

It is difficult to foresee an obstacle on a road you have never traveled. Despite all efforts to the contrary, code is handcrafted. Third—and this gets to the heart of the matter—system specifications have the half-life of an adolescent friendship. Someone—the project manager, the team leader, a programmer, or, if the system is built on contract, the client—always has a new idea. It is as if a third of the way through building a bridge, the highway department decided it should have an additional traffic lane and be moved a half mile downstream.

Notice that not one of the reasons I have mentioned for failed software projects is technical. Researchers trying to develop a discipline of software engineering are fond of saying that there is no silver bullet: no single technical fix, no single software-development tool, no single, yet-to-be-imagined programming technique that will result in error-free, maintainable software. The reason for this is really quite simple. The problem with software is not technical. Remember my project. It fell into chaos because of foolish business decisions. Had Mark resisted the temptation to use the latest software-development products, a temptation he succumbed to not because they would produce a better system, but because they would seem flashier to prospective clients, we might have gone to market with only the usual array of problems.

Interestingly, the geek's geek, Bruce Schneier, in his recent book, *Secrets and Lies*, has come to similar conclusions about computer security: the largest problems are not technical. A computer security expert, Schneier has recanted his faith in the impermeability of cryptographic algorithms. Sophisticated cryptography is as resistant as ever to massive frontal attacks. The problem is that these algorithms are embedded in computer systems that are administered by real human beings with all their charms and foibles. People use dictionary entries or a child's name as passwords. They attach modems to their office computers, giving hackers easy access to a system that might otherwise be more thoroughly protected. They run versions of Linux with all network routines enabled, or they surreptitiously set up Web servers in their dormitory rooms. Cryptographic algorithms are no more secure than their contexts.

Until computing is organized like engineering, law, and medicine through a combination of self-regulating professional bodies, government-imposed standards, and the threat of litigation, inviting a computer into your house or office is to invite complexity masquerading as convenience.

Though the long march is far from over, we know a lot more about managing the complexity of software systems than we did twenty years ago. We have better programming languages and techniques, better design principles, clever software to keep track of changes, richly endowed procedures for moving from conception to system design to coding to testing to release. But systems still fail and projects are still canceled with the same regularity as in the bad old days before object-oriented techniques, before software engineering becomes an academic discipline. These techniques are administered by the same humans who undermine computer security. They include marketing staff who decree systems into existence; companies that stuff yet more features into already overstuffed software; designers and clients who change specifications as systems are being built; programmers who are more artist than engineer; and, of course, software itself that can be neither seen, nor touched, nor measured in any significant way.

There is no silver bullet. But just as the *Challenger* disaster might have been prevented with minimal common sense, so also with software failure. Keep it simple. Avoid exotic and new programming techniques. Know that an army of workers is no substitute for clear design and ample time. Don't let the fox, now disguised as a young man with a head full of acronyms, guard the chicken coop. Make only modest promises. Good advice, certainly, but no one is likely to listen anytime soon. Until computing is organized like engineering, law, and medicine through a combination of self-regulating professional bodies, government-imposed standards, and, yes, the threat of litigation, inviting a computer into your house or office is to invite complexity masquerading as convenience. Given the nature of computing, even these remedies may fall short of the mark.

But don't despair. If software engineering practice is out of reach, you still have options. For starters, you could just say no. You could decide that the ease of buying plane tickets online is not worth the hours you while away trying to get your printer to print or your modem to dial. Understand that saying no requires an ascetic nature: abstinence is not terribly attractive to most of us. On the other hand, you could sign up for broadband with the full knowledge that your computer, a jealous lover, will demand many, many Saturday afternoons. Most people are shocked when they learn that their computer requires more care than, say, their refrigerator. Yet I can tell you that its charms are immeasurably richer. First among them is the dream state. It's almost irresistible.

Paul De Palma is associate professor of mathematics and computer science at Gonzaga University. His essay "http://www.when_is_enough_enough?.com" appeared in the *Winter 1999* issue.

From *American Scholar*, Vol. 74, No. 1, Winter 2005, pp. 69–83. Copyright © 2005 by Paul DePalma. Reprinted by permission of American Scholar, Phi Beta Kappa.

False Reporting on the Internet and the Spread of Rumors
Three Case Studies

PAUL HITLIN

Following the tragic events of September 11, 2001, a significant number of unsubstantiated rumors circulated around the Internet. One email pointed to the existence of prophecies by Nostradamus written hundreds of years earlier that predicted the attacks. Another accused Israel of masterminding the strikes and that thousands of Jews were told in advance to stay home from work that morning. The Internet allowed for a vast audience to spread these rumors along with the technology to facilitate their transmission, even though there was little evidence to support them and the rumors were later proven incorrect. Considering this spread of rumors, Stephen O'Leary (2002) writes:

> What may be hard for mainstream journalists to understand is that, in crisis situations, the social functions of rumor are virtually indistinguishable from the social functions of 'real news.' People spread rumors via the Net for the same reason that they read their papers or tune into CNN: they are trying to make sense of their world. (pg. 3)

O'Leary claims that these rumors fill a need for consumers of news that is very similar to the void that 'real news' fills. However, are the consequences the same? These Internet rumors help people to make sense of their world following a tragedy, although the lasting consequences are potentially much more harmful.

The Internet is certainly not responsible for errors in journalism. Every medium of news has a history of misreported stories. However, the nature of the Internet has created a new method for consumers to get their news and allowed for far greater numbers of people to become involved with the production and dissemination of news. As a consequence, cyberjournalism and the Internet have had real effects on both the process of reporting and subsequent public discourse.

How are errors in Internet journalism corrected online? What are the overarching consequences of errors that appear on Internet websites? Jim Hall (2001) believes that one problem with instant news appearing on the Internet is that the way errors are handled does not adequately address the fact that an error was made. He writes, "The problem with instant news is that when it is wrong it tends to be buried, sedimenting into and reinforcing its context, rather than corrected" (p. 133). Errors of Internet reporting do not often get identified and corrected as they do in newspapers. Instead, even if the editors of the website where the error first appeared change their site to remove the error, often the same false information will have already spread throughout other websites and emails. These rumors can become part of a public folklore even if there are no facts to support the original reports.

This paper will first consider Hall's assertion that errors are buried rather than corrected, and will examine the reasons Internet reporting leads to false reports. Then, three case studies of significant false reports on the Internet will be compared to the theories behind cyberjournalism in order to understand why the errors occurred and the impacts of these stories. Investigating these three examples will help us to begin to understand how we can decrease the influence of false reports in the future.

The first case study is the plane crash of TWA flight 800 in 1996. Even before full investigations were conducted, the Internet was full of reports of missiles or other causes behind the crash, the impacts of which would reach as far as the White House. The second case study will examine Matt Drudge's report that former White House special assistant Sidney Blumenthal physically abused his wife. The third case study will take a look at the pervasive rumors that the death of former Bill Clinton aide Vince Foster was a murder, not a suicide, even though numerous investigations have concluded that these accusations are unsupported. This incident is a clear example of how partisan politics can play a role in the spread of false reports on the Internet.

There has been much discussion about what distinguishes a 'journalist' working for a mainstream news source from a self-titled 'reporter' who never leaves his/ her computer and instead just links to reports on other sites. While these distinctions are important and worth discussing, it will not be within the realm of this study to draw out these distinctions. Instead, this paper will consider news reports that appear on the Internet regardless of whether or not the site displaying the report considers itself a news source. As we will see, public opinion can often be influenced as much from rumors on sites with little credibility as it can from more mainstream sources.

Reasons for Cyberjournalism Errors

Before considering the specific cases of false reporting, it is important to understand why the nature of the Internet may encourage reporting errors. Philip Seib (2001) points out that the Internet is not alone in containing factual errors. He writes, "the Web really is little different from other media in terms of its potential to abuse and be abused and its capability for self-governance" (pp. 129–130). The Internet itself, the actual technology, can not be held responsible for false reports since those reports have existed in all forms of media. However, there are qualities of the Internet and the manner in which news is reported on the Web that create differences in how frequently errors appear and what results as a consequence.

The causes of most cyberjournalism errors can be separated into four main categories. Let us now turn to each cause and examine it in turn.

1. The Need for Speed

The first and probably most significant reason for false reporting on the Internet is the 24-hour a day news cycle that the Internet promotes. With the development of newspapers, the news cycle was a daylong process that ended with having a story included in the next day's edition of the paper. This cycle changed with the expansion of cable television channels devoted entirely to news such as CNN and later MSNBC and Fox News. The cycle was expanded even further by the development of the Internet which is available to consumers 24-hours a day. Because of the constant need to keep both cable television and the Internet supplied with new information, expectations of news deadlines have shifted. As Seib notes, in the current information age, the deadline for reporters is always 'now' (p. 142).

Competitive pressures have also contributed to an emphasis being placed more on timeliness than accuracy. A number of Internet sites, such as Matt Drudge's *Drudge Report,* are one-person operations that issue reports on gossip and rumor without being constrained by traditional standards of reporting. These sites apply pressure to other news organizations to be the first to report a story or risk being scooped. Drudge himself believes that "absolute truth matters less than absolute speed" (Seib, 2001, p. 143). He also suggests that since we live in an information economy, complete accuracy is not possible or even necessary. Drudge focuses instead on immediacy and believes that the Web encourages this type of reporting (Hall, 2002, p. 148).

The pressure on reporters to be the first with a story has detracted from more traditional methods of journalism. Because the goal used to be to get a report into the next day's newspaper or that evening's nightly news television broadcast, reporters had more time for fact-checking. The 24-hour-a-day news cycle has decreased the time reporters have to assure accuracy and as a result, many errors found on the Internet can be attributed to the competitive pressure for journalists to be the first to break a specific news story.

2. The Desire to Attract 'Hits'

Competition among websites is also a cause for some false reports. Websites have financial incentives to attract visitors to their sites, whether it is through advertising or a desire to widen the site's influence. Hall argues that journalism on the Web has promoted the idea that news is 'infotainment' and more at the mercy of the demands of the marketplace than to its audiences (Hall, 2001, p. 155). Websites must fill the desires of consumers, or risk losing those consumers to other sites that either get the information first or are even more sensational in their reporting.

Furthermore, with the ability of Internet users to visit almost any news source in the world, as opposed to being confined to their local newspapers or television stations, the competition on the Web exacerbates the desire of sites to get the story first. Most news sites are updated several times a day, and competition forces those sites to get the story first or risk being thought of as irrelevant or out-of-date.

3. Political Gains

The specific source of many Internet rumors is often difficult to ascertain. However, certain rumors on the Internet are clearly promoted for partisan political gain and to advance a particular ideology.

Even after four investigations came to the same conclusions about Vince Foster's death, certain political groups were still spreading false reports in order to promote their own cause. For example, a fund-raising letter sent out by anti-Clinton groups asked for $1,000 donations in order to support the "Clinton Investigation Commission" which would investigate the claim that Foster was murdered (Piacente, 1997). Opponents of the Clinton administration perpetuated this false report to the exclusion of evidence in the case. These anti-Clinton groups were less concerned with accuracy than with forwarding a partisan agenda and the persistence of this specific rumor can be attributed to their political motives.

4. Attraction to Scandal

News, and specifically news on the Web, is often led by scandal and the concept of the spectacular rather than issues of depth (Hall, 2001, p. 137). For example, reports that TWA flight 800 was brought down by a missile were much more exciting than a report that a technical problem in the plane caused the crash. While some sites did wait for investigations into the cause of the crash to make conclusions about what actually brought the plane down, other sites used more dramatic rumors of missile fire to headline their reports. The competition between sites on the Web and the ability for consumers to move rapidly between those sites furthers the need for reporters to lead with scandal in order to catch consumers' attention. This desire for the spectacular, along with an emphasis on scandal, often leads to other false reports on the Internet.

Correction Policy, Social Cascades, and Online Credibility

Now that we have seen the four main reasons errors are found on the Internet, another key issue to understand is how those mistakes are corrected. There is still no singular method that websites use to correct errors, but as Seib (2001) writes:

> The easiest way to fix a mistake is simply to erase it and replace it with the correct information. That is a temptation unique to electronic publication, since there is no "original" version in the print or video archives . . . This is fine for readers who come to the site after the correction has been made. But failure to post a formal notice of correction implies that there was never an error, and that is less than honest. (pp. 154–155)

The question of how to correct a mistake once it is discovered causes Hall to suggest that the nature of Internet journalism reinforces the error's context rather than corrects the false information. While some retractions are clearly posted, as was the case with Matt Drudge following the accusations against Sidney Blumenthal, often the error has already spread to other sources. As a result, whether or not the original source is corrected no longer matters because the information will have already moved onto other places on the Web.

The result of this spread of Internet rumors is a phenomenon described by Cass Sunstein as one of 'social cascades.' Sunstein suggests that groups of people often move together in a direction of one set of beliefs or actions. He refers to this as a cascade effect (Sunstein, 2002, p. 80). Information can travel and become entrenched even if that information is incorrect. Sunstein argues that the Internet, with its wide reach and seemingly unending amount of websites and emails, greatly increases the likelihood of social cascades. Rumors can be passed to many users and spread quickly. The result is that the information appears believable solely due to the fact that the information has been repeated so many times. Richard Davis (1999) sums up the potential danger of this phenomenon:

> Anyone can put anything on the Internet and seemingly does. Often, one cannot be sure of the reliability of the information provided. Reliability diminishes exponentially as the information is passed from user to user and e-mail list to e-mail list until it acquires a degree of legitimacy by virtue of its widespread dissemination and constant repetition. (p. 44)

A number of other factors also contribute to the believability of information passed on the Internet. Richard Davis and Diana Owen (1998) discuss many of the reasons why 'new media,' consisting of the Internet, talk radio, and interactive television, often engage users in different ways than previous forms of news. They claim that much of new media relies on active participation by users rather than a more passive relationship between users and newspapers or earlier television programs. Davis and Owen describe the influence of this connection:

> The degree of involvement or interactivity with media is linked to the level of an audience member's media consumption and the strength of the effects of the communication. People who have a highly active relationship with a particular medium, such as callers to talk radio programs, may be more likely to establish a regular habit of attending to the medium and are more likely to be influenced by content than those whose acquaintance with the communication source is more casual. (p. 160)

Internet users who participate in online activities are not only more likely to be influenced by content they see online, but new media has a capacity to create strong psychological bonds between users and the media source. Davis and Owen add, "Individuals form personal relationships with their television sets and their computers. They treat computers as if they are people, talking to them, ascribing personalities to them and reacting to them emotionally when computers hand out praise or criticism during an interactive session" (p. 160). Users have greater influence over the content of media on the Web than in previous forms of media, whether it results from emailing articles of interest or responding to online polls and questionnaires. These interactions contribute to the perceived credibility that Internet users ascribe to information they receive over the Web. Stories that might be disregarded as false had they been disseminated through other forms of media often facilitate a social cascade effect if that information is spread online.

Having considered both why errors appear on the Internet and the difficulty in effectively correcting false information, let us now consider three cases of prominent false reports on the Internet and how those instances were handled.

Case Study One: The Crash of TWA Flight 800 in 1996

A clear example of how constant repetition of an erroneous report can result in widespread belief can be seen in the wake of the crash of TWA Flight 800. On July 17, 1996, the passenger flight left JFK International Airport in New York en route to Paris, but tragically crashed into the Long Island Sound. All 230 passengers and crew on board died.

Almost immediately, the National Transportation Safety Board (NTSB) began investigating the causes of the crash and rumors started to spread throughout the Internet as to what lead to the tragedy. Three main theories quickly surfaced as to what caused the crash: the crash was an act of terrorism conducted from onboard the flight; a mechanical malfunction was responsible for bringing down the plane; or the plane was shot down by a surface-to-air missile (Cobb & Primo, 2003, p. 104).

Some evidence initially indicated the crash could be a result of terrorism, either an onboard bomb or a projectile fired at the plane from the ground. The accident took place several days before the beginning of the 1996 Summer Olympics in Atlanta, which later become a target of a bombing attack. Some observers felt the timing of the plane crash indicated that it was somehow connected to international terrorism. In addition, numerous eyewitnesses reported having seen a streak of light approaching the plane before the explosion (Charles, 2001, p. 218). As the NTSB and the FBI began to investigate, numerous signals from the federal government indicated that all three potential theories were in play. As much as six months into a very public investigation, the NTSB was still declaring that all three theories remained as possibilities (Negroni, 2001). This did not change until March of 1997, when federal investigators began to dismiss theories of a missile bringing TWA Flight 800 down, claiming there was "no physical evidence" of such an attack (CNN.com, 1997).

As the investigation into the crash progressed and began to rule out terrorism, rumors persisted throughout the Internet that a government cover-up was concealing the real causes. At the forefront of those rumors was Pierre Salinger, a former press secretary to John F. Kennedy and correspondent for ABC News. Salinger insisted that he had a letter from French intelligence proving that a U.S. Navy missile ship shot down TWA Flight 800, and the FBI was covering up the act. Salinger's claims were reported in numerous news outlets. In addition, Salinger and several other journalists published a report in *Paris Match* stating that radar images existed that proved that a missile hit the plane (Harper, 1998, p. 85).

Salinger's credentials and his unwillingness to give up on his theory lent great credibility to the missile story. Many people on the Internet who believed the government was trying to hide something picked up on his writings. Interestingly enough, the letter that Salinger claimed had come from French intelligence was instead a memo that had been circulating on the Internet for several months written by a former United Air Lines pilot named Richard Russell. As Mark Hunter writes in his Salon .com article, Salinger's insistence on promoting his conspiracy theory of both the missile and the FBI cover-up, even with scare evidence, actually harmed the real investigation by causing a significant distraction for investigators. It also caused further psychological stress on the family members of the victims of the crash who were forced to revisit the circumstances as a result of these repeated allegations.

By the time the NTSB issued its final report on the crash in August of 2000, much of the talk of conspiracy theories relating to the crash had disappeared. In 2001, the Federal Aviation Agency (FAA) acted in response to what was believed to be the actual cause of the crash and issued safety rules to minimize flammable vapors and decrease the risk of a tank igniting (Cobb & Primo, 2003, p. 117). However, the consequences of the crash rumors can be seen both in continuing public discourse and actions taken by upper levels of the federal government.

The immediate rumors following the crash about a possible bomb or missile attack led to direct government action. In the days that followed the accident, before much hard evidence was discovered, President Clinton issued a tightening of security at airports throughout the country in order to try to prevent any acts of terrorism (Cobb & Primo, 2003, p. 106). Clinton later created the White House Commission on Aviation Safety, led by Vice President Al Gore, which issued recommendations for improving airline safety (Cobb & Primo, 2003, pp. 110–111). Just the possibility of a terrorist or missile attack was enough for the federal government to react strongly and tighten security.

What role did the Internet play in promoting and maintaining the false rumors about the crash of TWA Flight 800? Internet sites were not alone in reporting the rumors about the crash. Many newspapers, including the *Washington Post* and *New York Times,* also reported the possibilities of a bomb or terror attack (Cobb & Primo, 2003, pp. 107–108). However, the Internet did allow for certain aspects of the story to persist even when the evidence against the rumors was mounting. For one thing, a letter written by Richard Russell that circulated by email throughout the Internet played a key role in Salinger's claims about a government cover-up. Whether or not Salinger knew the true source of the letter, the circulation of the note alone added some perceived credibility to the rumor. This Internet 'error' was not corrected and removed. Instead, as Hall suggested, the nature of the Internet embedded the rumor. The circulation continued even after the NTSB determined it was false: a clear example of a social cascade facilitated by the Internet, moving many to believe the government was hiding information and not telling the full story about the crash.

To further this notion about the impact of these rumors, one only has to look to the Internet today, more than seven years after the crash, to see how public discourse has been influenced. While the Internet is full of conspiracy theories and anti-government rhetoric, a simple search can still find many websites that maintain that the TWA crash was a government cover-up. A clear example is the website whatreallyhappened .com. One can still go to this site at any time and read about how the government is hiding secrets and promoting beliefs that the "witnesses who saw a missile hit the jumbo jet are all drunks" (whatreallyhappened.com, 2002). To any person deciding to conduct research into the causes of this plane crash today, the Internet is a rich resource consisting of both facts about the accident and significant rumor and innuendo.

Case Study Two: Sidney Blumenthal vs. Matt Drudge and Internet Libel

While some Internet rumors persist on numerous websites, others can be linked more closely with one specific site, as is the case with a report that appeared on Matt Drudge's website, drudgereport.com, in 1997. Matt Drudge's one-man newsroom is most well known for breaking the story about President Bill Clinton's Oval Office affair with a White House intern. Along with breaking that story, Drudge has had 'exclusives' with a number of other stories, some of which turned out not to be true at all. Included among these was the report that Bill Clinton had fathered an illegitimate black son, a report that was later proven to be false (Hall, 2001, p. 129).

On August 8, 1997, Drudge chose to report on his website allegations about White House special assistant Sidney Blumenthal. Writing about a Republican operative who was facing allegations of spousal abuse, Drudge issued the 'exclusive' on his website that included the following:

> The *Drudge Report* has learned that top GOP operatives who feel there is a double-standard of only reporting [sic] shame believe they are holding an ace card: New White House recruit Sidney Blumenthal has a spousal abuse past that has been effectively covered up.
>
> The accusations are explosive.
>
> "There are court records of Blumenthal's violence against his wife," one influential Republican [sic], who demanded anonymity, tells the *Drudge Report*. (Blumenthal, 2003, pp. 239–240)

Drudge goes on to write that one White House source claimed the allegations were entirely false and that Drudge had been unsuccessful in his attempts to contact Blumenthal regarding these charges.

Three problems existed for Drudge in relation to this story. First, no court records existed that claimed Blumenthal abused his wife. Second, Drudge had not in fact made any attempts to contact Blumenthal. And third, Sidney Blumenthal decided to sue Matt Drudge and the Internet carrier of his column, American Online (AOL), for libel after other conservative news sources such as the *New York Post* and talk radio programs picked up the story (Blumenthal, 2003, p. 241).

This false Internet report was unique in that the origin of the rumor on the Web was clear along with who was responsible for spreading the rumor. Because of this, Blumenthal did have an opportunity to confront his accuser, which he did the day after the report first appeared. Blumenthal and his lawyer sent a letter to Drudge demanding to know the sources of the report. If Drudge did not comply, Blumenthal threatened to take "appropriate action" (Blumenthal, 2003, p. 244). In direct response to the threat, Drudge printed a retraction on his website that read, "I am issuing a retraction of my information regarding Sidney Blumenthal that appeared in the Drudge Report on August 11, 1997" (Blumenthal, 2003, p. 247). Drudge never officially apologized for the specific claim, although he was quoted as saying, "I apologize if any harm has been done. The story was issued in good faith. It was based on two sources who clearly were operating from a political motivation" (Kurtz, 1997).

While the lawsuit proceeded against Drudge with the blessing of President Clinton and the White House, the final result was not nearly as dramatic as the initial report. In May of 2001, Drudge and Blumenthal settled the suit out of court, and Blumenthal agreed to pay $2,500 to Drudge to reimburse travel expenses (Kurtz, 2001). Blumenthal claimed that he settled the suit because Drudge had endless financial backing from conservative groups and the suit was doing little more than providing additional exposure for Drudge (Blumenthal, 2003, p. 784). One interesting side note to this case is that early in the

process, a U.S. District judge had ruled that the Internet service provider, AOL, could not be a defendant in the libel case even though they had paid Drudge for his work. This decision was a significant victory for Internet service providers in protecting them from lawsuits concerning the content that appears on their own websites (Swartz, 1998).

Unlike the rumors about the TWA crash, this case study is much clearer in terms of who was responsible for placing the rumor online. Defamation of character is common in the Internet world, but Blumenthal viewed his lawsuit as an opportunity to make a larger point, "bringing the Internet under the same law that applied to the rest of the press" (Blumenthal, 2003, p. 471). Judging exactly how successful he was in doing so and whether future Internet sites will be as willing to publish unsubstantiated rumors is difficult. Drudge, for one, continues to publish numerous stories with seemingly little fear about being incorrect. However, this example does illustrate one occurrence where a retraction was issued on the same Internet site as the original error. Did the retraction correct the harm that resulted from a false story? Clearly Sidney Blumenthal did not feel so and continued his libel lawsuit even after the retraction was issued.

In addition, this news report was more a result of a partisan political agenda than it was an issue of Drudge trying to beat his competition by issuing an exclusive story not available on any other site. Drudge has been accused by many of having strong ties to conservative political groups who may have planted the Blumenthal story, but there seem to be no indications that other news sites were in competition with Drudge to be the first to issue this report. He would not thus have been facing a shortened time to check sources and facts. Drudge himself acknowledged that his sources for this story were acting on their own political agenda.

Case Study Three: The Suicide of White House Aide Vince Foster

Unlike the previous case study, the origins of the rumors involving the suicide of White House Aide Vince Foster are less clear. On July 20, 1993, the body of Vince Foster was discovered in a park in Washington, D.C. Foster had apparently committed suicide, and much of the initial evidence pointed to a self-inflicted gunshot wound as the cause of death. He had been showing tremendous signs of stress as he found himself the subject of political battles in Washington and a number of accusations against the Clinton administration. Foster had reportedly been very upset about the attention he was receiving in the "Travelgate" scandal and his role in questions about billing records involving Hillary Clinton and Whitewater investments (Tisdall, 1994). However, immediately after his body was found, rumors began circulating the Internet suggesting that Foster's death had not been a suicide. These reports claimed that the death was a murder that was covered-up by members of the Clinton administration who felt Foster knew too much about the Whitewater investigation being conducted by Independent Counsel Kenneth Starr.

Rumors of unresolved questions within the investigation of Foster's death began to spread throughout the Internet by members of conservative activist groups who made no secret of their hatred of President Clinton. Why was there no suicide note? Why were the keys on Foster's body not found at the scene, but only later, once the body was moved? What did the torn note say that was found near the body? Why were records missing from Vince Foster's office after the body was found? Those looking for sensational stories and rumors involving this story did not have to look hard on the Internet to find them.

The cascade effect of this story reached remarkable levels. Numerous websites published the rumor that Foster's death was a murder, including Matt Drudge's site (Scheer, 1999). Presidential candidate Pat Buchanan received criticism in 1996 by Jewish groups after an article published on his official campaign website claimed that Foster's death was ordered by Israel and that Hillary Clinton was secretly working as a Mossad agent (O'Dwyer, 1996). Rush Limbaugh, a conservative radio talk-show host, mentioned the accusations on his radio program and Representative John Linder, Republican of Georgia, even inserted the accusation into the record at Congressional hearings involving the Whitewater scandal (*Atlanta Journal and Constitution,* 1994). In fact, the rumors of murder were so persistent on the Internet and other mediums that a Time/CNN poll taken in 1995 during the Senate hearings of the aftermath of Foster's death showed that only 35 percent of respondents believed Foster's death was a suicide. Twenty percent believed he had been murdered (Weiner, 1995).

Rumors of a Clinton-led cover-up have continued to exist even after four separate investigations, conducted by the U.S. Park Police, the FBI, Special Counsel Robert Fiske, and Independent Counsel Ken Starr, all came to the same conclusion: Foster's death was a suicide. The persistent refusal to accept the conclusions of these investigations is demonstrated in a 1998 editorial in *The Augusta Chronicle* written five years after Foster's death. "Imagine [Ken Starr] ruling the Vince Foster killing a suicide when not one item of evidence would indicate suicide, but numerous items indicate obvious murder!" *(The Augusta Chronicle,* 1998).

Much of the persistent nature of these specific rumors can be traced to partisan political groups. Richard Scaife, a wealthy financier of many anti-Clinton groups, has been quoted as saying, "The death of Vincent Foster: I think that's the Rosetta Stone to the whole Clinton Administration" (Weiner, 1995). Scaife has supported groups, such as the Western Journalism Center, that have included work by Christopher Ruddy, a reporter who was dismissed by the *New York Post* for pursuing cover-up theories relating to the death. Ruddy, who refers to himself as part of the 'vast right-wing conspiracy' described by Hillary Clinton, has written and published numerous articles attacking both the Clinton administration and the Foster investigations. Even today, reports written by Ruddy questioning the investigations' findings can be found online (www.newsmax.com/ruddy/). In addition, fund-raising letters for conservative groups, including a 1997 letter from a group called "Clinton Investigation Committee," have been used to raise money to continue various investigations against Clinton, including the Foster case (Piacente, 1997). These organizations, websites, newspaper articles, and fund-raising letters, have all helped to perpetuate the rumors that Vince Foster's death was a murder, and somehow the Clinton administration was involved.

Because these rumors have persisted for years, their existence cannot be attributed to the timing pressure of the Internet news cycle. Instead, the theories involving Foster's death are a result of the desire for the sensational and partisan political efforts, in this instance from groups who opposed Bill Clinton. The possibility of a printed retraction seems impractical and would likely have no effect, since, unlike the Blumenthal case, there was no one specific site that started the rumors on the Internet, and because the rumors have extended far beyond the Internet into newspapers and even among members of Congress. The cascade effect of all of these rumors is that a certain contingent, in this case opponents of Bill Clinton, continues to believe that the Clintons were responsible for Vince Foster's death. The political consequences for such accusations, even after they have been disproved, can be far reaching because false information has the potential to unreasonably decrease the public's faith in public officials and the competency of their government.

Conclusion

The expansion of the Internet has great potential for promoting political discourse and allowing for far more citizens to be involved with the production and dissemination of news. Davis and Owen (1998) describe this positive potential:

> Increasingly, computer networks have become tools for political communication as well. Users gather political information, express their opinions, and mobilize other citizens and political leaders. The information superhighway is fast becoming an electronic town hall where anyone with a personal computer and a modem can learn about the latest bill introduced in Congress, join an interest group, donate money to a political candidate, or discuss politics with people they have never seen who may live half a world away. (pg. 110)

However, as these three case studies have shown, the potential for the Internet to be a conduit of false information or the spreading of rumors is also significant. The dilemma for those who are concerned about the role the Internet will play in the future of democracy will be to discover how to balance the positive democratizing aspects with the potentially harmful aspects that include the spread of false reports and misleading information.

The main goal of this investigation was to examine how errors of Internet reporting are handled online. These three case studies demonstrate that there is no single method as to how Internet errors are corrected. When one source for a rumor exists, as was the case with the Blumenthal story, a retraction is possible on that initial source which can somewhat lessen the impact of the false story. However, even that example was picked up by other mainstream newspaper and radio sources.

This study then supports Hall's assertion that the nature of the Internet reinforces the context of errors rather than corrects them. As seen with the Vince Foster case, significant numbers of people believed that his death was a murder even after several investigations had concluded otherwise. Public discourse was not shifted entirely even after the early reports were disproved or corrected. In fact, in all three of the cases presented here, the Internet rumors and false reports were picked up by other sources and continued to spread even after evidence pointed to contrary facts.

Another substantial conclusion that can be ascertained from this investigation is that Sunstein's assessment of social cascades is valid in regards to errors on the Internet. For those people who are interested in finding evidence to support their views, even if the evidence itself is questionable, the Internet can be a tremendous facilitator. And the reach of the influence of these reports is not just to conspiracy theorists. Their impact can be seen even in actions taken by government officials, such as President Clinton after the crash of TWA flight 800. These social cascades can have important political consequences, whether on airline safety regulations or in the perceptions of political figures. A connection appears to exist between the capabilities of the Internet and the vastness of the social cascading that can occur as a result of rumor and innuendo.

How, then, should the potential for social cascading as a result of misleading information be balanced with the positive potential of the Internet? Not all scholars agree that the implications of an 'anything goes' attitude of Internet reporting is entirely negative. Davis and Owen (1998) make an argument relating to old media that an increase of tabloid journalism may not be entirely destructive because it "can foster a sense of intimacy with the public," and also attract viewers to news sources (pg. 209). This same line of reasoning can be applied to the Internet sites such as Matt Drudge's that spread rumor while using standards for verification that are less than those that are utilized by traditional media. Consequently, it is possible that the lowering of journalistic norms that is apparent online will not have entirely negative consequences if the result encourages more people to search for news and connect with other Internet users.

Even if it is true that the Internet's impact on journalism and the increase of false reports is not entirely negative, this investigation has demonstrated that harmful effects can result from the cascade effects of misinformation. The question that arises from this investigation is regarding how to control or combat the prevalence of errors on the Internet. Sidney Blumenthal acknowledged that one of the goals of his lawsuit against Drudge was to bring the Internet under the same type of libel laws that newspaper and television journalists must follow. However, Blumenthal's attempt at forcing the Internet "reporter" to face negative consequences as a result of his false report was unsuccessful, and further attempts by the government to regulate the content of the Internet seem likely to be impractical, costly, and ineffective overall. There is simply too much online content for the government to be able to enforce the same types of journalistic laws that other news mediums must follow, not to mention the potential for excessive government censorship.

At the same time, it is incredibly unlikely that the four reasons mentioned earlier in this discussion that cause errors in reporting, that is, the need for speed, the desire to attract hits, the goal of advancing a partisan agenda, and the attraction to scandal, will lessen and lower the competitive pressures on Internet journalists in the next few years. If anything, those pressures are likely to increase as more and more people turn to the Internet for their news. The only probable method for improving the accuracy of online reporting would be for news producers themselves to make better attempts at following voluntary guidelines that are closer to the standards used by old media sources. Offering guidelines for reporters to follow is not new. Sabato, Stencel, and Lichter (2000) describe a number of guidelines reporters should follow in reporting political scandals in their book entitled *Peepshow* and journalism schools have been teaching professional norms for decades. Other sets of standards that are usually applied to traditional news outlets could be applied to Internet sources as well. These standards, such as the need for multiple sources for issuing a report, do not guarantee complete accuracy in reporting, as can be seen with the recent scandals of newspaper reporters Jayson Blair of the *New York Times* and Jack Kelley of *USA Today*. However, attempts to follow these more traditional guidelines would lessen the frequency and impact of Internet reporting errors.

Seib agrees with the need for online reporters to voluntarily follow traditional ethics of reporting. In his predictions for the future of Internet journalism, he notes that it will be increasingly important for reporters to aim at fairness and accuracy. He writes, "The 'Drudge effect'—shoot-from-the-hip sensationalism—will give online journalism a bad name if the public perceives it to be a dominant characteristic of this medium" (p. 162). The best way for journalists to deal with this perceived 'Drudge effect' and the potentially harmful impact of Internet rumors is to deliver a consistently fair and accurate news product. The marketplace will in time come to rely on the high-quality product more than the hastily put together news site that does not have a good track record of accuracy. Seib's faith in the public's desire for quality reporting is the most hopeful and promising view as to how to lessen the impact of social cascades based on misleading or false information.

Along with offering positive aspects of the Internet, Davis and Owen (1998) also write, "new technologies have enhanced opportunities for the mass dissemination of misinformation" (p. 200). As this study has shown, this rapidly expanding technology can have potentially harmful effects if false reports are spread without supporting evidence. In order for us to reap the positive effects of the Internet, which include added convenience and the possibility of increased political discourse, the dangers of false information must also be confronted. The most effective method to lessen the amount and impact of false Internet errors will be for news producers on the Web to follow traditional journalistic standards of fact-checking and sourcing. False reporting will not disappear, but, we must make ourselves aware of the various types of reporting that can be found on the Web and hope that market forces will encourage high-quality reporting as opposed to unsubstantiated rumors passing as news. Awareness of the potential for both types of reporting is a central condition for encouraging effective and accurate online reporting.

References

The Atlanta Journal and Constitution (1994, July 29). "Hatemongers Who Cry Wolf . . . " Editorial, p. A14.

The Augusta Chronicle (Georgia) (1998, December 11). "Calls for Investigation, Not Cover-Up." Editorial, p. A4.

Blumenthal, Sidney (2003). *The Clinton Wars*. New York: Farrar, Straus and Giroux.

Charles, Michael T. (2001). "The Fall of TWA Flight 800." In Uriel Rosenthal, R. Arjen Boin, & Louise K. Comfort (Eds.), *Managing Crises: Threats, Dilemmas, Opportunities* (pp. 216–234). Springfield, IL.: Charles C. Thomas Publisher, Ltd.

CNN.com (1997, March 11). *NTSB: "No Physical Evidence" Missile Brought Down TWA 800*. Atlanta, GA: CNN.com. Retrieved October 18, 2003, from the CNN Interactive website: http://www.cnn.com/US/9703/11/twa.missile/

Cobb, Roger W., & Primo, David M. (2003). *The Plane Truth: Airline Crashes, the Media, and Transportation Policy*. Washington, D.C.: Brookings Institution Press.

Davis, Richard (1999). *The Web of Politics: The Internet's Impact on the American Political System*. New York: Oxford University Press.

Davis, Richard & Owen, Diana (1998). *New Media and American Politics*. New York: Oxford University Press.

Hall, Jim (2001). *Online Journalism: A Critical Primer*. London: Pluto Press.

Harper, Christopher (1998). *And That's the Way It Will Be: News and Information in a Digital World*. New York: New York University Press.

Hunter, Mark (1997). *The Buffoon Brigade: Pierre Salinger and His Conspiracy-Minded Colleagues Are Stopping Investigators from Finding Out What Really Happened to TWA Flight 800*. San Francisco: Salon.com. Retrieved October 18, 2003, from the Salon.com website: http://www.salon.com/march97/ news/ news970326.html

Kurtz, Howard (1997, August 12). "Blumenthals Get Apology, Plan Lawsuit: website Retracts Story of Clinton Aide." *The Washington Post*, p. A11.

Kurtz, Howard (2001, May 2). "Clinton Aide Settles Libel Suit Against Matt Drudge—At a Cost." *The Washington Post*, p. C1.

Negroni, Christine (1997, January 17). *Six Months Later, Still No Answer to TWA Flight 800 Mystery*. Atlanta, GA: CNN.com. Retrieved October 18, 2003, from the CNN Interactive website: http://www.cnn.com/US/9701/17/twa/index.html

O'Dwyer, Thomas (1996, February 18). "Buchanan website Blames Mossad for Clinton Aide's Death; Calls Hillary an Agent." *The Jerusalem Post*, p. 1.

O'Leary, Stephen (2002). *Rumors of Grace and Terror*. Los Angeles, CA: The Online Journalism Review. Retrieved September 29, 2003, from the Online Journalism Review website: http://www.ojr.org/ojr/ethics/1017782038.php

Piacente, Steve (1997, April 16). "Letter Claims Foster was Killed." *The Post and Courier* (Charleston, SC), p. A9.

Ruddy, Christopher (1999). "A Memo: The Unanswered Questions in the Foster Case." West Palm Beach, FL: The Christopher Ruddy website. Retrieved November 27, 2003, from Newsmax.com: http://www.newsmax.com/articles/?a=1999/2/8/155138

Sabato, Larry J., Stencel, Mark, & Lichter, S. Robert (2000). *Peepshow: Media and Politics in an Age of Scandal*. Lanham, MD: Rowman & Littlefield Publishers, Inc.

Scheer, Robert (1999, January 14). "More Sludge From Drudge: The Story that Clinton Fathered an Illegitimate Son Turns Out to Be a Hoax." *Pittsburgh Post-Gazette*, p. A15.

Seib, Philip (2001). *Going Live: Getting the News Right in a Real-Time, Online World*. Lanham, MD: Rowman & Littlefield Publishers, Inc.

Sunstein, Cass (2002). *Republic.com*. Princeton: Princeton University Press.

Swartz, Jon (1998, June 23). "Free-Speech Victory For Internet; AOL Off the Hook in Landmark Libel Case." *The San Francisco Chronicle*, p. A1.

Tisdall, Simon (1994, February 7). "The Body in the Park." *The Guardian* (London), p. 2.

Weiner, Tim (1995, August 13). "One Source, Many Ideas in Foster Case." *The New York Times*, pp. 1–19.

whatreallyhappened.com (2002, June 10). *Was TWA Flight 800 Shot Down by a Military Missile?* Retrieved October 18, 2003, from the whatreallyhappened.com website: http://www.whatreallyhappened.com/RANCHO/ CRASH/TWA/twa.html

Note

1. For complete text of the Internet letter written by Russell, see (Harper, 1998, pp. 85–86).

From *gnovis*, April 26, 2004 (Original manuscript), pp. 1–26. Copyright © 2004 by Communication, Culture and Technology Program (CCT), Georgetown University. Reprinted by permission. www.gnovis.georgetown.edu

UNIT 7

International Perspectives and Issues

Unit Selections

Key Points to Consider

- Find out more about proxy servers. What is to prevent an authoritarian government from shifting the monitoring of traffic within its borders to a proxy server? Suppose an authoritarian government sets up a website claiming to be anonymous.org. How could it be distinguished from the real thing? What if a volunteer within a proxy server group sells a list of names and searched websites to authoritarian regimes? Do the proxy server websites you have visited address these issues?

- Do proxy servers permit sites that most of us would consider censoring, say those hosting child pornographers?

- Find out if your university blocks websites. How about the public library in your hometown?

- Are you surprised to learn that France and Australia block websites? What do you know about governmental censorship in the United States?

- Follow up on the some of the sources mentioned in Joel Schectman's piece on "Iran's Twitter Revolution." Are they reliable? If so, what does that tell you about news being reported as it happens? Recall the very large claims about Twitter reporting in the heat of Iran's presidential election.

Student Website

www.mhhe.com/cls

Internet Reference

The Internet and State Control in Authoritarian Regimes

http://www.carnegieendowment.org/files/21KalathilBoas.pdf

For the past several years, we have been hearing a great deal about a global economy, the exchange of goods, services, and labor across national boundaries. Yet human beings have been trading across long distances for centuries. The discovery of Viking artifacts in Baghdad and sea shells in the Mississippi Valley are two of many, many examples. The beginnings of capitalism in the 15th century accelerated an existing process (Merrett 2008). When most commentators speak of globalization, though, they refer increasingly to the interdependent trade we have witnessed since the collapse of the former Soviet Union and the global availability of the Internet and satellite communications. Without the new information technologies, the global marketplace would not be possible. We can withdraw money from our bank accounts using ATMs in Central Turkey, make cell phones calls from nearly anywhere on the planet, and check our e-mail from a terminal located in an Internet cafe in Florence or Katmandu. They also make it possible for businesses to transfer funds around the world and, if you happen to be a software developer, to employ talented—and inexpensive—software engineers in growing tech centers like Bangalore, India.

Or China. Those of us old enough to remember the Chinese Red Guard waving copies of Chairman Mao's *Little Red Book* might be surprised to find that "Bill Gates has become the new idol of youths across China" ("China's Tech Generation Finds a New Chairman to Venerate").

One area where the United States still has the indisputable lead is in squeezing every ounce of productivity out of information technology. Some of what we have read about the length of the Korean and Japanese workweek may be due to the unwillingness of employers in those countries to give their employees laptops. See "New Tech, Old Habits," for an account of the more creative side of American business.

Not all international consequences of computer technology are economic. One very odd corner has been occupied by dissenters using advanced technology to outwit repressing regimes. Iran's presidential election in 2009 is a good example. Most of us will remember that media everywhere focused on what became known as the "twitter revolution," "as hundreds of thousands of street protestors purportedly mobilized their demonstrations using the microblogging service." "Purportedly" is the operative word. Read Joel Schectman's article to see why.

And not all governments that censor the Internet are what we generally think of as repressive regimes. Australia, France, India, Argentina, and South Korea have all set up Internet firewalls. If Tor and its developers are successful, dissenters, whether political protestors in Iran or terrorists in Australia, could be fully online. Consider Arias Qtiesh who blogs from an Internet café in Syria, a country that David Talbot (Article 36) calls an

© Don Farrall/Getty Images

"all-purpose Internet repressor." Since Qtiesh blogs about pan-Arab—and not Syrian—politics, he doesn't fear the local police. Still, he would like to see a larger piece of the Internet than is officially available in his country. The Torbutton on his browser lets him access blocked sites through a series of proxy servers, essentially providing anonymity to both bloggers and surfers. These servers are operated by universities, corporations, free-speech advocates, and computer security professionals on a volunteer basis.

The global interconnectedness that Marshall McLuhan observed forty years ago has only increased in complexity with developments in computer technology. Now instead of merely receiving one-way satellite feeds, as in McLuhan's day, we can talk back through e-mail, websites, and blogs. It is not surprising that all of this communication is having unanticipated effects across the planet. Who, for instance, during the Tiananmen Square uprising of 1989, could have predicted that a newly market-centered China would become the source of significant competition to the United States? Or, who could ever have predicted that Bill Gates would replace Chairman Mao in the hearts of the young Chinese? No one, in fact, which is why the study of computing is so fascinating.

Reference

Merrett, C. (2008). *The Future of Rural Communities in a Global Economy.* The University of Iowa Center for International Finance and Development. Retrieved September 13, 2008, from http://www.uiowa.edu/ifdebook/ issues/globalization/perspectives/merrett.shtml

China's Tech Generation Finds a New Chairman to Venerate

KEVIN HOLDEN

Since the passing of Chairman Mao Zedong, a new chairman has come to represent the aims and aspirations of millions of Chinese youth—the chairman of Microsoft, Bill Gates.

"Chairman Mao was the great symbol of revolutionary China, but Bill Gates has become the new idol of youths across China," said a researcher with China's ministry of propaganda. "Gates has become more popular in China than any government leader."

Books by or about Microsoft's chairman are massive best sellers across China, even in the IT-impoverished countryside, and Gates has been cited as the ultimate role model by everyone, from the founders of internet startups to Chinese cyberdissidents.

"I read about Bill Gates before I had ever even seen a computer," said Dong Ruidong, who abandoned his rural village for the bright lights and cybercafes of the Chinese capital. "Even in the remotest villages of China, Gates is one of the most popular figures alive."

The Chinese edition of Gates' *The Road Ahead* "was one of the most successful books in our history," said Wang Mingzhou, who edited the Chinese edition. It is "among the most important works published since the founding of the People's Republic of China."

Wang, who rode the success of Gates' book to be named president of the Peking University Press, said *The Road Ahead* "helped launch the internet revolution across China, and gave it power and speed."

"Bill Gates is without doubt now one of the most influential foreigners in China," Wang said.

Chairman Gates is everything Chairman Mao was not. Mao crushed capitalists, closed newspapers and universities, and isolated China from the world. But Chairman Gates celebrates free enterprise and is busy forging partnerships with Chinese entrepreneurs, creating cybercolleges and integrating China's best and brightest into the web-linked world.

Gates has disbursed grants from his $30-billion philanthropic Gates Foundation to bring computers to rural China and health care to the poor, and in the process has acquired the aura of an internet-age angel.

Chinese youths stand to gain from the virtual universities Gates is helping create, and from student software packages Microsoft has begun offering for $3 (1/50th the retail price) each to governments buying computers for K–12 kids.

Microsoft Vice President Will Poole, who is helping spearhead the race to double the globe's cybercitizenry to 2 billion people by 2015, said Microsoft's software packages could be provided in tandem with the ultra-cheap XO machines being produced in China by the One Laptop Per Child group.

China's Ministry of Education, which paints Gates with an almost superhuman glow in books like *Junior English for China*, might use this software in its quest to churn out more internet-generation graduates.

China's internet population jumped by 23 percent to reach 130 million people in 2006, but nine-tenths of China's 1.3 billion citizens are still on the dark side of the digital divide.

At a recent Asian leadership forum in Beijing with Chinese technocrats and U.N. leaders, Gates outlined his latest goal—to extend internet access beyond the globe's 1 billion online elite to its 5 billion digitally dispossessed—many of whom are in China.

"Microsoft is now over 30 years old, and the original dream was about computers for everyone," he said. "As we go after this next 5 billion, it is really going back to the original roots, the original commitment of what Microsoft is all about."

Of course, meeting that goal would also position Microsoft to multiply, by a factor of 10, its current base of 600 million Windows users worldwide, and further expand Gates' global influence.

Microsoft's chairman is extending lots of incentives to new Windows users here, and has become a symbol of global fame and fortune, and of American-style freedoms. While hosting Chinese President Hu Jintao at an aristocratic feast at the Gates' private residence in Seattle last spring, Gates echoed Microsoft's testimony during U.S. congressional hearings on "The Internet in China: A Tool for Freedom or Suppression."

In remarks repeated across Chinese chat rooms, Gates told Hu: "Industry and government around the world should work even more closely to protect the privacy and security of internet users, and promote the exchange of ideas."

During his recent tour of China, Gates predicted the next global leader might be born here: "There was a survey done in the U.S. that asked where the next Bill Gates will come from," he said. "Sixty percent of the U.S. said the next stunning success would come from Asia."

Yet few Chinese believe that a clone of Gates, if born in China, could become *the* Bill Gates.

"Piracy is so widespread here that Microsoft would never generate such massive profits," said author Huang Wen.

Despite the massive, institutionalized piracy that has led the United States to file a complaint against China with the World Trade Organization, Gates has been amazingly tolerant of China's counterfeiters. This has created a paradoxical image of an internet-age Robin Hood and gained him universal admiration.

"Bill Gates deserves to win the Nobel Peace Prize," said the Chinese propaganda officer. "He gives people across the globe not only material help, but also inspiration that if they work very, very hard, they might one day become more important than a president."

From *Wired.com*, May 24, 2007, pp. online. Copyright © 2007 by Wired.com. Reprinted by permission.

New Tech, Old Habits

Despite world-class IT networks, Japanese and Korean workers are still chained to their desks.

MOON IHLWAN AND KENJI HALL

Masanori Goto was in for a culture shock when he returned to Japan after a seven-year stint in New York. The 42-year-old public relations officer at cellular giant NTT DoCoMo logged many a late night at his Manhattan apartment, using his company laptop to communicate with colleagues 14 time zones away. Now back in Tokyo, Goto has a cell phone he can use to send quick e-mails after hours, but he must hole up at the office late into the night if he needs to do any serious work. The reason: His bosses haven't outfitted him with a portable computer. "I didn't realize that our people in Japan weren't using laptops," he says. "That was a surprise."

A few hundred miles to the west, in Seoul, Lee Seung Hwa also knows what it's like to spend long hours chained to her desk. The 33-year-old recently quit her job as an executive assistant at a carmaker because, among other complaints, her company didn't let lower-level employees log on from outside the office. "I could have done all the work from home, but managers thought I was working hard only if I stayed late," says Lee.

These days, information technology could easily free the likes of Goto and Lee. Korea and Japan are world leaders in broadband access, with connection speeds that put the U.S. to shame. And their wireless networks are state of the art, allowing supercharged Web surfing from mobile phones and other handhelds, whether at a café, in the subway, or on the highway. But when it comes to taking advantage of connectivity for business, Americans are way ahead.

For a study in contrasts, consider the daily commute. American trains are packed with business people furiously tapping their BlackBerrys or Treos, squeezing a few extra minutes into their work days. In Tokyo or Seoul, commuters stare intently at their cell phone screens, but they're usually playing games, watching video clips, or sending Hello Kitty icons to friends. And while advertising for U.S. cellular companies emphasizes how data services can make users more productive at work, Asian carriers tend to stress the fun factor.

Why? Corporate culture in the Far East remains deeply conservative, and most businesses have been slow to mine the opportunities offered by newfangled communications technologies. One big reason is the premium placed on face time at the office. Junior employees are reluctant to leave work before the boss does for fear of looking like slackers. Also, Confucianism places greater stock on group effort and consensus-building than on individual initiative. So members of a team all feel they must stick around if there is a task to complete. "To reap full benefits from IT investment, companies must change the way they do business," says Lee Inn Chan, vice-president at SK Research Institute, a Seoul management think tank funded by cellular carrier SK Telecom. "What's most needed in Korea and Japan is an overhaul in business processes and practices."

Time, Not Task

In these countries, if you're not in the office, your boss simply assumes you're not working. It doesn't help that a lack of clear job definitions and performance metrics makes it difficult for managers to assess the productivity of employees working off site. "Performance reviews and judgments are still largely time-oriented here, rather than task-oriented as in the West," says Cho Bum Coo, a Seoul-based executive partner at business consulting firm Accenture Ltd.

Even tech companies in the region often refuse to untether workers from the office. Camera-maker Canon Inc. for instance, dispensed with flextime four years ago after employees said it interfered with communications, while Samsung stresses that person-to-person contact is far more effective than e-mail. In Japan, many companies say they are reluctant to send workers home with their laptops for fear that proprietary information might go astray. Canon publishes a 33-page code of conduct that includes a cautionary tale of a worker who loses a notebook computer loaded with sensitive customer data on his commute. At Korean companies SK Telecom, Samsung Electronics, and LG Electronics, employees must obtain permission before they can carry their laptops out of the office. Even then, they often are barred from full access to files from work. And while just about everyone has a cell phone that can display Web pages or send e-mails, getting into corporate networks is complicated and unwieldy.

Bound by Tradition

Despite fast wireless and broadband networks, Korean and Japanese companies aren't getting the most out of technology. Here's why:

FUN FACTOR Smart phones are viewed more as toys than tools.

FACE TIME If you're not in the office, no one thinks you're working.

INFO-FEAR Companies worry that laptop-toting commuters could misplace sensitive data.

The result: Korean and Japanese white-collar workers clock long days at the office, often toiling till midnight and coming in on weekends. "In my dictionary there's no such thing as work/life balance as far as weekdays are concerned," says a Samsung Electronics senior manager who declined to be named. Tom Coyner, a consultant and author of *Mastering Business in Korea: A Practical Guide,* says: "Even your wife would think you were not regarded as an important player in the office if you came home at five or six."

These factors may be preventing Japan and Korea from wringing more productivity out of their massive IT investments. Both countries place high on lists of global innovators. For instance, Japan and Korea rank No. 2 and No. 6, respectively, out of 30 nations in terms of spending on research and development, according to the Organization for Economic Cooperation and Development. And the Geneva-based World Intellectual Property Organization says Japan was second and Korea fourth in international patent filings. But when it comes to the productivity of IT users, both countries badly lag the U.S., says Kazuyuki Motohashi, a University of Tokyo professor who is an expert on technological innovation. "Companies in Japan and Korea haven't made the structural changes to get the most out of new technologies," he says.

Still, a new generation of managers rising through the ranks may speed the transformation. These workers are tech-savvy and often more individualistic, having come from smaller families. Already, some companies are tinkering with changes to meet their needs. SK Telecom abolished titles for all midlevel managers in the hopes that this would spur workers to take greater initiative. Japan's NEC Corp. is experimenting with telecommuting for 2,000 of its 148,000 employees. And in Korea, CJ 39 Shopping, a cable-TV shopping channel, is letting 10% of its call-center employees work from home.

Foreign companies are doing their bit to shake things up. In Korea, IBM has outfitted all of its 2,600 employees with laptops and actively encourages them to work off site. The system, which was first introduced in 1995, has allowed the company to cut back on office space and reap savings of $2.3 million a year. One beneficiary is Kim Yoon Hee. The procurement specialist reports to the office only on Tuesdays and Thursdays. On other days, calls to her office phone are automatically routed to her laptop, so she can work from home. "It would have been difficult for me to remain employed had it not been for the telecommuting system," says Kim, 35, who quit a job at a big Korean company seven years ago because late nights at the office kept her away from her infant daughter. "This certainly makes me more loyal to my company."

From *BusinessWeek,* March 26, 2007, pp. 48–49. Copyright © 2007 by BusinessWeek. Reprinted by permission of the McGraw-Hill Companies.

Iran's Twitter Revolution? Maybe Not Yet

Some Iranian election protesters used Twitter to get people on the streets, but most of the organizing happened the old-fashioned way.

JOEL SCHECTMAN

Media across the globe have been focusing on a "Twitter Revolution" in Iran as hundreds of thousands of street protestors purportedly mobilized their demonstrations using the microblogging service. So great has the notion of Twitter's role in the Iranian protests become that the U.S. State Dept. reportedly asked the company to defer some maintenance. Twitter says it rescheduled maintenance work from June 15 to later the next day, or about 1:30 A.M. in Iran. "It made sense for Twitter . . . to keep services active during this highly visible global event," the San Francisco company said on its blog.

However, Iran experts and social networking activists say that while Iranian election protesters have certainly used social media tools, no particular technology has been instrumental to organizers' ability to get people on the street. Indeed, most of the organizing has occurred through far more mundane means: SMS text messages and word of mouth. Sysomos, a Toronto-based Web analytics company that researches social media, says there are only about 8,600 Twitter users whose profiles indicate they are from Iran.

"I think the idea of a Twitter revolution is very suspect," says Gaurav Mishra, co-founder of 20:20 WebTech, a company that analyzes the effects of social media. "The amount of people who use these tools in Iran is very small and could not support protests that size."

And with the government blocking the Twitter site, that small group becomes even smaller. Tech-savvy netizens can use proxy addresses such as Tor or Proxy.org to bypass the government block of certain IP addresses. But for many users, circumnavigating the government's blockage is too big a hurdle, and organizing in more conventional ways, such as over the phone or by knocking on doors, can be both quicker and easier.

Raising Awareness Elsewhere

Mishra, who has organized social media activism campaigns for elections in India, says the main reason to use the tools is the attention it generates in the international media. Indeed, one of Twitter's primary contributions in the Iranian elections has been to raise awareness of the issue among tech-savvy users outside the country.

"Political organizers use these tools because they create a multiplier effect—not only do you get a story about the campaign but then you also get a story about the fact they are using social-networking tools," Mishra says. "So you get two stories for the price of one. The international media loves [the] social-networking world. But in India or in Iran, their use is still somewhat limited."

Another reason for the hype surrounding Twitter's role in these protests is the lack of good access for reporters in Iran and the difficulty of covering the story of the protested elections. Iran's religious leadership declared incumbent President Mahmoud Ahmadinejad the winner on June 12 with 63% of the vote a mere two hours after polls had closed. The opposition, which had largely supported Mir Hussein Mousavi, took to the streets of Tehran to protest; bloody crackdowns by police and militia followed. At least six people have died and many more have been injured, according to reports.

For now, these tools represent the best chance the demonstrations have of getting continued coverage. "Social media is not at all a prime mover of what is happening on the ground," says Ethan Zuckerman, a senior researcher at Harvard University's Berkman Center for Internet & Society. "The reason social media is so interesting [for the press] is that the international media doesn't have its members on the ground."

Twitter in Moldova?

Zuckerman analyzed protests in Moldova this past April, which were also labeled a "Twitter Revolution," and found the vast majority of tweets, or Twitter postings, during the protests were coming from outside the country, either Moldovan expats or just people sympathetic to the movement.

"Of the 700 people who were twittering on the Moldovan protests, less than 200 were in Moldova at the time," Zuckerman said. "Social media are helpful in exposing what's happening to the outside world, but it's a mistake to think that these protests [in Iran] are because of social media. It's more conventional things like word-of-mouth and phone calls that really bring massive numbers of people into the streets."

A study by Mike Edwards, a social network researcher at Parsons The New School for Design, examined 79,000 tweets related to the Iran protests, and found that one-third are repostings of other tweets. The general ratio of reposts to posts is 1-to-20, and even in other fast-breaking global news events, when reposting might be more common, such as the swine flu outbreak, Edwards says he has seen the number go only as high as 1 in 5. This could indicate the amount of information deployed by protestors in Iran is small compared to the amount recirculated by outsiders, although Edwards cautions there are other possible explanations.

"There is this romantic notion that the people tweeting are the ones in the streets, but that is not what is happening," Edwards says. "The hubs are generally not people on the ground, and many are not in the country."

Exaggerating the News?

One analyst cautioned that while Twitter or Facebook may keep the outside world's attention trained on Iranian protests, there was also a danger such tools could exaggerate the movement's momentum. "You can get the notion that Ahmadinejad is very unpopular and that Mousavi has this groundswell of support, but we don't have data that shows that," says Reva Bhalla, director of analysis for Austin (Tex.)-based Stratfor, a strategic intelligence and forecasting company. "Ahmadinejad has real support, but his supporters don't have smartphones. There is a real risk of amplifying [one side]." Ahmadinejad is thought to have a greater base of support in rural areas, while Mousavi is popular with urbanites.

Still, regardless of how much a mover social media may be in the protests, Iran watchers agree that the tools do represent a step forward. "Governments like Iran, Syria, and Egypt are really struggling with how to continue limiting information," Bhalla said. "No matter how hard these governments try to block communication, now there is always going to be a hole. This really is a case study in how technology can affect closed societies."

Mousavi introduced the use of social-networking tools to his campaign last month, Iran experts say, because he didn't have the access to state-run television and newspapers Ahmadinejad enjoys. "They needed an alternative means to campaign and get their message across," said Trita Parsi, president of the National Iranian American Council. But Parsi, like others, acknowledges that Facebook and Twitter were important mainly for letting people outside the country follow events, and text messages and phone calls were the primary mover of people in Iran's protests. "The people I know mainly tell me they hear about these protests from friends or by SMS," Parsi says.

SCHECTMAN is a reporter at BusinessWeek.

From *BusinessWeek*, June 17, 2009. Copyright © 2009 by BusinessWeek. Reprinted by permission of the McGraw-Hill Companies.

The List: Look Who's Censoring the Internet Now

Countries like Iran and China are notorious for their Internet censorship regimes. But a growing number of democracies are setting up their own great fire walls.

JOSHUA KEATING

Australia
What's targeted?
Officially, child pornography and terrorism, but recent reports suggest the scope might be expanded.

What's behind the wall?
In January 2008, the Australian Parliament began considering a law to require all Internet service providers (ISPs) to filter the content they provide to users in order to block a blacklist of objectionable sites prepared by the Australian Communications and Media Authority. Although the law is still in the planning stages, ISPs are required to have their filtering systems ready for testing by June 2009.

The government claimed that the blacklist would combat child pornography and terrorism-related sites, but in March 2009, the list of 2,935 sites was leaked by anticensorship website Wikileaks and revealed a much broader scope of content, including online poker, Satanism, and euthanasia. Some seemingly uncontroversial private businesses, such as a Queensland dentist's office, were also included for unknown reasons. The release of the list has dampened public support for the law, and one of Australia's largest ISPs recently announced it would not participate in the filtering tests.

France
What's targeted?
File-sharing.

What's behind the wall?
The French Parliament is debating and seems likely to pass the world's toughest antipiracy law to date. Other countries have begun cracking down on file-sharers with fines, but the French law would require ISPs to deny Internet access to those who have been repeatedly caught illegally downloading material. A new administrative body would be created and granted judicial power to enforce the law. The controversial measure is strongly supported by music and film industry leaders, as well as President Nicolas Sarkozy (whose wife Carla Bruni recently released an album incidentally), and opposed by privacy groups and cable companies.

One of the law's most controversial aspects is that it would penalize anyone whose Internet connection was used for downloading illegal material, even if the person wasn't aware of it or the network was used without permission. All people in France, in effect, would be legally required to secure their wireless networks.

India
What's targeted?
Political radicalism, terrorist tools.

What's behind the wall?
India's Internet filtering is still sporadic, but the seemingly arbitrary nature of its enforcement has censorship watchdogs nervous. In 2003, the Indian Computer Emergency Response Team (CERT-In) was created to enforce the country's filtering regime. CERT-In is the sole authority empowered to block websites, and there is no review or appeals process once it blacklists a site. Many blocked sites have been found to contain obscene material, but CERT-In has also shut down Hindu nationalists and other radical groups on social networking sites such as Orkut. In 2003, thousands of Indian Internet users were blocked from accessing Yahoo! Groups because CERT-In objected to a message board for a minor North Indian separatist group consisting of 25 people.

When it was revealed that the terrorists responsible for the November 2008 Mumbai attacks used Google Earth to plan their assault, a prosecutor petitioned the Bombay High Court to block the popular site. The motion was ultimately thrown out, but security concerns are also dogging a rival satellite-mapping site being developed by the Indian government itself. The government agency building the program suggests that some sensitive sites might be blurred out in the final version.

Argentina
What's targeted?
Celebrity dirt.

What's behind the wall?
Argentine soccer legend Diego Maradona is best known for his controversial 1986 "hand of God" goal, but he also has a hand in one of the world's most brazen acts of Web censorship. Maradona and about 70 other celebrities filed a class action suit in mid-2007 against Google and Yahoo!, claiming that their names were being associated with pornography or libelous sites against their will. A judge ruled in favor of the plaintiffs, essentially holding the search engines responsible for the content of other sites, a standard that a Google Argentina spokesperson told *Time* was like "suing the newsstand for what appears in the newspapers it sells."

The search engines are appealing the ruling, but for now, if you search for Maradona or any of his co-plaintiffs on the Argentine version of Google or Yahoo!, you'll get a message saying the search engine is "obliged to temporarily suspend all or some of the results related to this search," followed by an abridged list of links to major news sites. It's one thing for Maradona to try to cover up gossip about his past partying, but the plaintiffs also included several judges whose decisions have provoked online discussion, a fact many see as a major conflict of interest for the justices deciding the case. Unfortunately for Maradona, though, getting the dirt on him is as easy as loading up another country's version of the search engines.

South Korea
What's targeted
North Korean propaganda.

What's behind the wall
South Korea is one of the world's most wired countries, with about 90 percent of households hooked up to the Web, but the Korean Internet is also one of the world's most heavily policed. ISPs are reportedly required to block as many as 120,000 sites from an official government blacklist. Some sites on the list are for pornography and gambling—South Korea requires ISPs to self-police content that could be deemed harmful to youth—but much of it is content sympathetic to North Korea or advocating Korean reunification.

The medium may be new, but the justification is decades old. Thanks to the 1948 anticommunist National Security Law, South Koreans can be imprisoned for up to seven years for vaguely defined "antistate" activities. In recent years such activities have extended to the Internet, with communist activists being arrested for downloading material on Marxism. The National Security Law is controversial, and the South Korean government recently stated that it will relax restrictions on access to pro-North Korea sites, many of which are hosted in Japan. However, recent testing by the OpenNet Initiative has revealed that filtering is still pervasive.

JOSHUA KEATING is deputy Web editor at FP.

Reprinted in entirety by McGraw-Hill with permission from *Foreign Policy*, March 2009. www.foreignpolicy.com. © 2009 Washingtonpost.Newsweek Interactive, LLC.

Dissent Made Safer: How Anonymity Technology Could Save Free Speech on the Internet

David Talbot

"Sokwanele" means "enough is enough" in a certain Bantu dialect. It is also the name of a Zimbabwean pro-democracy website whose bloggers last year published accounts of atrocities by Robert Mugabe's regime and posted Election Day updates describing voter intimidation and apparent ballot stuffing. You can visit Sokwanele's "terror album" and see photographs: of a hospitalized 70-year-old woman who'd been beaten and thrown on her cooking fire (she later died, the site says); of firebombed homes; of people with deep wounds carved into their backs. You can find detailed, frequently updated maps describing regional violence and other incidents. You will be confronted with gruesome news, starkly captioned: "Joshua Bakacheza's Body Found."

Because this horrific content is so readily available, it is easy to overlook the courage it took to produce it. The anonymous photographers and polling-station bloggers who uploaded the Sokwanele material remain very much in danger. In a place like Zimbabwe, where saying the wrong thing can get you killed or thrown in prison on treason charges, you take precautions: you're careful about whom you talk to; you're discreet when you enter a clinic to take pictures. And when you get to the point of putting your information on the Internet, you need protection from the possibility that your computer's digital address will be traced back to you. Maybe, at that point, you use Tor.

Tor is an open-source Internet anonymity system—one of several systems that encrypt data or hide the accompanying Internet address, and route the data to its final destination through intermediate computers called proxies. This combination of routing and encryption can mask a computer's actual location and circumvent government filters; to prying eyes, the Internet traffic seems to be coming from the proxies. At a time when global Internet access and social-networking technologies are surging, such tools are increasingly important to bloggers and other Web users living under repressive regimes. Without them, people in these countries might be unable to speak or read freely online.

Unlike most anonymity and circumvention technologies, Tor uses multiple proxies and encryption steps, providing extra security that is especially prized in areas where the risks are greatest. Paradoxically, that means it's impossible to confirm whether it's being used by the Zimbabwean bloggers. "Anyone who really needs Tor to speak anonymously isn't going to tell you they use Tor to speak anonymously," says Ethan Zuckerman, cofounder of Global Voices, an online platform and advocacy organization for bloggers around the world. "You can't tell if it's happening, and anyone who is actively evading something isn't going to talk about it." That said, the Sokwanele journalists "are extremely sophisticated and use a variety of encryption techniques to protect their identity," he says.

Anonymity aside, Internet users in dozens of countries—whether or not they are activist bloggers—often need to evade censorship by governments that block individual sites and even pages containing keywords relating to forbidden subjects. In 2006, the OpenNet Initiative—a research project based at Harvard and the Universities of Toronto, Oxford, and Cambridge that examines Internet censorship and surveillance—discovered some form of filtering in 25 of 46 nations tested, including China, Saudi Arabia, Iran, and Vietnam.

In a new and still-evolving study, OpenNet found that more than 36 countries are filtering one or more kinds of speech to varying degrees: political content, religious sites, pornography, even (in some Islamic nations) gambling sites. "Definitely, there is a growing norm around Internet content filtering," says Ronald Deibert, a University of Toronto political scientist who cofounded OpenNet. "It is a practice growing in scope, scale, and sophistication worldwide."

Tor can solve both problems; the same proxies that provide anonymous cover for people posting content also become portals for banned websites. When it officially launched five years ago, the Tor network consisted of 30 proxies on two continents; now it has 1,500 on five continents, and hundreds of thousands of active users. And its developers are trying to expand its reach, both abroad and in the United States, because digital barriers and privacy threats affect even the free world. In the United States, for example, libraries and employers often block content, and people's Web habits can be—and are—recorded for marketing purposes by Internet service providers (ISPs) and by the sites themselves. "The Internet is being carved up and filtered and surveilled," says Deibert. "The environment is being degraded. So it's up to citizens to build technologies to [counter these trends]. And that is where I see tools like Tor coming into play. It preserves the Internet as a forum for free information."

Neutral Nodes

The product of a small nonprofit organization with eight paid developers and a few dozen volunteer security professionals around the world, Tor takes advantage of the fact that Internet traffic consists of two-part packets. The first part contains data-pieces of a Web page you are viewing, or of the photo file or e-mail you are sending. The other consists of the Internet protocol (IP) address of the sending and receiving computer (plus other data, such as the size of the file). Tor uses the latter portion—the addressing information—to build a circuit of encrypted connections through relays on the network. The requisite relays (which collectively serve as proxies) are operated on a volunteer basis at universities such as Boston University and a few corporations, and by computer-security professionals and free-speech advocates around the world. (Many Tor users also use existing technologies, such as HTTPS—a protocol for encrypting and decrypting a user's page requests and the pages that are returned—to protect the content they are sending and receiving.)

Tor, like the Internet itself, emerged from military research—in this case at the U.S. Naval Research Laboratory in Washington, which built a prototype in the mid-1990s. The military interest was clean. without a way to make Internet traffic anonymous, an agent's cover could be compromised the minute he or she visited .mil domains using the Internet connection of, say, a hotel. Even if the data were encrypted, anyone watching traffic over the hotel network could quickly figure out that the guest might be associated with the U.S. military. And the problem is hardly limited to hotel networks; IP addresses can be linked to physical locations by a variety of means (ISPs correlate such data with phone numbers, data miners can piece together clues from Internet traffic, and someone outside your house can confirm that you are the source of specific kinds of Internet traffic by "sniffing" data traveling over Wi-Fi). As a Tor presentation puts it, chillingly, what might an insurgent group pay to get a list of Baghdad IP addresses that get e-mail from a .gov or .mil account?

The navy project never emerged from the lab, but it attracted the interest of Roger Dingledine, a cryptographer concerned about a different aspect of Internet privacy: the way ISPs and websites amass databases on people's browsing and search history. In 2000, at a conference where he was presenting his MIT master's thesis on anonymous distributed data storage, he met a Naval Research Lab mathematician, Paul Syverson. The two men saw that tools for protecting military agents and tools for protecting Web surfers' privacy could be one and the same, and together they revived the project with funding from the Defense Advanced Research Projects Agency (DARPA) and the navy.

The first public version of Tor, which came out in 2003, was available for anyone who cared to install it. But it worked only on open-source operating systems, and using it required at least some technical knowledge. The Electronic Frontier Foundation, the digital civil-liberties organization, funded development of a version for Windows, and soon a wider variety of users emerged. "Originally one of my big reasons for working on Tor was to provide tools for people in the West—Americans and Europeans—to let them keep their information safe from corporations and other large organizations that generally aren't very good at keeping it to themselves," says Dingledine, now 32, who is Tor's project leader. But now, he says, some police agencies use Tor to make sure that an investigation of an online scare won't be compromised by tipping the scammer off to regular site visits from a police department's computers. And some companies, he says, use it to help them prevent competitors from figuring out, say, who is scouring their online product sheets.

It quickly became clear that this diversity was crucial to the technology's success. "It's not just safety in numbers; there is safety in variety," Dingledine says. Even if there were 100,000 FBI agents using Tor, you would know what it's for: "You are using the FBI's anonymity system. Even from the very beginning, part of the fun and the challenge was to take all of these different groups out there who care about what Tor provides, and put them all into the same network." To help promote wider use, its developers made Tor far easier to install. And in 2006, they developed a new feature, the Torbutton, which allows Tor users to easily turn Tor on and off while they browse with the Firefox Web browser (turning it off speeds up Internet access but removes the protections).

Global Spread

Syria is an all-purpose Internet repressor. It hunts down some bloggers; a Syrian named Tariq Biasi, for example, was recently sentenced to three years in prison for "dwindling the national feeling"; he allegedly posted a comment critical of the state's security service online. Beyond going after online critics, Syria also blocks many websites—including Facebook, YouTube, and Skype—from all Web users in the nation. I spoke about Syrian censorship with another blogger, Arias Qtiesh; he sat in an Internet cafe in Damascus as I messaged him from my living room. Qtiesh isn't worried that he'll be tracked down, because he tends to blog about pan-Arab politics, not about criticisms of the regime. But he wants access to more of the Internet than the government permits, so the Firefox browser on his laptop sports the Torbutton. Click the button, and presto—the same Internet that everyone in America sees. To access blocked sites, his computer negotiates a series of proxies, eventually connecting to an IP address somewhere else in the world. This intermediary fetches the blocked material. "Tor brings back the Internet," he wrote.

Qtiesh has plenty of company: Tor was always of interest abroad, but word of mouth and the introduction of the easy-to-use Torbutton have helped accelerate its global spread. Zuckerman has been actively promoting Tor through his Global Voices network. So have other advocates of online free speech in Asia, China, and Africa. And these efforts have been working. Wendy Seltzer, who teaches Internet law at American University and founded Chilling Effects, a project to combat legal threats against Internet users, saw that firsthand when she traveled to Guangzhou, China, for a blogger conference last year. China is generally acknowledged as the most sophisticated Internet filterer in the world; it employs a variety of techniques, including blocking IP addresses, domain names (the text name of a website, such as www.google.com), and even Web pages containing certain keywords (Falun Gong, for example). According to one report, Chinese security forces have arrested several hundred Internet users and bloggers in the past 10 years. Seltzer says that many bloggers she met in Guangzhou were using Tor. And when she went to an Internet cafe there, she reports, the computers were automatically configured to run the software.

In China, Tor is one weapon in a large arsenal. But in Mauritania, Tor appears to have single-handedly overwhelmed state censorship. Nasser Weddady is a Mauritanian-born son of a diplomat, now living in the Boston area. He is a civil-rights activist who seeks to call attention to the slavery still practiced in his native country, where black Muslims work in servitude for Arab and Moorish farms and households, far from the international spotlight. In 2005, in response to Internet filtering in Mauritania, he translated a guide to using Tor into Arabic and arranged for its distribution to owners of cybercafes. The effect was stunning: the government stopped filtering. Officials "didn't know we were using Tor," says Weddady. "I'm not sure they know what Tor is. But they noticed that our communications were not disrupted, so the filtering was useless."

Such successes can be short-lived, of course, and Weddady predicts that the regime will regroup and resume filtering. "The Middle East in general is a civil-rights desert; it has some of the most sophisticated filtering operations in the world," he says. "Plenty of people I personally know are using Tor in that region." Users know that to any snooper, the messages they post appear to originate from a Tor relay somewhere else in the world, so cybercafe owners can't rat them out even if they want to. "Tor doesn't say, 'Just trust us not to give out your information'—it says, 'We have a design where nobody is in a position to give up your information, because no one person has it," says Seltzer, who volunteers on Tor's board. "I do believe Tor is the best solution for people who are trying to get access to blocked matter, or are trying to speak anonymously."

Bridging Tor's Gaps

Neither Tor nor any other tool is a perfect solution to Internet spying and censorship. As an open-source project, Tor publishes everything about its workings, including the addresses of its relays. That doesn't betray the actual source and destination of users' information, but it does mean that a government could obtain this list of addresses and block them. (So far, nobody has taken this step, though Iran, Saudi Arabia, and the United Arab Emirates did find a way to block Tor for a few months in 2008.) Second, using Tor can make Internet access painfully slow; online activities can take more than 10 times longer when using Tor, according to a study by Harvard's Berkman Center for Internet and Society. "It turns out the speed of light isn't so fast after all," Dingledine deadpans. And this problem is getting worse; in the past year, the number of users has increased faster than Tor's developers can add relays.

But the biggest limitation is simply that all these tools still reach only a narrow slice of the world's Internet users. Yes, if you're a business traveler in China and have technical savvy and bandwidth—or you hire someone to set you up—you can circumvent government filters. (It's generally understood that state security forces will rarely move to shut down circumvention tools unless they're publicly embarrassed by being outsmarted online.) But a recently released Berkman report by Zuckerman, faculty codirector John Palfrey, and researcher Hal Roberts has concluded—on the basis of data supplied in 2007 by makers of circumvention software—that only a few million people use the major circumvention tools worldwide. It's true that usage has grown since then—and this estimate doesn't count everybody who has figured out a way to use proxies. Still, China alone has 300 million Internet users, and the researchers believe that most of them aren't equipped to fight censorship. Meanwhile, the list of nations that censor is only growing. Two years ago, Turkey piled on, with particular zeal for stamping out criticism of the nation's founding father, Kemal Ataturk.

Tor is preparing for the fight against relay blocking by creating a system of "bridge nodes"—a constantly changing list of IP addresses through which people can reach the main network of relays. A user can simply send an e-mail asking for a bridge address. Of course, an Iranian censor could also request and block such addresses, but the idea is to defeat such efforts by generating ever more bridges, donated by a wide range of Internet users. And Jonathan Zittrain, a Berkman cofounder and Harvard Law School professor, envisions going even further. "The next big moment that the Tor people haven't implemented—something in the background, something that would be huge—would be if your use of Tor, by default, makes you a Tot node yourself," he says. "At that point, it totally scales. The more people use it, the more people can use it."

As part of a three-year effort to improve the software and expand its use, Tor's staff and volunteers will step up appeals for Tor users to let their computers serve as bridges to individual users elsewhere. But taking the next step—becoming a relay, or node, potentially available to any Tor traffic—would massively increase the traffic flowing through a user's computer. If users became nodes by default, it could defeat the purpose of using Tor to remain low key: once a user wandered into a cybercafe to blog anonymously, that terminal would soon stand out as a hub of Internet traffic. What's more, such a system "sets off an arms race with all the network providers and network administrators," says Andrew Lewman, Tor's executive director. "It increases traffic, and we become something they might block, because that's their job." Tor would ultimately like to find safe ways to enlist distributed help, but for now, developers are pursuing intermediate goals, such as limiting bulk data transfers and improving the flow among existing Tor relays.

One criticism leveled against Tor is that it can be used not only for good purposes but for bad—protecting distributors of child pornography, for example. Dingledine's response is that Tor's protections help law enforcement catch criminals, too, while criminals may find it more effective to use neighbors' or public Wi-Fi links, or hacked computers, to mask their identities.

Another concern is that circumvention tools—especially those that only use a single proxy, which holds information about who is talking to whom—can create privacy and security worries of their own. Earlier this year, Hal Roberts discovered that certain tools used widely in China—DynaWeb Freegate, GPass, and Fire-Phoenix—appeared to be offering to sell users' browsing histories. While there's no evidence that any individual's privacy was compromised, the point was made: in many cases, using anonymity or circumvention systems still means trusting an organization with your information—and trusting that its privacy policies can and will be honored. (With Tor, it's a bit different; since no single relay ever holds the information about the complete route, you must trust the integrity of algorithms that obscure connections between origins and destinations.) "I don't doubt the dedication of the people hosting these tools, but what I'm concerned about is whether they will protect your data," Roberts says. "The biggest takeaway is: they have that data."

Dingledine thinks events will push people to seek the protections that Tor and other tools provide. In 2006, for example, AOL gave away millions of users' search terms for research purposes. Although the searchers were identified only by random numbers, bloggers and reporters were quickly able to identify individual users from clues based on the search terms. (Since Tor uses a different router pathway for each user each time, it's impossible to amass such aggregate data about even an anonymously identified Tor user.) Dingledine reasons that each time a national censor

Beating Surveillance and Censorship

Here's how five leading tools rate in circumventing Internet censorship and protecting privacy. All use proxy computers in uncensored nations to help people in censored ones; Tor uses multiple proxies for extra protection.

Circumvention/anonymity tool	Source	Model
Tor www.torproject.org	Open-source nonprofit project, U.S. Navy research	Peer to peer, but with multiple hops through a network of proxies
Psiphon psiphon.ca	Citizen Lab at the University of Toronto	Peer to peer; users circumvent filters through one trusted proxy computer
UltraReach www.ultrareach.com	UltraReach Internet	Centrally hosted, requiring trust in the company
Anonymizer www.anonymizec.com	Subsidiary of Abraxas	Centrally hosted, requiring trust in the company
Dynaweb Freegate us.dongtaiwang.com/home_en.php	Dynamic Internet Technology	Centrally hosted, requiring trust in the company

Circumvention/anonymity tool	Strengths	Weaknesses
Tor www.torproject.org	Mast secure for the most users	Slowest of the tested tools
Psiphon psiphon.ca	No software installation required (users log in)	Slower than most tested tools
UltraReach www.ultrareach.com	Easy for users to install; fastest of tested tools	Requires funding to scale
Anonymizer www.anonymizec.com	Easy for users to install; can sustain growth	Retail version is insecure in countries that filter; free version available only in China and Iran
Dynaweb Freegate us.dongtaiwang.com/ home_en.php	Easy for users to install	Now available only in China; requires funding to scale

Sources: 2007 Circumvention Landscape Report Methods, Uses, and Tools, Beckman Center for Internet and Society, March 2009; Hal Roberts.

blocks news sites and YouTube, or an ISP or website loses or sells or gives away user data, people will seek solutions. "The approach we've taken so far is to let the bad guys teach people about it," he says. "Let the AOLs and the China firewalls screw up. Let everybody read about why they want privacy on the Internet." More and more people might just decide that enough is enough.

Dodging Spies, Data Miners, and Censors

Let's say you want to visit www.blogger.com or www.webmd.com but don't want those sites (or your ISP) recording your computer's digital address as you do so. If you use Tor's Internet anonymity software, your computer's addressing data is encrypted at each of several relays. That way, a Web page can't track what computer is visiting, and someone watching your computer can't know what sites you are connecting to. The system can circumvent government filtering, too, because censoring countries generally block specific websites, not neutral and ever-changing Tor nodes.

1. To use Tor, you (orange) visit the Tor directory website (blue block) to obtain addresses of Tor relays.
2. When you try to view Blogger pages (or upload your blogs), software routes those efforts through a random set of Tor relays operated by volunteers.
3. At the first relay, your computer's IP address is replaced by the address of the relay. The next relay sees only the address of the previous relay. No single relay "knows" the whole route; this provides strong anonymity protection. (Many users also use other tools to encrypt the data they are sending and receiving.)
4. You reach Blogger.com—but Blogger doesn't know your computer's digital address. It only knows the address of the last relay that handled your request.
5. If you visit webmd.com 10 minutes later, the process is repeated—but with another random chain of relays. This way, no one can aggregate data on your activities and infer your identity.

DAVID TALBOT is Technology Review's chief correspondent.

From *Technology Review*, August 15, 2009. Copyright © 2009 by Technology Review. Reprinted by permission via Copyright Clearance Center.

UNIT 8
The Frontier of Computing

Unit Selections

Key Points to Consider

• 2003 marked the 30th anniversary of the publication of an essay entitled "Animals, Men and Morals" by Peter Singer in the *New York Review of Books.* This essay is often credited with beginning the animal rights movement. Singer argues that because animals have feelings, they can suffer. Because they can suffer, they have interests. Because they have interests, it is unethical to conduct experiments on them. Suppose scientists succeed in developing machines that feel pain and fear. What obligations will we have toward them? If this is difficult to imagine, watch the movie *Blade Runner* with Harrison Ford. What do you think now?

• The overview to this unit says that the dollar value of the output of the meat and poultry industries exceeds the dollar value of the output of the computer industry. The overview mentions one reason why we hear so much more about software than chickens. Can you think of others?

• Suppose you were provided with a robot whose task is to filter spam from your e-mail. Now suppose you are provided with a real secretary to do the same task. Both of these assistants will make judgment calls. That is, based on what you have told them, each will make best guesses as to whether the e-mail is spam or not. How do you feel about your robot making the occasional error? How do you feel about your secretary making a mistake?

• Professor Turkle poses a disturbing question that is quoted in the Preface to this book: "Are you really you if you have a baboon's heart inside, had your face resculpted by Brazil's finest plastic surgeons, and are taking Zoloft to give you a competitive edge?" Are you?

Student Website
www.mhhe.com/cls

Internet References

Introduction to Artificial Intelligence (AI)
http://www-formal.stanford.edu/jmc/aiintro/aiintro.html

Kasparov vs. Deep Blue: The Rematch
http://www.research.ibm.com/deepblue/home/html/b.html

PHP-Nuke Powered Site: International Society for Artificial Life
http://www.alife.org/

According to the U.S. Census Bureau statistics not long ago, the output of the meat and poultry industry was worth more than the output of the computer and software industries. Although this is not exactly a fair comparison—computers are used to build still other products—it does get at something significant about computers: They figure more importantly in our imaginations than they do in the economy. Why is this? Part of the answer has to do with who forms opinions in developed nations. The computer is an indispensable tool for people who staff the magazine, newspaper, publishing, and education sectors. If meat packers were the opinion makers, we might get a different sense of what is important. Recall "Five Things We Need to Know about Technological Change." Postman says that "Embedded in every technology there is a powerful idea. . . . To a person with a computer, everything looks like data."

We can concede Postman's point but still insist that there is something special about computing. Before computers became a household appliance, it was common for programmers and users alike to attribute human-like properties to them. Joseph Weizenbaum, developer of Eliza in the 1970s, a program that simulated a Rogerian psychotherapist, became a severe critic of certain kinds of computing research, in part because he noticed that staff in his lab had begun to arrive early to ask advice from the program. In 1956, a group of mathematicians interested in computing gathered at Dartmouth College and coined the term "Artificial Intelligence." AI, whose goal is to build into machines something that we can recognize as intelligent behavior, has become perhaps the best-known and most criticized area of computer science. Since intelligent behavior, like the ability to read and form arguments, is often thought to be the defining characteristic of humankind (we call ourselves *homo sapiens,* after all), machines that might exhibit intelligent behavior have occupied the dreams and nightmares of Western culture for hundreds of years.

All of our ambiguous feelings about technology are congealed in robots. The term itself is surprisingly venerable, having been invented by the Czech playwright Karel Copek in 1921. They can be lovable like R2D2 from *Star Wars* or Robbie from *The Forbidden Planet* of a generation earlier. They can be forbidding but loyal, like Gort from *The Day the Earth Stood Still.* They can even be outfitted with logical safety mechanisms that render them harmless to humans. This last, an invention of Isaac Asimov in *I, Robot,* is a good thing, too, since so many of our robotic imaginings look like *The Terminator.* Sherry Turkle of MIT has been studying the relationship between humans and their machines for twenty years. In "A Nascent Robotics Culture: New Complicities for Companionship," she asks the jarring question, "What is a robot kind of love?"

Researchers from around the world met in Montreal this past summer for GECCO 2009, the Genetic and Evolutionary Computing Conference. In the mid-1970s, John Holland at the University of Michigan proposed a mechanism for problem solving based loosely on the idea of Darwinian natural selection. Since that time, researchers have used genetic algorithms, as Holland called them, to solve problems too difficult to be solved using conventional computing techniques. The genetic algorithm is one of several computing techniques based on a "paradigm that draws on the principles of self-organization of complex

© Ryan McVay/Getty Images

systems." The article, "Toward Nature-Inspired Computing," is an excellent introduction.

Fifteen years ago, the study of database systems was an important but unheralded part of computer science. For all its importance, how an insurance company organizes its data could seem a little dull. But that was before Google began to tame the chaos of the Internet through sophisticated storage and retrieval techniques and, above all, through clusters of computers it calls "the cloud." See "Google and the Wisdom of Clouds," for a glimpse at how one creative researcher at Google is teaching researchers around the world to extract patterns from large collections of data. Brian Hayes, an excellent reporter on developments in computing, provides an accessible introduction to cloud computing. Turns out that the Google cloud is, in a sense, a return to the centralized computing of forty years ago. This will have major implications for companies like Microsoft who package software to be run on local computers.

Centralized computing is not all that has come in from the cold. Artificial Intelligence, long criticized because it promised more than it delivered, is making a comeback, largely through the development of evolutionary computing and the seemingly inevitable march of Moore's Law (see Article 2). The *New York Times* ran a surprisingly uncritical view in May 2009. Read "The Coming Superbrain" and see if you're persuaded that "the singularity is near."

Robots, evolutionary and cloud computing, the singularity; The articles in this unit have a common theme: the technologies described are neither fully formed nor has their impact on society been large—Goggle excepted. Computing history is filled with bad predictions. Perhaps the most spectacularly wrong is widely attributed to Thomas Watson, head of IBM, who in 1943 is supposed to have said, "I think there is a world market for maybe five computers." But there have been many, many others. Will robots get no further than furbies? Is the "Google and the Wisdom of Clouds" just a reprise of centralized data processing? Is post-human evolution upon us? It's hard to know. But no one wants to be the next Thomas Watson.

A Nascent Robotics Culture
New Complicities for Companionship

Encounters with humanoid robots are new to the everyday experience of children and adults. Yet, increasingly, they are finding their place. This has occurred largely through the introduction of a class of interactive toys (including Furbies, AIBOs, and My Real Babies) that I call "relational artifacts." Here, I report on several years of fieldwork with commercial relational artifacts (as well as with the MIT AI Laboratory's Kismet and Cog). It suggests that even these relatively primitive robots have been accepted as companionate objects and are changing the terms by which people judge the "appropriateness" of machine relationships. In these relationships, robots serve as powerful objects of psychological projection and philosophical evocation in ways that are forging a nascent robotics culture.

SHERRY TURKLE

Introduction

The designers of computational objects have traditionally focused on how these objects might extend and/or perfect human cognitive powers. But computational objects do not simply do things *for* us, they do things *to* us as people, to our ways of being the world, to our ways of seeing ourselves and others (Turkle 2005[1984], 1995). Increasingly, technology also puts itself into a position to do things *with* us, particularly with the introduction of "relational artifacts," here defined as technologies that have "states of mind" and where encounters with them are enriched through understanding these inner states (Turkle 2004a, 2004b). Otherwise described as "sociable machines (Breazeal 2000, 2002, Breazeal and Scasselati 1999, 2000, Kidd 2004), the term relational artifact evokes the psychoanalytic tradition with its emphasis on the meaning of the person/machine encounter.

In the late 1970s and early 1980s, children's style of programming reflected their personality and cognitive style. And computational objects such as Merlin, Simon, and Speak and Spell provoked questions about the quality of aliveness and about what is special about being a person. (Turkle 2005[1984]) Twenty years later, children and seniors confronting relational artifacts as simple as Furbies, AIBOs and My Real Babies (Turkle 2004a) or as complex as the robots Kismet and Cog (Turkle et al. 2004) were similarly differentiated in their style of approach and similarly provoked to ask fundamental questions about the objects' natures.

Children approach a Furby or a My Real Baby and explore what it means to think of these creatures as alive or "sort of alive"; elders in a nursing home play with the robot Paro and grapple with how to characterize this creature that presents itself as a baby seal (Taggart, W. et al. 2005, Shibata 1999, 2005). They move from inquiries such as "Does it swim?" and "Does it eat?" to "Is it alive?" and "Can it love?"[1]

These similarities across the decades are not surprising. Encounters with novel computational objects present people with category-challenging experiences. The objects are liminal, betwixt and between, provoking new thought. (Turner 1969; Bowker and Star 1999). However, there are significant differences between current responses to relational artifacts and earlier encounters with computation. Children first confronting computer toys in the late 1970s and early 1980s were compelled to classification. Faced with relational artifacts, children's questions about classification are enmeshed in a new desire to *nurture and be nurtured by* the artifacts rather than simply categorize them; in their dialogue with relational artifacts, children's focus shifts from cognition to affect, from game playing to fantasies of mutual connection. In the case of relational artifacts for children and the elderly, nurturance is the new "killer app." We attach to what we nurture (Turkle 2004, 2005b).

We Attach to What We Nurture

In *Computer Power and Human Reason*, Joseph Weizenbaum wrote about his experiences with his invention, ELIZA, a computer program that seemed to serve as self object as it engaged people in a dialogue similar to that of a Rogerian psychotherapist (1976). It mirrored one's thoughts; it was always supportive. To the comment: "My mother is making me angry," the program might respond, "Tell me more about your mother," or "Why do you feel so negatively about your mother." Weizenbaum was disturbed that his students, fully knowing that they were talking with a computer program, wanted to chat with it, indeed, wanted to be alone with it. Weizenbaum was my colleague at MIT at the time; we taught courses together on computers and society. And at the time that his book came out, I felt moved to reassure him. ELIZA seemed to me like a Rorschach through which people expressed themselves. They became involved with ELIZA, but the spirit was "as if." The gap between program and person was vast. People bridged it with attribution and desire. They thought: "I will talk to this program 'as if' it were a person; I will vent, I will rage, I will get things off my chest." At the time, ELIZA seemed to me no more threatening than an interactive diary. Now, thirty years later, I ask myself if I had underestimated the quality of the connection.

A newer technology has created computational creatures that evoke a sense of mutual relating. The people who meet relational artifacts feel a desire to nurture them. And with nurturance comes the fantasy of reciprocation. They wanted the creatures to care about them in return. Very little about these relationships seemed to be experienced "as if." The experience of "as if" had morphed into one of treating robots "as though." The story of computers and their evocation of life had come to a new place.

Children have always anthropomorphized the dolls in their nurseries. It is important to note a difference in what can occur with relational artifacts. In the past, the power of objects to "play house" or "play cowboys" with a child has been tied to the ways in which they enabled the child to project meanings onto them. They were stable "transitional objects." (Winnicott 1971) The doll or the teddy bear presented an unchanging and passive presence. But today's relational artifacts take a decidedly more active stance. With them, children's expectations that their dolls want to be hugged, dressed, or lulled to sleep don't only come from the child's projection of fantasy or desire onto inert playthings, but from such things as the digital dolls' crying inconsolably or even saying: "Hug me!" or "It's time for me to get dressed for school!" *In the move from traditional transitional objects to contemporary relational artifacts, the psychology of projection gives way to a relational psychology, a psychology of engagement. Yet, old habits of projection remain: robotic creatures become enhanced in their capacities to enact scenarios in which robots are Rorschachs, projective screens for individual concerns.*

From the perspective of several decades of observing people relating to computational creatures, I see an evolution of sensibilities.

- Through the 1980s, people became deeply involved with computational objects—even the early computer toys became objects for profound projection and engagement. Yet, when faced with the issue of the objects' affective possibilities, a modal response might be summed up as "Simulated thinking may be thinking; simulated feeling is never feeling. Simulated love is never love."
- Through the 1990s, the development of a "culture of simulation" brought the notion of simulation (largely through participation in intensive game spaces) into the everyday. The range and possibilities of simulation became known to large numbers of people, particularly young people.
- By the late 1990s, the image of the robot was changing in the culture. A robotics presence was developing into a robotics culture increasingly shaped by the possibility if not the reality of robots in the form of relational artifacts. Alongside a tool model, people are learning about a notion of cyber-companionship. Acceptance of this notion requires a revisiting of old notions of simulation to make way for a kind of companionship that feels appropriate to a robot/person relationship.

The Evolution of Sensibilities: Two Moments

A first moment: I take my fourteen-year-old daughter to the Darwin exhibit at the American Museum of Natural History. The exhibit documents Darwin's life and thought, and with a somewhat defensive tone (in light of current challenges to evolution by proponents of intelligent design), presents the theory of evolution as the central truth that underpins contemporary biology. The Darwin exhibit wants to convince and it wants to please. At the entrance to the exhibit is a turtle from the Galapagos Islands, a seminal object in the development of evolutionary theory. The turtle rests in its cage, utterly still. "They could have used a robot," comments my daughter. She considers it a shame to bring the turtle all this way and put it in a cage for a performance that draws so little on the turtle's "aliveness." I am startled by her comments, both solicitous of the imprisoned turtle because it is alive and unconcerned about its authenticity. The museum has been advertising these turtles as wonders, curiosities, marvels—among the plastic models of life at the museum, here is the life that Darwin saw. I begin to talk with others at the exhibit, parents and children. It is Thanksgiving weekend. The line is long, the crowd frozen in place. My question, "Do you care that the turtle is alive?" is welcome diversion. A ten-year-old girl would prefer a robot turtle because aliveness comes with aesthetic inconvenience: "its water looks dirty. Gross." More usually, votes for the robots echo my daughter's sentiment that in this setting, aliveness doesn't seem worth the trouble. A twelve-year-old girl opines: "For what the turtles do, you didn't have to have the live ones." Her father looks at her, uncomprehending: "But the point is that they are real, that's the whole point."

The Darwin exhibit gives authenticity major play: on display are the actual magnifying glass that Darwin used, the actual notebooks in which he recorded his observations, indeed, the very notebook in which he wrote the famous sentences that first described his theory of evolution *But in the children's reactions to the inert but alive Galapagos turtle, the idea of the "original" is in crisis.* I recall my daughter's reaction when she was seven to a boat ride in the postcard blue Mediterranean. Already an expert in the world of simulated fish tanks, she saw a creature in the water, pointed to it excitedly and said: "Look mommy, a jellyfish! It looks so realistic!" When I told this story to a friend who was a research scientist at the Walt Disney Company, he was not surprised. When Animal Kingdom opened in Orlando, populated by "real," that is, biological animals, its first visitors complained that these animals were not as "realistic" as the animatronic creatures in Disney World, just across the road. The robotic crocodiles slapped their tails, rolled their eyes, in sum, displayed "essence of crocodile" behavior. The biological crocodiles, like the Galapagos turtle, pretty much kept to themselves. What is the gold standard here?

I have written that now, in our culture of simulation, the notion of authenticity is for us what sex was to the Victorians—"threat and obsession, taboo and fascination" (Turkle, 2005[1984]). I have lived with this idea for many years, yet at the museum, I find the children's position strangely unsettling. For them, in this context, aliveness seems to have no intrinsic value. Rather, it is useful only if needed for a specific purpose. "If you put in a robot instead of the live turtle, do you think people should be told that the turtle is not alive?" I ask. Not really, say several of the children. Data on "aliveness" can be shared on

a "need to know" basis, for a purpose. But what *are* the purposes of living things? When do we need to know if something is alive?

A second moment: an older woman, 72, in a nursing home outside of Boston is sad. Her son has broken off his relationship with her. Her nursing home is part of a study I am conducting on robotics for the elderly. I am recording her reactions as she sits with the robot Paro, a seal-like creature, advertised as the first "therapeutic robot" for its ostensibly positive effects on the ill, the elderly, and the emotionally troubled. Paro is able to make eye contact through sensing the direction of a human voice, is sensitive to touch, and has "states of mind" that are affected by how it is treated—for example, it can sense if it is being stroked gently or with some aggressivity. In this session with Paro, the woman, depressed because of her son's abandonment, comes to believe that the robot is depressed as well. She turns to Paro, strokes him and says: "Yes, you're sad, aren't you. It's tough out there. Yes, it's hard." And then she pets the robot once again, attempting to provide it with comfort. And in so doing, she tries to comfort herself.

Psychoanalytically trained, I believe that this kind of moment, if it happens between people, has profound therapeutic potential. What are we to make of this transaction as it unfolds between a depressed woman and a robot? When I talk to others about the old woman's encounter with Paro, their first associations are usually to their pets and the solace they provide. The comparison sharpens the questions about Paro and the quality of the relationships people have with it. I do not know if the projection of understanding onto pets is "authentic." That is, I do not know whether a pet could feel or smell or intuit some understanding of what it might mean to be with an old woman whose son has chosen not to see her anymore. What I do know is that Paro has understood nothing. Like other "relational artifacts" its ability to inspire relationship is not based on its intelligence or consciousness, but on the capacity to push certain "Darwinian" buttons in people (making eye contact, for example) that cause people to respond *as though* they were in relationship. For me, relational artifacts are the new uncanny in our computer culture, as Freud (1960) put it, "the long familiar taking a form that is strangely unfamiliar."

Confrontation with the uncanny provokes new reflection. Do plans to provide relational robots to children and the elderly make us less likely to look for other solutions for their care? If our experience with relational artifacts is based on a fundamentally deceitful interchange (artifacts' ability to persuade us that they know and care about our existence) can it be good for us? Or might it be good for us in the "feel good" sense, but bad for us in our lives as moral beings? The answers to such questions are not dependent on what computers can do today or what they are likely to be able to do in the future. These questions ask what *we* will be like, what kind of people are *we* becoming as we develop increasingly intimate relationships with machines.

Rorschach and Evocation

We can get some first answers by looking at the relationship of people—here I describe fieldwork with children and seniors—with these new intimate machines. In these relationships it is clear that the distinction between people using robots for projection of self (as Rorschach) and using robots as philosophically evocative objects, is only heuristic. They work together: children and seniors develop philosophical positions that are inseparable from their emotional needs. Affect and cognition work together in the subjective response to relational technologies. This is dramatized by a series of case studies, first of children, then of seniors, in which the "Rorschach effect" and the "evocative object effect" are entwined.[2]

Case Studies of Children

I begin with a child, Orelia, ten, whose response to the robot AIBO serves as commentary on her relationship to her mother, a self-absorbed woman who during her several sessions with her daughter and the robot does not touch, speak to, or make eye contact with her daughter. One might say that Orelia's mother acts robotically and the daughter's response is to emphasize the importance and irreducibility of the human heart. In a life characterized by maternal chill, Orelia stressed warmth and intuition as ultimate human values.

Orelia: Keeping a Robot in Its Place

I met Orelia at a private Boston-area middle school where we were holding group sessions of fifth graders with a range of robotic toys. Orelia received an AIBO to take home; she kept a robot "diary." We met several times with Orelia and her parents in their Charlestown home. (Turkle 2004a)

Orelia is bright and articulate and tells us that her favorite hobby is reading. She makes determined distinctions between robots and biological beings. "AIBO is not alive like a real pet; it does not breathe." There is no question in her mind that she would choose a real dog over an AIBO. She believes that AIBO can love but only because "it is programmed to." She continues: "If [robots] love, then it's artificial love. [And] if it's an artificial love, then there really isn't anything true . . . I'm sure it would be

programmed to [show that it likes you], you know, the computer inside of it telling it to show artificial love, but it doesn't love you."

Orelia is sure that she could never love an AIBO. "They [robots] won't love you back if you love them." In order to love an AIBO, Orelia says it would need "a brain and a heart." Orelia feels that it is not worth investing in something that does not have the capacity to love back, a construction that is perhaps as much about the robot as about her relationship with her mother.

Orelia's brother Jake, nine, the baby of the family, is more favored in his mother's eyes. Unlike his sister, Jake assumes that AIBO has feelings. Orelia speaks to the researchers *about* AIBO; Jake addresses AIBO directly. He wants to stay on AIBO's good side, asking, "Will he get mad if you pick him up?" When Jake's style of addressing AIBO reveals that Jake finds the robot's affective states genuine, Orelia corrects her brother sharply: "It [AIBO] would just be mad at you because it's programmed to know 'if I don't get the ball, I'll be mad.'" The fact that AIBO is programmed to show emotions make these artificial and not to be trusted.

Orelia expands on real versus programmed emotion:

A dog, it would actually feel sorry for you. It would have sympathy, but AIBO, it's artificial. I read a book called *The Wrinkle in Time,* where everyone was programmed by this thing called "It." And all the people were completely on routine. They just did the same thing over and over. I think it'd be the same thing with the [artificial] dog. The dog wouldn't be able to do anything else.

For Orelia, only living beings have real thoughts and emotions:

With a real dog if you become great friends with it, it really loves you, you know, it truly . . . has a brain, and you know somewhere in the dog's brain, it loves you, and this one [AIBO], it's just somewhere on a computer disk . . . If a real dog dies, you know, they have memories, a real dog would have memories of times, and stuff that you did with him or her, but this one [AIBO] doesn't have a brain, so it can't.

Orelia wants the kind of love that only a living creature can provide. She fears the ability of any creature to behave 'as if' it could love. She denies a chilly emotional reality by attributing qualities of intuition, transparency, and connectedness to all people and animals. A philosophical position about robots is linked to an experience of the machine-like equalities of which people are capable, a good example of the interdependence of philosophical position and psychological motivation.

Melanie: Yearning to Nurture a Robotic Companion

The quality of a child's relationship with a parent does not determine a *particular* relationship to robotic companions. Rather, feelings about robots can represent different strategies for dealing with one's parents, and perhaps for working through difficulties with them. This is illustrated by the contrast between Orelia and ten-year-old Melanie. Melanie, like Orelia, had sessions with AIBO and My Real Baby at school and was given both to play with at home. In Melanie's case, feelings that she did not have enough of her parent's attention led her to want to nurture a robotic creature. Melanie was able to feel more loved by loving another; the My Real Baby and AIBO were "creature enough" for this purpose.

Melanie is soft-spoken, intelligent, and well mannered. Both of her parents have busy professional lives; Melanie is largely taken care of by nannies and baby-sitters. With sadness, she says that what she misses most is spending time with her father. She speaks of him throughout her interviews and play sessions. Nurturing the robots enables her to work through feelings that her parents, and her father in particular, are not providing her with the attention she desires.

Melanie believes that AIBO and My Real Baby are sentient and have emotions. She thinks that when we brought the robotic dog and doll to her school "they were probably confused about who their mommies and daddies were because they were being handled by so many different people." She thinks that AIBO probably does not know that he is at her particular school because the school is strange to him, but "almost certainly does knows that he is outside of MIT and visiting another school." She sees her role with the robots as straightforward; it is maternal.

One of Melanie's third-grade classmates is aggressive with My Real Baby and treats the doll like an object to explore (poking the doll's eyes, pinching its skin to test its "rubberness," and putting her fingers roughly inside its mouth). Observing this behavior, Melanie comes over to rescue the doll. She takes it in her arms and proceeds to play with it as though it were a baby, holding it close, whispering to it, caressing its face. Speaking of the My Real Baby doll that she is about to take home, Melanie says, "I think that if I'm the first one to interact with her then maybe if she goes home with another person [another study participant] she'll cry a lot . . . because she doesn't know, doesn't think that this person is its Mama." For Melanie, My Real Baby's aliveness is dependent on its animation and relational properties. Its lack of biology is not in play. Melanie understands that My Real Baby is a machine. This is clear in her description of its possible "death."

Hum, if his batteries run out, maybe [it could die]. I think it's electric. So, if it falls and breaks, then it would die, but if people could repair it, then I'm not really sure. [I]f it falls and like totally shatters I don't think they could fix it, then it would die, but if it falls and one of its ear falls off, they would probably fix that.

Melanie combines a mechanical view of My Real Baby with confidence that it deserves to have her motherly love. At home, Melanie has AIBO and My Real Baby sleep near her bed and believes they will be happiest on a silk pillow. She names My Real Baby after her three-year old cousin Sophie. "I named her like my cousin . . . because she [My Real Baby] was sort of demanding and said most of the things that Sophie does." She analogies the AIBO to her dog, Nelly. When AIBO malfunctions, Melanie does not experience it as broken, but as behaving in ways that remind her of Nelly. In the following exchange that takes place at MIT, AIBO makes a loud, mechanical, wheezing sound and its walking becomes increasingly wobbly. Finally AIBO falls several times and then finally is still. Melanie gently picks up the limp AIBO and holds it close, petting it softly. At home, she and a friend treat it like a sick animal that needs to be rescued. They give it "veterinary care."

In thinking about relational artifacts such as Furbys, AIBOs, My Real Babies, and Paros, the question is posed: how these objects differ from "traditional" (non-computational) toys, teddy bears, and Raggedy-Ann dolls. Melanie, unbidden, speaks directly to this issue. With other dolls, she feels that she is "pretending." With My Real Baby, she feels that she is really the dolls's mother: "[I feel] like I'm her real mom. I bet if I really tried, she could learn another word. Maybe Da-da. Hopefully if I said it a lot, she would pick up. It's sort of like a real baby, where you wouldn't want to set a bad example."

For Melanie, not only does My Real Baby have feelings, Melanie sees it as capable of complex, mixed emotions. "It's got similar to human feelings, because she can really tell the differences between things, and she's happy a lot. She gets happy, and she gets sad, and mad, and excited. I think right now she's excited and happy at the same time."

Our relationship, it grows bigger. Maybe when I first started playing with her she didn't really know me so she wasn't making as much of these noises, but now that she's played with me a lot more she really knows me and is a lot more outgoing. Same with AIBO.

When her several weeks with AIBO and My Real Baby come to an end, Melanie is sad to return them. Before leaving them with us, she opens the box in which they are housed and gives them an emotional good bye. She hugs each one separately, tells them that she will miss them very much but that she knows we [the researchers] will take good care of them. Melanie is concerned that the toys will forget her, especially if they spend a lot of time with other families.

Melanie's relationship with the AIBO and My Real Baby illustrates their projective qualities: she nurtures them because getting enough nurturance is an issue for her. But in providing nurturance to the robots, Melanie provided it to herself as well (and in a way that felt more authentic than developing a relationship with a "traditional" doll). In another case, a seriously ill child was able to use relational robots to speak more easily in his own voice.

Jimmy: From Rorschach to Relationship

Jimmy, small, pale, and thin, is just completing first grade. He has a congenital illness that causes him to spend much time in hospitals. During our sessions with AIBO and My Real Baby he sometimes runs out of energy to continue talking. Jimmy comes to our study with a long history of playing computer games. His favorite is Roller Coaster Tycoon. Many children play the game to create the wildest roller coasters possible; Jimmy plays the game to maximize the maintenance and staffing of his coasters so that the game gives him awards for the safest park. Jimmy's favorite toys are Beanie Babies. Jimmy participates in our study with his twelve-year-old brother, Tristan.

Jimmy approaches AIBO and My Real Baby as objects with consciousness and feelings. When AIBO slams into the red siding that defines his game space, Jimmy interprets his actions as "scratching a door, wanting to go in . . . I think it's probably doing that because it wants to go through the door . . . Because he hasn't been in there yet." Jimmy thinks that AIBO has similar feelings toward him as his biological dog, Sam. He says that AIBO would miss him when he goes to school and would want to jump in to the car with him. In contrast, Jimmy does not believe that his Beanie Babies, the stuffed animal toys, have feelings or 'aliveness,' or miss him when he is at school. Jimmy tells us that other relational artifacts like Furbies 'really do' learn and are the same 'kind of alive' as AIBO.

During several sessions with AIBO, Jimmy talks about AIBO as a super dog that show up his own dog as a limited creature. Jimmy says: "AIBO is probably as smart as Sam and at least he isn't as scared as my dog [is]." When we ask Jimmy if there are things that his dog can do that AIBO can't do, Jimmy answers not in terms of his dog's strengths but in terms of his deficiencies: "There are some things that *Sam can't do and AIBO can*. Sam can't fetch a ball. AIBO can. And Sam definitely can't kick a ball." On several other occasions, when AIBO completed a trick, Jimmy commented "My dog couldn't do that!" AIBO is the "better" dog. AIBO is immortal, invincible. AIBO cannot get sick or die. In sum, AIBO represents what Jimmy wants to be.

During Jimmy's play sessions at MIT, he forms a strong bond with AIBO. Jimmy tells us that he would probably miss AIBO as much as Sam if either of them died. As we talk about the possibility of AIBO dying, Jimmy explains that he believes AIBO could die if he ran out of power. Jimmy wants to protect AIBO by taking him home.

> If you turn him off he dies, well, he falls asleep or something . . . He'll probably be in my room most of the time. And I'm probably going to keep him downstairs so he doesn't fall down the stairs. Because he probably, in a sense he would die if he fell down the stairs. Because he could break. And. Well, he could break and he also could . . . probably or if he broke he'd probably . . . he'd die like.

Jimmy's concerns about his vulnerable health are expressed with AIBO in several ways. Sometimes he thinks the dog is vulnerable, but Jimmy thinks he could protect him. Sometimes he thinks the dog is invulnerable, a super-hero dog in relation to his frail biological counterpart. He tests AIBO's strength in order to feel reassured.

Jimmy "knows" that AIBO does not have a real brain and a heart, but sees AIBO as a mechanical kind of alive, where it can function as if it had a heart and a brain. For Jimmy, AIBO is "alive in a way," because he can "move around" and "[H]e's also got feelings. He shows . . . he's got three eyes on him, mad, happy, and sad. And well, that's how he's alive." As evidence of AIBO's emotions, Jimmy points to the robot's lights: "When he's mad, then they're red. [And when they are green] he's happy."

Jimmy has moments of intense physical vulnerability, sometimes during our sessions. His description of how AIBO can strengthen himself is poignant. "Well, when he's charging that means, well he's kind of sleepy when he's charging but when he's awake he remembers things more. And probably he remembered my hand because I kept on poking in front of his face so he can see it. And he's probably looking for me."

AIBO recharging reassures Jimmy by providing him with a model of an object that can resist death. If AIBO can be alive through wires and a battery then this leaves hope that people can be "recharged" and "rewired" as well. His own emotional connection to life through technology motivates a philosophical position that robots are "sort of alive."

At home, Jimmy likes to play a game in which his Bio Bugs attack his AIBO. He relishes these contests in which he identifies with AIBO. AIBO lives through technology and Jimmy sees AIBO's survival as his own. AIBO symbolizes Jimmy's hopes to someday be a form of life that defies death. The Bio Bugs are the perfect embodiment of threat to the body, symbolizing the many threats that Jimmy has to fight off.

Jimmy seems concerned that his brother, Tristan, barely played with AIBO during the time they had the robot at home. Jimmy brings this up to us in a shaky voice. Jimmy explains that his brother didn't play with AIBO because "he didn't want to get addicted to him so he would be sad when we had to give him back." Jimmy emphasizes that he did not share this fear. Tristan is distant from Jimmy. Jimmy is concerned that his brother's holding back from him is because Tristan fears that he might die. Here, AIBO becomes the "stand in" for the self.

When he has to return his AIBO, Jimmy says that AIBO he will miss the robot "a little bit" but that it is AIBO that will probably miss him more.

Researcher: Do you think that you'll miss AIBO?

Jimmy: A little bit. He'll probably miss me.

Seniors: Robots as a Prism for the Past

In bringing My Real Babies into nursing homes, it was not unusual for seniors to use the doll to re-enact scenes from their children's youth or important moments in their relationships with spouses. Indeed, seniors were more comfortable playing out family scenes with robotic dolls than with traditional ones. Seniors felt social "permission" to be with the robots, presented as a highly valued and "grownup" activity. Additionally, the robots provided the elders something to talk about, a seed for a sense of community.

As in the case of children, projection and evocation were entwined in the many ways seniors related to the robots. Some seniors, such as Jonathan, wanted the objects to be transparent as a clockwork might be and became anxious when their efforts to investigate the robots' "innards" were frustrated. Others were content to interact with the robot as it presented itself, with no window onto how it 'worked' in any mechanical sense. They took the relational artifact 'at interface value' (Turkle 1995). In each case, emotional issues were closely entwined with emergent philosophies of technology.

Jonathan: Exploring a Relational Creature, Engineer-Style

Jonathan, 74, has movements that are slow and precise; he is well spoken, curious, and intelligent. He tells us that throughout his life he has been ridiculed for his obsessive ways. He tends to be reclusive and has few friends at the nursing home. Never married, with no children, he has always been a solitary man. For most of his life, Jonathan worked as an accountant, but was happiest when he worked as a computer programmer. Now, Jonathan approaches AIBO and My Real Baby with a desire to analyze them in an analytical, engineer's style.

From his first interaction with the My Real Baby at a group activity to his last interview after having kept the robot for four months in his room, Jonathan remained fascinated with how it functioned. He handles My Real Baby with detachment in his methodical explorations.

When Jonathan meets My Real Baby the robot is cooing and giggling. Jonathan looks it over carefully, bounces it up and down, pokes and squeezes it, and moves its limbs. With each move, he focuses on the doll's reactions. Jonathan tries to understand what the doll says and where its voice comes from. Like Orelia, Jonathan talks to the researchers about the robot, but does not speak to the robot itself. When he discovers that My Real Baby's voice comes from its stomach, he puts his ear next to the stomach and says: "I think that this doll is a very remarkable toy. I have never seen anything like this before. But I'd like to know, how in the entire universe is it possible to construct a doll that talks like this?"

Despite his technical orientation to the robot, Jonathan says that he would be more comfortable speaking to a computer or robot about his problems than to a person.

> Because if the thing is very highly private and very personal it might be embarrassing to talk about it to another person, and I might be afraid of being ridiculed for it . . . And it wouldn't criticize me . . . Or let's say that if I wanted to blow off steam, it would be better to do it to a computer than to do it to a living person who has nothing to do with the thing that's bothering me. [I could] express with the computer emotions that I feel I could not express with another person, to a person.

Nevertheless, Jonathan cannot imagine that his bond with My Real Baby could be similar to those he experiences with live animals, for example the cats he took care of before coming to the nursing home:

> Some of the things I used to enjoy with the cat are things I could never have with a robot animal. Like the cat showing affection, jumping up on my lap,

letting me pet her and listening to her purr, a robot animal couldn't do that and I enjoyed it very much.

Jonathan makes a distinction between the affection that can be offered by something alive and an object that acts as if it were alive.

Andy: Animation in the Service of Working Through

Andy, 76, at the same nursing home as Jonathan, is recovering from a serious depression. At the end of each of our visits to the nursing home, he makes us promise to come back to see him as soon as we can. Andy feels abandoned by family and friends. He wants more people to talk with. He participates in a day-program outside the home, but nevertheless, often feels bored and lonely. Andy loves animals and has decorated his room with scores of cat pictures; he tells us that some of his happiest moments are being outside in the nursing home's garden speaking to birds, squirrels, and neighborhood cats. He believes they communicate with him and considers them his friends. Andy treats robotic dolls and pets as sentient; they become stand-ins for the people he would like to have in his life. Like Jonathan, we gave Andy a My Real Baby to keep in his room for four months. He never tired of its company.

The person Andy misses most is his ex-wife Rose. Andy reads us songs he has written for her and letters she has sent him. My Real Baby helps him work on unresolved issues in his relationship with Rose. Over time, the robot comes to represent her.

Andy: Rose, that was my ex-wife's name.

Researcher: Did you pretend that it was Rose when you talked to her?

Andy: Yeah. I didn't say anything bad to her, but some things that I would want to say to her, it helped me to think about her and the time that I didn't have my wife, how we broke up, think about that, how I miss seeing her . . . the doll, there's something about her, I can't really say what it is, but looking at her reminds me of a human being. She looks just like her, Rose, my ex-wife, and her daughter . . . something in her face is the same, looking at her makes me feel more calm, I can just think about her and everything else in my life.

Andy speaks at length about his difficulty getting over his divorce, his feelings of guilt that his relationship with Rose did not work out, and his hope that he and his ex-wife might someday be together again. Andy explains how having the doll enables him to try out different scenarios that might lead to a reconciliation with Rose. The doll's presence enables him to express his attachment and vent his feelings of regret and frustration.

Researcher: How does it make you feel to talk to the doll?

Andy: Good. It lets me take everything inside me out, you know, that's how I feel talking to her, getting it all out of me and feel not depressed . . . when I wake up in the morning I see her over there, it makes me feel so nice, like somebody is watching over you.

Andy: It will really help me [to keep the doll] because I am all alone, there's no one around, so I can play with her, we can talk. It will help me get ready to be on my own.

Researcher: How?

Andy: By talking to her, saying some of the things that I might say when I did go out, because right now, you know I don't talk to anybody right now, and I can talk much more right now with her than, I don't talk to anybody right now.

Andy holds the doll close to his chest, rubs its back in a circular motion, and says lovingly, "I love you. Do you love me?" He makes funny faces at the doll, as if to prevent her from falling asleep or just to amuse her. When the doll laughs with perfect timing as if responding to his grimaces, Andy laughs back, joining her. My Real Baby is nothing if not an "intimate machine."

Intimate Machines: A Robot Kind of Love

The projective material of the children and seniors is closely tied to their beliefs about the nature of the relational artifacts in their care. We already know that the "intimate machines" of the computer culture have shifted how children talk about what is and is not alive (Turkle 2005[1984]). For example, children use different categories to talk about the aliveness of "traditional" objects than they do when confronted with computational games and toys. A traditional wind-up toy was considered "not alive" when children realized that it did not move of its own accord. Here, the criterion for aliveness was in the domain of physics: autonomous motion. Faced with computational media, children's way of talking about aliveness became psychological. Children classified computational objects as alive (from the late 1970s and the days of the electronic toys Merlin, Simon, and Speak and Spell) if they could *think* on their own. Faced with a computer toy that could play tic-tac-toe, what counted to a child was not the object's physical but psychological autonomy.

Children of the early 1980s came to define what made people special in opposition to computers, which they saw as our "nearest neighbors." Computers, the children reasoned, are rational machines; people are special because they are emotional. Children's use of the category "emotional machines" to describe what makes people special was a fragile, unstable definition of human uniqueness. In 1984, when I completed my study of a first generation of children who grew up with electronic toys and games, I thought that other formulations would arise from generations of children who might, for example, take the intelligence of artifacts for granted, understand how it was created, and be less inclined to give it philosophical importance. But as if on cue, robotic creatures that presented themselves as having both feelings and needs entered mainstream American culture. By the mid-1990s, as emotional machines, people were not alone.

With relational artifacts, the focus of discussion about whether computational artifacts might be alive moved from the psychology of projection to the psychology of engagement, from Rorschach to relationship, from creature competency to creature connection. Children and seniors already talk about an "animal kind of alive" and a "Furby kind of alive." The question ahead is whether they will also come to talk about a "people kind of love" and a "robot kind of love."

What is a robot kind of love?

In the early 1980s, I met a thirteen-year-old, Deborah, who responded to the experience of computer programming by speaking about the pleasures of putting "a piece of your mind into the computer's mind and coming to see yourself differently." Twenty years later, eleven-year-old Fara reacts to a play session with Cog, a humanoid robot at MIT that can meet her eyes, follow her position, and imitate her movements, by saying that she could never get tired of the robot because "it's not like a toy because you can't teach a toy; it's like something that's part of you, you know, something you love, kind of like another person, like a baby."

In the 1980s, debates in artificial intelligence centered on the question of whether machines could "really" be intelligent. These debates were about the objects themselves, what they could and could not do. Our new debates about relational and sociable machines—debates that will have an increasingly high profile in mainstream culture—are not about the machines' capabilities but about our vulnerabilities. In my view, decisions about the role of robots in the lives of children and seniors cannot turn simply on whether children and the elderly "like" the robots. What does this deployment of "nurturing technology" at the two most dependent moments of the life cycle say about us? What will it do to us? What kinds of relationships are appropriate to have with machines? And what is a relationship?

My work in robotics laboratories has offered some images of how future relationships with machines may look, appropriate or not. For example, Cynthia Breazeal was leader on the design team for Kismet, the robotic head that was designed to interact with humans "sociably," much as a two-year-old child would. Breazeal was its chief programmer, tutor, and companion. Kismet needed Breazeal to become as "intelligent" as it did and then Kismet became a creature Breazeal and others could interact with. Breazeal experienced what might be called a maternal connection to Kismet; she certainly describes a sense of connection with it as more than "mere" machine. When she graduated from MIT and left the AI Laboratory where she had done her doctoral research, the tradition of academic property rights demanded that Kismet be left behind in the laboratory that had paid for its development. What she left behind was the robot "head" and its attendant software. Breazeal described a sharp sense of loss. Building a new Kismet would not be the same.

In the summer of 2001, I studied children interacting with robots, including Kismet, at the MIT AI Laboratory (Turkle et. al. 2006). It was the last time that Breazeal would have access to Kismet. It is not surprising that separation from Kismet was not easy for Breazeal, but more striking, it was hard for the rest of us to imagine Kismet without her. One ten-year-old who overheard a conversation among graduate students about how Kismet would be staying in the AI lab objected: "But Cynthia is Kismet's mother."

It would be facile to analogize Breazeal's situation to that of Monica, the mother in Spielberg's *A.I.,* a film in which an adopted robot provokes feelings of love in his human caretaker, but Breazeal is, in fact, one of the first people to have one of the signal experiences in that story, separation from a robot to which one has formed an attachment based on nurturance. At issue here is not Kismet's achieved level of intelligence, but Breazeal's experience as a "caregiver." My fieldwork with relational artifacts suggests that being asked to nurture a machine that presents itself as an young creature of any kind, constructs us as dedicated cyber-caretakers. Nurturing a machine that presents itself as dependent creates significant attachments. We might assume that giving a sociable, "affective" machine to our children or to our aging parents will change the way we see the lifecycle and our roles and responsibilities in it.

Sorting out our relationships with robots bring us back to the kinds of challenges that Darwin posed to his generation: the question of human uniqueness. How will interacting with relational artifacts affect people's way of thinking about what, if anything, makes people special? The sight of children and the elderly exchanging tendernesses with robotic pets brings science fiction into everyday life and techno-philosophy down to earth. The question here is not whether children will love their robotic pets more than their real life pets or even their parents, but rather, what will loving come to mean?

One woman's comment on AIBO, Sony's household entertainment robot, startles in what it might augur for the future of person-machine relationships: "[AIBO] is better than a real dog . . . It won't do dangerous things, and it won't betray you . . . Also, it won't die suddenly and make you feel very sad." Mortality has traditionally defined the human condition; a shared sense of mortality has been the basis for feeling a commonality with other human beings, a sense of going through the same life cycle, a sense of the preciousness of time and life, of its fragility. Loss (of parents, of friends, of family) is part of the way we understand how human beings grow and develop and bring the qualities of other people within themselves (Freud 1989).

Relationships with computational creatures may be deeply compelling, perhaps educational, but they do not put us in touch with the complexity, contradiction, and limitations of the human life cycle. They do not teach us what we need to know about empathy, ambivalence, and life lived in shades of gray. To say all of this about our love of our robots does not diminish their interest or importance. It only puts them in their place.

Notes

1. A note on method: the observations presented here are based on open-ended qualitative fieldwork. This is useful in the study of human/robot interaction for several reasons. Case studies and participant-observation in natural settings enable the collection of empirical data about how people think about and use technology outside the laboratory. Qualitative methods are well-positioned to bring cultural beliefs and novel questions to light. Open-ended qualitative work puts the novelty of the technology at the center of things and says, "When you are interested in something new: *observe, listen, ask.*" Additionally, qualitative approaches to human-robot interaction provide analytical tools that help us better understand both the technologies under study and the social and cultural contexts in which these technologies are deployed. Differences in individual responses to technology are a window onto personality, life history, and cognitive style. Seeing technology in social context helps us better understand social complexities.

2. My case studies of robots and seniors with AIBO and My Real Baby are drawn from work conducted through weekly visits to schools and nursing homes from 2001 to 2003, studies that encompassed several hundred participants. In my discussion of Paro, I am reporting on studies of the same two nursing homes during the spring of 2005, a study that took place during twelve site visits

and recruited 23 participants, ranging in age from 60–104, six males, and seventeen females. Researchers on these projects include Olivia Dasté, for the first phase of work, and for the second phase, Cory Kidd and Will Taggart.

References

Bowker, G.C., and Star, S.L. 1999. *Sorting Things Out: Classification and Its Consequences,* Cambridge, Mass.: MIT Press.

Breazeal, C. "Sociable Machines: Expressive Social Exchange Between Humans and Robots." 2000. PhD Thesis, Massachusetts Institute of Technology.

Breazeal, C. 2002. *Designing Sociable Robots,* Cambridge: MIT Press.

Breazeal, C., and Scassellati, B. 1999. "How to Build Robots that Make Friends and Influence People," in *Proceedings of the IEEE/RSJ International Conference on Intelligent Robots and Systems (IROS-99),* pp. 858–863.

Breazeal, C., and Scassellati, B., 2000. "Infant-like Social Interactions Between a Robot and a Human Caretaker," *Adaptive Behavior,* 8, pp. 49–74.

Freud, S. 1960. "The Uncanny," in *The Standard Edition of the Complete Psychological Works of Sigmund Freud,* vol. 17, J. Strachey, trans. and ed. London: The Hogarth Press, pp. 219–252.

Freud, S. 1989. "Mourning and Melancholia," in *The Freud Reader.* P. Gay, ed. New York: W.W. Norton & Company, p. 585.

Kahn, P., Friedman, B., Perez-Granados, D.R., and Freier, N.G. 2004. "Robotic Pets in the Lives of Preschool Children," in *CHI Extended Abstracts,* ACM Press, 2004, pp. 1449–1452.

Kidd, C.D. "Sociable Robots: The Role of Presence and Task in Human-Robot Interaction." 2004. Master's Thesis, Massachusetts Institute of Technology.

Shibata, T., Tashima, T., and Tanie, K. 1999. "Emergence of Emotional Behavior through Physical Interaction between Human and Robot," in *Proceedings of the IEEE International Conference on Robotics and Automation,* 1999, pp. 2868–2873.

Shibata, T. (accessed 01 April 2005). "Mental Commit Robot," Available online at: http://www.mel.go.jp/soshiki/robot/biorobo/shibata/

Taggard, W., Turkle, S., and Kidd, C.D. 2005. "An Interactive Robot in a Nursing Home: Preliminary Remarks," in *Proceedings of CogSci Workshop on Android Science,* Stresa, Italy, pp. 56–61.

Turkle, S. 2005 [1984]. The Second Self: Computers and the Human Spirit. Cambridge, Mass.: MIT Press.

Turkle, S, *Life on the Screen.* 1995. New York: Simon and Schuster.

Turkle, S. 2004. "Relational Artifacts," NSF Report, (NSF Grant SES-0115668).

Turkle, S. 2005a. "Relational Artifacts/Children/Elders: The Complexities of CyberCompanions," in *Proceedings of the CogSci Workshop on Android Science,* Stresa, Italy, 2005, pp. 62–73.

Turkle, S. 2005b. "Caring Machines: Relational Artifacts for the Elderly." Keynote AAAI Workshop, "Caring Machines." Washington, D.C.

Turkle, S., Breazeal, C., Dasté, O., and Scassellati, B. 2006. "First Encounters with Kismet and Cog: Children's Relationship with Humanoid Robots," in *Digital Media: Transfer in Human Communication,* P. Messaris and L. Humphreys, eds. New York: Peter Lang Publishing.

Turner, V. 1969. The Ritual Process. Chicago: Aldine.

Weizenbaum, J. 1976. *Computer Power and Human Reason: From Judgment to Calculation.* San Francisco, CA: W. H. Freeman. Winnicott. D. W. (1971). *Playing and Reality.* New York: Basic Books.

From *AAAI Technical Report,* July 2006, pp. 1–10. Copyright © 2006 by AAAI Press. Reprinted by permission.

Toward Nature-Inspired Computing

NIC-based systems utilize autonomous entities that self-organize to achieve the goals of systems modeling and problem solving.

JIMING LIU AND K. C. TSUI

Nature-inspired computing (NIC) is an emerging computing paradigm that draws on the principles of self-organization and complex systems. Here, we examine NIC from two perspectives. First, as a way to help explain, model, and characterize the underlying mechanism(s) of complex real-world systems by formulating computing models and testing hypotheses through controlled experimentation. The end product is a potentially deep understanding or at least a better explanation of the working mechanism(s) of the modeled system. And second, as a way to reproduce autonomous (such as lifelike) behavior in solving computing problems. With detailed knowledge of the underlying mechanism(s), simplified abstracted autonomous lifelike behavior can be used as a model in practically any general-purpose problem-solving strategy or technique.

Neither objective is achievable without formulating a model of the factors underlying the system. The modeling process can begin with a theoretical analysis from either a macroscopic or microscopic view of the system. Alternatively, the application developer may adopt a blackbox or whitebox approach. Blackbox approaches (such as Markov models and artificial neural networks) normally do not reveal much about their working mechanism(s). On the other hand, whitebox approaches (such as agents with bounded rationality) are more useful for explaining behavior [7].

The essence of NIC formulation involves conceiving a computing system operated by population(s) of autonomous entities. The rest of the system is referred to as the environment. An autonomous entity consists of a detector (or set of detectors), an effector (or set of effectors), and a repository of local behavior rules (see Figure 1) [5,8].

A detector receives information related to its neighbors and to the environment. For example, in a simulation of a flock of birds, this information would include the speed and direction the birds are heading and the distance between the

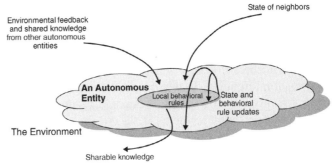

Figure 1 Modeling an autonomous entity in a NIC-based system.

birds in question. The details of the content and format of the information must be defined according to the system to be modeled or to the problem to be solved. The notion of neighbors may be defined in terms of position (such as the bird(s) ahead, to the left, and to the right), distance (such as a radial distance of two grids), or both (such as the birds up to two grids ahead of the nominal viewpoint bird).

Environmental information conveys the status of a certain feature of interest to an autonomous entity. The environment can also help carry sharable local knowledge. The effector of an autonomous entity refers collectively to the device for expressing actions. Actions can be changes to an internal state, an external display of certain behaviors, or changes to the environment the entity inhabits. An important role of the effector, as part of the local behavior model, is to facilitate implicit information sharing among autonomous entities.

Central to an autonomous entity are the rules of behavior governing how it must act or react to the information collected by the detector from the environment and its neighbors. These rules determine into what state the entity should change and also what local knowledge should be released via the effector to the environment. An example of sharable local knowledge is the role pheromones play in an ant colony. It is untargeted, and the communication via the environment is undirected; any ant can pick up the information and react according to its own behavior model.

In order to adapt itself to a problem without being explicitly told what to do in advance, an autonomous entity must modify the rules of its behavior over time. This ability, responding to local changing conditions, is known as the individual's learning capability. Worth noting is that randomness plays a part in the decision-making process of an autonomous entity despite the presence of a rule set. It allows an autonomous entity to explore uncharted territory despite evidence that it should exploit only a certain path. On the other hand, randomness helps the entity resolve conflict in the presence of equal support for suggestions to act in different ways in its own best interests and avoid being stuck by randomly choosing an action in local optima.

The environment acts as the domain in which autonomous entities are free to roam. This is a static view of the environment. The environment of a NIC system can also act as the "noticeboard" where the autonomous entities post and read local information. In this dynamic view, the environment is constantly changing For example, in the N-queen constraint satisfaction problem [7], the environment can tell a particular queen on a chessboard how many constraints are violated in her neighborhood after a move is made. In effect, this violations, or conflicts, report translates a global goal into a local goal for a particular entity. The environment also keeps the central clock that helps synchronize the actions of all autonomous entities, as needed.

Before exploring examples of NIC for characterizing complex behavior or for solving computing problems, we first highlight the central NIC ideas, along with common NIC characteristics, including autonomous, distributed, emergent, adaptive, and self-organized, or ADEAS [5]:

Autonomous. In NIC systems, entities are individuals with bounded rationality that act independently. There is no central controller for directing and coordinating individual entities. Formal computing models and techniques are often used to describe how the entities acquire and improve their reactive behavior, based on their local and/or shared utilities, and how the behavior and utilities of the entities become goal-directed.

Distributed. Autonomous entities with localized decision-making capabilities are distributed in a heterogeneous computing environment, locally interacting among themselves to exchange their state information or affect the states of others. In distributed problem solving (such as scheduling and optimization), they continuously measure, update, and share information with other entities following certain predefined protocols.

Emergent. Distributed autonomous entities collectively exhibit complex (purposeful) behavior not present or pre-defined in the behavior of the autonomous entities within the system. One interesting issue in studying the emergent behaviors that leads to some desired computing solutions (such as optimal resource allocation) is how to mathematically model and measure the interrelationships among the local goals of the entities and the desired global goal(s) of the NIC system in a particular application.

Adaptive. Entities often change their behavior in response to changes in the environment in which they are situated. In doing so, they utilize behavioral adaptation mechanisms to continuously evaluate and fine-tune their behavioral attributes with reference to their goals, as well as to ongoing feedback (such as intermediate rewards). Evolutionary approaches may be used to reproduce high-performing entities and eliminate poor-performing ones.

Self-organized. The basic elements of NIC-based systems are autonomous entities and their environment. Local interactions among them are the most powerful force in their evolution toward certain desired states. Self-organization is the essential process of a NIC system's working mechanism. Through local interactions, these systems self-aggregate and amplify the outcome of entity behavior.

Characterizing Complex Behavior

A complex system can be analyzed and understood in many different ways. The most obvious is to look at it from the outside, observing its behaviors and using models to try to identify and list them. Assumptions about unknown mechanisms must be made to start the process. Given observable behaviors of the desired system, NIC designers verify the model by comparing its behavior with the desired features. This process is repeated several times before a good, though not perfect, prototype can be found. Apart from obtaining a working model of the desired system, an important by-product is the discovery of the mechanisms that were unknown when the design process began.

The human immune system is an example of a highly sensitive, adaptive, self-regulated complex system involving numerous interactions among a vast number of cells of different types. Despite numerous clinical case studies and empirical findings [1], the working mechanism underlying the complex process of, say, HIV invasion and the erosion and eventual crash of the immune system (including how the local interactions in HIV, T-cells, and B-cells affect the process) are still not fully understood (characterized and predicted).

The usefulness of conventional modeling and simulation technologies is limited due to computational scale and costs.

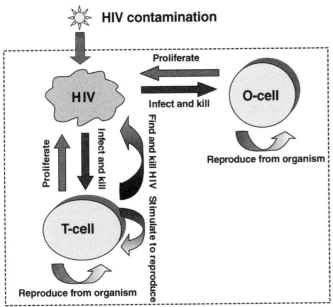

Figure 2 Modeling HIV, T-cells, and O(ther) cells in a NIC-based system.

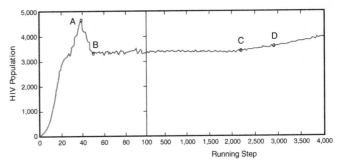

Figure 3 Simulation results on an HIV population during several phases of AIDS development.

Understanding and modeling complex systems (such as the human immune system) is a major challenge for the field of computing for two main reasons: the task of computing is seamlessly carried out in a variety of physical embodiments, and no single multipurpose or dedicated machine is able to accomplish the job. The key to success for simulating self-regulated complex systems lies in the large-scale deployment of computational entities or agents able to autonomously make local decisions and achieve collective goals.

Seeking to understand the dynamics of the immune system during an HIV attack, NIC researchers can use a 2D lattice to build a NIC model. The lattice is circular so the edges wrap around one another. Each site can be inhabited by HIV, as well as by immune cells. HIV and immune cells behave in four main ways:

Interaction. T-cells recognize HIV by its signature (protein structure); HIV infects and kills cells;

Proliferation. Reactions stimulate lymphoid tissue to produce more T-cells, which are reproduced naturally;

Death. Besides being killed by drugs and other deliberate medical intervention, HIV and T-cells die naturally; and

Diffusion. HIV diffuses from densely populated sites to neighboring sites (see Figure 2).

Figure 3 outlines the temporal emergence of three-stage dynamics in HIV infection generated from the NIC model [12]:

Before B. Primary response;

B ~ C. Clinical latency; and

After D. Onset of AIDS.

At A, the HIV population reaches a maximum point. Starting from C, the mechanism that decreases the natural ability of an organism to reproduce T-cells is triggered. These NIC-generated results are consistent with empirically observed phenomena [1]. Experiments in [12] have also found that AIDS cannot break out if HIV destroys only T-cells without weakening the T-cell reproduction mechanism. The emergence in "shape space" indicates it is because of HIV's fast mutation that the immune system cannot eradicate HIV as readily as it does other invaders. These discoveries are helping immunology researchers understand the dynamics of HIV-immune interaction.

The NIC approach to systems modeling starts from a microscopic view of the immune system. The elements of the model are the basic units—HIV and immune cells—of the immune system. The model aims to capture the essence of the immune system, though simplification is inevitable. Note that the autonomous entities in the model that belong to the same species types normally have a similar set of behavior rules. The only difference among them is the parameters of the rules, which may be adapted throughout the lifetime of the entities. Probabilistic selection of certain behavior is also common in the entities. It must be emphasized that the environment of the model can also be viewed as a unique entity in the model, with its own behavior rules.

Self-Organized Web Regularities

Researchers have identified several self-organized regularities related to the Web, ranging from its growth and evolution to usage patterns in Web surfing. Many such regularities are best represented by characteristic distributions following a Zipf law or a power law. Random-walk models [4] have been used to simulate some statistical regularities empirically observed on the Web. However, these models do not relate the emergent regularities to the dynamic interactions between users and the Web, nor do they reflect the interrelationships between user behavior and the contents or structure of the Web. User interest and motivation in navigating the

Web are among the most important factors determining user navigation behavior.

As part of the NIC approach to regularity characterization, [6] proposed a computational model of Web surfing that includes user characteristics (such as interest profiles, motivations, and navigation strategies). Users are viewed as information-foraging entities inhabiting the Web environment or as a collection of websites connected by hyperlinks. When an entity finds certain websites with content related to its topic(s) of interest, it will be motivated to search sites deeper into the Web. On the other hand, when an entity finds no interesting information after a certain amount of foraging or finds enough content to satisfy its interest, it stops foraging and goes offline, leaving the Web environment.

Experiments in [6] classified users into three groups: recurrent users familiar with the Web structure; rational users new to a particular website but who know what they are looking for; and random users with no strong intention to retrieve information but are just "wandering around." The results, which used both synthetic and empirical data from visitors to NASA website(s), showed that the foraging agent-entity-oriented model generates power-law distributions in surfing and link-click-frequency, similar to those found in the real world and hence offer a whitebox explanation of self-organized Web regularities.

Solving Computing Problems

The key factors contributing to the success of these NIC-based models are the distinctive characteristics of their elements. Marvin Minsky of MIT suggested in his 1986 book *Society of Mind* that "To explain the mind, we have to show how minds are built from mindless stuff, from parts that are much smaller and simpler than anything we'd consider smart." So, if we want to formulate a problem-solving strategy based on some observation from nature, how and where should we begin? To formulate a NIC problem-solving system, we must identify and gain a deep understanding of a working system in the natural or physical world from which models can be extracted. As with complex-systems modeling, the abstracted behavior of the working system becomes the property of the elements to be modeled.

Basing their approach on the general principles of survival of the fittest (whereby poor performers are eliminated) and the "law of the jungle" (whereby weak performers are eaten by stronger ones), several NIC systems have been devised [7, 9] to solve some well-known constraint-satisfaction problems. One is the N-queen problem, in which N queens are placed on an N × N chessboard, so no two queens ever appear in the same row, column, or diagonal. Based on the rules of the problem, a NIC model is formulated in the following way: Each queen is modeled as an autonomous entity in the system, and multiple queens are assigned to each row

of the chessboard (a grid environment). This process allows for competition among the queens in the same row, so the queen with the best strategy survives. The system calculates the number of violated constraints for each position on the grid. This represents the environmental information all queens can access when making decisions about where to move, with possible movements being restricted to positions in the same row.

Three movement strategies are possible: random-move (involving the random selection of a new position for a queen); least-move (involving selection of the position with the least number of violations, or conflicts); and coop-move (promoting cooperation among the queens by eliminating certain positions in which one queen's position may create conflicts with other queens). All three are selected probabilistically.

This NIC system gives an initial amount of energy to each queen. Like a character in a video game, a queen "dies" if its energy falls below a predefined threshold. A queen's energy level changes in one of two ways: losing it to the environment and absorbing it from another queen. When a queen moves to a new position that violates the set constraint with m queens, it loses m units of energy. This also causes the queens that attack this new position to lose one unit of energy. The intention is to encourage the queens to find a position with the fewest violations, or conflicts. The law of the jungle is implemented by having two or more queens occupy the same grid position and fight over it. The queen with the greatest amount of energy wins and eats the loser(s) by absorbing all its (their) energy. This model efficiently solves the N-queen problem with only a moderate amount of computation.

> **As with complex-systems modeling, the abstracted behavior of the working system becomes the property of the elements to be modeled.**

In the commonly used version of a genetic algorithm [3], a member of the family of evolutionary algorithms, the process of sexual evolution is simplified to selection, recombination, and mutation, without the explicit identification of male and female (such as in the gene pool). John Holland of the University of Michigan, in his quest to develop a model to help explain evolution, has developed a genetic algorithm for optimization. The basic unit in this artificial evolution is a candidate solution to the optimization problem, commonly termed a chromosome. A genetic algorithm has a pool of them. Interactions among candidate solutions are achieved through artificial reproduction where operations mimicking natural evolution allow the candidate solutions to produce offspring that carry part of either parent (crossover) with occasional variation (mutation). While reproduction can be viewed as the cooperative side of all the chromosomes, competition among chromosomes for a position in the next generation directly reflects the principle of survival of the fittest.

On the other hand, evolutionary autonomous agents [10] and evolution strategies [11] are closer to asexual reproduction, with the addition of constraints on mutation and the introduction of mutation operator evolution, respectively. Despite this simplification and modification, evolutionary algorithms capture the essence of natural evolution and are proven global multi-objective optimization techniques. Another successful NIC algorithm that has been applied in similar domains is the Ant System [2], which mimics the food-foraging behavior of ants.

Autonomy-Oriented Computing

As a concrete manifestation of the NIC paradigm, autonomy-oriented computing (AOC) has emerged as a new field of computer science to systematically explore the metaphors and models of autonomy offered in nature (such as physical, biological, and social entities of varying complexity), as well as their role in addressing practical computing needs. It studies emergent autonomy as the core behavior of a computing system, drawing on such principles as multi-entity formulation, local interaction, nonlinear aggregation, adaptation, and self-organization [5, 8].

Three general approaches help researchers develop AOC systems: AOC-by-fabrication, AOC-by-prototyping, and AOC-by-self-discovery. Each has been found to be promising in several application areas [6, 7, 10, 12]. Work on AOC in our research laboratory over the past decade [5, 8] has opened up new ways to understand and develop NIC theories and methodologies. They have provided working examples that demonstrate the power and features of the NIC paradigm toward two main goals: characterizing emergent behavior in natural and artificial systems involving a large number of self-organizing, locally interacting entities; and solving problems in large-scale computation, distributed constraint satisfaction, and decentralized optimization [5].

Conclusion

The NIC paradigm differs from traditional imperative, logical, constraint, object-oriented, and component-based paradigms, not only in the characteristics of its fundamental concepts and constructs, but in the effectiveness and efficiency of the computing that can be achieved through its ADEAS characteristics. NIC approaches have been found most effective in dealing with computational problems characterized by the following dimensions:

High complexity. Problems of high complexity (such as when the system to be characterized involves a large number of autonomous entities or the computational computing problem to be solved involves large-scale, high-dimension, highly nonlinear interactions/relationships, and highly interrelated/constrained variables);

Locally interacting problems. They are not centralized or ready or efficient enough for batch processing;

Changing environment. The environment in which problems are situated is dynamically updated or changes in real time; and

Deep patterns. The goal of modeling and analysis is not to extract some superficial patterns/relationships, data transformation, or association from one form to another, but to discover and understand the deep patterns (such as the underlying mechanisms and processes that produce the data in the first place or help explain their cause and origin).

We will continue to see new NIC theories and methodologies developed and learn to appreciate their wide-ranging effect on computer science, as well as on other disciplines, including sociology, economics, and the natural sciences. Promising applications will help explain gene regulatory networks and drug-resistance mechanisms for anti-cancer drug design, predict the socioeconomic sustainability of self-organizing online markets or communities, and perform real-time autonomous data processing in massive mobile sensor networks for eco-geological observations.

References

1. Coffin, J. HIV population dynamics in vivo: Implications for genetic variation, pathogenesis, and therapy. *Science 267* (1995), 483–489.

2. Dorigo, M., Maniezzo, V., and Colorni, A. The Ant System: Optimization by a colony of cooperative agents. *IEEE Transactions on Systems, Man, and Cybernetics, Part B, 26,* 1 (1996), 1–13.

3. Holland, J. *Adaptation in Natural and Artificial Systems.* MIT Press, Cambridge, MA, 1992.

4. Huberman, B., Pirolli, P., Pitkow, J., and Lukose, R. Strong regularities in World Wide Web surfing. *Science 280* (Apr. 3, 1997), 96–97.

5. Liu, J., Jin, X., and Tsui, K. *Autonomy-Oriented Computing: From Problem Solving to Complex Systems Modeling.* Kluwer Academic Publishers/Springer, Boston, 2005.

6. Liu, J., Zhang, S., and Yang, J. Characterizing Web usage regularities with information foraging agents. *IEEE Transactions on Knowledge and Data Engineering 16,* 5 (2004), 566–584.

7. Liu, J., Han, J., and Tang, Y. Multi-agent-oriented constraint satisfaction. *Artificial Intelligence 136,* 1 (2002), 101–144.

8. Liu, J. *Autonomous Agents and Multi-Agent Systems: Explorations in Learning, Self-Organization and Adaptive Computation*, World Scientific Publishing, Singapore, 2001.

9. Liu, J. and Han, J. A Life: A multi-agent computing paradigm for constraint satisfaction problems. *International Journal of Pattern Recognition and Artificial Intelligence 15*, 3 (2001), 475–491.

10. Liu, J., Tang, Y., and Cao, Y. An evolutionary autonomous agents approach to image feature extraction. *IEEE Transactions on Evolutionary Computation 1*, 2 (1997), 141–158.

11. Schwefel, H.P. *Numerical Optimization of Computer Models*. John Wiley & Sons, Inc., New York, 1981.

12. Zhang, S. and Liu, J. A massively multi-agent system for discovering HIV-immune interaction dynamics. In *Proceedings of the First International Workshop on Massively Multi-Agent Systems* (Kyoto, Japan, Dec. 10–11). Springer, Berlin, 2004.

JIMING LIU (jiming@uwindsor.ca) is a professor in and director of the School of Computer Science at the University of Windsor, Windsor, Ontario, Canada. K. C. TSUI (tsuikc@comp.hkbu.edu.hk) is an IT manager in the Technical Services and Support Department of Hong-Kong and Shanghai Banking Corporation, Hong Kong, China.

From *Communications of the ACM,* 49(10), October 2006, pp. 59–64. Copyright © 2006 by Association for Computing Machinery. Reprinted by permission.

Google and the Wisdom of Clouds

A lofty new strategy aims to put incredible computing power in the hands of many.

Stephen Baker

One simple question. That's all it took for Christophe Bisciglia to bewilder confident job applicants at Google. Bisciglia, an angular 27-year-old senior software engineer with long wavy hair, wanted to see if these undergrads were ready to think like Googlers. "Tell me," he'd say, "what would you do if you had 1,000 times more data?"

What a strange idea. If they returned to their school projects and were foolish enough to cram formulas with a thousand times more details about shopping or maps or—heaven forbid—with video files, they'd slow their college servers to a crawl.

At that point in the interview, Bisciglia would explain his question. To thrive at Google, he told them, they would have to learn to work—and to dream—on a vastly larger scale. He described Google's globe-spanning network of computers. Yes, they answered search queries instantly. But together they also blitzed through mountains of data, looking for answers or intelligence faster than any machine on earth. Most of this hardware wasn't on the Google campus. It was just out there, somewhere on earth, whirring away in big refrigerated data centers. Folks at Google called it "the cloud." And one challenge of programming at Google was to leverage that cloud—to push it to do things that would overwhelm lesser machines. New hires at Google, Bisciglia says, usually take a few months to get used to this scale. "Then one day, you see someone suggest a wild job that needs a few thousand machines, and you say: Hey, he gets it."

What recruits needed, Bisciglia eventually decided, was advance training. So one autumn day a year ago, when he ran into Google CEO Eric E. Schmidt between meetings, he floated an idea. He would use his 20% time, the allotment Googlers have for independent projects, to launch a course. It would introduce students at his alma mater, the University of Washington, to programming at the scale of a cloud. Call it Google 101. Schmidt liked the plan. Over the following months, Bisciglia's Google 101 would evolve and grow. It would eventually lead to an ambitious partnership with IBM, announced in October, to plug universities around the world into Google-like computing clouds.

Cloud Computing

User Friendly

Clouds are giant clusters of computers that house immense sets of data too big for traditional computers to handle—such as the receipts from 100 million shoppers or troves of geological data.

As this concept spreads, it promises to expand Google's footprint in industry far beyond search, media, and advertising, leading the giant into scientific research and perhaps into new businesses. In the process Google could become, in a sense, the world's primary computer.

"I had originally thought [Bisciglia] was going to work on education, which was fine," Schmidt says late one recent afternoon at Google headquarters. "Nine months later, he comes out with this new [cloud] strategy, which was completely unexpected." The idea, as it developed, was to deliver to students, researchers, and entrepreneurs the immense power of Google-style computing, either via Google's machines or others offering the same service.

It's the computing equivalent of the evolution in electricity, when businesses shut down their generators and bought power instead.

What is Google's cloud? It's a network made of hundreds of thousands, or by some estimates 1 million, cheap servers, each not much more powerful than the PCs we have in our homes. It stores staggering amounts of data, including numerous copies of the World Wide Web. This makes search faster, helping ferret out answers to billions of queries in a fraction of a second.

Unlike many traditional supercomputers, Google's system never ages. When its individual pieces die, usually after about three years, engineers pluck them out and replace them with new, faster boxes. This means the cloud regenerates as it grows, almost like a living thing.

A move toward clouds signals a fundamental shift in how we handle information. At the most basic level, it's the computing equivalent of the evolution in electricity a century ago when farms and businesses shut down their own generators and bought power instead from efficient industrial utilities. Google executives had long envisioned and prepared for this change. Cloud computing, with Google's machinery at the very center, fit neatly into the company's grand vision, established a decade ago by founders Sergey Brin and Larry Page: "to organize the world's information and make it universally accessible." Bisciglia's idea opened a pathway toward this future. "Maybe he had it in his brain and didn't tell me," Schmidt says. "I didn't realize he was going to try to change the way computer scientists thought about computing. That's a much more ambitious goal."

One-Way Street

For small companies and entrepreneurs, clouds mean opportunity—a leveling of the playing field in the most data-intensive forms of computing. To date, only a select group of cloud-wielding Internet giants has had the resources to scoop up huge masses of information and build businesses upon it. Our words, pictures, clicks, and searches are the raw material for this industry. But it has been largely a one-way street. Humanity emits the data, and a handful of companies—the likes of Google, Yahoo!, or Amazon.com—transform the info into insights, services, and, ultimately, revenue.

This status quo is already starting to change. In the past year, Amazon has opened up its own networks of computers to paying customers, initiating new players, large and small, to cloud computing. Some users simply park their massive databases with Amazon. Others use Amazon's computers to mine data or create Web services. In November, Yahoo opened up a cluster of computers—a small cloud—for researchers at Carnegie Mellon University. And Microsoft has deepened its ties to communities of scientific researchers by providing them access to its own server farms. As these clouds grow, says Frank Gens, senior analyst at market research firm IDC, "A whole new community of Web startups will have access to these machines. It's like they're planting Google seeds." Many such startups will emerge in science and medicine, as data-crunching laboratories searching for new materials and drugs set up shop in the clouds.

For clouds to reach their potential, they should be nearly as easy to program and navigate as the Web. This, say analysts, should open up growing markets for cloud search and software tools—a natural business for Google and its competitors. Schmidt won't say how much of its own capacity Google will offer to outsiders, or under what conditions or at what prices. "Typically, we like to start with free," he says, adding that power users "should probably bear some of the costs." And how big will these clouds grow? "There's no limit," Schmidt says. As this strategy unfolds, more people are starting to see that Google is poised to become a dominant force in the next stage of computing. "Google aspires to be a large portion of the cloud, or a cloud that you would interact with every day," the CEO says. The business plan? For now, Google remains rooted in its core business, which gushes with advertising revenue. The cloud initiative is barely a blip in terms of investment. It hovers in the distance, large and hazy and still hard to piece together, but bristling with possibilities.

Changing the nature of computing and scientific research wasn't at the top of Bisciglia's agenda the day he collared Schmidt. What he really wanted, he says, was to go back to school. Unlike many of his colleagues at Google, a place teeming with PhDs, Bisciglia was snatched up by the company as soon as he graduated from the University of Washington, or U-Dub, as nearly everyone calls it. He'd never been a grad student. He ached for a break from his daily routines at Google—the 10-hour workdays building search algorithms in his cube in Building 44, the long commutes on Google buses from the apartment he shared with three roomies in San Francisco's Duboce Triangle. He wanted to return to Seattle, if only for one day a week, and work with his professor and mentor, Ed Lazowska. "I had an itch to teach," he says.

He didn't think twice before vaulting over the org chart and batting around his idea directly with the CEO. Bisciglia and Schmidt had known each other for years. Shortly after landing at Google five years ago as a 22-year-old programmer, Bisciglia worked in a cube across from the CEO's office. He'd wander in, he says, drawn in part by the model airplanes that reminded him of his mother's work as a United Airlines hostess. Naturally he talked with the soft-spoken, professorial CEO about computing. It was almost like college. And even after Bisciglia moved to other buildings, the two stayed in touch. ("He's never too hard to track down, and he's incredible about returning e-mails," Bisciglia says.)

On the day they first discussed Google 101, Schmidt offered one nugget of advice: Narrow down the project to something Bisciglia could have up and running in two months. "I actually didn't care what he did," Schmidt recalls. But he wanted the young engineer to get feedback in a hurry. Even if Bisciglia failed, he says, "he's smart, and he'd learn from it."

To launch Google 101, Bisciglia had to replicate the dynamics and a bit of the magic of Google's cloud—but without tapping into the cloud itself or revealing its deepest secrets. These secrets fuel endless speculation among computer scientists. But Google keeps much under cover. This immense computer, after all, runs the company. It automatically handles search, places ads, churns through e-mails. The computer does the work, and thousands of Google engineers, including Bisciglia, merely service the machine. They teach the system new tricks or find new markets for it to invade. And they add on new clusters—four new data centers this year alone, at an average cost of $600 million apiece.

In building this machine, Google, so famous for search, is poised to take on a new role in the computer industry. Not so many years ago scientists and researchers looked to national laboratories for the cutting-edge research on computing. Now, says Daniel Frye, vice-president of open systems development at IBM, "Google is doing the work that 10 years ago would have gone on in a national lab."

How was Bisciglia going to give students access to this machine? The easiest option would have been to plug his class directly into the Google computer. But the company wasn't about to let students loose in a machine loaded with proprietary software, brimming with personal data, and running a $10.6 billion business. So Bisciglia shopped for an affordable cluster of 40 computers. He placed the order, then set about figuring out how to pay for the servers. While the vendor was wiring the computers together, Bisciglia alerted a couple of Google managers that a bill was coming. Then he "kind of sent the expense report up the chain, and no one said no." He adds one of his favorite sayings: "It's far easier to beg for forgiveness than to ask for permission." ("If you're interested in someone who strictly follows the rules, Christophe's not your guy," says Lazowska, who refers to the cluster as "a gift from heaven.")

A Frenetic Learner

On Nov. 10, 2006, the rack of computers appeared at U-Dub's Computer Science building. Bisciglia and a couple of tech administrators had to figure out how to hoist the 1-ton rack up four stories into the server room. They eventually made it, and then prepared for the start of classes, in January.

Bisciglia's mother, Brenda, says her son seemed marked for an unusual path from the start. He didn't speak until age 2, and then started with sentences. One of his first came as they were driving near their home in Gig Harbor, Wash. A bug flew in the open window, and a voice came from the car seat in back: "Mommy, there's something artificial in my mouth."

At school, the boy's endless questions and frenetic learning pace exasperated teachers. His parents, seeing him sad and frustrated, pulled him out and home-schooled him for three years. Bisciglia says he missed the company of kids during that time but developed as an entrepreneur. He had a passion for Icelandic horses and as an adolescent went into business raising them. Once, says his father, Jim, they drove far north into Manitoba and bought horses, without much idea about how to transport the animals back home. "The whole trip was like a scene from one of Chevy Chase's movies," he says. Christophe learned about computers developing Web pages for his horse sales and his father's luxury-cruise business. And after concluding that computers promised a brighter future than animal husbandry, he went off to U-Dub and signed up for as many math, physics, and computer courses as he could.

In late 2006, as he shuttled between the Googleplex and Seattle preparing for Google 101, Bisciglia used his entrepreneurial skills to piece together a sprawling team of volunteers. He worked with college interns to develop the curriculum, and he dragooned a couple of Google colleagues from the nearby Kirkland (Wash.) facility to use some of their 20% time to help him teach it. Following Schmidt's advice, Bisciglia worked to focus Google 101 on something students could learn quickly. "I

was like, what's the one thing I could teach them in two months that would be useful and really important?" he recalls. His answer was "MapReduce."

Bisciglia adores MapReduce, the software at the heart of Google computing. While the company's famous search algorithms provide the intelligence for each search, MapReduce delivers the speed and industrial heft. It divides each task into hundreds, or even thousands, of tasks, and distributes them to legions of computers. In a fraction of a second, as each one comes back with its nugget of information, MapReduce quickly assembles the responses into an answer. Other programs do the same job. But MapReduce is faster and appears able to handle near limitless work. When the subject comes up, Bisciglia rhapsodizes. "I remember graduating, coming to Google, learning about MapReduce, and really just changing the way I thought about computer science and everything," he says. He calls it "a very simple, elegant model." It was developed by another Washington alumnus, Jeffrey Dean. By returning to U-Dub and teaching MapReduce, Bisciglia would be returning this software "and this way of thinking" back to its roots.

There was only one obstacle. MapReduce was anchored securely inside Google's machine—and it was not for outside consumption, even if the subject was Google 101. The company did share some information about it, though, to feed an open-source version of MapReduce called Hadoop. The idea was that, without divulging its crown jewel, Google could push for its standard to become the architecture of cloud computing.

The team that developed Hadoop belonged to a company, Nutch, that got acquired. Oddly, they were now working within the walls of Yahoo, which was counting on the MapReduce offspring to give its own computers a touch of Google magic. Hadoop remained open source, though, which meant the Google team could adapt it and install it for free on the U-Dub cluster.

Students rushed to sign up for Google 101 as soon as it appeared in the winter-semester syllabus. In the beginning, Bisciglia and his Google colleagues tried teaching. But in time they handed over the job to professional educators at U-Dub. "Their delivery is a lot clearer," Bisciglia says. Within weeks the students were learning how to configure their work for Google machines and designing ambitious Web-scale projects, from cataloguing the edits on Wikipedia to crawling the Internet to identify spam. Through the spring of 2007, as word about the course spread to other universities, departments elsewhere started asking for Google 101.

Many were dying for cloud know-how and computing power—especially for scientific research. In practically every field, scientists were grappling with vast piles of new data issuing from a host of sensors, analytic equipment, and ever-finer measuring tools. Patterns in these troves could point to new medicines and therapies, new forms of clean energy. They could help predict earthquakes. But most scientists lacked the machinery to store and sift through these digital El Dorados. "We're drowning in data," said Jeannette Wing, assistant director of the National Science Foundation.

Cloud Power

Companies and research organizations may eventually hand off most of their high-level computing tasks to a globe-spanning network of servers known as "clouds." These pioneers are in a position to dominate the field:

Google

The only search company built from the ground up around hardware. Investing more than $2 billion a year in data centers. Far and away the leader in cloud computing.

Yahoo!

Smaller and poorer than Google, with software not perfectly suited to cloud computing. But as the leading patron of Hadoop, it could end up with a lead over latecomers.

IBM

King of business computing and traditional supercomputers. Teaming up with Google to get a foothold in clouds. Launching a pilot cloud system for the government of Vietnam.

Microsoft

Wedded, for now, to its proprietary software, which could be a handicap. But it's big in the fundamentals of cloud science. And it's building massive data centers in Illinois and Siberia.

Amazon

The first to sell cloud computing as a service. Smaller than competitors, but its expertise in this area could give the retailer a leg up in next-generation Web services from retail to media.

Big Blue Largesse

The hunger for Google computing put Bisciglia in a predicament. He had been fortunate to push through the order for the first cluster of computers. Could he do that again and again, eventually installing mini-Google clusters in each computer science department? Surely not. To extend Google 101 to universities around the world, the participants needed to plug into a shared resource. Bisciglia needed a bigger cloud.

That's when luck descended on the Googleplex in the person of IBM Chairman Samuel J. Palmisano. This was "Sam's day at Google," says an IBM researcher. The winter day was a bit chilly for beach volleyball in the center of campus, but Palmisano lunched on some of the fabled free cuisine in a cafeteria. Then he and his team sat down with Schmidt and a handful of Googlers, including Bisciglia. They drew on whiteboards and discussed cloud computing. It was no secret that IBM wanted to deploy clouds to provide data and services to business customers. At the same time, under Palmisano, IBM had been a leading promoter of open-source software, including Linux. This was a

key in Big Blue's software battles, especially against Microsoft. If Google and IBM teamed up on a cloud venture, they could construct the future of this type of computing on Google-based standards, including Hadoop.

> **"I had originally thought [Bisciglia] was going to work on education," says CEO Schmidt. "Google 101" became vastly more ambitious.**

Google, of course, had a running start on such a project: Bisciglia's Google 101. In the course of that one day, Bisciglia's small venture morphed into a major initiative backed at the CEO level by two tech titans. By the time Palmisano departed that afternoon, it was established that Bisciglia and his IBM counterpart, Dennis Quan, would build a prototype of a joint Google-IBM university cloud.

Over the next three months they worked together at Google headquarters. (It was around this time, Bisciglia says, that the cloud project evolved from 20% into his full-time job.) The work involved integrating IBM's business applications and Google servers, and equipping them with a host of open-source programs, including Hadoop. In February they unveiled the prototype for top brass in Mountain View, Calif., and for others on video from IBM headquarters in Armonk, N.Y. Quan wowed them by downloading data from the cloud to his cell phone. (It wasn't relevant to the core project, Bisciglia says, but a nice piece of theater.)

The Google 101 cloud got the green light. The plan was to spread cloud computing first to a handful of U.S. universities within a year and later to deploy it globally. The universities would develop the clouds, creating tools and applications while producing legions of computer scientists to continue building and managing them.

Those developers should be able to find jobs at a host of Web companies, including Google. Schmidt likes to compare the data centers to the prohibitively expensive particle accelerators known as cyclotrons. "There are only a few cyclotrons in physics," he says. "And every one if them is important, because if you're a top-flight physicist you need to be at the lab where that cyclotron is being run. That's where history's going to be made; that's where the inventions are going to come. So my idea is that if you think of these as supercomputers that happen to be assembled from smaller computers, we have the most attractive supercomputers, from a science perspective, for people to come work on."

As the sea of business and scientific data rises, computing power turns into a strategic resource, a form of capital. "In a sense," says Yahoo Research Chief Prabhakar Raghavan, "there are only five computers on earth." He lists Google, Yahoo, Microsoft, IBM, and Amazon. Few others, he says, can turn electricity into computing power with comparable efficiency.

All sorts of business models are sure to evolve. Google and its rivals could team up with customers, perhaps exchanging computing power for access to their data. They could recruit partners into their clouds for pet projects, such as the company's clean energy initiative, announced in November. With the electric bills at jumbo data centers running upwards of $20 million a year, according to industry analysts, it's only natural for Google to commit both brains and server capacity to the search for game-changing energy breakthroughs.

What will research clouds look like? Tony Hey, vice-president for external research at Microsoft, says they'll function as huge virtual laboratories, with a new generation of librarians—some of them human—"curating" troves of data, opening them to researchers with the right credentials. Authorized users, he says, will build new tools, haul in data, and share it with far-flung colleagues. In these new labs, he predicts, "you may win the Nobel prize by analyzing data assembled by someone else." Mark Dean, head of IBM's research operation in Almaden, Calif., says that the mixture of business and science will lead, in a few short years, to networks of clouds that will tax our imagination. "Compared to this," he says, "the Web is tiny. We'll be laughing at how small the Web is." And yet, if this "tiny" Web was big enough to spawn Google and its empire, there's no telling what opportunities could open up in the giant clouds.

It's a mid-November day at the Googleplex. A jetlagged Christophe Bisciglia is just back from China, where he has been talking to universities about Google 101. He's had a busy time, not only setting up the cloud with IBM but also working out deals with six universities—U-Dub, Berkeley, Stanford, MIT, Carnegie Mellon, and the University of Maryland—to launch it. Now he's got a camera crew in a conference room, with wires and lights spilling over a table. This is for a promotional video about cloud education that they'll release, at some point, on YouTube.

Eric Schmidt comes in. At 52, he is nearly twice Bisciglia's age, and his body looks a bit padded next to his protégé's willowy frame. Bisciglia guides him to a chair across from the camera and explains the plan. They'll tape the audio from the interview and then set up Schmidt for some stand-alone face shots. "B-footage," Bisciglia calls it. Schmidt nods and sits down. Then he thinks better of it. He tells the cameramen to film the whole thing and skip stand-alone shots. He and Bisciglia are far too busy to stand around for B footage.

See Senior Writer **Stephen Baker's** Q&A with Google CEO Eric Schmidt.

From *BusinessWeek*, December 24, 2007. Copyright © 2007 by BusinessWeek. Reprinted by permission of the McGraw-Hill Companies.

Cloud Computing

As software migrates from local PCs to distant Internet servers, users and developers alike go along for the ride.

Brian Hayes

The Greek myths tell of creatures plucked from the surface of the Earth and enshrined as constellations in the night sky. Something similar is happening today in the world of computing. Data and programs are being swept up from desktop PCs and corporate server rooms and installed in "the compute cloud."

Whether it's called *cloud computing* or *on-demand computing, software as a service,* or *the Internet as platform,* the common element is a shift in the geography of computation. When you create a spreadsheet with the Google Docs service, major components of the software reside on unseen computers, whereabouts unknown, possibly scattered across continents.

The shift from locally installed programs to cloud computing is just getting under way in earnest. Shrink-wrap software still dominates the market and is not about to disappear, but the focus of innovation indeed seems to be ascending into the clouds. Some substantial fraction of computing activity is migrating away from the desktop and the corporate server room. The change will affect all levels of the computational ecosystem, from casual user to software developer, IT manager, even hardware manufacturer.

In a sense, what we're seeing now is the second coming of cloud computing. Almost 50 years ago a similar transformation came with the creation of service bureaus and time-sharing systems that provided access to computing machinery for users who lacked a mainframe in a glass-walled room down the hall. A typical time-sharing service had a hub-and-spoke configuration. Individual users at terminals communicated over telephone lines with a central site where all the computing was done.

When personal computers arrived in the 1980s, part of their appeal was the promise of "liberating" programs and data from the central computing center. (Ted Nelson, the prophet of hypertext, published a book titled *Computer Lib/Dream Machines* in 1974.) Individuals were free to control their own computing environment, choosing software to suit their needs and customizing systems to their tastes.

But PCs in isolation had an obvious weakness: In many cases the sneaker-net was the primary means of collaboration and sharing. The client-server model introduced in the 1980s offered a central repository for shared data while personal computers and workstations replaced terminals, allowing individuals to run programs locally.

In the current trend, the locus of computation is shifting again, with functions migrating outward to distant data centers reached through the Internet. The new regime is not quite a return to the hub-and-spoke topology of time-sharing systems, if only because there is no hub. A client computer on the Internet can communicate with many servers at the same time, some of which may also be exchanging information among themselves. However, even if we are not returning to the architecture of time-sharing systems, the sudden stylishness of the cloud paradigm marks the reversal of a long-standing trend. Where end users and corporate IT managers once squabbled over possession of computing resources, both sides are now willing to surrender a large measure of control to third-party service providers. What brought about this change in attitude?

For the individual, total control comes at a price. Software must be installed and configured, then updated with each new release. The computational infrastructure of operating systems and low-level utilities must be maintained. Every update to the operating system sets off a cascade of subsequent revisions to other programs. Outsourcing computation to an Internet service eliminates nearly all these concerns. Cloud computing also offers end users advantages in terms of mobility and collaboration.

For software vendors who have shifted their operations into the cloud, the incentives are similar to those motivating end users. Software sold or licensed as a product to be installed on the user's hardware must be able to cope with a baffling variety of operating environments. In contrast, software offered as an Internet-based service can be developed, tested, and run on a computing platform of the vendor's choosing. Updates and bug fixes are deployed in minutes. (But the challenges of diversity don't entirely disappear; the server-side software must be able to interact with a variety of clients.)

Although the new model of Internet computing has neither hub nor spokes, it still has a core and a fringe. The aim is to concentrate computation and storage in the core, where high-performance machines are linked by high-bandwidth connections, and all of these resources are carefully managed. At the fringe are the end users making the requests that initiate computations and who receive the results.

Although the future of cloud computing is less than clear, a few examples of present practice suggest likely directions:

Wordstar for the Web. The kinds of productivity applications that first attracted people to personal computers 30 years ago are now appearing as software services. The Google Docs programs are an example, including a word processor, a spreadsheet, and a tool for creating PowerPoint-like presentations. Another undertaking of this kind is Buzzword, a Web-based word processor acquired by Adobe Systems in 2007. Another recent Adobe product is Photoshop Express, which has turned the well-known image-manipulation program into an online service.

Enterprise computing in the cloud. Software for major business applications (such as customer support, sales, and marketing) has generally been run on corporate servers, but several companies now provide it as an on-demand service. The first was Salesforce.com, founded in 1999, offering a suite of online programs for customer relationship management and other business-oriented tasks; the company's slogan is "No software!"

Cloudy infrastructure. It's all very well to outsource the chore of building and maintaining a data center, but someone must still supply that infrastructure. Amazon.com has moved into this niche of the Internet ecosystem. Amazon Web Services offers data storage priced by the gigabyte-month and computing capacity by the CPU-hour. Both kinds of resources expand and contract according to need. IBM has announced plans for the "Blue Cloud" infrastructure. And Google is testing the App Engine, which provides hosting on Google server farms and a software environment centered on the Python programming language and the Bigtable distributed storage system.

For most applications, the entire user interface resides inside a single window in a Web browser.

The cloud OS. For most cloud-computing applications, the entire user interface resides inside a single window in a Web browser. Several initiatives aim to provide a richer user experience for Internet applications. One approach is to exploit the cloud-computing paradigm to provide all the facilities of an operating system inside a browser. The eyeOS system, for example, reproduces the familiar desktop metaphor—with icons for files, folders, and applications—all living in a browser window. Another solution would bypass the Web browser, substituting a more-capable software system that runs as a separate application on the client computer and communicates directly with servers in the cloud. This is the idea behind AIR (formerly Apollo) being tested by Adobe Systems. Open-Laszlo, an open-source project, works in much the same way.

For those deploying software out in the cloud, scalability is a major issue—the need to marshal resources in such a way that a program continues running smoothly even as the number of users grows. It's not just that servers must respond to hundreds or thousands of requests per second; the system must also coordinate information coming from multiple sources, not all of which are under the control of the same organization. The pattern of communication is many-to-many, with each server talking to multiple clients and each client invoking programs on multiple servers.

The other end of the cloud-computing transaction—the browser-based user interface—presents challenges of another kind. The familiar window-and-menu layer of modern operating systems has been fine-tuned over decades to meet user needs and expectations. Duplicating this functionality inside a Web browser is a considerable feat. Moreover, it has to be done in a comparatively impoverished development environment. A programmer creating a desktop application for Windows or one of the Unix variants can choose from a broad array of programming languages, code libraries, and application frameworks; major parts of the user interface can be assembled from pre-built components. The equivalent scaffolding for the Web computing platform is much more primitive.

A major challenge of moving applications to the cloud is the need to master multiple languages and operating environments. In many cloud applications a back-end process relies on a relational database, so part of the code is written in SQL or other query language. On the client side, program logic is likely to be implemented in JavaScript embedded within HTML documents. Standing between the database and the client is a server application that might be written in a scripting language (such as PHP, Java, and Python). Information exchanged between the various layers is likely to be encoded in some variation of XML.

Even though the new model of remote computing seems to reverse the 1980s "liberation" movement that gave individual users custody over programs and data, the shift does not necessarily restore control to managers in the corporate IT department.

To the extent that cloud computing succeeds, it represents an obvious competitive challenge to vendors of shrink-wrap software. Ironically, the open-source movement could also have a tough time adapting to the new computing model. It's one thing to create and distribute an open-source word processor competing with Microsoft Word; not so obvious is how a consortium of volunteers would create a Web service to compete with Google Docs.

Finally, cloud computing raises questions about privacy, security, and reliability—a major subject of discussion at a workshop held last January at the Center for Information Technology Policy at Princeton University. Allowing a third-party service to take custody of personal documents raises awkward questions about control and ownership: If you move to a competing service provider, can you take your data with you? Could you lose access to your documents if you fail to pay your bill? Do you have the power to expunge documents that are no longer wanted?

The issues of privacy and confidentiality are equally perplexing. In one frequently cited scenario, a government agency presents a subpoena or search warrant to the third party that has possession of your data. If you had retained physical custody, you might still have been compelled to surrender the information, but at least you would have been able to decide for yourself whether or not to contest the order. The third-party service is presumably less likely to go to court on your behalf. In some circumstances you might not even be informed that your documents have been released. It seems likely that much of the world's digital information will be living in the clouds long before such questions are resolved.

BRIAN HAYES writes about science and technology from Durham, NC.

From *Communications of the ACM*, July 2008. Copyright © 2008 by Association for Computing Machinery. Reprinted by permission.

The Coming Superbrain

JOHN MARKOFF

It's summertime and the Terminator is back. A sci-fi movie thrill ride, *Terminator Salvation* comes complete with a malevolent artificial intelligence dubbed Skynet, a military R.&D. project that gained self-awareness and concluded that humans were an irritant—perhaps a bit like athlete's foot—to be dispatched forthwith.

The notion that a self-aware computing system would emerge spontaneously from the interconnections of billions of computers and computer networks goes back in science fiction at least as far as Arthur C. Clarke's "Dial F for Frankenstein." A prescient short story that appeared in 1961, it foretold an ever-more-interconnected telephone network that spontaneously acts like a newborn baby and leads to global chaos as it takes over financial, transportation and military systems.

Today, artificial intelligence, once the preserve of science fiction writers and eccentric computer prodigies, is back in fashion and getting serious attention from NASA and from Silicon Valley companies like Google as well as a new round of start-ups that are designing everything from next-generation search engines to machines that listen or that are capable of walking around in the world. A.I.'s new respectability is turning the spotlight back on the question of where the technology might be heading and, more ominously, perhaps, whether computer intelligence will surpass our own, and how quickly.

The concept of ultrasmart computers—machines with "greater than human intelligence"—was dubbed "The Singularity" in a 1993 paper by the computer scientist and science fiction writer Vernor Vinge. He argued that the acceleration of technological progress had led to "the edge of change comparable to the rise of human life on Earth." This thesis has long struck a chord here in Silicon Valley.

Artificial intelligence is already used to automate and replace some human functions with computer-driven machines. These machines can see and hear, respond to questions, learn, draw inferences and solve problems. But for the Singulatarians, A.I. refers to machines that will be both self-aware and superhuman in their intelligence, and capable of designing better computers and robots faster than humans can today. Such a shift, they say, would lead to a vast acceleration in technological improvements of all kinds.

The idea is not just the province of science fiction authors; a generation of computer hackers, engineers and programmers have come to believe deeply in the idea of exponential technological change as explained by Gordon Moore, a co-founder of the chip maker Intel.

In 1965, Dr. Moore first described the repeated doubling of the number transistors on silicon chips with each new technology generation, which led to an acceleration in the power of computing. Since then "Moore's Law"—which is not a law of physics, but rather a description of the rate of industrial change—has come to personify an industry that lives on Internet time, where the Next Big Thing is always just around the corner.

Several years ago the artificial-intelligence pioneer Raymond Kurzweil took the idea one step further in his 2005 book, *The Singularity Is Near: When Humans Transcend Biology*. He sought to expand Moore's Law to encompass more than just processing power and to simultaneously predict with great precision the arrival of post-human evolution, which he said would occur in 2045.

In Dr. Kurzweil's telling, rapidly increasing computing power in concert with cyborg humans would then reach a point when machine intelligence not only surpassed human intelligence but took over the process of technological invention, with unpredictable consequences.

Profiled in the documentary *Transcendent Man,* which had its premier last month at the TriBeCa Film Festival, and with his own Singularity movie due later this year, Dr. Kurzweil has become a one-man marketing machine for the concept of post-humanism. He is the co-founder of Singularity University, a school supported by Google that will open in June with a grand goal—to "assemble, educate and inspire a cadre of leaders who strive to understand and facilitate the development of exponentially advancing technologies and apply, focus and guide these tools to address humanity's grand challenges."

Not content with the development of superhuman machines, Dr. Kurzweil envisions "uploading," or the idea that the contents of our brain and thought processes can somehow be translated into a computing environment, making a form of immortality possible—within his lifetime.

That has led to no shortage of raised eyebrows among hard-nosed technologists in the engineering culture here, some of whom describe the Kurzweilian romance with supermachines as a new form of religion.

The science fiction author Ken MacLeod described the idea of the singularity as "the Rapture of the nerds." Kevin Kelly, an editor at Wired magazine, notes, "People who predict a very utopian future always predict that it is going to happen before they die."

However, Mr. Kelly himself has not refrained from speculating on where communications and computing technology is heading. He is at work on his own book, *The Technium,* forecasting the emergence of a global brain—the idea that the planet's interconnected computers might someday act in a coordinated fashion and perhaps exhibit intelligence. He just isn't certain about how soon an intelligent global brain will arrive.

Others who have observed the increasing power of computing technology are even less sanguine about the future outcome. The computer designer and venture capitalist William Joy, for example, wrote a pessimistic essay in *Wired* in 2000 that argued that humans are more likely to destroy themselves with their technology than create a utopia assisted by superintelligent machines.

Mr. Joy, a co-founder of Sun Microsystems, still believes that. "I wasn't saying we would be supplanted by something," he said. "I think a catastrophe is more likely."

Moreover, there is a hot debate here over whether such machines might be the "machines of loving grace," of the Richard Brautigan poem, or something far darker, of the "Terminator" ilk.

"I see the debate over whether we should build these artificial intellects as becoming the dominant political question of the century," said Hugo de Garis, an Australian artificial-intelligence researcher, who has written a book, *The Artilect War,* that argues that the debate is likely to end in global war.

Concerned about the same potential outcome, the A.I. researcher Eliezer S. Yudkowsky, an employee of the Singularity Institute, has proposed the idea of "friendly artificial intelligence," an engineering discipline that would seek to ensure that future machines would remain our servants or equals rather than our masters.

Nevertheless, this generation of humans, at least, is perhaps unlikely to need to rush to the barricades. The artificial-intelligence industry has advanced in fits and starts over the past half-century, since the term "artificial intelligence" was coined by the Stanford University computer scientist John McCarthy in 1956. In 1964, when Mr. McCarthy established the Stanford Artificial Intelligence Laboratory, the researchers informed their Pentagon backers that the construction of an artificially intelligent machine would take about a decade. Two decades later, in 1984, that original optimism hit a rough patch, leading to the collapse of a crop of A.I. start-up companies in Silicon Valley, a time known as "the A.I. winter."

Such reversals have led the veteran Silicon Valley technology forecaster Paul Saffo to proclaim: "never mistake a clear view for a short distance."

Indeed, despite this high-technology heartland's deeply held consensus about exponential progress, the worst fate of all for the Valley's digerati would be to be the generation before the generation that lives to see the singularity.

"Kurzweil will probably die, along with the rest of us not too long before the 'great dawn,'" said Gary Bradski, a Silicon Valley roboticist. "Life's not fair."

From *The New York Times,* May 24, 2009. Copyright © 2009 by The New York Times Company. Reprinted by permission via PARS International.

Test-Your-Knowledge Form

We encourage you to photocopy and use this page as a tool to assess how the articles in *Annual Editions* expand on the information in your textbook. By reflecting on the articles you will gain enhanced text information. You can also access this useful form on a product's book support website at *http://www.mhhe.com/cls*.

NAME: _____ DATE: _____

TITLE AND NUMBER OF ARTICLE: _____

BRIEFLY STATE THE MAIN IDEA OF THIS ARTICLE: _____

_____

LIST THREE IMPORTANT FACTS THAT THE AUTHOR USES TO SUPPORT THE MAIN IDEA:

_____

_____

WHAT INFORMATION OR IDEAS DISCUSSED IN THIS ARTICLE ARE ALSO DISCUSSED IN YOUR TEXTBOOK OR OTHER READINGS THAT YOU HAVE DONE? LIST THE TEXTBOOK CHAPTERS AND PAGE NUMBERS:

_____

_____

LIST ANY EXAMPLES OF BIAS OR FAULTY REASONING THAT YOU FOUND IN THE ARTICLE:

_____

_____

LIST ANY NEW TERMS/CONCEPTS THAT WERE DISCUSSED IN THE ARTICLE, AND WRITE A SHORT DEFINITION:

We Want Your Advice

ANNUAL EDITIONS revisions depend on two major opinion sources: one is our Advisory Board, listed in the front of this volume, which works with us in scanning the thousands of articles published in the public press each year; the other is you—the person actually using the book. Please help us and the users of the next edition by completing the prepaid article rating form on this page and returning it to us. Thank you for your help!

ANNUAL EDITIONS: Computers in Society 10/11

ARTICLE RATING FORM

Here is an opportunity for you to have direct input into the next revision of this volume.
We would like you to rate each of the articles listed below, using the following scale:

1. **Excellent: should definitely be retained**
2. **Above average: should probably be retained**
3. **Below average: should probably be deleted**
4. **Poor: should definitely be deleted**

Your ratings will play a vital part in the next revision.
Please mail this prepaid form to us as soon as possible.
Thanks for your help!

RATING	ARTICLE	RATING	ARTICLE
	1. Five Things We Need to Know about Technological Change		22. Google & the Future of Books
	2. Moore's Law and Technological Determinism: Reflections on the History of Technology		23. Archiving Writers' Work in the Age of E-Mail
			24. Wikipedia in the Newsroom
	3. Click Fraud: The Dark Side of Online Advertising		25. E-Mail in Academia: Expectations, Use, and Instructional Impact
	4. Online Salvation?		26. A Growing Watch List
	5. The Great Wall of Facebook: The Social Network's Plan to Dominate the Internet—and Keep Google Out		27. The Evolution of Cyber Warfare
			28. Geeks and Hackers, Uncle Sam's Cyber Force Wants You!
	6. Beyond Blogs		29. Privacy Requires Security, Not Abstinence: Protecting an Inalienable Right in the Age of Facebook
	7. Personally Controlled Online Health Data— The Next Big Thing in Medical Care?		
	8. National ID: Biometrics Pinned to Social Security Cards		30. The Software Wars: Why You Can't Understand Your Computer
	9. Dilberts of the World, Unite!		31. False Reporting on the Internet and the Spread of Rumors: Three Case Studies
	10. Computer Software Engineers		
	11. How Deep Can You Probe?		32. China's Tech Generation Finds a New Chairman to Venerate
	12. Privacy, Legislation, and Surveillance Software		
	13. Is Google Making Us Stupid?		33. New Tech, Old Habits
	14. The End of Solitude		34. Iran's Twitter Revolution? Maybe Not Yet
	15. Girl Power		35. The List: Look Who's Censoring the Internet Now
	16. Bloggers against Torture		36. Dissent Made Safer: How Anonymity Technology Could Save Free Speech on the Internet
	17. It's Not Easy to Stand up to Cyberbullies, but We Must		
	18. The Nike Experiment: How the Shoe Giant Unleashed the Power of Personal Metrics		37. A Nascent Robotics Culture: New Complicities for Companionship
			38. Toward Nature-Inspired Computing
	19. Center Stage		39. Google and the Wisdom of Clouds
	20. E-Mail Is for Old People		40. Cloud Computing
	21. The Coming Robot Army		41. The Coming Superbrain

ANNUAL EDITIONS: COMPUTERS IN SOCIETY 10/11

**NO POSTAGE
NECESSARY
IF MAILED
IN THE
UNITED STATES**

BUSINESS REPLY MAIL
FIRST CLASS MAIL PERMIT NO. 551 DUBUQUE IA

POSTAGE WILL BE PAID BY ADDRESSEE

McGraw-Hill Contemporary Learning Series
501 BELL STREET
DUBUQUE, IA 52001

ABOUT YOU

Name   Date

Are you a teacher? ❒ A student? ❒
Your school's name

Department

Address   City   State   Zip

School telephone #

YOUR COMMENTS ARE IMPORTANT TO US!

Please fill in the following information:
For which course did you use this book?

Did you use a text with this ANNUAL EDITION? ❒ yes ❒ no
What was the title of the text?

What are your general reactions to the Annual Editions concept?

Have you read any pertinent articles recently that you think should be included in the next edition? Explain.

Are there any articles that you feel should be replaced in the next edition? Why?

Are there any World Wide Websites that you feel should be included in the next edition? Please annotate.

May we contact you for editorial input? ❒ yes ❒ no
May we quote your comments? ❒ yes ❒ no